# THE FUTURE OF DIGITAL DATA, HERITAGE AND CURATION



*The Future of Digital Data, Heritage and Curation* critiques digital cultural heritage concepts and their application to data, developing new theories, curatorial practices and a more-than-human museology for a contemporary and future world.

Presenting a diverse range of case examples from around the globe, Cameron offers a critical and philosophical reflection on the ways in which digital cultural heritage is currently framed as societal data worth passing on to future generations in two distinct forms: digitally born and digitizations. Demonstrating that most perceptions of digital cultural heritage are distinctly western in nature, the book also examines the complicity of such heritage in climate change, and environmental destruction and injustice. Going further still, the book theorizes the future of digital data, heritage, curation and the notion of the human in the context of the profusion of new types of societal data and production processes driven by the intensification of data economies and through the emergence of new technologies. In so doing, the book makes a case for the development of new types of heritage that comprise AI, automated systems, biological entities, infrastructures, minerals and chemicals – all of which have their own forms of agency, intelligence and cognition.

*The Future of Digital Data, Heritage and Curation* is essential reading for academics and students engaged in the study of museums, archives, libraries, galleries, archaeology, cultural heritage management, information management, curatorial studies and digital humanities.

**Fiona R. Cameron** is Senior Research Fellow at the Institute for Culture and Society, Western Sydney University, Australia. Her research is directed to the figuration of museum and digital cultural heritage theory and curatorial practice for a more-than-human world.

# THE FUTURE OF DIGITAL DATA, HERITAGE AND CURATION

## in a More-than-Human World

*Fiona R. Cameron*

Routledge
Taylor & Francis Group
LONDON AND NEW YORK

First published 2021
by Routledge
2 Park Square, Milton Park, Abingdon, Oxon OX14 4RN

and by Routledge
605 Third Avenue, New York, NY 10158

*Routledge is an imprint of the Taylor & Francis Group, an informa business*



*British Library Cataloguing-in-Publication Data*
A catalogue record for this book is available from the British Library

*Library of Congress Cataloging-in-Publication Data*
A catalog record has been requested for this book

ISBN: 978-0-367-71164-1 (hbk)
ISBN: 978-0-367-69058-8 (pbk)
ISBN: 978-1-003-14960-6 (ebk)

Typeset in Bembo
by Taylor & Francis Books

In loving memory of Hazel

# CONTENTS

# FIGURES

# ACKNOWLEDGMENTS

*The Future of Digital Data, Heritage and Curation in a More-than-Human World* has been in progress over many years. It has been a thrilling but also a very demanding undertaking in which many iterations preceded this final production.

I have greatly benefited from the rich collegial interdisciplinary and intellectual culture of the Institute for Culture and Society at Western Sydney University during the course of the monograph's development. I would especially like to thank esteemed scholar and colleague Tony Bennett who has provided generous support and advice throughout its duration. Special thanks also to Ned Rossiter and Liam Magee. The activities of the Digital Life ICS research theme program and the series of workshops on AI and automation they convened were inspirational and informed the theoretical direction of my work.

I have been fortunate to hold a number of fellowships at leading intellectual centres for the advancement of the environmental humanities and museum research. In 2010, I was awarded a Rachel Carson Fellowship and spent six months at the Rachel Carson Center, a joint research centre between Munich's Ludwig-Maximilians-Universität and the German Deutsches Museum of Science and Technology under the inspiring leadership of Professor Drs Christof Mauch and Helmuth Trischler. I was also fortunate to have a research residency at the Deutsches Museum Research Institute in two consecutive years that assisted in the development of the book. I also held a visiting fellow position at KTH Environmental Humanities Lab, Stockholm, in 2018 under the directorship of Dr Marco Armiero. These opportunities further developed my skills and expertise in new materialisms, media ecology and the environmental humanities all of which informed the book's theoretical framework.

In 2018 I was fortunate to receive a professorial appointment at Linköping University in my capacity as Investigator on *In Orbit: When Collections go Online* with colleagues principal Bodil Axelsson, Sheenagh Pietrobruno and Katherine

Hauptman, Director of the Swedish History Museum. This position and grant emerged out of long-term, ongoing collaborations with TEMAQ and more recently SEEDBOX staff. These connections and grant advanced my research in the digital and environmental humanities and facilitated the completion of the book chapter, "Theorizing digitizations in global computational infrastructures" published in H. Lewi, W. Smith, S. Cooke and D. vom Lehn (Eds.) *The Routledge International Handbook of New Digital Practices in Galleries, Libraries, Archives, Museums and Heritage Sites*. London: Routledge, pp.55–67. This piece of writing introduces some of the book's key concepts.

I would also like to thank colleagues in Chile, Sweden, Norway and Germany and the PhD students who also contributed to this book through their generous responses to the monograph's multifarious theoretical elements and figurations presented in workshops and conferences, notably, ICS events, *Knowledge, Culture Ecologies*, Santiago 2017, *Knowledge Culture Technology*, Lüneburg, Germany, and *Cultural Institutions, Online Collections and Digital Media: Critical Perspectives, Theories and Methods* masterclass at Linköping University, May, 2018. I would like to thank Britta Brenna for her invitation to present this work at the *Museum: A Culture of Copies* workshop at the Department of Culture Studies and Oriental Languages, University of Oslo in June 2018.

This book emerged since 1999 through four Australian Research Council (ARC) grants of which I was lead Chief Investigator. These included the ARC SPIRT grant, *Themescaping virtual collections* (SPIRTC00107832), *Reconceptualising heritage collections* (LP0561202), ARC Sesquicentenary grants, *Knowledge objects* and *Globalizing museums*. My publications and scholarship on digital cultural heritage theory, object concepts, collections documentation and interpretive paradigms, notably the highly influential co-edited collection, *Theorizing Digital Cultural Heritage: A Critical Discourse* (with Sarah Kenderdine, MIT Press 2007), all outputs of these projects, are precursors to this book. A very special thanks to the Australian Research Council who funded these digital heritage research projects.

The book's first paragraphs were formed while a visiting scholar at the Deutsches Museum Research Institute in Munich in September 2014. For this opportunity I would like to thank Director, Helmut Trischler for his support for this project.

Special thanks to the staff at Villa Crawford, Sant'Agnello on the Amalfi Coast. Much of my sustained writing was conducted there in the silence and tranquillity of the convent and its grounds.

Special thanks also to David Kelly for his excellent editorial work on the final draft and to Marie-Louise Taylor for her precision on the book's referencing.

I would also like to express my gratitude to Fiona Stewart and Philip Nitschke of Exit International; Candice Cranmer, Australian Centre for the Moving Image, Museum of Applied Arts and Sciences; Stephen Pierce, Mary Huang and Jenna Fizel who generously supplied images of their work without charge. Thank you to colleague Ned Rossiter who supplied several excellent images of data centres and infrastructures gathered as part of his research for the Australian Research Council Discovery Project, *Data Centres and the Governance of Labour and Territory*

(DP160103307). A special thank you also to Helen Pritchard who supplied the image for the front cover of the Critter compiler exhibited at Medea Malmo (2016) and Sussex University Digital Humanities Lab (2016) as part of the Ecologies of Intimacy event.

I would like to express my gratitude to Heidi Lowther, Editor for Museum & Heritage Studies – Library, Archival & Information Science – Conservation – Digital Humanities for her unwavering enthusiasm for the book project from the outset. Special thanks to all those blind assessors who reviewed the proposal and manuscript draft through its two rounds of review.

And finally I would like to thank lovely friends, Rick Lum, Audrey Rhoda, Corrine Shaw, Michael Saunders, Rob Marshall, Louise and Rossario Grasso, Tracey and Stu Nome and of course to "Bowie" who offered support throughout this long book journey.

# 1

# INTRODUCTION

## Refiguring digital cultural heritage and curation in a more-than-human world

Waking around 5.30am each morning, former President Donald Trump routinely turned on his television and tuned into CNN, Fox News or MSNBC in the White House master bedroom. Propped up on his pillow in night attire Trump grabbed his iPhone, often tweeting from his personal account handle @realDonaldTrump or his presidential account, inspired or infuriated by what he saw and heard.[1]

Trump used Twitter to rule: to break news; to boast; to thank supporters; to spread propaganda; to announce policy and military commands; to insult; and to threaten. His impulsive and sometimes outlandish outbursts included threats to the Iranian president after Mr Rouhani cautioned the US about the nation's hostile

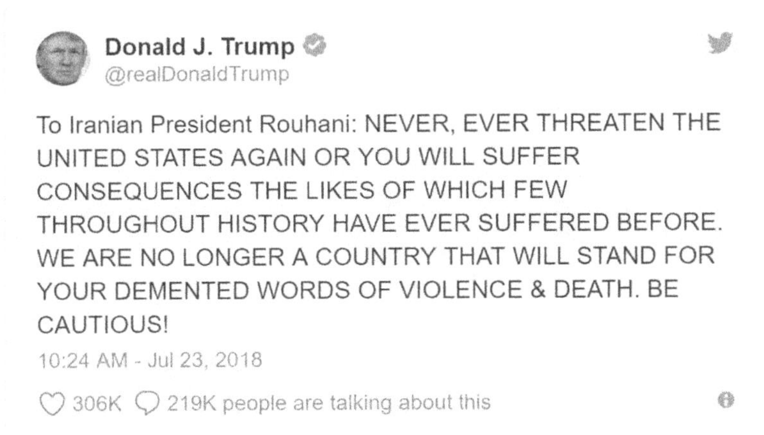


**FIGURE 1.1** Donald Trump's tweet to Iranian President Rouhani, July 23, 2018 via Twitter.

policies towards Iran;[2] a proclamation to stop sales of 3D plastic guns and threats to shut down government if the Democrats didn't agree to fund the wall between Mexico and the US.

As the coronavirus continued to assert itself, reproducing and spreading insidiously at alarming rates, Trump in the face of this escalating crisis referred to Covid-19 as a Chinese virus thereby deepening a US-China diplomatic confrontation over the outbreak and angering Chinese government officials. The World Health Organization in response warned against using such terms to describe the crisis, in an effort to prevent racial discrimination against Chinese people.[3] While making the final adjustments to this manuscript news broke that Trump and his wife Melania had tested positive for Covid-19 on the 2nd of October 2020. In a tweet released at 2.45 pm he wrote, "Tonight @FLOTUS and I tested positive for COVID-19. We will begin our quarantine and recovery process immediately. We will get through this TOGETHER."

All Trump's tweets, from the strange or mundane to those seen as insulting and threatening and his most recent Covid-19 diagnosis have been designated as historical data worth preserving in the archive because they are official statements and therefore a record of his presidency.[4] Historically many presidents have edited, and even destroyed, records, diaries, letters, and emails, unintentionally or intentionally, to protect themselves, their privacy, and their political allies. But since the NARA directive, the White House is now legally obligated to preserve all original tweets.[5]

Trump's tweets as historical data worth preserving are surprisingly new forms of digital cultural heritage, that is, whether they are his policies and opinions launched through the platform or the re-tweets and responses they elicit, including those that are critical and racist.

But rather than locked away in the archive, their heritagization took a different turn predicated on their continuing existence within the world of serendipitous experience. Trump's tweets are used throughout the book not only to expand thinking in regard to the types and forms of digital cultural heritage that are emerging but also as an example of heritage out in the world as a means to rethink practices relating to objects, objecthood, the archive and curating in a more-than-human world.

Our very existence has become datafied. Digital data is omnipresent in what we do and how we experience life: how we record our lives, how we spend our leisure time, how we conduct our work and love lives. How we view ourselves as biological species is also a question of data, from the 3D digital imaging of ourselves as a foetus before we enter the world, to digitally mediated diagnoses as to when and how we might die, and even how we might conduct ourselves as digital humans after death.[6] Our every move, our activities, and actions are monitored, monetized, and bureaucratized, made subject to machinic calculations and used to create identity profiles and on-sold by global oligarchs such as Google and Facebook.[7] The use of drones equipped with infrared cameras to check and monitor the temperatures of quarantined citizens in Fuxin, Liaoning Province[8] in an effort to prevent the coronavirus asserting itself illustrates how our bodily functions, biochemical processes and the virus itself are interpenetrated and converted into data for the purposes of surveillance and reporting. Drones are used to disinfect, control crowds, monitor, traffic, dispose of medical waste and deliver supplies[9], all producing their own data as Covid heritage in the making.

Data is embedded in our devices, from the cars we drive to the domestic appliances, the stoves, fridges, and washing machines we use in the seemingly private spaces of our homes. Smart machines embedded with artificial intelligence unleash their capacities onto the world. Computers win Poker, even beating professional players.[10] AI is replacing humans' labour in the manufacturing and sex industries.[11] Even mundane things such as our phones and elevators contain embedded AI. Our decision-making capacities have also become algorithmically inflected and personalized, from the items we are encouraged to purchase to the programmes we are recommended on Netflix.

A new species of cell zombie (oblivious to the world and others around them and its dangers while glued to their phone) has emerged as an outcome of our addiction to connectivity. Data is able to be produced and accessed anywhere while on the move. As smartphones become integrated into our lives, we are witnessing a digital image explosion in which hundreds of billions of them now circulate on internets and through social media platforms. Smartphones have also become regimes of control, evident with the rise of digital profiling and personalization, but most alarmingly these devices are linked to an emerging digital dictatorship in China, a social credit system where points are accumulated or lost depending on our online or offline choices and behaviour.[12]

The networked capacities and smart properties in all manner of digital machines and commonplace devices we use all create data. Vitally, data production is no longer a human capacity and never really was. All manner of things produce and archive data online and offline, from social bots on social media sites to sex robots, autonomous weapons, embedded medical devices used to predict an epileptic seizure, automated systems in banks, and the machine learning capacities on social media sites such as Facebook that structure our choices and what we might remember. The production of data by all these entities is discussed in Chapter 7. Even bacteria are creating data, as made evident through bio art experimentations.[13]

Due to the rise of data economies, the emergence of data as a modality for governing and for profit generation, the interpenetration of the digital into everyday life alongside the replacement of traditional forms of heritage such as books, paper records, correspondence, photographs, film, sound recordings and artefacts, in digital format, has led to a burgeoning of digital data, much of which has the potential to become heritage of the contemporary world.

*Digital cultural heritage* is conceived as all digital data that a society sees as important to retain and keep as a source of knowledge for future generations. Digital data therefore is the new cultural heritage of life, one that is increasingly threatened and therefore valued.

Significant digital data as a new type of digital cultural heritage product emerges as two distinct forms: *digitally born,* derived from data only existing in digital format, and *digital surrogates*[14] (now popularly known as digitizations), or digital reproductions of pre-existing works.[15] This is a distinction that was first made official by UNESCO (United Nations Educational, Scientific and Cultural Organization) in 2003.

Digital cultural heritage is viewed as human productions and about human concerns first and foremost. We generally consider ourselves as beings who make, own, and use objects;[16] use digital media; use digital resources; make digital things; live in a digital society; and use a variety of digital media objects whose seemingly "immaterial" qualities and indeed their technics are taken for granted until they break down. Born-digital heritage and its collection therefore are about what we have done; what we value; how we thought about something; and what we experienced in the past that we now see as significant. Collecting digital data is a series of actions directed to framing the past and making judgments about what should be carried forward to the future. In broader societal terms digital cultural heritage is about our social relations, about our economic life and transactions, about our history, how we identify ourselves, our opinions and our politics.

Cultural heritage objects have been described by cultural theorist John Plotz as "the eloquent signifiers by which western culture makes the social known to itself."[17] Now digital data is made subject to the same systems of meaning. Accordingly, digital cultural heritage categorization implies that things are metaphysically stable. Nouns stabilize their role as signifiers. Heritage descriptors and narratives of its history define their subject. Here, data through heritage production emerges in new forms as lofty, western, and humanist.

Digital data in a heritage framework and within heritage institutions focuses on the formal technical qualities of digital data and hardware. It is framed according to computer science, information theory, and digital communication, and concerned with internet-mediated networking and the use of tools for cultural communication from personalization and locational intelligence to data analytics. The future of the digital and its entanglement with heritage remains focused on the development of higher-quality digitizations, visualizations, more effective digital communication strategies and literacies, and the iterative application of digital technologies and emerging trends across all areas of operation and practice. Attention has been directed to all these things while digital machines and data languish in museum storerooms, and billions of files lie like sediment in the cloud, in hard drives and all manner of devices. Data in itself as a form of heritage has to date received little attention, especially in regard to its theorization.

We are currently witnessing a turn to born-digital objects, digital hybrid objects or variable media, and an interest in digital materiality as bits central to preservation strategies as the essence of our contemporary past and our future. Alongside this is an emerging interest in the other-than-western cultural contexts and meanings of digital things that challenge west-centred notions of heritage that are routinely attached to them. But at the same time, we must take heed of a profusion of forms that are currently being produced due to the rise of algorithmic mediations and all manner of AI smart data and machines. Such trends, as yet largely unacknowledged in the heritage field, direct our attention away from an anthropocentric notion of digital cultural heritage to that of the more-than-human and non-human forms of data production. This represents a shift in heritage as human-centred productions to new types of humanism that acknowledge our profound entanglements with data.

Accordingly, digital cultural heritages are not simply temporal forms of human memory, human categories of intelligibility, ephemeral, immaterial, material, or technical things. Digital cultural heritage is no longer solely a reflection of human creativity mediated through data and technical systems but also encompasses the creative impulses of a wide range of other-than-human actors. Furthermore, digital cultural heritage can no longer be thought of as human–machine productions or even strictly a product of human intelligence. Emerging genres of digital data and digital machines are all potential heritages. AI, machine learning, and social bots are all involved in heritage-like making practices, and at the same time many are potential objects of heritage. New hybrid forms are emerging such as 3D printed materials.[18] Therefore, the category of heritage producers and productions must be expanded to include the technical, the machinic, the more-than-human and the non-human as new figurations and configurations.

Digital data is a term used in the broadest sense to encapsulate our digital interface with the world. Technically speaking, the smallest unit of digital information is called a bit and is embedded in layered, modular architectures and all manner of digital machines exhibiting properties of decomposability, adaptability, traceability, and interoperability.[19] Often represented by a single binary number or value as a 0 or 1, as on and off switches, bits are instructions that are stored within, manipulated by, and communicated through digital systems that appear as images or sounds.

Strikingly, digital data as heritage is not just the new fabric of human life, it is radically embedded in the vast and sprawling ecological circumstances of life itself.[20] As digital data becomes more ubiquitous and its production accelerated due to the Covid-19 pandemic with physical distancing requiring new platforms for interaction, people create more data and by implication digital cultural heritage. Covid-19 is emerging as a new curatorial agent in museum spaces, providing the impetus for the widespread implementation of new technologies such as AI and machine learning. Museum professionals muse on the future of museum experiences in light of viral contagion, gesturing towards more virtual experiences, a broader application of digital devices to access information, collections visualizations, virtual reality and augmented reality, the development of new applications, digitized exhibits and networked sociality.[21] The experience "Gogh by Car", a digital art installation in a 4,000-square-foot warehouse in Toronto designed by artist Massimiliano Siccardi and composed by musician Luca Longobardi, allowed guests to drive into a completely immersive projection of 400 high resolution images of *Starry Night, Café Terrace at Night, Irises, Almond Blossoms* and *Sunflowers.*[22] With fourteen cars present simultaneously in the space to experience the 35-minute show, viewing art from inside a car provided a safe environment distanced from surfaces, viral clouds and people who might be contagious.

Digital data and by implication digital cultural heritage, is not only habitual or everyday, reaching deep into our human worlds used to structure, monitor and anticipate our lives, but is profoundly ecological, interpenetrating deep time, the geological, technological, and biological substrates of our very existence on Earth.[23] Digital cultural heritage therefore becomes a question born of the ecological complexity of planetary and even interplanetary scope rather than a bounded thing.

Curation then, I argue, becomes a matter of eco-curation enacted by the interrelatedness of all manner of coordinates, from micro-technical operations such as bitstreams, rare earth minerals, colours, metadata and algorithms, and the chemicals in microchips and computer hardware, to electrical impulses, to machine learning and AI, to humans, viruses and global computational infrastructures such as cables, data centres, and smartphones.[24] All these coordinates have efficacy in different ways that can transform, produce a variety of effects that are not always known in advance, to become what I refer to collectively as domains of influencing.[25]

Within these domains of influencing, and as we delegate more of our decision-making responsibilities to machines as part of complex ecological entanglements, we witness the rise of the more-than-human user. Human curatorial agency is also re-worked as one of influencing in eco-curatorial domains. Digital curation therefore becomes one of ecological design.

Digital data and therefore digital cultural heritage production is also a crisis of habitability in the Technosphere[26], a subsystem of the Anthropocene implicated in resource and human exploitation; in data and e-waste production; carbon pollution and global heating, and in the excesses of capitalism. We therefore must curb our data production in order to mitigate such problems. Practices that promote ecologically-friendly consumption and production again become a question of ecological compositional design through the mapping and tracking of infrastructures, supply chains, distribution networks, and consumption patterns across vast distances.

The ecological implications of digital data, its production, and our addiction to connectivity are even reaching deep into our fleshly bodies. Access to data and data processing machines is becoming a biological matter. The air we breathe holds traces of minerals, hazardous chemicals and toxic metals. Cancers are induced in e-waste dumps where the processing of obsolete hardware toxifies environments and people. Brain cancers induced by smartphone use and electromagnetic sensitivities are on the rise as people become addicted to their smart devices and are made subject to clouds of electromagnetic radiation through the wifi networks that envelop us. I was one of those sensitive canaries. Data and its production has had an impact on my health. Through neuroplasticity practice, I have rewired my biological computer, removing past neuro-memories etched into my neural networks and re-setting the structure of my smart brain's hardware and software with astonishing results. I use my digital belongings, digital photographs of my visits to Villa Crawford (a convent on the Amalfi Coast) while writing this book to prompt memory recall and to induce euphoric feelings of intense joy that are then used in future visualizations to change my brain. The potency of such images derives from a combination of the location, my soul home, southern Italy, with the spectacular beauty of the setting, the emphatically calming, joyous and reverential energy circulating within the walls of the convent, and the many friendships that blossomed during the course of my visits. This image of myself with Mount Vesuvius in the background and Villa Crawford to the right is one of those brain-changing personal heritages.

Such events and practices highlight our human positionality in data economies. We – our brains and bodies – are too chemical, energetic, material, and technospheric. Our brains and bodies and actions are scripted into big data. We become raw materials in digital systems.

The heritage sector I argue is no longer the sole arbiter of digital cultural heritage. Heritage-like practices exist across all domains, especially in data economies, in government and research sectors, and in vintage gaming communities, all of which make decisions about what data should be archived for the future or kept active. All of these sectoral practices exhibit different intents concerning why they

**FIGURE 1.2** The author at Villa Crawford, Sant'Agnello, Amafi Coast, Italy, July 2018. Photo credit: Fiona Cameron.

save data and for what purpose. In data economies, historical digital data is also used to anticipate our future, but not in the normative sense as containing the essence of the past to shore up future life. Historical data is made subject to machine learning to anticipate capitalist futures based on what came before.[27]

Digital cultural heritage is becoming smarter, faster, and more complex. Many different forms of intelligence are embedded in digital heritage. Interpretive communities are no longer solely human. Intelligence involves the capacities of many other coordinates, from AI to machines to the elemental and to electrical currents. Cognition also becomes a matter of sensing and of calculation. Here we move from the digital as symbolic and as a category of heritage to also include sensing and the calculative.

In this introductory Chapter 1, I outline the monograph's key themes, aims and position thereby acting as a signpost for the discussions and concepts that emerge across the book. Broadly the monograph contends that new thinking and conceptual frameworks are required to assist in how to collect, document and keep digital data (born-digital, and digitizations including online resources) emblematic of our current social, political, technical, and cultural worlds for the long term. As a result, the monograph, the first of its type, undertakes a bold, innovative, timely re-theorization and refiguration of digital cultural heritage's conceptual frameworks and methods especially relating to current heritage and museum professional practice and digital curation. This is achieved against a background of very current, emerging data forms, formations, platforms, the development of AI and automation, political, environmental and cultural events and situations. These refigurations, novel in themselves, are inspired by emerging scholarship across a range of fields from the critical posthumanities, media ecology, theories of automation and algorithmic governance, the digital and environmental humanities and new materialisms alongside the ontological turn in the social sciences and humanities, all of which act as levers for rethinking digital cultural heritage otherwise as imbricated in planetary life.

In my philosophical re-examination of digital cultural heritage, this book addresses many of the outmoded ideas, issues and gaps which continue to form the basis of the different aspects of museum and gallery practice, and heritage policy and management. To this end the monograph proposes new vocabularies for digital cultural heritage, challenging traditional humanist approaches that drive the conceptual understanding and practical application of the digital and its heritagization. Here I move beyond existing frames of critique, reference, and representation. These existing frames include the analysis of what objects stand for; the postcolonial and post-structuralist critique of practices, knowledge production, and power relations; the analysis of digital media as a medium of communication and the description of the logical structures of media and its preservation; and outmoded binary concepts of the virtual and real, the tangible and the intangible, the digital and analogue, and online and offline as situated practices.

Digital cultural heritage I argue operates beyond the realm of what we can see and what we know. In this regard, the qualities we ascribe to things, the marks of their maker, their production history, their association with an event, and their aesthetics are turned on their head. What holds true here is that the properties of digital cultural heritage are of a different nature, activated in an ever-expanding mesh of materials, queries and processes, infrastructures, and ideas, planetary crises, temporal frameworks and so forth.

Emerging out of these lines of critique, I also re-work the human-centeredness of heritage practice through an engagement with the Critical Posthumanities and inspired by the work of Rosi Braidotti[28] in refiguring human agency. I argue that heritage are now practices of life itself in the broadest sense. Digital cultural heritage and museum systems are no longer located solely in the national or local or the human or technical; rather, they are embedded and deeply entangled in dynamic, burgeoning meshes of diverse people, cultural contexts and realities, technological developments, global infrastructures, automations, human and non-human processes, planetary crises, geopolitical contexts and events.[29]

In contrast to outdated humanist, materialist, Eurocentric approaches, I argue that we need to understand digital cultural heritage and frame a museology through a lens which is ecological and "more than human", and as creative forms of practice alongside non-western digital practices or realities if we are to fully grasp and enact new forms of curatorship and management for a contemporary and future world. Accordingly, I develop new theories of digital cultural heritage as ecological compositions and curation as cuts into the complexity, flow, and duration of life itself.[30] Ecological compositions, through their unique human, non-human and more-than-human coordinates and eco-curating processes, exceed current human-centred notions of heritage; they are things that operate in excess of human meanings, habits, or projects. Heritage also includes the non-human and more-than-human as both data producers and curatorial influencers. Here digital cultural heritage as a knowledge practice and its documentation is always contingent and emergent rather than contained or completed. Digital cultural heritage and curation no longer just represent our social life, it is life, it shapes our lives and our future predicaments.

In the first content chapter, Chapter 2, *The official birth of digital data as universal heritage*, I chart the history and birth of digital cultural heritage as an official heritage through the library and archive sector and its formation through the UNESCO Charter on Digital Heritage of 2003. Here I advance a discussion and critique of the framing of data as a universal heritage through UNESCO as the peak body on matters relating to the framing of data as digital cultural heritage and its preservation. In progressing this line of enquiry, I examine how live digital data becomes first historical and then heritage through the lens of the standard heritage object and how it is produced conceptually through a series of standardizing procedures created by UNESCO. These standardizations frame digital data as a universal heritage through categorizations according to the assumption that a global citizenship of common interests and beliefs exists, that the essence of human history is now cultural memory in a digital form, and that digital data is the dominant fabric of contemporary life. These forms of standardization are further refined according to substance designations, as immaterial software objects them as material bitstreams, and according to two type-categories, the born-digital and the digitization. Central to this is the framing of historical data as globally endangered; as a heritage form that embodies the past; as significant cultural information worthy of generational remittance; heritagized through the act of removing data from its worldly contexts alongside its archival interment, and through the emergence of new professions directed to controlling, securing, and managing it. I also examine how the ubiquity of data and its subversion as heritage is part of a broader heritagization drive, colloquially called "creeping heritage," where almost anything now has the potential to become heritage.[31] Furthermore, I chart the emergence of the European Union's regional preservation strategies and the rise of Google's Cultural Institute as a new corporate and sovereign entity in digital preservation to rival UNESCO's hegemony. I then examine what happens when digital cultural heritage in its UNESCO heritage form collides with informal heritage-like practices in other sectors and out in the world. These preservation practices I argue capitalize on the interactive, mutable, and dynamic character of digital data, and thereby challenge the very notion of digital cultural heritage.

UNESCO's vision for a global digital cultural heritage, I contend, is founded on the idea of a universal human cosmopolitanism, forms of cultural expression, and a series of discrete spatial scales and entities from individuals and institutions to communities and nations. Using the example of the *300* movie and the British Museum's Forgotten Empire exhibition as pithy case studies that link heritage, museums and algorithmic governance, I explain how digital cultural heritage escapes UNESCO's imaginary of heritage as institutionally and nationally based, geographically located, and human centred, and the very idea that data can conform to heritage frameworks. Rather I illustrate how digital cultural heritage crosses multiple national territories, becoming subject to machinic jurisdictions, is distributed and becomes embroiled in worldly concerns. Social relations within these geoscapes, rather than being seen as comprising solely human users and their narratives, now also encompass storable data, earth minerals, calculable and predictive entities such as sensors, switches, code, robots, algorithmic automations, cables, data centres, and technological capitalism.[32] Fixed hierarchies of scale and notions of the national, the global, and a human-centred cosmopolitanism collapse and are replaced by what I call domains of influencing, a process that more accurately resembles the current global computational infrastructure and its dissonant entanglements. Accordingly, digital cultural heritage and its users in global geoscapes become more-than-human, comprising machines, switches, algorithms, robots, codes, sensors.

In conclusion I rework western notions of digital cultural heritage using digitizations as examples to disrupt the copy–analogue binary and to illustrate how digital data in different cultural contexts serve different cultural purposes and hold many meanings. Using powerful non-western examples, the digitization of Malagan masks belonging to the Nalik people of New Ireland, New Guinea[33], and Maori *taonga*, the Te Kani-a-Takirau ancestral house from Aotearoa New Zealand,[34] I contend that we must view digital cultural heritage as different types of digital realities and in doing so disrupt the very idea of heritage as a common language and framework of standardization.

Digital cultural heritage is a distinctly late modern idea and encapsulates how we think about the past and the future and how we frame risk; it reveals how we use data to connect with the past, and how we seek to use them to fortify our future. In Chapter 3, *Digital data as the heritage of the modern world*, I argue accordingly that digital data as heritage are products of contemporary modern life. To do this I draw on contemporary heritage scholarship in related fields, UNESCO documentation, literature on digital preservation and media ecology. Digital cultural heritage, like other forms of heritage, I argue, is born out of discourses and experiences of late modernity: the experiences of intensified globalization and rapid progress; the desire for technological novelty; and planned obsolescence, technical fragility and disruption. Its birth emerges on the one hand as a result of technical innovation and on the other with the threat of loss and rupture from the past through planned technical obsolescence due to capitalist aspirations alongside a nostalgia for old and obsolete things. Accordingly, digital data as the fabric of contemporary life *becomes* the past and at the same time, hyper-imminently about to disappear.

Critically here, the timescales in which digital cultural heritage in its humanist form is created and becomes something worth saving for the future are conflated. Heritage practice becomes anticipatory. Digital data is conceptualized as heritage because it is viewed as significant, but at the same time it is rendered obsolete even before it is produced. To explain the phenomenon, I use examples from the Smithsonian Archive and President Trump's tweets where the loss of his presidential records is anticipated even before he produces them. The temporal distance between when digital data is made and when it becomes heritage in many cases is foregone.

Digital cultural heritage is deeply complicit with data economies and the future of global capitalism itself. Using policy examples, the European Commission Digital Agenda for Europe 2010 strategy, the Europeana platform, and the 2014 research report *Challenges and Opportunities for Australia's Galleries, Libraries, Archives and Museums* that illustrates the connections between digital cultural heritage and economy, I argue that digital cultural heritage, as a heritage of the future, is put to work to fortify capitalism. Digital data as digital cultural heritage alongside digital labour, become new commodities within data markets and are exploited by global corporations such as Google and Facebook. I also examine how collections as they circulate online powered by algorithms become inadvertently and also purposely aligned with technological capitalism, using the case of the U-bra from Fantasy Lingerie and Sydney's Museum of Applied Arts and Sciences' "Nu-U bra", and the Metropolitan Museum's digital marketing campaigns through their collections on Pinterest. In observing trends across sectors, I make a case for the emergence of heritage-like practices, the saving and archiving of data in data economies and in government bureaucracies such as the taxation, public health, education, and research sectors and in corporations as distinctive dispositions emerging from late modernity each of which aims to keep data according to different timeframes and for different reasons. Heritage-making practices in heritage institutions operate within these broader heritage-like dispositions but represent a distinctive set of standardizing and archiving practices directed towards saving data for eternity. Due to their proliferation, I reframe heritage-like regimes as a broader trend characterized as significant societal data worth saving, archiving, keeping active and alive in the world.

Finally, I examine heritage-like practices in the private realm and the type of attachments we have to our digital mementos; the emergence of smartphone zombies, the mobile archive, and citizen journalism. To do this I draw on potent examples of personal data becoming historical, first Alan Stacey's photographs of the terrorist attacks in the London underground on July 7, 2005, then the Whakaari/White Island volcanic eruption in New Zealand's Bay of Plenty on December 9, 2019, its capture on an iPhone video by Allessandro Kauffmann and finally Mia Ayliffe-Chung's Facebook digital memorial in the afterlife.[35]

In Chapter 4, *Object concepts in digital cultural heritage*, I examine and critique the framing of digital cultural heritage as objects conceptually and in practice. The idea that digital data has an objecthood or essence has been central to the emergence of digital cultural heritage historically. I first unravel the idea of the object in computer science, information theory, digital art preservation, and in heritage and museological thinking. I track existing and emerging genres of objects and new forms of object-centred thinking from the interfacial image; to immaterial, virtual, and informational objects; to technical ecosystems, and to material bits, using case studies such as *lifeSigns*, a variable media game from the Australian Centre for the Moving Image[36], social media photographs,[37] Stephen Hawking's voice-output assisted speech technology[38], and World of Warcraft[39] that potentially illustrate these various forms. I argue that thinking about digital cultural heritage as having an objecthood – conceptualized as possessing a fundamental original, authentic form and function, and framed according to humanist forms of knowledge, is limiting. In conclusion, I disrupt the very idea of digital cultural heritage as objects and the accompanying focus on humanist and technology-centred concerns and instead argue that they encapsulate other registers of significance, temporality, and agency such as planetary technological infrastructures, material agency, non-human, elemental, and earthly processes, all of which are invisible figures in their constitution. To illustrate the different agencies involved and their conjoinment beyond the human, I draw on examples of digital cultural heritage in the Smithsonian's 9/11 collection, notably the jump seat belt from American Airlines 11 aircraft that was propelled into the North Tower of New York's World Trade Center. Throughout the book I draw on examples from various 9/11 publicly-held collections. The role of museums and archives in the development of these collections and their public availability operated as a means of understanding what the day meant to many, for those who were victims, others who lost love ones and for many of us who were involuntary eyewitnesses. Furthermore, the power of the collections, images and recordings fused into our collective memory by endless repetition called for a repository, one that many of us could trust to translate and render the event accessible beyond the terror in which it wrought.

In Chapter 5, *From objects to ecological formations*, I reframe digital cultural heritage as ecological compositions through a series of conceptual moves. With the expansion of the digital economy; new types of digital platforms and media types such as Twitter, Facebook, Instagram; mobile applications; technological capitalism; the development of automations, AI, machine learning; cloud computing, the World Wide Web, and multiple internets; the destructive forces of media waste; the mining of rare earth minerals and the advent of climate change, digital cultural heritage is drawn into the vast and more complex ecological circumstances of life itself. As a result, I make a case for an ever-expanding range of coordinates and subjects to enter the field beyond our micro-level concerns in respect to code, bitstreams, platforms, file formats, media, and the interface. Accordingly, I develop new concepts and theories for digital cultural heritage as a post-object concept, the ecological composition drawing on previous research and experimentations I have done on a range of other collection types and curatorial practice[40] deriving inspiration from the Critical Posthumanities and ontological forms of thinking. This refiguration and its novel method is described in detail in the chapter narrative. As a result ecological compositions, digital cultural heritage, both online and offline, become dynamic processes as multi-scaled, extensive radically interoperable webs of heterogeneous coordinates, forces, and agencies that are often unpredictable, unknowable and planetary in their extent and effects. Within these complex ecological circumstances, curating is no longer authorial in a conventional sense as a series of actions by humans or automated systems. Rather I develop a new curatorial theory inspired broadly by scholarship in computational design and new materialisms in which curatorial agency becomes the interrelatedness of the vitalities of more-than- and other-than-human coordinates together emerging as forms of eco-systemic curating. To empirically frame the ecological composition and its method in novel ways, I use two examples: first, the analogue and digitization of the American Airlines Flight 11 jump seat belt, framing the digitization as a unique ecological composition different but also related to its so-called original. The second example is US President Donald Trump's tweets:, "Mexico must pay for the wall", and a series of tweets about North Korea and nuclear capacity, to illustrate heritage in its emergence as an ecological composition in its full and distributed complexity.

Further, in Chapter 6, *Digital data and artefactual production*, I propose a series of conceptual and practical adjustments to digital curation and artefactual production based on the ecological composition. Heritage institutions have been slow to collect and curate digital cultural heritage – both variable media (digital machines with embedded data) and historical data residing on internets – due to difficulties of dealing with the affordances of data in a material and object-centred curatorial regime perceived as under threat from technical extinction. Using examples of the assisted suicide machine Deliverance, currently on exhibition at the Science Museum in London, and a robotic arm from a surgery machine at the Smithsonian

Institution and related literature on digital collecting, I argue data and devices are often collected as material fragments to represent their physical form, their auric and cultural significance, intended never to or unable to be booted up again.

At the same time, digital data as digital cultural heritage is founded on the belief in the existence of an original structure, material fabric comprising its bitstreams, operating systems and its technical supports, and more recently a belief in the containment of its functionality as close as possible to its original aesthetic and behaviour. To illustrate this, I draw on current best-practice preservation practices of containment and their policy documents at the Smithsonian Institution archive, the Australian Centre for the Moving Image, the National Museum of Australia, and the Victoria and Albert Museum, London. In each of these case examples the making of artefacts through technical standardization in the archive has been put to work to uphold the notion of the museum as a repository for rare and valuable collections and more recently for maintaining the original's behaviour. Despite this, an artefactual and representational legacy remains that locks data and its technical supports into a specific set of object, material, modern historical narrative, and signification systems so it can operate as the embodiment of social and cultural life.

When refigured as ecological compositions, digital data (both digitizations and born-digital forms) cannot always be possessed in a conventional artefactual sense. Curating ecological compositions represents a challenge to heritage practices, because in thinking about digital data in this way we must also shift from a disposition based on modern time and human-centric concerns, framed around authenticity, aura, the original, and history, to thinking of an unruly dispersed ecological composition with its own temporal frameworks and histories. Practices of cloning, migration, and emulation in digital preservation, I argue, rather than a genealogy of copying and preserving, produces new ecological compositions in which all stages in their preservation process produce new works and at the same time actuate new curatorial practices that embrace change, renewal, and the making of new things.

Working with Trump's tweet warning North Korea about nuclear testing and the risk of war, re-released recordings from the Wikileaks 9/11 collection, the US Library of Congress September 11 Digital Archive and emails from survivors trapped in the World Trade Center[41]all of which are either re-addressed or remain active out in the world, I explore the potential for new curatorial practices. In doing so I make a case and propose methods for three qualitatively different "archiving" approaches. These are, first, making the artefactual as a moment in its duration; second, keeping digital cultural heritage active while operating within the realm of the original and authentic; and third, keeping ecological compositions active in their duration out in the world with or without restrictions and where the world becomes the archive.

Following on from this discussion, in Chapter 7, *Curating inside the archive and out in the world*, I formulate new collecting, documentation, and interpretive practices that support an ecological, process-based and emergent curatorial system. In doing so I seek to propose a set of modifications to curatorial practice by inducting the "ecological composition" concept into the way we produce what we call digital cultural heritage, thereby revising our social relationships to digital data by opening them up to the full agency of the world. Such revised practices include the use of automated curatorial systems, documentation, and collecting based on the intents of many interested parties and cuts into the duration of the ecological composition as a collecting and documentation procedure better suited to material and processual forms of investigation drawing inspiration from ontology, Critical Posthumanities scholarship, media ecology and new materialisms. I examine the potential for schemaless databases as tools to activate and collect data in many formats and forms, data analytics and visualizations for documentation, and automated systems to trace and search all these things in unstructured ways.

In doing so I recalibrate curation practices according to post-object thinking, to eco-curation, to cognition beyond that of the human within newly-visible domains of influencing on internets, and to the archive as a worldly practice, using Trump's tweets, bond futures databases[42], and Harmony the sex robot[43] as examples that operate across space and time, and engage many different constituencies including the non-human. Western-ness, human-ness and the technical are no longer at the centre of curation practices. Rather, I conceptualize an open and process-based curatorial system, encompassing the idea of these activities and the curator as comprising more-than-human collectives, agencies, and communities, and at the same time attentive to process, the creation of new things, and a reconceptualization of digital cultural heritage as dynamic ecological compositions. These tasks challenge the basic common and shared references for what heritage and indeed digital cultural heritage is in the West as past-, present-, and future-directed things, as the original, and as artefactual. I make a case for the emergence of the more-than-human curator as influencer, and curating as eco-systemic. Naming, categorizing, and editing is then re-read as influencing, transforming, tracking, contextualizing, and recontextualizing; remixing, emulating, collaborating, and moderating. Authenticity I argue emerges in different genres, from tracking the original through encryption or through blockchain technology in and outside the museum archive to retaining the original alongside the intent of its creator. But significantly here, I contend that authenticity may not even be something to aspire to, as it does not resonate as an overriding concern across all digital realities.

A profusion of new types of societal data and potential heritage forms and their producers is emerging as a result of technological development driven by the intensification of data economies, the emergence of new types of artificial intelligence, algorithms, machine learning, automated systems, and maker cultures. In Chapter 8, *The rise of more-than-human digital cultural heritage in the Technosphere*, I argue that an ever-expanding repertoire of societal data and therefore potential heritage forms are emerging. Within this milieu of technological innovation and the ever-expanding ecological circumstances in which data resides, a broader range of agencies are involved in its production. Emerging from these new forms of writing, recording, memory capture, knowledge production, and anticipatory programming, and through interactions between agencies and systems both human and non-human, the array of data forms involving more-than- and non-human intelligence and cognitive systems that arise challenge current understandings of heritage. A prevalent question in regard to these technical developments is whether data produced by a range of producers becoming historical can be regarded as worthy of heritagization.

Robots, super smart Sophia, Harmony the sex robot, drones, embedded medical devices, automated weapons, bacteria, and automated messaging from banks within the World Trade Center prior to its collapse, as well as automated curation systems, are examples of new more-than and non-human knowledge producers all of which produce data, much of which is saved. In this chapter I discuss all these conjoined entities and make a case for the development of new types of heritage comprising artificial intelligence, automated systems, biological entities, and new materials.

As a result, the notion of human-ness as the central feature and figure in heritage making is displaced. Digital cultural heritage can no longer be considered solely a product of human expression and social life in digital format; indeed, it never was entirely. Human agency and associated definitions of heritage therefore must be recalibrated. Here I draw inspiration from Rosi Braidotti's view of the posthuman subject[44] to read algorithmically driven AI, big data, social bots, automated heritage and maker cultures as empirical case studies that acknowledge the embedded, embodied and affective position of human agency of thinking, reasoning, training, classifying and creating in heritage production. That is not as a singular capacity made possible by technics but as part of eco-curatorial collectives. To do this I advance new concepts and terms for these kinds of more-than-human heritage and investigate the novel forms of humanisms embedded within their ecological compositions. To illustrate different forms of humanisms, I use a range of examples from social bots and the Pizzagate meme as an example of a situated human embedded form (a cyberattack on the Clinton campaign during the US Presidential Election in 2016), maker cultures and 3D printing of couture, Covid-19 face masks, a 3D-printed suicide machine, the Sarco, 3D digitizations of collections as the convergence of materialisms, the human and the technical, and the use of personal data as raw material in data markets as examples of human-ness in all their facets becoming more-than-human digital cultural heritage. All these emerging heritage forms currently operate outside UNESCO definitions. I explain how this data boom generated by all manner of people, AI, and machines has planet-wide ecological implications in the Technosphere, the technical system of the Anthropocene. Digital cultural heritage therefore is implicated in the global problem of unrestrained data production by all manner of producers, excessive demands for more storage, and the burgeoning problem of data waste. I also discuss digital cultural heritage as a problem deeply embedded in the geological substrates of life, in the contemporary climate crisis and environmental destruction through the lens of the Technosphere. Here we witness the emergence of a new type of heritage, the technofossil, the hard parts of data recovered from the archeological sites in the future that have been lost, discarded, and forgotten, such as computer discs recovered from the World Trade Center rubble.

In the conclusion *Framing a more-than-human digital museology,* and drawing on the examples and arguments I make in each of the chapters, I challenge the idea that humanist heritage is a universal definition but rather it becomes merely one form of digital reality which operates among others. In doing so I disrupt its universal claims and its binary figurations. I also reclaim digital cultural heritage as ecological, as of the earth, as more-than- and other-than-human, as a story of deep time and planetary crises and futures yet to come. Digital heritage therefore becomes a practice and technic of life itself. As a result, digital cultural heritage is no longer immaterial or digital memory traces of human expression. It is enmeshed in the broader material history of human–non-human entanglements of planetary extent and impact, from geological mineral deposits made when the universe was created to rare earth elements used in technical systems to their becoming technofossils. Digital cultural heritage, therefore operates as different genres, as humanist, and as more-than-human ecological forms with their own praxes and museological formations that do not necessarily replace each other.

Digital museology in a more-than-human frame becomes a way of being in and becoming with the world. To explain this, I develop a new workable framework, terms, and methods for a more-than-human digital heritage and digital museology within a distributed ecological refiguration, thereby generating a new set of practices and values and ways of framing what we call digital data in an interconnected world. These new concepts, terms and practices include the ecological composition, coordinates, thingness, eco-curating, domains of influencing, cutting, and tracing within and across the ecological composition, and the idea of the world as archive and archiving. Curatorial principles of containment, authenticity, and history are re-worked. When we let go of endangerment and loss as the defining characteristics of heritage, the question then becomes one of renewal, creativity, and new productions.

Heritage and indeed digital cultural heritage, I concur, has always been more-than-human and more-than digital. Data has always been produced by all manner of entities, but this process and the entities involved are expanding. In a more-than-human frame, the human as the pivotal agent in heritage-making is decentred. As a result, new humanisms emerge where human agency or humanness becomes embodied and embedded in ecological compositions as a series of traces across and through them, from writing code to making hardware and infrastructures, from mining minerals to all manner of cultured materials. Modern time and historicity rather become the operation of a series of durational temporalities embedded within their ecological formations that are both non-linear and multi-scalar.

Curatorial work therefore becomes a matter of crafting and composing, of thinking and making ontologies. Curatorial praxis becomes the cut, a method, documentation, and interpretive strategy that seeks to record its processes tethered to the logic of keeping digital data active and continuing. The digital cataloguing of historical data in the archive become emergent processes, and on the other hand processes of renewal, of reuse, and involving the production of new compositions. The world is also a dynamic, circulating archive enabling ecological compositions to run, to renew, to distribute, to proliferate, to create data, and also to pass away. Aura in a more-than-human frame is reworked as a medium of perception born out of the observed, affective, and temporal emergent characteristics of eco-curating processes.

Digital cultural heritage, their usefulness and their reuse in the future will not be solely a legacy of preserved originals. The digital cultural heritage legacies that will be significant for future generations are not only what we seek to make and contain as the artefactual but what is passed on as a dynamic ecological composition in duration – that is, as societal data worth continuing. All this is an invitation to re-address the idea of material and stability and at the same time view digital cultural heritage as renewal and a creative practice, drawing inspiration from digital art practice in which new things are born out of what we currently view as multiple and never-ending cycles of death. An endangered digital cultural heritage is no longer solely concerned with obsolescence, loss, and extinction but equally about creative practice, and signals the difference between modern and non-representational understandings of heritage.

Broadly speaking, cultural practices share a common disposition towards societal data as something of significance worth keeping, maintaining in its aliveness as continuing. Drawing on a broader definition of societal data, a space opens up in which to consider why data is worth saving, and its significance and usefulness in the context of a broader repertoire of digital realities.

## Notes

1 Maggie Haberman, Glenn Thrush and Peter Baker, "Inside Trump's Hour-by-Hour Battle for Self-Preservation," *The New York Times*, Dec 9, 2017, https://www.nytimes.com/2017/12/09/us/politics/donald-trump-president.html.
2 ABC/wires, "Donald Trump Threatens Iran President with Consequences 'few throughout history have suffered'," *ABC News*, July 23, 2018, https://www.abc.net.au/news/2018-07-23/donald-trump-threatens-iran-consequences-few-history-have-seen/10025538.
3 Lily Kuo, "Trump Sparks Anger by Calling Coronavirus the 'Chinese Virus'," *The Guardian*, Tuesday, March 17, 2020, https://www.theguardian.com/world/2020/mar/17/trump-calls-covid-19-the-chinese-virus-as-rift-with-coronavirus-beijing-escalates.
4 AP, "Donald Trump's Tweets are Presidential Records, but What Happens When They Get Deleted or Altered?" *ABC News*, Jan 24, 2017, https://www.abc.net.au/news/2017-01-24/donald-trump-tweets-presidential-records-deletions-edits/8206920; Darren Samuelsohn, "Trump's Tweets Represent Legal Liabilities," *Politico*, Sept 27, 2017, https://www.politico.com/story/2017/09/27/trump-delete-tweets-legal-issues-243212; Shontavia Johnson, "Donald Trump's Tweets Are Now Presidential Records," *US News*, Feb 1, 2017, https://www.pri.org/stories/2018-02-19/donald-trumps-tweets-are-now-presidential-records.
5 Olivia Beavers, "White House Will Preserve All of Trump's Tweets: Report," *The Hill*, March 4, 2017, https://thehill.com/homenews/administration/327125-white-house-will-preserve-all-of-trumps-tweets-reports.
6 Andrew Burt and Samuel Volchenboum, "How Health Care Changes When Algorithms Start Making Diagnoses," *Harvard Business Review*, May 8, 2018.

7 Shoshana Zuboff, *The Age of Surveillance Capitalism.* London: Profile Books, 2019.
8 Mohit Sagar, "How Drones are Assisting Government in China Fight COVID-19," *Opengov*, March 11, 2020, https://opengovasia.com/how-drones-are-assisting-government-in-china-fight-covid-19/
9 Sagar, "How Drones are Assisting Government in China Fight COVID-19,"
10 Sean Greene, Computers can now challenge – and beat professional poker players at Texas hold 'em, *Los Angeles Times*, March 7, 2017, https://www.latimes.com/science/sciencenow/la-sci-sn-computers-poker-20170307-story.html#:
11 Max Opray, "Robots May Change the Sex Industry but Could They Replace Intimacy?" *The Guardian*, April 5, 2017 https://www.theguardian.com/sustainable-business/2017/apr/05/robots-may-change-the-sex-industry-but-could-they-replace-intimacy
12 Alexandra Ma, "China Has Started Ranking Citizens with a Creepy 'Social Credit' System - Here's What You Can Do Wrong, and the Embarrassing, Demeaning Ways They Can Punish You," *Business Insider, Australia*, October 30, 2018, https://www.businessinsider.com.au/china-social-credit-system-punishments-and-rewards-explained-2018-4?r=US&IR=T
13 Helen Pritchard, *Critter Compiler Executing Practices*, 2015, https://research.gold.ac.uk/24852/1/Critter_Compiler_Executing_Practices.pdf
14 Ross Parry, *Recoding the Museum: Digital Heritage and the Technologies of Change.* (Abingdon: Routledge, 2007), 68.
15 Abdelaziz Abid, "Safeguarding our Digital Heritage: A New Preservation Paradigm," in *Preserving the Digital Heritage: Principles and Policies*, eds. Yola de Lusenet and Vincent Wintermans, Selected Papers of the International Conference organized by the Netherlands National Commission for UNESCO and The European Commission for Preservation and Access, The Hague, 4–5 November 2005 (Netherlands National Commission for UNESCO and The European Commission for Preservation and Access, 2005), 2, http://www.ica.org/sites/default/files/WG_2007_PAAG-preserving-the-digital-heritage_EN.pdf, 9.
16 For a discussion of mass-produced objects and the values we attach to them see Daniel Miller, "Materiality: An Introduction," in *Materiality*, ed. Daniel Miller (Durham, NC: Duke University Press, 2005), 1–50.
17 John Plotz, "Can the Sofa Speak? A Look at Thing Theory," *Criticism* 47, no. 1 (2005): 110.
18 *Technology Quarterly*, "More than Just Digital Quilting," *The Economist*, December 3, 2011, http://www.economist.com/node/21540392.
19 Trevor Owens, *Theory and Craft of Digital Preservation* (Baltimore: Johns Hopkins University, 2018), 2–12.
20 For a discussion of museum collections and digitizations as ecological compositions see Fiona Cameron, "Theorizing Digitizations in Global Computational Infrastructures," in *The Routledge International Handbook of New Digital Practices in Galleries, Libraries, Archives, Museums and Heritage Sites*, eds. Hannah Lewi, Wally Smith, Steven Cooke and Dirk vom Lehn (Abingdon: Routledge, 2019); and Fiona Cameron, "Posthuman Museum Practices," in *Posthuman Glossary*, eds. Rosi Braidotti and Maria Hlavajova (London: Bloomsbury Academic, 2018), 349–351.
21 Jerry Vanek, "How will Museums Change after Covid-19?", *SmithGroup*, May 20, 2020, https://www.smithgroup.com/perspectives/2020/how-will-museums-change-after-covid-19
22 Amanda McGowan, "Go by Car to this Toronto art exhibit," *The World*, May 29, 2020, https://www.pri.org/stories/2020-05-29/gogh-car-toronto-art-exhibit
23 For a discussion of museum collections and digitizations as ecological compositions see Cameron, "Theorizing Digitizations in Global Computational Infrastructures"; and Cameron, "Posthuman Museum Practices".
24 Cameron, "Theorizing Digitizations in Global Computational Infrastructures."
25 Cameron, "Theorizing Digitizations in Global Computational Infrastructures."
26 Peter Haff, "Technology as a Geological Phenomenon: Implications for Human Well-Being," in *A Stratigraphical Basis for the Anthropocene?*, eds. C. N. Waters, J. Zalasiewicz,

M. Williams, Michael Ellis and Andrea Snelling, volume 395, no. 1, (London: Geological Society London Special Publications, May 2014), http://dx.doi.org/10.1144/SP395.

27 See Wendy Hui Kyong Chun, *Updating to Remain the Same: Habitual New Media* (Cambridge, MA: The MIT Press, 2017) for a discussion of the use of historical big data to predict future scenarios as a scenario of updating to remain the same.

28 Rosi Braidotti, *Posthuman Knowledge* (Cambridge, UK: Polity Press, 2019).

29 Fiona Cameron, "Object-orientated Democracies: Conceptualising Museum Collections in Networks," *Museum Management and Curatorship* 23, no. 3 (2008): 229–243; Fiona Cameron, "Liquid Governmentalities, Liquid Museums and the Climate Crisis," in *Hot Topics, Public Culture, Museums*, ed. Fiona Cameron and Lynda Kelly (Newcastle, UK: Cambridge Scholars Publishing, 2010), 112–128.

30 For a discussion of museum collections and digitizations as ecological compositions see Cameron, "Theorizing Digitizations in Global Computational Infrastructures"; and Cameron, "Posthuman Museum Practices".

31 See David Lowenthal, *The Past is a Foreign Country* (Cambridge, UK: Cambridge University Press, 1999); and Rodney Harrison, *Heritage: Critical Approaches* (Abingdon: Routledge, 2013) for a discussion of the idea of "creeping heritage."

32 For a discussion of social action on the internet see Yuk Hui, "Infrastructure and Automatic Participation," Techno-Collectivities. International Conference, University of Konstanz, June 9–11, 2016, University of Konstanz, Germany; also see Benjamin Bratton, *The Stack: On Software and Sovereignty* (Cambridge, MA: The MIT Press, 2015), 219.

33 Laurie Frey, "Digital Repatriation – Malagan Mask Makers in Papua New Guinea try out new way of dealing with cultural property ownership," *The Heritagist*, last modified Dec 18, 2012, http://www.theheritagist.com/2012/12/digital-repatriation-malagan-mask.html; "PNG's Malagan Masks to be Digitally Repatriated," *ABC News*, updated Dec 12, 2012, http://www.abc.net.au/news/2012-12-12/an-pngs-malagan-masks-to-be-digitalise/4423464.

34 Wayne Ngata, Hera Ngata-Gibson and Amiria Salmond, "Te Ataakura: Digital *taonga* and Cultural Innovation," *Journal of Material Culture* 17, 3 (2013): 242–243.

35 Adam Stacey, "Images of 7 July: Tunnel Horror," *BBC World News*, July 2, 2006, http://news.bbc.co.uk/2/hi/uk_news/5102860.stm; Allessandro Kauffmann video of the White Island eruption on December 10, 2019, https://www.nzherald.co.nz/nz/news/article.cfm?c_id=1&objectid=12293107. Tiffany Black, "What Happens to Your Facebook Profile When You Die?" accessed March 1, 2017, http://facebook.about.com/od/Profiles/ss/What-Happens-To-Your-Facebook-Profile-When-You-Die.htm; "About Mia Ayliffe-Chung," Facebook profile, accessed March 1, 2017, https://www.facebook.com/MiMiChung7/videos/vb.560643167/10154370825748168/?type=2&theater.

36 Candice Cranmer, "Preserving Time-based Media: A Case Study with Troy Innocent's lifeSigns: Eco-System of Signs & Symbols," *ACMI Labs*, April 11, 2018, https://labs.acmi.net.au/preserving-time-based-media-a-case-study-with-troy-innocents-lifesigns-eco-system-of-signs-3e2f0b3ae2.

37 Kajsa Hartig, Bente Jensen, Anni Wallenius and Elisabeth Boogh, "Collecting the Ephemeral Social Media Photograph for the Future: Why Museums and Archives Need to Embrace New Work Practices for Photography Collections," MW18 Conference, Vancouver, Canada, April 18th–21st, 2018, https://mw18.mwconf.org/paper/collecting-the-ephemeral-social-media-photograph-for-the-future-why-museums-and-archives-need-embrace-new-work-practices-for-photography-collections/.

38 Stephen Hawking website, http://www.hawking.org.uk/the-computer.html.

39 Trevor Owens, *The Theory and Craft of Digital Preservation.* (Baltimore: Johns Hopkins University, 2018).

40 Fiona Cameron, *Museum Practices and the Posthumanities: Curating for Earthly Habitability* (Abingdon: Routledge Environmental Humanities Series, forthcoming); Fiona Cameron, "Theorizing Digitizations in Global Computational Infrastructures," in *The Routledge International Handbook of New Digital Practices in Galleries, Libraries, Archives,*

*Museums and Heritage Sites*, eds. Hannah Lewi, Wally Smith, Steve Cooke and Dirk vom Lehn (Abingdon: Routledge, 2019), 55–67. Fiona Cameron, "Stirring Up Trouble: Museums as Provocateurs and Change Agents in Polycentric Alliances for Climate Change Action," in *Addressing the Challenges in Communicating Climate Change Across Various Audiences*, eds. Walter Leal Filho, Bettina Lackner and Henry McGhie (New York: Springer, 2019) 647–673; Fiona Cameron, "Posthuman Museum Practices," in *Posthuman Glossary*, eds. Rosi Braidotti and Maria Hlavajova (London: Bloomsbury Academic, 2018), 349–351; Fiona Cameron, "The Liquid Museum: New Ontologies for a Climate Changed World," in *Museum Theory: An Expanded Field*, eds. Andrea Witcomb and Kylie Message (Oxford, UK: Blackwell Publishing, 2015), 345–362; Fiona Cameron and Sarah Mengler, "Transvisuality, Geopolitics and Cultural Heritage in Global Flows: The Israeli–Palestinian Conflict and the Death of the Virtual Terrorist," in *Transvisuality: Dimensioning the Visual*, eds. Tore Kristensen, Anders Michelsen and Frauke Wiegand (Liverpool, UK: Liverpool University Press, 2015) 59–72; Fiona Cameron, "Theorizing More-Than-Human Collectives for Climate Change Action in Museums," *L'Internationale Online Climate Change Special Issue* to coincide with the UNFCCC meeting in Paris, 30 November – 11 December 2015, http://www.internationaleonline.org/research/politics_of_life_and_death/48_theorising_more_than_human_collectives_for_climate_change_action_in_museums; Fiona Cameron, "From 'Dead Things' to Immutable, Combinable Mobiles: H.D. Skinner, the Otago Museum and University and the Governance of Māori Populations," *History and Anthropology* Special Issue, 25, no. 2 (March 2014): 208–226; Fiona Cameron, "We Are On Nature's Side? Experimental Work in Rewriting Narratives of Climate Change for Museum Exhibitions," in *Climate Change and Museum Futures*, eds. Fiona R. Cameron and Brett Neilson (Abingdon: Routledge Museum Research Series, 2014), 51–77; Fiona Cameron, "Ecologizing Experimentations: A Method and Manifesto for Composing a Post-humanist Museum," in *Climate Change and Museum Futures*, eds. Fiona R. Cameron and Brett Neilson (Abingdon: Routledge Museum Research Series, 2014), 16–33; Fiona Cameron, "Climate Change, Agencies and the Museum and Science Centre Sector," *Museum Management and Curatorship* 27, no. 4 (October 2012): 317–339 (Best paper award for 2012); Fiona Cameron, "Liquid Governmentalities, Liquid Museums and the Climate Crisis," in *Hot Topics, Public Culture, Museums*, eds. Fiona Cameron and Lynda Kelly (Newcastle, UK: Cambridge Scholars, 2010), 112–128; Fiona Cameron, "Object-orientated Democracies: Conceptualising Museum Collections in Networks," *Museum Management and Curatorship* 23, no. 3 (2008): 229–243.

41 "email497.xml," *The September 11 Digital Archive*, http://911digitalarchive.org/items/show/39760.

42 For an ethnography of bond markets see Iain Hardie and Donald MacKenzie, "Assembling an Economic Actor: The *Agencement* of a Hedge Fund," *The Sociological Review* 55, no. 1 (February 2007): 57–80.

43 Sean Keach, "Dirty Droid, Harmony Sex Robot Gets 'Mind-Blowing X-Mode' Upgrade Making It Even MORE Lifelike," *The Sun*, Oct 5, 2018, https://www.thesun.co.uk/tech/7073748/harmony-sex-robot-release-date-app-sexbot-doll/.

44 Rosi Braidotti, *Posthuman Knowledge* (Cambridge, UK: Polity Press, 2019), 12.

## Bibliography

ABC/wires. "Donald Trump Threatens Iran President with Consequences 'few throughout history have suffered'." *ABC News*, July 23, 2018. https://www.abc.net.au/news/2018-07-23/donald-trump-threatens-iran-consequences-few-history-have-seen/10025538.

ABC. "PNG's Malagan Masks to be 'Digitally Repatriated'." *ABC News*, updated December 12, 2012. http://www.abc.net.au/news/2012-12-12/an-pngs-malagan-masks-to-be-digitalise/4423464.

Abid, Abdelaziz. "Safeguarding our Digital Heritage: A New Preservation Paradigm." In *Preserving the Digital Heritage: Principles and Policies*, edited by Yola de Lusenet and Vincent Wintermans, Selected Papers of the International Conference organized by the Netherlands National Commission for UNESCO and The European Commission for Preservation and Access, The Hague, 4–5 November 2005 (Netherlands National Commission for UNESCO and The European Commission for Preservation and Access, 2005), 2. http://www.ica.org/sites/default/files/WG_2007_PAAG-preserving-the-digital-heritage_EN.pdf.

AP. "Donald Trump's Tweets are Presidential Records, but What Happens When They Get Deleted or Altered?" *ABC News*, Jan 24, 2017. https://www.abc.net.au/news/2017-01-24/donald-trump-tweets-presidential-records-deletions-edits/8206920.

Beavers, Olivia. "White House Will Preserve All of Trump's Tweets: Report." *The Hill*, March 4, 2017. https://thehill.com/homenews/administration/327125-white-house-will-preserve-all-of-trumps-tweets-reports.

Billock, Jennifer. "How Will Covid-19 Change the Way Museums Are Built?" *Smithsonian Magazine*, September 16, 2020. https://www.smithsonianmag.com/travel/how-will-covid-19-change-way-future-museums-are-built-180975022/.

Black, Tiffany. "What Happens to Your Facebook Profile When You Die?" *Facebook*, accessed March 1, 2017. http://facebook.about.com/od/Profiles/ss/What-Happens-To-Your-Facebook-Profile-When-You-Die.htm.

Braidotti, Rosi. *Posthuman Knowledge*. Cambridge, UK: Polity Press, 2019.

Bratton, Benjamin. *The Stack: On Software and Sovereignty*. Cambridge, MA.: The MIT Press, 2015.

Burt, Andrew and Samuel Volchenboum. "How Health Care Changes When Algorithms Start Making Diagnoses." *Harvard Business Review*, May 8, 2018. https://hbr.org/2018/05/how-health-care-changes-when-algorithms-start-making-diagnoses.

Cameron, Fiona. "Liquid Governmentalities, Liquid Museums and the Climate Crisis." In *Hot Topics, Public Culture, Museums*, edited by Fiona Cameron and Lynda Kelly, 112–128. Newcastle, UK: Cambridge Scholars Publishing, 2010.

Cameron, Fiona. "Object-orientated Democracies: Conceptualising Museum Collections in Networks." *Museum Management and Curatorship* 23, no. 3 (2008): 229–243.

Cameron, Fiona. "Posthuman Museum Practices." In *Posthuman Glossary*, edited by Rosi Braidotti and Maria Hlavajova, 349–351. London: Bloomsbury Academic, 2018.

Cameron, Fiona. "Theorizing Digitizations in Global Computational Infrastructures." In *The Routledge International Handbook of New Digital Practices in Galleries, Libraries, Archives, Museums and Heritage Sites*, edited by Hannah Lewi, Wally Smith, Steve Cooke and Dirk vom Lehn, 55–67. Abingdon: Routledge, 2019.

Cameron, Fiona. "Climate Change, Agencies and the Museum and Science Centre Sector." *Museum Management and Curatorship* 27, no. 4 (2012): 317–339 (Best paper award for 2012).

Cameron, Fiona. "Ecologizing Experimentations: A Method and Manifesto for Composing a Post-humanist Museum." In *Climate Change and Museum Futures*, edited by Fiona Cameron and Brett Neilson, 16–33. Abingdon: RoutledgeMuseum Research Series, 2014.

Cameron, Fiona. "From 'Dead Things' to Immutable, Combinable Mobiles: H.D. Skinner, the Otago Museum and University and the Governance of Māori Populations." *History and Anthropology* Special Issue, 25, no. 2 (2014): 208–226.

Cameron, Fiona. *Museum Practices and the Posthumanities: Curating for Earthly Habitability*. Abingdon: Routledge Environmental Humanities Series, forthcoming.

Cameron, Fiona. "Stirring Up Trouble: Museums as Provocateurs and Change Agents in Polycentric Alliances for Climate Change Action." In *Addressing the Challenges in*

*Communicating Climate Change Across Various Audiences*, edited by Walter Leal Filho, Bettina Lackner and Henry McGhie, 647–673. New York: Springer, 2019.

Cameron, Fiona. "The Liquid Museum: New Ontologies for a Climate Changed World." In *Museum Theory: An Expanded Field*, edited by Andrea Witcomb and Kylie Message, 345–362. Oxford, UK: Blackwell Publishing, 2015.

Cameron, Fiona. "Theorizing Digitizations in Global Computational Infrastructures." In *The Routledge International Handbook of New Digital Practices in Galleries, Libraries, Archives, Museums and Heritage Sites*, edited by Hannah Lewi, Wally Smith, Steve Cooke and Dirk vom Lehn, 55–67. Abingdon: Routledge, 2019.

Cameron, Fiona. "Theorizing More-Than-Human Collectives for Climate Change Action in Museums." *L'Internationale Online Climate Change Special Issue* to coincide with the UNFCCC meeting in Paris, 30 November – 11 December2015. http://www.internationaleonline.org/research/politics_of_life_and_death/48_theorising_more_than_human_collectives_for_climate_change_action_in_museums.

Cameron, Fiona. "We Are On Nature's Side? Experimental Work in Rewriting Narratives of Climate Change for Museum Exhibitions." In *Climate Change and Museum Futures*, edited by Fiona Cameron and Brett Neilson, 51–77. Abingdon: RoutledgeMuseum Research Series, 2014.

Cameron, Fiona and Sarah Mengler. "Transvisuality, Geopolitics and Cultural Heritage in Global Flows: The Israeli–Palestinian Conflict and the Death of the Virtual Terrorist." In *Transvisuality: Dimensioning the Visual*, edited by Tore Kristensen, Anders Michelsen and Frauke Wiegand, 59–72. Liverpool, UK: Liverpool University Press, 2015.

Chun, Wendy Hui Kyong. *Updating to Remain the Same: Habitual New Media.* Cambridge, MA: The MIT Press, 2017.

Cranmer, Candice. "Preserving Time-based Media: A Case Study with Troy Innocent's life-Signs: Eco-System of Signs & Symbols." *ACMI Labs*, April 11, 2018. https://labs.acmi.net.au/preserving-time-based-media-a-case-study-with-troy-innocents-lifesigns-eco-system-of-signs-3e2f0b3ae2.

Fisher, Marc, John Woodrow Cox and Peter Hermann. "Pizzagate: From Rumor, to Hashtag, to Gunfire." *The Washington Post*, Dec 7, 2016. https://www.chron.com/national/article/Pizzagate-From-rumor-to-hashtag-to-gun-re-10779741.php.

Frey, Laurie. "Digital Repatriation – Malagan Mask Makers in Papua New Guinea try out new way of dealing with cultural property ownership." *The Heritagist*, last modified Dec 18, 2012. http://www.theheritagist.com/2012/12/digital-repatriation-malagan-mask.html.

Greene, Sean. "Computers can now challenge – and beat professional poker players at Texas hold 'em," *Los Angeles Times*, March 7, 2017. https://www.latimes.com/science/sciencenow/la-sci-sn-computers-poker-20170307- story.html#:

Haberman, Maggie, Glenn Thrush and Peter Baker. "Inside Trump's Hour-by-Hour Battle for Self-Preservation." *The New York Times*, Dec 9, 2017. https://www.nytimes.com/2017/12/09/us/politics/donald-trump-president.html.

Haff, Peter. "Technology as a Geological Phenomenon: Implications for Human Well-Being." In *A Stratigraphical Basis for the Anthropocene?*, edited by C. N. Waters, J. Zalasiewicz, M. Williams, Michael Ellis and Andrea Snelling, volume 395, no. 1. London: Geological Society London Special Publications, May 2014. http://dx.doi.org/10.1144/SP395.

Hardie, Iain, and Donald MacKenzie. "Assembling an Economic Actor: The *Agencement* of a Hedge Fund." *The Sociological Review* 55, no. 1 (2007): 57–80.

Harrison, Rodney. *Heritage: Critical Approaches*. Abingdon: Routledge, 2013.

Hartig, Kajsa, Bente Jensen, Anni Wallenius, and Elisabeth Boogh. "*Collecting the Ephemeral Social Media Photograph for the Future: Why Museums and Archives Need to Embrace New Work Practices for Photography Collections*." MW18 Conference, Vancouver, Canada,

April 18th–21st, 2018. https://mw18.mwconf.org/paper/collecting-the-ephemeral-social-media-photograph-for-the-future-why-museums-and-archives-need-embrace-new-work-practices-for-photography-collections/.

Hui, Yuk. "*Infrastructure and Automatic Participation.*" Techno-Collectivities. International Conference, University of Konstanz, June 9–11, 2016, University of Konstanz, Germany.

Johnson, Shontavia. "Donald Trump's Tweets Are Now Presidential Records." *US News*, Feb 1, 2017. https://www.pri.org/stories/2018-02-19/donald-trumps-tweets-are-now-presidential-records.

Kauffmann, Allessandro. "White Island eruption." 2019. Video, embedded in https://www.nzherald.co.nz/nz/news/article.cfm?c_id=1&objectid=12293107.

Keach, Sean. "Dirty Droid, Harmony Sex Robot Gets 'Mind-Blowing X-Mode' Upgrade Making It Even MORE Lifelike." *The Sun*, Oct 5, 2018. https://www.thesun.co.uk/tech/7073748/harmony-sex-robot-release-date-app-sexbot-doll/.

Kember, Sarah and Joanna Zylinska. *Life after New Media: Mediation as a Vital Process*. Cambridge, MA: The MIT Press, c. 2012.

Kuo, Lily. "Trump Sparks Anger by Calling Coronavirus the 'Chinese Virus'." *The Guardian*, March 17, 2020. https://www.theguardian.com/world/2020/mar/17/trump-calls-covid-19-the-chinese-virus-as-rift-with-coronavirus-beijing-escalates.

Lowenthal, David. *The Past is a Foreign Country*. Cambridge, UK: Cambridge University Press, 1999.

Ma, Alexandra. "China Has Started Ranking Citizens with a Creepy 'Social Credit' System – Here's What You Can Do Wrong, and the Embarrassing, Demeaning Ways They Can Punish You," *Business Insider, Australia*, October 30, 2018. https://www.businessinsider.com.au/china-social-credit-system-punishments-and-rewards-explained-2018-4?r=US&IR=T.

McGowan, Amanda. "Go by Car to this Toronto art exhibit," *The World*, May 29, 2020. https://www.pri.org/stories/2020-05-29/gogh-car-toronto-art-exhibit.

Miller, Daniel. "Materiality: An Introduction." In *Materiality*, edited by Daniel Miller, 1–50. Durham, NC: Duke University Press, 2005.

Ngata, Wayne, Hera Ngata-Gibson, and Amiria Salmond. "Te Ataakura: Digital *taonga* and Cultural Innovation." *Journal of Material Culture* 17, 3 (2013): 229–244.

Opray, Max. "Robots May Change the Sex Industry but Could They Replace Intimacy?" *The Guardian*, April 5, 2017. https://www.theguardian.com/sustainable-business/2017/apr/05/robots-may-change-the-sex-industry-but-could-they-replace-intimacy.

Owens, Trevor. *The Theory and Craft of Digital Preservation*. Baltimore: Johns Hopkins University, 2018.

Parry, Ross. *Recoding the Museum: Digital Heritage and the Technologies of Change*. Abingdon: Routledge, 2007.

Plotz, John. "Can the Sofa Speak? A Look at Thing Theory." *Criticism* 47, no. 1 (2005): 108–118.

Pritchard, Helen. *Critter Compiler Executing Practices*, 2015. https://research.gold.ac.uk/24852/1/Critter_Compiler_Executing_Practices.pdf.

Sagar, Mohit. "How Drones are Assisting Government in China Fight COVID-19," *Opengov*, March 11, 2020. https://opengovasia.com/how-drones-are-assisting-government-in-china-fight-covid-19/.

Samuelsohn, Darren. "Trump's Tweets Represent Legal Liabilities." *Politico*, Sept 27, 2017. https://www.politico.com/story/2017/09/27/trump-delete-tweets-legal-issues-243212.

Stacey, Adam. "Images of 7 July: Tunnel Horror," *BBC World News*, July 2, 2006. http://news.bbc.co.uk/2/hi/uk_news/5102860.stm.

Technology Quarterly. "More than Just Digital Quilting" *The Economist*, December 3, 2011. https://www.economist.com/technology-quarterly/2011/12/03/more-than-just-digital-quilting.
Vanek, Jerry. "How will Museums Change after Covid-19?", *SmithGroup*, May 20, 2020. https://www.smithgroup.com/perspectives/2020/how-will-museums-change-after-covid-19.
Zuboff, Shoshana. *The Age of Surveillance Capitalism*. London: Profile Books, 2019.

# 2

# THE OFFICIAL BIRTH OF DIGITAL DATA AS UNIVERSAL HERITAGE

Digital data is perceived as the stuff of contemporary life on which our future prospects depend. The impetus for embedding and attributing heritage value to digital data therefore arises from the exponential increase in the quantity and diversity of cultural materials that are now produced in digital format and where no analogue equivalent is apparent.

This chapter is dedicated to promoting a critical discussion of the birth of digital cultural heritage as a universal heritage through the library, archive sector and through UNESCO's (United Nations Educational, Scientific and Cultural Organization) bureaucratic mechanisms. The aim here is to develop a better understanding of digital cultural heritage whose genre as a subset of heritage and as a new technical object is both ambiguous and theoretically undersubscribed. In addition, the emergence of digital data as heritage I assert challenges our understanding of what heritage is and the traditions of heritage practice.

In the course of this chapter, I identify the context and milieu in which digital cultural heritage comes to be, and problematize and disrupt digital cultural heritage as an idea, its theoretical bases and its human-centeredness. To do this I explore the following questions. What is digital cultural heritage and how does digital data then become subject to heritagization through the UNESCO charter? How does digital data operate as a universal heritage in an increasingly complex and digitally mediated world in contrast to the informal practices of heritagization occurring in other public and private spaces? How is digital cultural heritage narrated in conventional heritage frameworks, and how do these agendas challenge or re-enforce established norms? Here digital data and its framing as heritage is my central concern. In conclusion I explore a series of case examples in which UNESCO's universal vision of digital cultural heritage and its globalizing agenda is usurped, challenged, reframed and overturned.

## "Creeping heritage"

The creation of digital cultural heritage as an official heritage by UNESCO in 2003 and, at around the same time, of intangible heritage were procedures tantamount to what historian David Lowenthal calls "creeping heritage."[1] Creeping heritage is a consequence of a cultural milieu where heritage is perceived as ubiquitous. Here the material substrates in which cultural expression is made explicit in contemporary life have expanded and diversified greatly, at the same time replacing older forms based on materials such as paper and wood. Now almost anything can be attributed heritage status if it is valued, seen as endangered, and earmarked for preservation. Further to this, other forms of cultural expression of a "non-material kind" are being inducted into UNESCO's heritage stable as worthy of preservation, such as intangible cultural heritage,[2] after pressure from UNESCO's North Asian members.

Digital cultural heritage is profusing because data and computers are now central to the enactment of contemporary life. But digital heritage and its ubiquity relate not only to the types and forms of data classified as significant repositories of cultural memory; rather, they are by their very nature constitutive of the dominating contemporary memory of life. The production and dispersal of large amounts of data about us and our everyday lives, recorded and operationalized through large-scale systems, for example, constitute a deeper, more pervasive industrialization and commodification of memory in digital format. All these materials are potentially heritage in the making if they meet certain criteria.

## Refiguring digital data as digital cultural heritage

Digital cultural heritage as a concept and as a method for transforming digital data into heritage is still taken almost as a given, and as a result remains largely untouched by critical discourse.[3] In this discussion I expand on my 2005 critique of digital cultural heritage in respect to its co-relation with modern heritage frameworks as a subgroup of heritage products.[4]

The discussion in this section is directed towards a deeper interrogation of digital cultural heritage and its political affiliations, with the specific purpose of illuminating the powerful and loaded system of definition that is enshrined in charters and practices that led to its birth and subsequent emergence. What we witness here, and as I will explain in detail later, is the melding of heritage narratives as a representational affordance with a new type of materiality, digital code.

*Digital cultural heritage* is conceived as all digital data that a society sees as of enduring value that is important enough to retain, keep, preserve and pass on to future generations. Once tagged as heritage, digital materials are understood as intellectual and cultural resources having lasting cultural value and significance, and constitute a heritage that should be protected and preserved for current and future generations.[5] Digital cultural heritage comprises specific types of computer-based cultural materials representative of societal activity from the past.[6] Digital cultural heritage is from a technical point of view a computational "object".

As digital data is inducted into heritage frames, it immediately becomes historical data and then representational things that document, stand for, and embody human cultural life. Accordingly, digital cultural heritage is understood as digital data that is able to sustain social life, embody human knowledge, expression and experience in support of social pursuits and most importantly memory recall.

Digital data as a form of heritage was made official by UNESCO in 2003 and was subsequently inducted into their stable of heritages that year. Because digital data such as websites, blogs, discussion lists, and so forth often only exist on the world-wide web, they have been viewed by UNESCO as fragile, risky, and an unstable platform.[7]

UNESCO was established in 1945 under the auspices of the United Nations and the Charter of the United Nations as a post-war initiative directed to the reconstruction of Europe's intellectual and moral foundations after the devastating consequences of World War 2.[8] In the aftermath of war, UNESCO was viewed as a civilizing organization of global reach that could promote peace through cooperation directed towards the development of global standards in education, in science, in communication, and in cultural pursuits promoting universal respect for human rights, justice, law and supporting fundamental freedoms.[9] UNESCO began with a utopian agenda, but these aspirations soon conflated into an intergovernmental agency directed towards the provision of technical assistance for cultural reconstruction and the conservation of buildings, museums, libraries, and art. UNESCO at that time capitalized on the post-war reconstruction, recovery, and heritage-making movements and folded its aspirations into a project devoted to making a "heritage of humanity" which it could circumscribe and whose preservation it could direct.[10] Such regulatory processes were aimed at decisions such as what from the past is deemed worthy of recovery; what best reflects the new global order; and how the past might be managed for the betterment of humankind into the future.[11] Today UNESCO remains the primary international body whose mandate is to encourage and enable the preservation and enjoyment of the cultural, scientific, and information heritage of the global populace[12] including digital data and in particular those forms that exist online because they are viewed as fragile, risky, and unstable.[13]

## The emergence of digital data as universal heritage: The early years

A substantive and excellent literature traces the growth of cultural heritage as a concept and its politics. Cultural heritage refers to sites such as monuments and buildings, museum collections, archives, manuscripts, and practices that have cultural, historical, aesthetic, archaeological, scientific, ethnological, or anthropological value to groups and individuals. They are all things that a society inherits from the past and intends to keep and pass on to future generations.[14]

Archaeologist and heritage theorist Rodney Harrison charts the emergence of material heritage, tracing the idea from its inception in Euro-American conservation movements in the eighteenth century to its materialization as an all-encompassing, universal concept and as a professional practice culminating in the World Heritage Convention of 1972.[15] In a similar manner, the idea that digital data should be a new type of cultural heritage emerged out of the conservation movements of the library and archive sector and their attempts to deal with digital techniques and the new materials produced with them.

In 2000, the International Federation of Library Associations (IFLA) was the first official organization to attribute heritage status to digital data, motivated by the burgeoning of digital publications, activated by the threat of their obsolescence, and as a response to an urgent need for the sector to adapt to this new environment.[16] In the same year a Committee on Digital Preservation was established during the Conference of Directors of National Libraries (CDNL) to raise awareness within the library community and more widely of the urgent need to safeguard digital cultural heritage, and to develop an international research agenda for digital longevity.[17] Here the emergence of digital cultural heritage was founded on the notion of societal risk on one hand and of salvage on the other.

The attribution of heritage status to digital data as a global societal concern within the archive sector was catalysed by the International Council on Archives at its XIV International Congress (Seville, Spain, September 2000) through a resolution that encouraged national archivists to institute digital preservation programs that could ensure access to the content and functionality of authentic electronic records into the future. The rights of a global citizenship to access such records in perpetuity was one of the drivers behind their agenda.[18]

As the impetus grew for transforming digital data into a new form of heritage, the Conference of Directors of National Libraries (CDNL) Committee on Digital Preservation drafted the UNESCO Resolution on Digital Preservation.[19] The circumstances in which data emerged as a distinctive type of heritage are outlined below in their submission to UNESCO:

> *Preservation of Digital Heritage*
>
> *The General Conference*
> *Recalling* that the preservation of and access to the cultural heritage is one of UNESCO's major concerns,
>
> *Considering* that, with respect to the preservation of the cultural heritage, UNESCO has initiated several international conventions and recommendations, including the Convention for the Protection of the World Cultural and Natural Heritage, and has moreover established the "Memory of the World" programme specifically aimed at preservation and access of documentary heritage,
>
> *Considering* that many of the world's cultural, educational and scientific resources are increasingly produced, distributed and accessed only in digital form,
>
> *Considering* that government and public administration depend more and more on continued access to digital records and documents not available in any other form,

> *Considering* that digital information is highly susceptible to both technical obsolescence –of hardware, software and data formats- and physical decay,
> *Considering* that as the digital information economy rushes to adopt newer formats, older information formats become obsolete at an alarmingly fast rate,
> *Considering* that maintaining on-going access to digital information resources is complex and costly, requiring long-term commitment,
> *Considering* that libraries and archives have traditionally been responsible for safeguarding the intellectual and cultural heritage and the administrative record of nations and are committed to long-term access...[20]

This CDNL document called on UNESCO to recognize digital data as a form of documentary heritage to be protected and inducted into its stable of heritages alongside other types and forms of universal heritage within its Memory of the World Program. This call was prompted by a perceived shift in the material foundations of cultural and social life from paper documentary records to digital data. The value of data within this framework was limited to its role as emblematic of cultural life in a digital form. Its distinctiveness from other types of heritages was premised on its digital materiality.

To ensure ongoing access to digital data for the long term beyond the short-term horizon of profit-driven corporate entities, libraries and archives were nominated to become the institutional location for preservation. These institutions' traditions of salvage and storage in regard to other types of paper records and their experience with the development of standards across collection genres were considered to make them suitable and trusted repositories. Strikingly we see a shift from concerns in respect to physical decay to ones that recognized the problem of technical obsolescence. This is because digital information is not subject to gradual decay. While paper-based information may be preserved by benign neglect, digital resources either exist or are lost forever.[21] But paradoxically, and in contrast to paper records, the frequent use and widespread circulation of digital information enhances the chances of its survival.

The focus of the document is clearly on the born-digital: "Materials created in digital form are also called 'born-digital materials' and include for instance all types of websites and databases, electronic records, e-journals, digital photographs and audio-visual materials and digital text archives."[22] Digital resources were made subject to technical forms of preservation and classified by type, media, and technical medium. Recommendations made by the CDNL Committee on Digital Preservation were resolved in the 2001 UNESCO resolution on the Preservation of Digital Heritage:

> *Considering* that the preparation of standard-setting instruments in the field of culture and information is an important and universally valued task of UNESCO, lying at the very heart of its mandate.
> *Recalling* that the preservation of the digital heritage constitutes an important aspect of UNESCO's Draft Medium-Term Strategy for 2002–2007 (31 C/4)

> as stated in paragraphs 208, 209, 210 and 211 of that document, which includes the launching of an international campaign to safeguard endangered digital memory and the drafting of guidelines for the preservation of digital heritage and for preserving materials in digital form, Also recalling UNESCO's determination, as expressed in the Draft Medium-Term Strategy (31 C/4) under strategic objective 12, paragraph 171, to give encouragement to the formation or strengthening of existing networks of archives, libraries and other documentation services through institutional support and to the establishment of a world network of developers and users of digital information management and processing tools,
>
> Invites the Director-General: (a) to prepare for the 164th session of the Executive Board a discussion paper containing elements of a draft charter on the preservation of digital heritage. This draft charter should be submitted for adoption to the General Conference at its 32nd session in 2003...[23]

First, the ratification of the Committee's recommendations by UNESCO acknowledged that digital data was an endangered heritage and a globally collective digital memory that must be preserved across national, regional, and global scales. Second, the document inducts digital heritage into UNESCO's strategic programme of preservation as a priority; prompts the launch of an international campaign to safeguard endangered digital memory; and calls for the development of standardizing instruments and the strengthening of documentary heritage networks.

The digital surrogate or digitization itself was not attributed heritage status; rather, the digitization was seen to exist solely to serve other forms of documentary heritage. For UNESCO digitizations are put to work to replicate a fragile cultural memory imprinted in other material forms reminiscent of previous eras such as paper, parchment, and film.[24] Digitization programs under the auspices of UNESCO did precede the declaration. The UNESCO Slave Trade Archives project for example, launched in 1999[25] and funded by the Norwegian Agency for Development Cooperation (NORAD) and involving 11 countries, is an early example of a large-scale digitization preservation initiative that sought to improve the conservation and accessibility of trans-national slave trade documents and artefacts.

## UNESCO and the birth of digital cultural heritage

The first reference to born-digital data as an official digital cultural heritage across the broader heritage sector is evident in the 2002 UNESCO document produced for the United Nations Year for Cultural Heritage.[26] In the following year, UNESCO created the Charter on the Preservation of Digital Heritage for the establishment of digital cultural heritage as an official, common and universal heritage.[27] The UNESCO General Conference adopted Resolution 34 at its 31st session on October 15, 2003, thereby drawing attention to the emerging digital heritage and the need for an international campaign to safeguard endangered digital memory.[28] Its opening declaration included these observations:

> *Recognizing* that such resources of information and creative expression are increasingly produced, distributed, accessed and maintained in digital form, creating a new legacy – the digital heritage...
>
> *Aware* that access to this heritage will offer broadened opportunities for creation, communication and sharing of knowledge among all peoples. Understanding that this digital heritage is at risk of being lost and that its preservation for the benefit of present and future generations is an urgent issue of worldwide concern...[29]

The development of the briefing document was led by the National Library of Australia.[30]

Here UNESCO's dominant globalizing principle, the invocation of a universal digital cultural memory, seeks to galvanize people around digital cultural heritage as a collective memory and to unify this field of heritage making through a set of standardizing procedures, regimes, and objects. Motivated by a belief in a world citizenship and a humanity mobilized around a digital heritage, UNESCO sought to frame and secure a post-national, transnational digital memory in the service of humanity's future across domains of practice.

Digital cultural heritage emerges as a result of a dialogue between UNESCO and heritage professionals. Through these dialogues, and by transposing heritage concepts onto digital resources, digital data became caught up in heritage procedures enmeshed in West-centred values: technical, economic, aesthetic, conceptual systems and of time. The impetus to attribute an elevated status of heritage to digital resources (and thus situate them alongside other heritages already recognized) was a desire to safeguard them and institute preservation mechanisms to digital data augmentation deemed to be at risk, now or in the future.

The heritagization of digital cultural materials is also demonstrative of the use by UNESCO of global and globalizing processes as a means to frame digital data as heritage and its preservation as a global concern across scales and cultures, and importantly to ensure it remains accessible to the public. To do this, the preamble of the charter signals a shift in the management of digital cultural heritage from individual institutions and nations to the global sphere as a heritage collectively owned. In this vein, it calls for a globally coordinated campaign of preservation "on the part of governments, creators, publishers, relevant industries and heritage institutions."[31]

For UNESCO it is an agenda of heroic rescue from the perils of an impending digital dark age. The creation and bureaucratization of digital resources in heritage terms is pragmatic. It is a way of categorizing a burgeoning and globally dispersed stockpile of digital content and of discriminating between that which is deemed significant and valuable and that which is not.

The rationale for globalizing heritage is explicitly established in the UNESCO statement that "Digital heritage emanates from different communities, industries, sectors and regions... [and] may exist in any language, in any part of the world, and in any area of human knowledge or expression."[32] Further to this, UNESCO insists as expressed in Article 9 ("Promoting cultural diversity"), that the digital heritage of all regions, countries, and communities should be preserved and made accessible, creating over time a balanced and equitable representation of all peoples, nations, cultures, and languages. The regimes of digital cultural heritage-in-the-making span not only all cultures but all domains of social and material life and all areas of production and consumption, from commerce and the law to academia; to government institutions and government itself; to art, design, and the creative industries; and to online gaming and the personal realm, including all forms of social media. The specificity of digital materials as heritage forms becomes customized according to the specific sets of criteria operating as abstractions of social life.

Digital cultural heritage is established through the UNESCO charter as a practice and a schema that seeks to establish digital data as universal heritage through standardization procedures in which data in all its multifarious variations is refigured according to a series of overarching values and categories for worldly bureaucratic purposes in line with and in support of an emerging globally networked information society. The entire apparatus of abstraction and simplification that UNESCO sought and still seeks to promote through its conventions, recommendations, charters, and declarations, collectively described by the organization as normative instruments,[33] operates as standardization procedures directed towards making digital data into a universal heritage for perpetuity. To achieve this, UNESCO's approach was distinctly technocratic, technical, and utopian. In doing so, UNESCO sought to generalize the particular. Standardizing procedures were put to work to create a series of common characteristics and properties out of diverse data to enable heritage bureaucrats to rise above and abstract the particular cultural nuances inherent in it. Standards also sought to formulate categories that had the potential to fold the different values and views that people hold about digital data into compatible systems of understanding and thereby allow federated access and discovery across vast distances, territories and institutions. These standardizing processes, presented as agreed international standards for best practice involving narrative schemas and material practices, were transferred over from other types of heritage and imposed on digital data as normative forms and praxes. With the acknowledgement by UNESCO in 2003 of digital data as a specific type of heritage (discussed in Chapter 4), born-digital items have gradually been acknowledged as having heritage value within institutions and therefore as worthy of collecting and preserving.

The first mode of standardization was born out of the observation that the foundation of human social communication systems, memory functions, forms of capital accumulation, meaning-making capabilities through culture, language, and experience and associated forms of expression was rapidly becoming embedded in data enacted through digital media and made operable through complex infrastructural systems. Accordingly, the creation of digital materials as heritage reinforced the demarcation of things based on materials (either immaterial digital or the material analogue). Using the term digital as an identifier drew on conventions of substance. Like the analogue object, digital cultural heritage (whether born or surrogate) also acts as a reservoir of meaning – a direct link to its creation, to a formative event, to a person or another type of referent. Here modern and humanist notions of material, value, time, temporality, and historicity were imposed on digital data.

Like other types of heritage, born-digital heritage is backward-looking, involving the conservation of things that already exist, because it is from and of the past. It follows, therefore, that the emphasis is on preserving and saving data rather than on the production of new work. Because data as heritage is seen as something that exists, is (already) there, the task of the heritage professional was simply to collect and order digital materials. Their value only accrues in relation to the past that is made for them in the present. The past therefore becomes known through selected materials.

Digitizations, on the other hand, are viewed as copies of analogue sources and are new works that are created and built. Through mass digitization projects, heritage institutions become deeply involved in the production of new heritage. But the digitization's deferential role in respect to the analogue renders invisible the circumstances of their creation. The concealment of the reproduction's unique attributes and the production of a copy without visible signs of its making complete the very act of conjoinment with its so-called real source. It becomes historical data of its source and does not uphold a history of its own.

The categorization and promotion by UNESCO of the separate categories of tangible and intangible heritage are reminiscent of the application of the philosophical principles that underpin the neoliberal industrialized world, founded on and driven by hubris and the rationalist dualism of French philosopher René Descartes. The styles of thought promoted by Descartes' thinking emphasize a dualistic metaphysics in the service of a hierarchical division of the world into immaterial, mental things (mind) and material things (matter).[34]

The theory of the mind (intellect, consciousness, reason, subjectivity, moral conscience) became emblematic of a humanity where the modern individual was placed above other people, beings, and things.[35]

Within this framework, heritage is assigned by UNESCO to categories: intangible heritage[36] embracing non-material and living forms of human creativity such as oral traditions, social practices, rituals, knowledge, and skills to produce things (each being products of the mind); and material things, tangible heritage, as objects, monuments, and so forth.

With the creation of digital cultural heritage a second mode of standardization emerges: the digital as a category of heritage in-between, a technical heritage that is both ethereal, a product of the mind – for example, information and digital code – and material, dependent on computer hardware to bring it to life. Such binary oppositions are evident in media, manifest as comparisons between new digital and old analogue media, and distinctions made between interactive – information, the virtual, the immaterial, convergence and data – and non-interactive – the stable and inert analogue, material and physical matter.

A third mode of standardization is the concept of endangerment. Both the born and the replicant (digitization) as forms of heritage emerge in the context of risk, in which the latter has a secondary status. Here the sources of risk and therefore memory loss are identified as the passage of time, decay, the fragility of materials and digital networks; the uncertainty of technological change; and rapid technological obsolescence in the context of the very platforms in which these materials were created. The specific considerations and processes that activate digital preservation and archiving campaigns are detailed in Article 3 of the Charter, concerning the threat of loss:

> ...the world's digital heritage is at risk of being lost to posterity. Contributing factors include the rapid obsolescence of the hardware and software which brings it to life, uncertainties about resources, responsibility and methods of maintenance and preservation, and the lack of supportive legislation... To preserve digital heritage, measures will need to be taken throughout the digital informational life cycle, from creation to access. Long-term preservation of digital heritage begins with the design of reliable systems and procedures to produce authentic and stable digital objects...[37]

The Charter expressly refers to the quality of this new heritage as digital software at risk of obsolescence. Software and hardware, while demarcated in the Charter as binary opposites operate as interdependent cultural and technological actants, alongside their imperfections both placing digital data at risk, but in different ways. The Charter foregrounds a series of uncertain or potential threats to digital cultural resources, thereby articulating an affective atmosphere of urgency. Critically, the invocation of urgency provided the impetus to establish a more global sense of the digital as a form of potential heritage, collectively valued and owned.

> Digital technology is constantly evolving and new versions of software replacing earlier ones in the context where the net is constantly being rebuilt, all these things leading to a loss of the contemporary expressions of living culture, intangible heritage.[38]

The loss of digital data is presented as perilous, not only in terms of an impending death of significant digital materials that has the potential to undermine the cultural fabric of global communities, but also as a more immediate and catastrophic threat to the continuation of cultural life itself. Here digital data has a specific role in anchoring the experience and knowledge of late modernity in perpetuity. The past and its making through the heritagization of digital data are therefore presented as stabilizing, enacted through a curatorial process of selection, captured, uprooted, gathered up, relocated, reconstructed, and represented within a selective heritage tradition.

This preoccupation with digital obsolescence, that is, the loss of digital formats, programs and technology as a research agenda in the early years and into the present, is an outcome of Jeff Rothenberg's 1995 article in *Scientific American*, "Ensuring the Longevity of Digital Documents." Rothenberg's call to action through the promotion of technology and technical solutions for digital preservation was taken up by the library and archive sector in the US and Europe and later UNESCO. This focus on digital obsolescence directed thought and action in particular ways, to the detriment of core tasks of selecting and collecting digital cultural heritage.[39] Furthermore, UNESCO's technical disposition directed towards salvage and conservation – both pragmatic pursuits in the face of obsolescence – were deemed more important than conceptualizing and theorizing these "objects" in new and different ways according to their affordances.

In doing so, the Charter not only created new forms of value, to be attributed to digital data on the basis of their cultural content and what they symbolize, but also sought to have those digital resources deemed significant, removed from everyday life, rendered redundant in their originating use contexts to become bureaucratized through a digital archiving campaign. Accordingly, the fourth mode of standardization directs institutions to remove so-called significant data from society by means of its collection, documentation, and storage in heritage institutions. In doing so, UNESCO seeks to unify and centralize endangered data knowledge about society as a public good to benefit all humanity. By quarantining and standardizing digital data in this manner, it is claimed that its so-called defining and authentic characteristics are assured and maintained.

Digital data comes in an infinite number of variations and formats. A fifth mode of standardization is thus the demarcation of digital cultural heritage as type categorizations and accompanying forms of value. These variations are standardized by selecting and arranging digital data on the basis of type categories according to their specific qualities, media formats, and societal functions through sets of authenticating procedures. The UNESCO resolution sets up a binary opposition between the materiality of digital software as information and the multifarious material qualities of the analogue.

The very foundation of cultural capital in heritage practice and in museum culture is framed around the selection and attribution of value to all manner of collections as material evidence of the passage of time and as symbols of cultural life. These authenticating practices directed to the maintenance of the original through artefactual encapsulation to be discussed in Chapter 6 collectively uphold the authority of the institution. In order to maintain the original's superior standing, the culture of modern heritage regimes and the museum is one of demarcating and maintaining clear-cut categorizations between originals and reproductions. The UNESCO charter seeks to uphold this division by instituting separate categories and descriptors for the born-digital original and digital copies of the analogue.

To support these demarcations, the Charter elicits new sub-categories within the digital cultural heritage register. These two distinctive types are: *digitally born*, and *digital surrogates* (now popularly known as digitizations).[40] Each type is defined on the basis of its origin and history of production, and according to the intent of its creation.

UNESCO prioritizes "*Digitally born*" resources as a type where "there is no other format but the digital original"[41] and which is ephemeral in nature. Such digital materials include digital texts; organizational and personal records of activity; transactions; correspondence; datasets collected to record and analyse scientific, geospatial, spatial, sociological, demographic, educational, health, environmental and other phenomena; learning objects; software tools such as databases; models; simulations and software applications; digitally-generated artworks and documentary photographs; scans, still and moving images; audio recordings; graphics; web sites; blog posts; social media pages in a wide and growing range of formats.[42] With no apparent non-digital counterparts, digital cultural resources are seen as highly vulnerable to degradation and loss.[43]

On the other hand, the *digital surrogate* is a copy captured from already existing analogue sources for the specific purposes of representation or research. Such digitizations can be captured images; 3D scanned objects; or digital videos of performances as representations of intangible heritage and visualizations of historical structures and environments.[44] While these collections may appear less vulnerable, many according to the National Library of Australia guidelines "hold the only surviving version of an original that has since been damaged, lost, or dispersed."[45]

The widely held view is that to digitize heritage is to actualize collections digitally. Digital copying therefore involves the careful step-by-step digital capture of the sources' surface features and form, digital reprocessing, and display using advanced imaging technology. Digitizing collections becomes an automated copying procedure rather than a creative or inventive act.

The way we perceive digitizations and classify them within heritage frameworks as new forms of collection copying follows the habits and routines of earlier types of reproduction. Such procedures become categorically intuitive and therefore unquestioned. Within this regime of value, born-digital heritage is founded on an artefactual notion of identity, and digitization is founded on an informational one. Such practices frame digitizations as having historical and heritage value that is as culturally significant but not authentic, or as originals in their own right. Their material composition or processes of production remain largely irrelevant for interpretative purposes because it is made and put to work to authenticate its analogue source.

The status of the digitization changed between 2002 and 2003. In UNESCO's Charter of 2003, the surrogate became heritage. This move represented the heritagization of copying culture. Digitizations are not considered historical data in their own right or worthy of inter-generational transmittance in the way that born-digital objects are given heritage status. Digitizations that merge with their original source become historical data and therefore heritage items. This shift in value may have occurred because originals are always endangered, and digitized copies were seen to act against their disappearance. Whether a digitization, and in particular one of the simple-image variety becomes historical data and potentially heritage is a subjective judgment based on whether it is considered unique, worth saving, keeping, and passing on. Simple images and even 3D representations become heritage by default if they are copies of the analogue source and are preserved. Indeed, billions of digitizations reside in databases and circulate in the worldly archive, with decisions as to their value left to institutions and individuals. Those that are kept by default become heritagized.

Digital copies may be coupled to their source through their semblance, but like other copies they are never the same as each other because they comprise different digital files made up of bits of various sizes and formats, appear on different platforms, devices, browsers, and monitors, and at different resolutions, are subject to different routing, algorithmically driven personalization schemas, are updated in the cloud on a regular basis, and so forth.

Accordingly, digital cultural heritage, both the born and surrogate, while an endangered digital memory, also becomes a technical heritage on one hand and a social object on the other. A sixth mode of standardization therefore is the compilation of digital cultural heritage as cultural information, as forms of human knowledge and expression, and as historical texts. To this end, practices of standardization are directed towards the identification of certain types of digital cultural materials and their segregation into a discrete system of value. Each selected item therefore shares similar rhetorical qualities and truths as significant examples of human knowledge and cultural expression. Digital cultural heritage therefore operate at once as data, and as evidential facts symbolic of their utility and social significance. Here the born-digital is most clearly distinguished from the digitization as being artefactual because it is framed as a singular unique entity that embodies its own temporal and historical framework equivalent to other material heritage. As with other heritage, the designation of digital cultural heritage privileges its human-centred rhetorical and social function, not its material composition (with the exception of preservation) or other things interior and anterior to it. Rather it is defined on the basis of what it does and can do to uphold societal memory and social practice. The Charter's description of this form of heritage as cultural knowledge and information seeks to promote the idea of digital data as embodying significant cultural knowledge as well as acting as social texts, symbols, and metaphors, and our engagement with them primarily as a communicative act and activity. Digital cultural heritage therefore comprises a new form of language (through code) for writing culture. Like other types of artefacts such as archaeological collections[46] emphasis is placed on data and its role as a social text and as symbols from which socio-cultural insights into the past might be acquired.

Born-digital heritage is therefore defined within the single dimension and hierarchical relation of human subject–object relations acting as passive representations of contemporary social life and directed towards how digital cultural heritage can serve people's need for symbolic referents and memorializing rituals. Past narratives and stories embodied as code are central to their role as a memory resource. These forms of valuation, as part of heritagization processes and standard object procedures, become embedded in data, naturalized and obviate alternative perspectives on what digital data means or how it is valued differently in the world. Born-digital materials within UNESCO's heritage assemblage come into their own because they have the potential to cite a point of origin in the course of their history as testimony to their significance and therefore gain the ability to activate an auric response because they can be connected to a person, location, an event. Through the identification of their original form and origin, their authenticity can be assured. Aura, according to a conventional heritage reading of Walter Benjamin's concept, is tied to a work of art's authenticity, defined on the basis of its discernible point of origin and its subsequent history: "the essence of all that is transmissible from its beginning, ranging from its substantive duration to its testimony to the history that it has experienced."[47] With the attribution of heritage to digital data, origin and authenticity become the definable markers of aura above conventional substance. Similarly, the term digital is used to demarcate and describe these things materially.

Accordingly, registers of comparability include representational approaches founded on objecthood that are privileged above other worldviews in respect to the value and importance of digital data, the material, affective qualities of digital media and their non-human and more-than-human elements. The production of digital cultural heritage objecthood through preservation also seek to render data inanimate, removed from the complex more-than-human ecosystems which they comprise in their lived context, thereby ensuring their availability as a tangible readable entity. The act of heritagization itself represents a shift from the practical use contexts in which digital data resides to their re-emergence like other artefacts, as socio-cultural props and empirical devices directed to sustaining cultural life and through which the user might gain insights into the past.

A seventh mode of standardization within the heritage-making register is the invocation of cultural significance, the past, and generations yet to arrive. Digital cultural heritage as a symbolic descriptor ascribed to digital data has a very specific trajectory that emerges from the conventional political language of heritage and heritage preservation to which these types of heritage become attuned.[48] UNESCO combines the politics and symbolism of cultural heritage with digital data in the Charter in the formulation "our legacy from the past, what we live with today, and what we pass on to future generations." Heritage is something that is, or should be, passed from generation to generation because it is valued.[49] Not all digital materials are, according to UNESCO, of enduring value, but those earmarked as significant require active preservation approaches if these digital cultural heritages are to be maintained.[50]

These standardizing procedures define digital data as materials that support the invocation of a longing for that which has gone before and therefore act as a spiritual anchoring and as something worthy of generational remittance. Cultural significance is transformed into a bureaucratic instrument used to discriminate between stockpiles of data and thereby to determine what constitutes valued heritage. Article 7 explains this further in the clause "Selecting what to keep":

> As with all documentary heritage, selection principles may vary between countries, although the main criteria for deciding what digital materials to keep would be their significance and lasting cultural, scientific, evidential or

> other value. "Born digital" materials should clearly be given priority. Selection decisions and any subsequent reviews need to be carried out in an accountable manner, and be based on defined principles, policies, procedures and standards ... Member states need appropriate legal and institutional frameworks to secure the protection of their digital heritage...[51]

The drive to preserve through UNESCO's bureaucratic apparatus seeks in the first instance to frame a global digital memory[52] field that is better able to promote the creation and sharing of heritage. An eighth mode of standardization therefore invokes not only universalizing principles directed to the creation of a universal heritage but also the sharing of heritage. The Charter focuses on the expansion and enhancement of access to such materials through technical innovation, its production in multiple formats, and the universalizing characteristics of digital data and the web as a mode and site for cultural production across territories and diverse communities. The Charter also acknowledges the emergence of new media ecologies made possible by the valency of the software and therefore the opportunities this medium offers for its distribution, access, sharing, and its co-production by multiple users, who are conceived solely as the human kind.

But these standardizing procedures in which type categorizations, fixed meanings, and objects are produced go against the material and computational efficacy of digital data and media. Digital data are processes that have the ability to transform and refashion relations, meanings, and descriptors in lively and unexpected ways.[53] They comprise a very diverse range of digital forms in respect to their technical features, as a consequence of their diverse functions and uses.

This very act of heritagization instituted by UNESCO and the notion of digital data having an objecthood map onto the object-orientated museum culture, thereby occasioning the framing of digital cultural heritage "objects" in representational terms in a way that obscures computational processes.

But it is no longer useful to view digital data-as-heritage as pre-existing artefacts able to represent the world. They might still have a role in representing contemporary life, like any other type of heritage, but digital data-as-heritage can take on other roles in their active state outside conventional heritage preservation programs to be discussed in the following chapters.

The assumption of the existence of a shared universal heritage invoked a set of rights in respect to their access. The standardization process also generated an array of organizational responsibilities, expectations, and practices. As a result UNESCO calls for a consensus among heritage, library, and archive institutions on how to do this work.[54] To further this, the perceived risk to cultural life, paired with preservation, also acts as a lever for the emergence of the digital archive and new forms of professionalism adapted from those used to managing analogue or tangible resources (i.e. historic cities and towns, historic landscape, archaeological sites, ancient buildings, museum collections, archives, and libraries). The same bureaucratic processes are put to work directed to the creation, ordering, management, and dissemination of digital assets.[55] This new digital cultural heritage field, according to UNESCO, "integrates the traditional expertise of heritage management, museology, history and archaeology, and the powerful new tools of digital information technologies."[56] Here ICTs (information and communication technologies) blend with heritage discourses, disciplines, representational schemas, and management systems. Additionally, they are composed as tools and software best able to democratize the heritage field beyond the confines of professional expertise and disciplinary specialisms.

Protocols for the identification and extraction of heritage items from the vast pool of digital data included strategies for developing international metadata, archival and preservation standards, programs that sought to make this data accessible and the emergence of new professions, languages and technical solutions to do this work. Even global publics are rendered as a universal citizenry and interpretive community where digital cultural memory becomes freely available to the world.

UNESCO's agency in the making and maintaining of digital cultural heritage as standard objects is enabled through the commingling of bureaucratic mechanisms such as legislation, collecting policies and procedures, modes of discrimination and ordering and administered through sanctioned bodies and through professional forms of expertise such as museums and libraries.

Accordingly, and through the charter, digital cultural heritage operates as a dispersed dynamic assemblage of entangled elements and forces, epistemologies, heritage principles, digital data, media, technologies, policies, human bodies, standard objects, and computers. The planned obsolescence of technology threatens to pull apart this heritage assemblage, whereas the valuation system and preservation procedures embodied in the Charter act as a way to cohere it.

UNESCO's regime of world heritage-making instituted in the World Heritage Convention of 1972 has come under fire from academics, activists, and indigenous peoples because of dissatisfaction with its universalizing mission that fails to respect sovereignty and incorporate other world views and ethical principles, and rights of inclusion, access, and use.[57]

This critique identifies that what has come to constitute heritage is a western genealogical project. Making digital data into heritage objects involves a series of prior philosophical, political, ideological and bureaucratic decisions by UNESCO about their objecthood, how their structure (software and computer hardware) is stabilized, how the selection, naming, categorization and the meaning given to digital resources is enacted, and the professional expertise required to institute these procedures and processes. The formulation and stabilization of digital data as heritage objects enable them to gain cultural value as authentic markers of what they stand for. Human thought also resides in their social construction, that is, the narratives that circumscribe why specific data is significant historically, stylistically and culturally. Significance is further underwritten by heritage values such as perceived loss, salvage, cultural memory, and cultural investments in the future. These processes are functional outcomes of how heritage subjects are imagined and how digital cultural heritage objects are formed.

The intensifying global production of digital data emerges as an equally burdensome challenge in digital preservation, as does obsolescence, a problem partly deriving from the ability to collect and store more granular and voluminous amounts of data[58] and the lack of appropriate and easy solutions for their preservation. There has been a tenfold increase in all the world's data since 2017. More than four billion people are now using the internet. Because of the vast amounts of data currently being produced daily, the selection and collection of significant historical data from this indeterminable stockpile residing in all manner of spaces and devices becomes ever more problematic. This situation has been driven by individuals' appetite to self-publish, as smartphones and cameras enable people to record and document the minutiae of their lives and post them on Twitter, Instagram, and Facebook alongside the bit trails we leave on websites, social media sites, and search engines. Furthermore, the burgeoning of data economies, the production of cultural life in digital format, the digital consumption of music and film and the rise of computing devices in everyday objects able to send, receive and produce data, alongside public and private sector authorities' interest in the capture of information about our lives as taxpayers and citizens in health, education, employment, and other domains contribute to data proliferation. The requirement and desire to make public information freely available alongside the emergence of open data strategies and repositories for its reuse contribute to the exponential increase in data copying.[59] The conduct of research using digital technologies, from the documentation of assets such as natural resources and the big-data modelling of real world problems such as climate change to mass digitization projects from collections data to medical imaging is also expanding locations for data production. Further to this, the apparatus of control-society intelligence gathering from surveillance cameras; GPS biometric technologies; electronic fingerprint evidence alongside a range of automated processes is all data with potential heritage-like value. Importantly, the overwhelming focus on digitizing collections to make them web accessible has diverted institutional resources from collecting born-digital materials.[60]

The dynamics, circumstances and events that enabled the digital cultural heritage composition to emerge include: the exponential growth of the internet and its infrastructures, new communicative technologies, the creation of digital cultural materials as new forms of cultural expression; the globalization of technology; and new modes of global capital accumulation entrenched in the digital and informational economy alongside the drive for novelty and its binary, obsolescence. Because digital data such as websites, blogs, discussion lists, and so forth often only exist on the world wide web, they have been viewed by UNESCO as fragile, risky, and an unstable platform.[61]

The preservation of digital cultural heritage in the context of global crises has subsequently been fine-tuned through regional programs such as the Joint Programming Initiative on Cultural Heritage and Global Change (Europe) and the Europeana digital collections comprising more than 50 million digitized items.[62]

## UNESCO's Current Agenda

The salvage and framing of digital data as standard objects as a remit to avert digital obsolescence remains UNESCO's preoccupation. At the Memory of the World Conference in Vancouver in September 2012, the urgency of this matter was expressed as a pressing need to establish a roadmap for the digital preservation of digital information. These discussions led to the UNESCO/UBC Vancouver Declaration on Digitization and Preservation of December 2012. In this declaration we see a shift from a sole focus on technical concerns to the preservation of data and its value for society alongside the study of societal and cultural histories and practices. This sociological interest is pursued through strategies that seek to raise awareness of the value of digital data and the reasons why it should be preserved, alongside access to digital information as a fundamental question of human rights.[63]

In addition to this it was also acknowledged that the heritage sector lacks the skills and expertise to carry out such tasks, and more fundamentally that it remains ill-equipped to deal with this new type of technical heritage. To support this the Declaration enshrines a new type of digital citizenship as a ninth mode of standardization in which individuals are seen as having fundamental rights to have access to, seek, receive, and impart information in digital format. Here the trustworthiness and integrity of documentary heritage were deemed prerequisites to exercising these rights. The rights of Indigenous people and the control and ownership of their digital cultural heritage were also recognized. The Declaration also prescribed legal and institutional frameworks to manage copyright and access to such materials. The 2003 UNESCO Charter on the preservation of digital cultural heritage was subsequently amended to include clauses on access to documentary heritage.[64]

Further to this action plan, and through a tenth mode of standardization, the Declaration made explicit reference to the identification and induction of exemplary, key born-digital documentary heritage into its register of the Memory of the World (MoW) Program: "By progressively identifying, recognizing and highlighting significant and irreplaceable documentary heritage" through the MoW register, "the larger objectives of preservation, access and awareness are promoted and advanced." The inscription of an item on any MoW register is an affirmation by UNESCO of its permanent value and significance.[65]

UNESCO sought to promote collaborations between the information industry, public authorities, cultural heritage institutions, and civil society. In doing so, UNESCO acknowledged the important role that the private sector, in collaboration with heritage organizations and civil society, can play in digital preservation alongside strategies to raise awareness of personal data as heritage worth saving, the importance of personal archiving, and the need to ensure analogue content is made available in digital format. Critically, urgency as a motivational logic remains at the forefront of such preservation efforts. Of importance was the articulation of an obligation on the part of cultural heritage institutions to ensure the reliability, authenticity, copyright ownership, and future use of digital information, and to develop policies for all aspects of the management and preservation of digital materials. Here the formulation of standard objects through the Charter took a more systematic turn. A further set of standardizing procedures was instituted in the form of metadata standards for describing and managing digital data as well as enabling interoperability between multiple repositories and their digital contents. The Memory of the World also encouraged the implementation of national and international standards initiatives to ensure that digital data could be retained for the long term.[66] But more importantly, the Memory of the World Register and its MoW logo operate as a standardizing procedure directed to certifying certain types of digital data as globally significant. Securing an authentic record through the preservation of digital heritage was therefore seen as of the upmost importance.

For the purposes of the Memory of the World Register, the MoW defines "a document as having two components or aspects: the information content and the carrier on which it resides," arguing that "both may be of great variety and, in the context of inscribed documents, of different degrees of importance."[67] But it takes the view that, in the case of digital or "machine-readable documents – all audiovisual documents except analogue photographs and all digital documents – the carrier, although necessary to physically hold the information, is of lesser, and often of no importance in the context of Memory of the World."[68] This represents a shift in emphasis from the technological carrier to the preservation of historical data as cultural information embedded in software, because new modes of preservation promoted by UNESCO involve the "migration from one storage platform and carriers to the next."[69]

UNESCO's latest agenda PERSIST (Platform to Enhance the Sustainability of the Information Society Transglobally) is a collaborative project with the International Federation of Library Associations and Institutions (IFLA), International Council of Archives (ICA), and other partners to address globally pressing questions in respect to digital strategies, techniques, selection, responsibility, and the division of labour in initiating and completing such tasks.[70] The programme was launched at the conference "A Digital Roadmap for Long-Term Access to Digital Heritage" in The Hague in December 2013 with three foci: content, technology, and policy. Central to this is a focus on different strategies for digital preservation, from applications to support new solutions that call for emulation and virtualization to the tracking of file formats and digital content via documentation, validation, testing, and migration.

The informational paradigm is now driving preservation with this shift from technological solutions to the collection and use of information. The approach is narrow in focus based on an informational thesis and the collection of information bits – digital materiality. Critically, while here we witness a shift from immateriality to bits, all these things remain informational. This more recent focus on collecting digital data as bits within the UNESCO agenda operates as an eleventh mode of standardization that can be traced directly to the positioning paper "The Paradox of Selection in the Digital Age," presented at the PERSIST session at the IFLA World Library and Information Conference (WLIC) on August 17–23, 2014, in Lyon, France.[71]

Overall, the agenda of the paper's authors is directed towards shifting the focus of preservation strategies from technology to the selection of information as bits in respect to their use over that of content, informed by Negroponte's work. But added to this, the use of digital information therefore becomes the focus of selection as a key indicator of societal significance. They couch this shift in terms of different types of materialities - from collecting atoms to collecting bits:

> The really valuable parts of the web are not the bits which contain the "content" (text, pictures, film.) but the bits that capture our on-line behaviour. Businesses have succeeded in distinguishing between useless and useful information in the digital mass.[72]

At the 2015 UNESCO General Conference, there was a recognition of the complexity and the mutual incommensurability of digital cultural heritage "objects" that are at the same time dynamic, complex systems. The acknowledgment of the complexity inherent in preservation raises important questions in regard to the collecting, description, management, and theorization of digital cultural heritage, all of which the Conference recognized as remaining unresolved:

> Taking into account the rapid evolution of technology, and the challenge of establishing models and processes for preserving digital heritage objects including complex ones, such as multi-media works, interactive hypermedia, online dialogues and dynamic data objects from complex systems, mobile content and future emerging formats…[73]

Again, UNESCO's aim is to design a universal technical system and metadata standards that can solve all digital preservation problems. Digital cultural heritage and preservation cannot be reduced to a series of normative procedures and standard objects. Solutions must take account of each as dynamic, complex processes out in the world rather than as an authentic original locked down in the archive. The production of standard objects becomes a diversion in many cases. There is no singular solution; rather, multiple approaches must be undertaken on a continuum between the authentic original saved in the archive and its lively career in its becoming. I discuss the implications of becoming-preservation and becoming-documentation as an emergent process in Chapter 7. In addition, specific cultural practices relating to death and renewal must be applied to collection and preservation strategies. Within the UNESCO schema, digital preservation is never completed, because of the emphasis on maintaining the original. Such a rubric is governed by understanding the risks inherent in losing content or losing the ability to render and interact with it. In the end, we can never save everything. Some things are meant to be ephemeral, such as the many emails which stand in for phone conversations. Indeed, Snapchat, an image messaging and multimedia mobile application, acknowledges the ephemeral character of most of our interactions by arranging for messages to be available only for a short period of time before they disappear. The overriding question is how can a preoccupation with inventory and control based on the creation of standard objects and procedures operate in a context where digital data defies such a logic?

## Disrupting UNESCO's sovereignty and heritage practices

Despite all this, UNESCO's work in digital cultural heritage remains in service of the idea of data preserved as authentic and the original. The UNESCO system seeks to stabilize and fix digital data as forms of information and cultural expression in space and time. This philosophical disposition is made manifest through prescriptions for managing digital data to ensure that it remains understandable, therefore readable or manifest from the commands of its making, in order to uphold institutional relevance and societal usefulness. This is achieved by saving and protecting original data through documentation and supporting metadata in the context of the secure archive.

But other approaches to digital preservation in vintage gaming fields thrive outside the archive and disrupt the very idea of conventional material authenticity, aura, and the original. Such practices by so-called rogue archivists seek to overcome the death of digital data through an entirely different set of philosophies and practices. Here the focus is on the preservation of the working function of digital data by capitalizing on its digital affordances and continuous re-use, in contrast to the privileging by formal heritage institutions of the authentic form of the object as its preservation. The death of digital data is therefore averted for the time being.

In gaming circles, the continual use of games played and replayed on different platforms over decades becomes the preservation strategy. In doing so, emulators both transform and preserve software as variants. The explosion in the numbers of emulators and participatory media has shifted the management of digital data as cultural legacies to diverse communities of interest, thereby empowering them to make decisions about what is worthy to preserve and what should be deleted.[74] Accordingly, copyright, the desire to own and protect data by heritage institutions, acts as an anti-preservationist strategy.

Interestingly, both approaches are underpinned by the same concerns, namely the fragility of technical platforms, the risk posed to significant digital data worth saving, and the desire to preserve games for perpetuity. Similarly, preservation is driven by the desire to preserve things so they might be used in the future. What is different here is the intent, that is between the commitments to "the original" and "salvage for posterity" that drive heritage preservation and the continued use contexts that drive gaming forms.

### *The rise of more-than- and other-than-human domains of influencing and the more-than-human user*

Democratizing heritage is framed in the UNESCO charter as a series of processes that seek to facilitate the ability to enhance research, management, and the involvement of audiences, tourists, and communities in the material remains of the past.[75] To support this ICTs are framed as technical supports put to work to build digital cultures to support economic development; as a medium for the expression of cultural identity; and as a technological schema to facilitate cross-cultural communication, cultural tourism, and educational enrichment.

In order to operationalize these aspirations UNESCO imagines its global regime of cybernetic power and digital cultural heritage, the transnational flows of information, policy, preservation strategies, and community engagement, as occupying a singular coherent space organized hierarchically from individuals and local communities to nations, regions, and global civil society, from within which action can be mobilized. But in reality the internet operates as multiple meta-territorial domains of infinite reach and depth populated by diverse agents of the human, more-than-human and non-human kind, mobilizing all manner of social, economic, cultural, and political possibilities, frictions, and resistances.

Media theorist Benjamin Bratton uses the concept of the Stack as a way of explaining the emergence of global computational apparatus and new governing structures as a coherent and all-encompassing technological megastructure of life.[76] The Stack concept while universalizing in its conception is a useful lever for identifying how digital cultural heritage as an idea is integrated into contemporary culture, not just as emergent products of the UNESCO charter but also integrated into governance structures, geopolitical configurations and even environmental crises. Here I re-work Bratton's Stack as multiple, more-than- and other-than-human domains of influencing involving human, more-than-human and non-human actors.

As a result, digital cultural heritage (born-digital and digitizations), operate as a series of uneven and chaotic interactions on these multiple internets as an outcome of the convergence of these domains of influencing, producing new sovereign and geopolitical realities that are often unplanned and unexpected. These domains of influencing comprise the interactions of multiple actors, from multi-scaled energy sources and rare earth mineral sources, data centres, server farms, museums, undersea fibre-optic cable networks, cloud infrastructures, and platforms to users, sensors, robots, algorithms, automations, molecules, and bits, databases, and interfaces, addressing systems, and as modes of computation such as applications, automations and machine learning, smart grids, and the Internet of Things. Interactions in and across these domains of influencing on a micro and macro scale, and through their chaotic and unpredictable lines of flight, disrupt and transcend the supposedly ordered geographies of nation, of territory, and of homeland. Furthermore, the logic of global space in which UNESCO and universal heritage operate becomes not a hierarchical and ordered series of entities and processes but rather multiple and interacting geoscapes.

Within the Stack geoscapes arise, Bratton explains, as multiple contested territories based on the aggregation of encounters and relationships between people, things and material events, that often remain unresolved.[77] They involve the circulation of images, ideas, plans, projections, claims, ideologies, cultural perspectives, aspirations, economic agendas, and forecasts that cross borders and geographical locations. Within heritage assemblages, geoscapes are made actionable through more-than-human and other-than-human domains of influencing that are often not necessarily planned in advance and also used opportunistically by politically-motivated groups.

One example of the operation of these domains of influencing and the emergence of a geoscape in which digital cultural heritage is ideologically implicated is the case of the movie *300: Rise of an Empire* and its representation of the Battle of Thermopylae between the Persians and Spartans in 480BC.[78] Through the Google search engine digitizations of Persian objects were used as signifiers of Iranian cultural identity but in the case of *300* these artefact representations were mobilized differently to counter negative representations of ancient Persia.

> All of Tehran was outraged. Everywhere I went yesterday, the talk vibrated with indignation over the film *300* – a movie no one in Iran has seen but everyone seems to know about since it became a major box office surprise in the U.S. As I stood in line for a full hour to buy ajeel, a mixture of dried fruits and nuts traditional to the start of Persian new year festivities, I felt the entire queue, composed of housewives with pet dogs, teenagers, and clerks from a nearby ministry, shake with fury…
>
> I returned home to discover my family in a similar state of pique. My sister-in-law sat behind her laptop, sending off an e-mail petition against the film to half of Tehran, while my husband leafed through a book on the Achaemenid Empire, noting that Herodotus had estimated the Persian army at 120,000 men, not one million as the film claimed. The morning newspaper lay on the table with the headline "*300* AGAINST 70 MILLION!" (the population of the country). It was echoed by the evening news: "Hollywood has opened a new front in the war against Iran."
>
> Top officials and parliament have scorned the film as though it were a matter of state, and for the first time in a long while, taxi drivers are shaking their fists in agreement when the state news comes on. Agreeing that *300* is egregious drivel is fairly easy. I'm relatively mellow as Iranian nationalists go, and even I found myself applauding when the government spokesman described the film as fabrication and insult.[79]

Human users who searched for the film were diverted away through search engine spiders to a website, Project 300,[80] that displayed contemporary Iranian art, documentaries and links to the British Museum's *Forgotten Empire*. *Forgotten Empire* was an exhibition celebrating the Persian Empire and its artefactual legacies from the period under the Achaemenid Great Kings (550–330 BC). The exhibition comprised 321 artefacts, including art and architectural elements from the royal palaces at Persepolis. All these "treasures" are legacies of the Great Kings removed from Persia after the conquest of their empire by Alexander of Macedon. Here, Iranians involved in Project 300 exploited the modes of power afforded by more-than- and other-than-human domains of influencing that underpin global cybernetic space. Through these actions, collection digitizations were used to project positive representations of Persian civilization during the period in question and bolster contemporary national narratives of pride.[81]

The *300* movie fiasco assembled what the Project 300 activists considered the truth or what Bruno Latour calls "matters of fact."[82] Digitizations of Persian objects as interfacial images through their circulation across these domains of influencing enabled the performance of diverse narratives operating as indisputable facts of Persian sophistication and prowess from an Iranian point of view, and at the same time became matters of concern around the *300* movie as an arena within a broader geopolitical space.[83] Here the political configuration that cohered around the *300* movie and Project 300 represented the aggregation of the agencies of these domains of influencing in which participants, nonhumans as well as humans, gathered. The *300* movie incident represents the conative actions of electrical currents, extensive networks of cables and data infrastructures such as cloud platforms, address systems, automations, materials, algorithms, sensors, bots, code, curators, the *Forgotten Empire* exhibition, Iranian nationals, users and so forth. While Iranian citizens were not directly involved in the making of the movie and the majority had never seen it, these more-than- and other-than-human domains of influencing brought them together with Project 300.

The user is generally conceived as a human actor within an infosphere in which cultural communication is enabled by ICTs and where digitizations, for example, act as a human-centred object of knowledge and a social text. Further to this, museums and other heritage institutions view users as independent curatorial agents able to express their own thoughts, actions, desires, and opinions in a democratic manner, and view digitizations as singular, coherent and visual metaphors of cultural identity through their representational role in respect to their material original. But we know that the human is always collectively formed, as an eco-systemic entity, whether that be through the exchange of genetic material in biological evolution or in a psychological setting as the emerging consequences of the embedded cultural and social contexts from which our lives are constituted. Occasions such as *300* become not only a social, cultural affair but also a collective more-than-human and other-than-human political and machinic event. Participation in such events is open to all manner of human, more-than-human and other-than-human agents including AI and social bots. It is clear therefore that the interaction of all these things, rendered possible through the actions of multiple intelligent agents and more recently machine learning as well, not only collapses the notion of the user as an independent agent of self-mastery but also renders their actions as chaotic, frictious, uncertain, and unplanned. Human curatorial acts are no longer central to this. While human agency does not dissolve, it rather operates in lively ways in collaboration with more-than-human, non-human agents and subjects.

UNESCO's vision of a global digital cultural heritage is founded on the notion of a human cosmopolitanism and informationalization, a moral manifesto for the planet where nations and citizens come together to save a universal heritage. Furthermore,

UNESCO promotes the idea that users are human "masters of data," thereby promoting a solely human frame of reference and rendering invisible the multifarious more-than-human actants that comprise "the user." Events such as the *300* example illustrate how more-than-human and other-than-human domains of influencing redefine borders away from geographical territories based on nation states and a human-focused global citizenship. Geographical territories are collapsed by the actions of these domains of influencing, and multiple interfaces accumulate into new types of networks and territories.

The domains and computational infrastructures of which digital cultural heritage is now part activate political and ideological wars over identity as an emerging more-than-human and machinic form of curatorial agency. Here we witness the emergence of a more-than-human global cosmopolitanism that also encompasses more-than-human machines such as switches, robots, codes, sensors, and so forth.

## *Challenging digital cultural heritage as a concept and practice in non-western cultural contexts*

UNESCO promotes digital cultural heritage as a universal concern even though it is a distinctly Eurocentric and humanist concept. This is indeed representative of what feminist philosopher Rosi Braidotti calls a mental habit of universalism[84] and in this instance visions of the human and the digital continue to promulgate in a hegemonic, colonial and Enlightenment form. While the UNESCO charter acknowledges that forms of cultural expression vary across the globe, the bureaucracy fails to adequately take account of the different values and attitudes that others may hold in respect to born-digital heritage and digitizations, and the different relationships they may develop with them, although this is slowly changing. It is well recognized that UNESCO's notions of universal heritage and heritage management in regard to material and intangible heritage are often in conflict with Indigenous and local practices.[85] Media scholar Sheenagh Pietrobruno has poignantly illustrated this, in the context of her examination of intangible cultural expression promoted through YouTube, by uncovering a conflict between official heritages as sanctioned by UNESCO and local practices among Turkish Mevlevi whirling dervishes. Search results on YouTube revealed that algorithmic agency was directed towards the privileging of UNESCO's versions of these cultural performances. Positioned solely as a masculine act in official records, the unofficial heritages of local, living communities show these performances to be non-gendered forms of cultural expression.[86]

By examining non-western cultural approaches to digital data, and in particular digitizations, and the interpretation of these objects in the context of the standardizing principles progressed by UNESCO, the very notion of digital cultural heritage as a universalizing imperative is called into question.

With the rise of ubiquitous computing and digital access in remote communities alongside better imaging quality, the ability to produce 3D models in smaller file sizes that are easily downloadable has made possible the new field of digital repatriation, by which heritage institutions can repatriate collections in digital form to source communities such as the Nalik people in New Ireland, Papua New Guinea. Museum scholar and anthropologist Graeme Were, formerly of Queensland University, explains, "Some clans want the return of their cultural property whereas others acknowledge that museums have the resources to preserve them and returning such items might incite bitter disputes over ownership."[87] The digital repatriation of 3D-rendered images of cultural artefacts is often a highly problematic and contentious topic for Indigenous source communities. The moral arguments for and against digital repatriation are not ones I seek to explore here. Rather I am interested in what purpose digitizations or copies serve in other cultural contexts.

Debates in regard to the digitization of cultural collections and their repatriation gesture towards a different rendering of digitizations in ways that are both conjoint with and distinct from their role as a copy. The 3D project and application "mobile museum," for example, was directed towards the digital replication of two Malagan funerary masks and a totem originating from New Ireland and held in museums in Germany and Australia, items selected by the clan themselves. The clan decided not to request the return of the physical objects because in their originating cultural context they were meant to be destroyed after funerary rituals were performed. The life force of these masks is considered very potent and people were concerned about the effects of their repatriation for their communities.[88] Three-dimensional images were not seen as dangerously powerful in the way the material object was.[89]

The aim of the project was therefore to strengthen clan cultural identity and connections with the past by restituting and revitalizing cultural knowledge about these artefacts and the Kastom rituals associated with them, much of which had dissipated due to colonial incursions and global pressures.[90] Imaging was produced according to how people sought to view or use them, and to who would be granted access. The project digitally captured the technical knowledge involved in creating them and the types of materials used in their manufacture.[91]

In the digitization's role as informational, certain features were foregrounded for the specific purposes of cultural revitalization. The fine details of the "real" object were captured from all angles, with particular emphasis placed on its paint, imagery, and carving techniques. Thus the digitizations were clearer than the masks and totem themselves, more detailed, less potent, and able to be viewed at close range.

The digitizations of the masks operated as an interface rather than just as an image of the real. The image also differed from its source through its interactive functionality, allowing clan members to zoom in and out to examine the image from all angles from the details of its production, to their carvings. The metadata attached to the mask operated as an entry point to other aligned images and information. The mask and totem's informational qualities become hyper-real. They are not substitutes for the real, rather they offer different experiences. This is in stark contrast to their value in a conventional heritage setting where the digitization operates as an exact transcription of its original, to be seen as inferior.

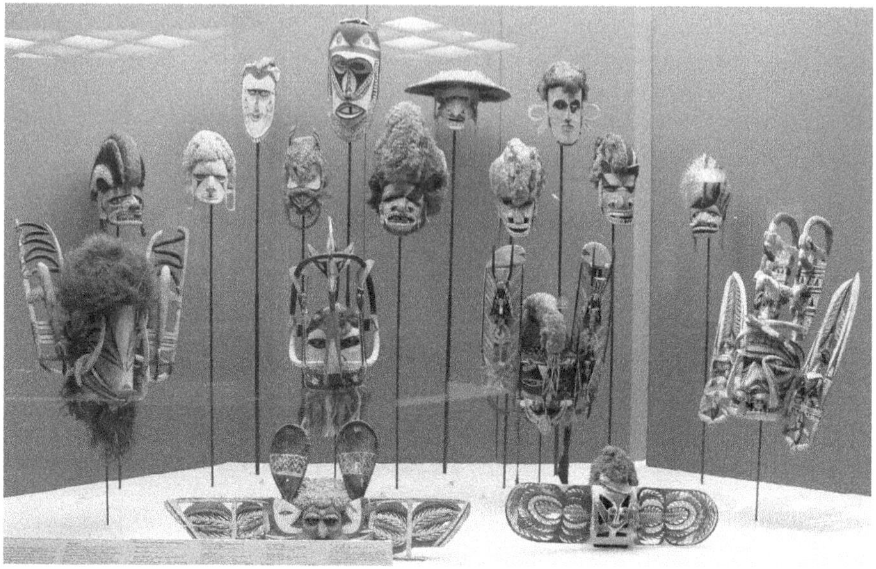

**FIGURE 2.1** Malagan Masks at the Ethnologisches Museum Berlin, 2006. Image from Wikimedia Commons.
Photo credit: Andreas Praefcke.

Here another set of culturally inscribed meanings than merely historical or heritage data are attached to digitized collections in source communities. Digitizations fold into different valuation registers in respect to their use and cultural values and include those of the secret, sacred, and spiritual. In this case, the Malagan masks comprised more than just the aura of the original. They were not seen as the same as the physical objects because they lacked their spiritual potency, a power that has the potential to bring harm. But on the other hand, they had cultural value different from but equivalent to the source, as acts of and for cultural revitalization.

Clearly digitizations do not operate according to the same inventory of value held by their source parent. Different regimes of heritage-like practices exist and operate according to distinctive indices of meaning and indeed being, and it's not always about preserving the source parent in perpetuity. It is not merely a matter of the way digitizations are interpreted in any given context as representative of differing beliefs. No singular value system or universe exists which all human life and diverse cultural perspectives occupy. Rather, cultural theorist John Law argues that cultures express and enact different realities or universes as possible worlds as a series of fractiverses[92] rather than operating as plural interpretations within a one-world or universal framework. In a digital context then cultural practices attach a different role, significance or relevance to digital data, in turn formulating different practices in relation to them. Here I work with the fractiverse concept as a way of framing a world which multiple digital cultural "realities" inhabit. In doing so, the fractiverse opens up a space to more deeply interrogate these different digital cultural realities as the effects of contingent and multifarious culturally inflected norms, values, enactments, and sets of relations. The term "fractiverse" also better explains why and how different approaches to human–nature relations exist, why different groups differently frame and respond to digitizations and digital data and why they see them as important to keep and pass on.

Fractiverse is a concept that can be put to work to explain how different heritage practices operate in disciplinary contexts such as science, history, and art. It can also illuminate how the different knowledge practices that lie behind the notion of heritage require different prioritized responses and seemingly attract competing interests. Overall it explains why global digital heritage management schemes based on a universal heritage are difficult to devise.

The concept comes with its difficulties, however. By rejecting the idea of one universe in which plural interpretations of digital cultural heritage exist, we also refuse the possibility of any overarching standardizing logic, or grand theory such as digital world heritage that can adjudicate between these different digital realities. The connections that exist between these realities can be thought of as different modes of existence. Each has its own unique system of coordinates and ecological circumstances which operate together as a series of intersecting lines and relations that must be taken into account when implementing digital heritage projects.

For example, the digitization has a very distinctive meaning and role in Māori lifeworlds, where it comprises a different but also overlapping set of coordinates (the latter being its technicity such as file formats, bitstreams, and computational infrastructures). Both the parent source and its digitization operate in the same way as material collections. In Māori culture, anthropologist and elder Paul Tapsell explains, many collection items are viewed as *taonga* (treasured possessions), are seen as living embodiments of people, are handed on to succeeding generations, and have an ongoing, active role in ensuring that kinship ties such as *iwi, hapu*, and *whanau* (tribal, sub-tribal and family) identity and lineages through *whakapapa* (genealogy) remain intact.[93] Digital *taonga* therefore form part of a political and cultural project, a way of asserting *mana* (control). They are put to work to promote and uphold principles such as *whanaungatanga* (the establishment of close connections between people) and *manaakitanga* (hospitality). The aim here is to reunite people with their *taonga*, artefacts, genealogies, and ancestors, from many of which they have long been separated, through digitizations.

Like the Nalik people, Māori tribal group Te Aitanga a Hauiti create digital surrogates, digital *taonga* for the purposes of cultural, artistic, and economic revitalization and put them to work in support of the continuation of traditional knowledge and art forms. In a practical sense, digitizations are used to revisit, rekindle, and restore knowledge of their ancestral *taonga* (artefacts) in a context where many of these items are dispersed among collections throughout New Zealand and overseas. Knowing the provenance of these items is imperative if they are to support *whakapapa* (kinship connections). Digitizations also have an important role in countering the effects of western museum cultural colonization by preserving and re-establishing authority over cultural identity and expression.

Te Aitanga a Hauiti elders Wayne Ngata and Hera Ngata-Gibson and collaborator Amiria Salmond explain that to assert authority over digital collections for example is to express cultural rights and interpretive authority in regard to the fundamental ways in which Māori life worlds are organized, how ancestors are connected with *whakapapa*, and about which of those connections matter most.[94]

But there is an element of heritage-like thinking in these efforts. Digital technologies are seen as powerful tools for preserving *taonga* and information about them for the benefit and use of future generations. But they are more than just information or historical data. Digitizations produce the real in a very different way. The genealogy and the relations to which digitization refers are more important than conventional aura, the historical testimony of any given artefact manifested through its material presence and location in a temporal framework. In this sense the digitization also produces the real, the lived reality of ancestral connections.

The hologram of the ancestral house Te Kani-a-Takirau, for example, embodies Te Kani-a-Takirau, a notable Māori tribal leader (1790s- c.1856) from the Hapu Matua of the Te Aitanga A Hauiti iwi on the East Cape of New Zealand. Te Kani was a well-known tribal leader who refused to sign the treaty of Waitangi in 1840, an agreement that worked against Māori sovereign claims to land and natural resources.[95]

The digitization of the ancestral house *Te Kani* according to Ngata is as much a *taonga* to the *tangata whenua* (people of the land) who know or are related to this ancestor and his or her history as the carved wooden panels from which it was made and now located in various museums in New Zealand, the US, and Europe.[96] Digital *Te Kani* therefore comprises interrelated, material agencies, such as the electro-magnetic and physical properties of its earthly mineral substrate, including memory inscribed in ferrite cores, quartz, and silicon, and the programmed inscription of code, to human bodies and minds, computers, algorithms, ancestors, heritage definitions, whakapapa, emotions, land, and so forth.

Here an interdependent relationship exists between knowledge of *Te Kani-a-Takirau*'s *whakapapa*, his ancestral biography, computers, codes, electromagnetic fields, and algorithms as a way of distributing knowledge of what it is and who he is. *Te Kani a Takirau* is composed of a range of differing, overlapping, and entangled coordinates from things in common across worldings, such as technologies and materials, to divergent ideas about the cosmos and the symbolic as representative of different understandings of dependences between humans, things, knowledge practices, and the environment.

For Toi Hauiti, reassembling *taonga* digitally such as Te Kani-a-Takirau for example, Ngata explains, is just as important as, and perhaps even more important than, bringing all its pieces together.[97] Here "digitizations" are considered no less "real" than any other object-forms. They are not merely copies. Rather they contain prior contexts and bundles of relations within them in which each has the capacity and power to generate effects and connections with *whakapaka* and their ancestors that together encourage the flourishing of Te Rawheoro's legacy and Te Aitanga a Hauiti's well-being and *mana*.[98] For Toi Hauiti, the digitization's aura is the recognition of *Te Kani-a-Takirau* as their ancestor and his ability to sustain kinship relations by means of his distribution in digital machinic networks. Te Kani's aura is also his presence as a digitization and the affectual qualities he invokes as a technique to re-enforce these feelings of connection. Accordingly, ancestral values, while promoting a different type of humanism, are seen as more potent than the presence of the real-source.

Working within this expanded field of digital cultural heritage, it becomes a more diverse range of coordinates and practices comprising human bodies, desires, thoughts, materials, ancestors, digital codes, family, relationships, global computational infrastructures, and so forth. Here Maori people profoundly challenge the very notion of digital cultural heritage by destabilizing the idea that digital heritage making and value represent the loss of, the salvage of, and the mourning of the past. Toi Hauiti challenges the separation of digital and material heritage in which the former is inferior alongside the belief in the notion of substance dualisms and human subject–object binary forms of assessment and engagement. Additionally, their rendering of the digital collapses along with modernist and heritage notions of linear and progressive time. Instead, the past present and future becomes entangled.

Above all, such a rendering of Te Kani digitally gestures towards the necessity for different types of approaches to the management of digital cultural heritage as ones crafted in accordance with specific cultural terms and realities. For many the digitization may serve to deceive due to its perfection and the merging of meaning with its source parent, but this is not the case for Māori. No such violence or disruption occurs. Only feelings of love, joy, and connection with Te Kani their ancestor, are felt.

So we may ask, how do we assemble together different types of heritage practices that work to produce different pasts, presents and futures? First, digital realities must be viewed as made up of different coordinates that overlap and intersect and where each is acknowledged as representative of different modes of existence in which the digital resides. Such an approach must be acknowledged in documentation procedures.

The informational aspects of digitizations are critical across all contexts because of their ability to visually illustrate and make connections, but they are no longer merely historical surrogates of the real. They operate within a wider range of cultural, social, economic, and political values and issues.

Clearly we must view digital productions differently in the field according to their own registers of value and meaning. In doing so we are then able to acknowledge ontological plurality in digital heritage practice and work with digital cultural practices that do not necessary sit within heritage and museological ways of thinking, or indeed that may usurp them. These things are not heritage because they do not adhere to values of the original, artefactural authentic, or the auric in the traditional sense of its relationship to modern history. But in a museum setting such digital realities may garner heritage values.

What emerges from this discussion is that digitizations, and indeed born-digital heritage, are described and experienced informationally, technically, and energetically according to a range of sensibilities and assigned different fractiverse-inflected registers of value. These registers of value and meaning include a digitization's role in representing the prismatic form and characteristics of its source replicated in silica, as bits, as data, as electromagnetic waves, as interactive, as aesthetic, as affectual, as tools of cultural revitalization, and as the embodiment of ancestors, and so forth. No digital reality is strictly digital, strictly heritage, strictly nature, strictly culture, strictly material, or strictly virtual.

## *Usurping UNESCO's Archival Sovereignty and Jurisdiction*

UNESCO's archival sovereignty and jurisdiction within this emerging digital cultural heritage commons is being usurped by Google's Cultural Institute, the arts and cultural division of the IT corporation established in 2011. Google has become the dominant power in the governance, production, and logistical distribution of global digital cultural heritage in its digitized form. The search engine giant has achieved this by harnessing its vast resources and funding capabilities and directing them towards the development of large-scale digitization projects. Justified as an act of common good to preserve the world's heritage, Google seeks to gather the digitized collections together and bring vast numbers of images to a global online audience.[99] Google's goal is to preserve and organize the world's information and make it universally accessible and useful within a global infosphere. Digitizing collections is presented as a morally neutral and value-free practice directed to sustaining the fabric of social and cultural life. The publication of these collections through multiple platforms also provides fast access and an ever-multiplying consumable and shareable heritage while at the same time producing big data.

Working with over 2000 institutions in 80 countries, Google has digitized millions of artworks and museum collections as high-resolution images and produced 60 Street View 360-degree images of galleries. Google claims its activities are a non-commercial endeavour and that rights to the images legally remain with the institutions.[100] Partners include the British Museum, the Museo Galileo in Florence, the Auschwitz-Birkenau State Museum, and the Museum of Polish History in Warsaw, to name a few. Google's new art and culture app available on smartphones now places the collections of thousands of museums into the hands of millions of potential users.[101] Interestingly, while claiming these digitization projects are a non-commercial activity, Google's domination of the search engine market alongside the Google Cultural Institute's globally-directed mass art and heritage digitization project together allow them to gather personal data from those who access collections through cookies that are then used for profit-targeted advertising.

These mass digitization projects embody a universalizing imperative. The production of a universal digital heritage and cultural memory is operationalized through the preservation of analogue forms via conveyor-belt-style digitization projects. To achieve this, Google uses standardized formats and procedures made actionable through the specially designed Google Art Camera, a custom-built camera intended to capture "ultra-high resolution 'gigapixel' images" of artworks. Here, through a standard template and format, collections are made into standard objects; disparate collections of different kinds, from different sources and cultural contexts, are unified as standardized digital copies in Google databases, published on standard platforms and narrated through standard storytelling tools. These mass digitization projects are discernible acts of heritage production and heritage proliferation directed to recording entire collections and the creation of millions of files stored in server farms, in databases and made available through collections interfaces.

Google's mass digitization project seeks to build cultural capital and promulgate the uniqueness, rarity, and aura of the original. Like other digitizations, Google's digital copies of analogue collections have no acknowledged history of their own because they carry the historicity and aura of the analogue source. Replicating the real's informational aura through digital imaging down to the source's finest detail is an act intended to capture the essence of the original. The image becomes the past. The image becomes the object itself and becomes what is valued. The image seeks to mediate our understanding of the past and make the world known to us. These very acts of transcription mean that the original becomes many as copies of copies proliferate. Historical data burgeons and as a result digital cultural heritage profuses. The digitization, through its proliferating copies, becomes the original's ever-multiplying surrogates and is put to work to assure the continuation of that original in perpetuity.

The digitization as an informational object is viewed as commensurate with its material source in the sense that they hold common elements and meanings. The informational object provides access to an institution's collection. The interface operates as a visible store room. Digitizations become the collections stored in museums. They are heritage by virtue of their role as informational copies in their own right, a status conferred by their conjoinment with their source.

Through an analysis of Norwegian digital museum platform DigitaltMuseum and Google's Art Project, Ole Marius Hylland argues that the emergence of large-scale digitization projects replaces authenticity with the desire for accessibility.[102] While this might appear to be the case, to act as an informational object all digitizations must be informationally faithful to their source in order for them to have value as a representation of that source. So rather than a replacement of authenticity with accessibility, it is informational accuracy that becomes a digitization's authenticity in respect to its source. The status of the digitization as a good informational surrogate is central to its distribution and access. It is not a surrendering of authenticity but rather its melding with the aura of its source. Whether the digitization operates as document, as a salvage strategy, as a mediator for collections access, or as historical data, all of these roles are based on the view that a solid image stands for the artefact. Through the act of copying, the digitization holds the real's significance and politics and does not appear to have its own.

## *The politics of digitizations*

Locked away in archives, material collections are largely immune from political incursions. By loosening the stranglehold of analogue material through its surrogate, the digitization's highly dynamic, generative, rhizomic, and distributed disposition enable, create, and intensify political frictions. Digitizations, like born-digital collections, do not remain in an original fixed form and cannot be contained within databases; rather, they escape, reproduce, move, and clash within contested domains, and continue to evolve, mutate, and proliferate. The circulation of digitizations made possible through their address and the dynamic machinic systems and powerful algorithms they are nestled within have potentially more far-reaching political consequences than perhaps their material referents could possibly achieve.

The politics of digitization has been played out in multifarious ways and not always to promote acts of cultural expression or cross-cultural understanding, as UNESCO seeks to assert and promulgate. Going against the grain of UNESCO's aspirations and recommendations, the documentary heritage of others seen as significant and of enduring value central to community identity and memory is at times deliberately destroyed in acts directed to inflicting harm and cultural impoverishment. Recent media interest in online responses to the destruction of physical sites in the Middle East and North Africa, for example were lent support by new digitization initiatives. These violent acts of destruction have been met by efforts to digitally preserve threatened places and objects through volunteer programs such as The Million Image Database using proprietary 3D imaging kits available through its site. In doing so, such projects have sought to act against groups that attempt to dictate or rewrite history and impose their own narratives and political ideologies on others through the destruction of cultural sites.[103]

In August 2015, monuments in the city of Palmyra, a world heritage site, were deliberately destroyed by ISIS in an act of cultural desecration.[104] In these instances, images and videos of the destruction of heritage sites by ISIS were placed on the internet and circulated within machinic geoscapes at ever-increasing speeds. The ability to view these acts of destruction digitally has invoked what digital media scholar Martijn Stevens describes as intense emotions of shock, of horror, of loss, and of despair at a distance.[105]

UNESCO denounced the destruction at Palmyra as a war crime. Shortly after the site's recapture in March 2016, Iconem, a French company specializing in the digitization of archaeological sites, in partnership with the Syrian DGAM (Direction-Générale des Antiquités et des Musées), surveyed the damage to the temples of Bel and Baalshamin, the Monumental Arch, the Valley of Tombs, and the museum.[106] These were the sites that held the most cultural value and therefore became the target of ISIS's violence. As a mitigating strategy, three-dimensional virtual reconstructions were made of them.[107]

Both projects draw our attention to the role that rapidly developing digital imaging technologies might play in the 3D imaging of sites in conflict zones as an ideological project of both restitution but also as an anticipatory act of heritagization in the event of their destruction.

The Libyan revolution of 2011 is another case in point. Digitizations of heritage items were put to work for ideological purposes, this time to denigrate Gaddafi's regime. The Jimahirya Museum, Libya's National Museum in Tripoli, comprises collections of Roman Art and the revolutionary memorabilia of Gaddafi's regime. In the upstairs gallery the walls were covered with images of the early days of the revolution.

> Brushing aside curators' preference for classical antiquity, Libya's leader gave pride of place in the first gallery to the Volkswagen Beetle he drove in the sixties and the open-top Jeep that swept him to power in 1969.
>
> ...At 11.30pm on 20 August 2011, as rebels launched their first attack on the Libyan capital, 20 armed men entered the museum, located in the Red Castle, at the corner of former Green Square.
>
> ...the rebels spotted the colonel's vintage cars and...wreaked their revenge. The windows of the sky blue Beetle were smashed; thousands of shards of glass now lie on the floor and over the dark upholstered seats where the ambitious young Gaddafi sat, driving officers to meetings and distributing political pamphlets. The headlamps are also damaged but the period gearstick, glovebox, running boards, speedometer and steering wheel remain intact.
>
> Mustafa Turjman, head of research...said: "It was a revolution – you can't resist. It was better to let the rebels in than have them enter by force. When they saw the objects belonging to Gaddafi they couldn't resist.
>
> "The rebels asked staff to remove all the things belonging to Gaddafi. We were happy to do it because this museum is for classical antiquity. The objects of Gaddafi were forced upon us. He wanted to take advantage of the classical things, which were the main attraction for tourists, so they would pass and see his objects and activities."[108]

Following the destruction of Gaddafi's collections in the Jimahirya Museum in 2011, images of his damaged cars were put online as a political statement and testimony of the overthrow of his regime. The sky-blue Beetle became interpenetrated with digital code as a testament to the car's political associations, and launched into machinic geoscapes. Here the digitization of the Beetle acted as the carrier of information, the ideology of its source and owner, and at the same time became a revolutionary itself.

The data politics of a digitization appearing on an interface is of a different kind than the physical object. While its interpretive narratives resemble its source host, when the image of the Beetle and its politics comprise the types of operations that are internal to data, its patterns, co-relations, predictions, aesthetics and automations and the powerful algorithms that drive it, alongside the multiple devices and global computational infrastructures in which it is embedded. The

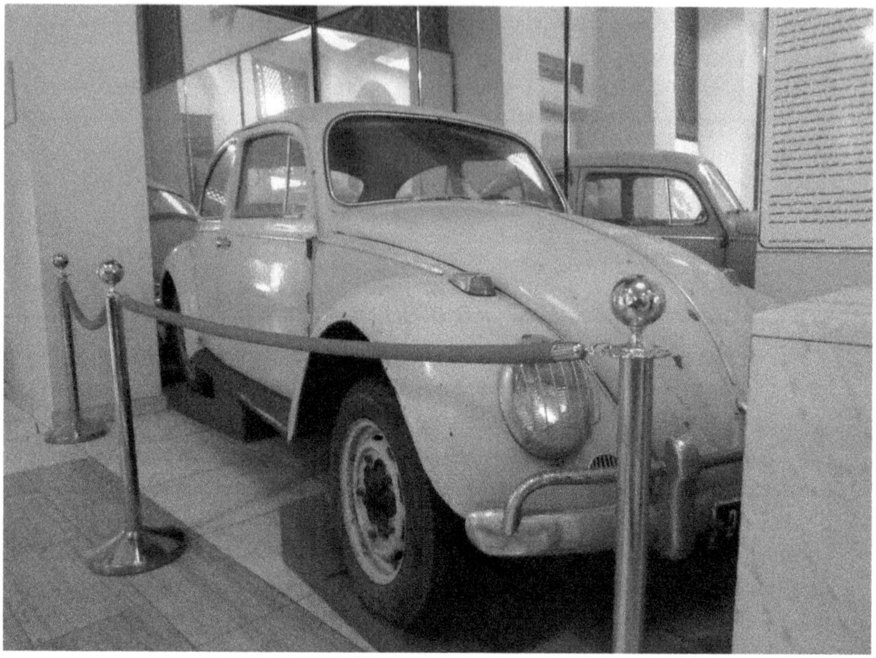

**FIGURE 2.2** Muammar Gaddafi's Volkswagen Beetle, the Jimahirya Museum, Libya's National Museum in Tripoli, 2010. Image from Wikimedia Commons. Photo credit: Franzfoto.

image of Gaddafi's car is less a fixed image representing the car in its damaged state as a set of image processing and display operations alongside the aesthetic practices produced by its neural network of processes that lay behind and beyond it. It also becomes a politic of its machine capacities, the automated processes and operational systems that enable it to appear as an image in which its interpretive narratives are directed on one hand and also that which comprises its unseen. Therefore, its politics becomes the small processes that enable and direct human and machinic behaviours and close down others, such as the search engine logics and recommendations that distribute its image alongside the capacity of certain materials such as silicon to conduct electrons at certain speeds and the bitmaps that store colour values that enable its emergence as an image. The image's formal characteristics as a numerical form, as bits of zeros and ones programmable through algorithmic manipulation, enable its variability, mutability, and rhizomic distribution so the image can then become entangled with bodies, minds, and ideologies. The different communication systems in which the Beetle appears through the internet and social media platforms such as Facebook enable different forms of cultural and machinic expression. The media languages it embodies and the visual rendering that is made visible have their own aesthetics and material effects. Here the politics of the digitization emerges as a politic of the more-than-human machinic kind.

Heritage institutions are therefore no longer fully able to demarcate and map all the narrative and machinic interpretations that comprise the heritage object, as they have attempted to do in the past.

Today the notion of heritage and what constitutes it even within the auspices of the UNESCO charter have become more flexible. For UNESCO anything considered important enough to be passed on to the future can be considered to have heritage value of some kind.[109] In the following Chapter 3, I argue that digital heritage and its emergence is a distinctly modern phenomenon and the cultural ideas, concepts and concerns that underlay its production, and the emergence of heritage-like practices across domains and sectors is emblematic of this milieu.

## Notes

1 Lowenthal, *The Past is a Foreign Country*. (Cambridge, UK, Cambridge University Press, 1999)
2 Laurajane Smith and Natsuko Akagawa, *Intangible Heritage* (Abingdon: Routledge, 2009).
3 Fiona Cameron, "Decolonizing the Past: The Politics of New Heritage," in *Proceedings of the New Heritage: Beyond Verisimilitude Conference*, eds. Yehula Kalay, Thomas Kvan and Janice Affleck (Hong Kong: University of Hong Kong, 2006), 198.
4 Cameron, "Decolonizing the Past," 199.
5 Sarah C.C. Choy, Nicholas Crofts, Robert Fisher, Ngian Lek Choh, Susanne Nickel, Clément Oury and Katarzyna Ślaska, "The UNESCO/PERSIST Guidelines for the Selection of Digital Heritage for Long-term Preservation," March 2016, 5, https://unesdoc.unesco.org/ark:/48223/pf0000244280.
6 Titia van der Werf and Bram van der Werf, "The Paradox of Selection in the Digital Age." Paper presented at: IFLA WLIC 2014 – Lyon – Libraries, Citizens, Societies: Confluence for Knowledge in Session 138 – UNESCO Open Session. In: IFLA WLIC 2014, 16–22 August 2014, Lyon, France, http://library.ifla.org/1042/1/138-vanderwerf-en.pdf, 9.
7 UNESCO, "United Nations Year for Cultural Heritage." http://unesdoc.unesco.org/images/0012/001271/127155eo.pdf.
8 Lynn Meskell, *A Future in Ruins: UNESCO, World Heritage and the Dream of Peace* (Oxford: Oxford University Press, 2018), xv.
9 Meskell, *A Future in Ruins*, xvi.
10 Meskell, *A Future in Ruins*, xvii.
11 Meskell, *A Future in Ruins*, xvi.
12 Meskell, *A Future in Ruins*, xvi.
13 UNESCO, "United Nations Year for Cultural Heritage."
14 National Library of Australia, "Guidelines for the Preservation of Digital Heritage," Information Society Division, UNESCO, March 2003, 109–110, http://unesdoc.unesco.org/images/0013/001300/130071e.pdf.
15 Rodney Harrison, *Heritage: Critical Approaches* (Abingdon: Routledge, 2013).
16 International Federation of Libraries Associations and Institutions Newsletter, http://www.ifla.org/archive/VII/s1/news/apr00.pdf.
17 UNESCO, *TEXT of the draft UNESCO RESOLUTION on DIGITAL PRESERVATION Proposed by the Conference of Directors of National Libraries (CDNL), The Hague, June 2001*, www.aes.org/technical/documentDownloads.cfm?docID=107.
18 *TEXT of the draft UNESCO RESOLUTION on DIGITAL PRESERVATION.*
19 Conference of Directors of National Libraries: *Minutes of the Twenty-Eighth Meeting of CDNL, held on Wednesday 22 August 2001, at 10.00am, at The Boston Public Library,*

*Boston, United States of America*, http://www.cdnl.info/sites/default/files/docs/2002_cdnl_minutes_2001.pdf.

20 Conference of Directors of National Libraries. *Minutes*

21 Yola de Lusenet and Vincent Wintermans, *Preserving the Digital Heritage: Principles and Policies*, Selected Papers of the International Conference organized by the Netherlands National Commission for UNESCO and The European Commission for Preservation and Access, The Hague, 4–5 November 2005 (Netherlands National Commission for UNESCO and The European Commission for Preservation and Access, 2005), 2, http://www.ica.org/sites/default/files/WG_2007_PAAG-preserving-the-digital-heritage_EN.pdf, 9.

22 UNESCO, *TEXT of the draft UNESCO RESOLUTION on DIGITAL PRESERVATION.*

23 *Records of the General Conference, 31st Session, Paris, 15 October – 3 November 2001, v. 1 Resolutions*, Preservation of the Digital Heritage, Resolution 34, Paris. (UNESCO 2002), 71.

24 UNESCO, "United Nations Year for Cultural Heritage," http://unesdoc.unesco.org/images/0012/001271/127155eo.pdf.

25 UNESCO, "Slave Trade Archives" project, http://www.unesco.org/new/en/communication-and-information/memory-of-the-world/projects/full-list-of-projects/slave-trade-archives-project/.

26 UNESCO, "United Nations Year for Cultural Heritage."

27 UNESCO, "Charter on the Preservation of Digital Heritage," last modified 15 October 2003, http://portal.unesco.org/en/ev.php-URL_ID=17721&URL_DO=DO_TOPIC&URL_SECTION=201.html, 1.

28 UNESCO, "Charter on the Preservation of Cultural Heritage."

29 UNESCO, "Charter on the Preservation of Cultural Heritage."

30 UNESCO, "Concept of Digital Heritage," http://www.unesco.org/new/en/communication-and-information/access-to-knowledge/preservation-of-documentary-heritage/digital-heritage/concept-of-digital-heritage/, 1.

31 UNESCO, "Charter on the Preservation of Cultural Heritage."

32 UNESCO, "Charter on the Preservation of Digital Heritage."

33 Ray Edmondson, "Recommendation Concerning the Preservation of, and Access to, Documentary Heritage Including in Digital Form: Implementation Guidelines," prepared for UNESCO, 2015, https://en.unesco.org/sites/default/files/2015_mow_recommendation_implementation_guidelines_en.pdf, 3.

34 René Descartes, *Meditations on First Philosophy in which the Existence of God and the Immortality of the Soul are Demonstrated* (New York: Classic Books [1641] 2009).

35 Bruno Latour, *We Have Never Been Modern* (Hertfordshire: Harvester Wheatsheaf, 1993).

36 UNESCO, "What is Intangible Heritage?" http://www.unesco.org/culture/ich/en/what-is-intangible-heritage-00003.

37 UNESCO, "Charter on the Preservation of Digital Heritage."

38 UNESCO, "Charter on the Preservation of Digital Heritage."

39 van der Werf, "The Paradox of Selection in the Digital Age," 15.

40 Abdelaziz Abid, "Safeguarding our Digital Heritage: The UNESCO Charter," https://slideplayer.com/slide/3870548/; de Lusenet and Wintermans, *Preserving the Digital Heritage: Principles and Policies*, 2.

41 UNESCO, "Charter on the Preservation of Digital Heritage."

42 UNESCO, "Charter on the Preservation of Digital Heritage," 1.

43 National Library of Australia, "Guidelines for the Preservation of Digital Heritage," 30.

44 Tamara Brizard, Willem Derde and Neil Silberman, *Basic Guidelines for Cultural Heritage Professionals in the Use of Information Technologies* (Stockholm: The Interactive Institute, Know How Books, 2007), http://www.enamecenter.org/files/documents/Know-how%20book%20on%20Cultural%20Heritage%20and%20ICT.pdf, 3.

45 National Library of Australia, "Guidelines for the Preservation of Digital Cultural Heritage," 30.
46 Liana Chua and Amiria Salmond, "Artefacts in Anthropology," in *The SAGE Handbook of Social Anthropology*, eds. Richard Fardon, Olivia Harris, Trevor H.J. Marchand, Mark Nuttall, Cris Shore, Veronica Strang and Richard A. Wilson (London: Sage Publications, 2012), 102.
47 Walter Benjamin, *The Work of Art in the Age of Mechanical Reproduction* (Cambridge, MA: Harvard University Press [1934] 2008), 221.
48 Cameron, "Decolonizing the Past," 198.
49 UNESCO, "United Nations Year for Cultural Heritage."
50 UNESCO, "Concept of Digital Heritage"; JPICH, "Joint Programming Initiative Cultural Heritage and Global Change," http://www.heritageportal.eu/About-Us/The-JPICH/.
51 UNESCO, "Charter on the Preservation of Digital Heritage," 3.
52 UNESCO, "Concept of Digital Heritage."
53 Matthew Fuller and Andrew Goffey, "The Unknown Objects of Object-Orientation," in *Objects and Materials*, eds. Penny Harvey, Eleanor Conlin Casella, Gillian Evans, Hannah Knox, Christine McLean, Elizabeth B. Silva, Hicholas Thoburn and Kath Woodward (Abingdon: Routledge, 2014), 218.
54 UNESCO, "United Nations Year for Cultural Heritage."
55 JPICH, "JPI Cultural Heritage and Global Change," http://www.jpi-culturalheritage.eu/wp-content/uploads/Strategic-Research-Agenda.pdf, 5; David Lowenthal, *The Past is a Foreign Country* (Cambridge, UK: Cambridge University Press, 1999); Harrison, *Heritage: Critical Approaches*, 3.
56 UNESCO, "Charter on the Preservation of Digital Heritage," 3.
57 Meskell, *A Future in Ruins*, xviii.
58 Dirk Helbing, Bruno S. Frey, Gerd Gigerenzer, Ernst Hafen, Michael Hagner, Yvonne Hofstetter, Jeroen van den Hoven, Roberto V. Zicari and Andrej Zwitter, "Will Democracy Survive Big Data and Artificial Intelligence?" *Scientific American*, Feb 25, 2017, https://www.scientificamerican.com/article/will-democracy-survive-big-data-and-artificial-intelligence/, 2.
59 van der Werf, "The Paradox of Selection in the Digital Age," 3.
60 van der Werf, "The Paradox of Selection in the Digital Age," 7, 15.
61 UNESCO, "United Nations Year for Cultural Heritage."
62 Europeana Collections, https://www.europeana.eu/portal/en/about.html.
63 *UNESCO/UBC VANCOUVER DECLARATION, The Memory of the World in the Digital Age: Digitization and Preservation, 26 to 28 September 2012 Vancouver, British Columbia, Canada,*http://www.unesco.org/new/fileadmin/MULTIMEDIA/HQ/CI/CI/pdf/mow/unesco_ubc_vancouver_declaration_en.pdf.
64 *UNESCO/UBC VANCOUVER DECLARATION, The Memory of the World in the Digital Age.*
65 UNESCO, *Memory of the World Register Companion*, 3, https://en.unesco.org/sites/default/files/memory_of_the_world_register_companion_en.pdf.
66 *Memory of the World Register Companion*, 3.
67 *Memory of the World Register Companion*, 3.
68 *Memory of the World Register Companion*, 3.
69 *Memory of the World Register Companion*, 3.
70 UNESCO, Draft Report on the PERSIST session at the 4th Annual Conference of the International Council of Archives (ICA) "Evaluation of Strategies of Digital Preservation & UNESCO's Role in Facing the Technical Challenges", Girona, 13 October 2014, https://www.unesco.nl/sites/default/files/dossier/report_girona_session_persist.pdf.
71 UNESCO, Report from the PERSIST session at WLIC, Lyon, August 2014, https://www.unesco.nl/sites/default/files/dossier/report_of_unesco_persist_session_at_wlic_lyon_2014.pdf.
72 Report from the PERSIST session at WLIC, Lyon, August 2014.

73 UNESCO, *Records of the General Conference, 38$^{th}$ Session, Paris, 3–18 November 2015, Annex V Recommendation Concerning the Preservation of, and Access to, Documentary Heritage including in Digital Form*, 163–167, http://unesdoc.unesco.org/images/0024/002433/243325e.pdf.

74 Richard Rinehart and Jon Ippolito, *Re-collection: Art, New Media, and Social Memory* (Cambridge, MA: The MIT Press, 2014).

75 Brizard, Derde and Silberman, *Basic Guidelines for Cultural Heritage Professionals in the Use of Information Technologies,* 3.

76 Benjamin Bratton, *The Stack: On Software and Sovereignty* (Cambridge, MA.: The MIT Press, 2015), 66. Bratton proposes his Stack as a coherent and all-encompassing technological megastructure of life. This theoretical framing is problematic because of its totality but is also useful in thinking about the extensiveness of digital cultural heritage. The Stack, Bratton explains, "takes different forms at different scales—from energy and mineral sourcing and subterranean cloud infrastructure to urban software and universal addressing systems; from interfaces…to users…and the arrival of legions of sensors, algorithms, and robots…these different genres of computation—smart grids, cloud platforms, mobile apps, smart cities, the Internet of Things, automation—can be seen not as so many species evolving on their own, but as forming a coherent whole: an accidental megastructure called the Stack that is both a computational apparatus and a new governing structure." .

77 Bratton, *The Stack*, 246. Bratton develops the idea of the geoscape: "A geoscape is a contested terrain of contested terrains, a shifting landscape made up of shifting landscapes: images, maps, projections and plans, irredentist land claims, borders, and jurisdictions, strata and striations, imagined worlds, macroeconomic forecasts, projected homes and homelands, addressing systems and various terra incognita. All of these can, but not necessarily, enter into irregular public exchanges…geoscapes are a form of content that cannot *not* be designed and designed for…When advanced technologies of globalization, closely associated with secular cosmopolitics, are employed opportunistically by political theologies for their own particular purposes, then unplannable and unresolved territories, jurisdictions and programs are put into play."

78 Fiona Cameron, "Object-Orientated Democracies: Conceptualising Museum Collections in Networks," *Museum Management and Curatorship* 23, no. 3 (August 2008): 229–243.

79 Azadeh Moaveni, "300 Sparks an Outcry in Iran," *Time*, Tuesday, March 13, 2007, http://content.time.com/time/world/article/0,8599,1598886,00.html.

80 Project 300, http://300themovie.info/.

81 Moaveni, "300 Sparks an Outcry in Iran."

82 For a discussion of matters of fact and matters of concern see Bruno Latour, "Why Has Critique Run out of Steam? From Matters of Fact to Matters of Concern," *Critical Inquiry* 30 (Winter 2004): 237.

83 Cameron, "Object-Orientated Democracies."

84 Rosi Braidotti, *Posthuman Knowledge*. (Cambridge, UK: Polity, 2019), 12.

85 Sheenagh Pietrobruno, "Between Narrative and Lists: Performing Digital Intangible Heritage through Global Media," *International Journal of Heritage Studies* 20, 7–8 (2014): 742–759; Smith and Akagawa, *Intangible Heritage*; UNESCO, "Incorporating Intangible Heritage in Education, 'a Win-Win Situation'," *Intangible Cultural Heritage*, https://ich.unesco.org/en/news/incorporating-intangible-heritage-in-education-a-win-win-situation-00220.

86 Pietrobruno, "Between Narrative and Lists."

87 Laurie Frey, "Digital Repatriation – Malagan Mask Makers in Papua New Guinea try out new way of dealing with cultural property ownership," *The Heritagist*, last modified Dec 18, 2012, http://www.theheritagist.com/2012/12/digital-repatriation-malagan-mask.html.

88 ABC, "PNG's Malagan Masks to be 'Digitally Repatriated'," *ABC News*, updated Dec 12, 2012, http://www.abc.net.au/news/2012-12-12/an-pngs-malagan-masks-to-be-digitalise/4423464.

89 ABC, "PNG's Malagan Masks to be 'Digitally Repatriated'."
90 ABC, "PNG's Malagan Masks to be Digitally Repatriated."
91 Stefan Armbruster, "Digital Repatriation of Artefacts a 'Thorny Issue'," *SBS News*, updated Aug 26, 2013, http://www.sbs.com.au/news/article/2012/12/10/digital-repatriation-artefacts-thorny-issue.
92 For a discussion of cultural perspectives as different reals and the universe comprising multiple fractiverses see John Law, "What's Wrong with a One-World World," *Heterogeneities.net* (2011), http://www.heterogeneities.net/publications/Law2011WhatsWrongWithAOneWorldWorld.pdf.
93 Paul Tapsell, *Ko Tawa: Māori Treasures of New Zealand* (Auckland: David Bateman in association with Auckland War Memorial Museum Tamaki Paenga Hira, 2006).
94 Wayne Ngata, Hera Ngata-Gibson and Amiria Salmond, "Te Ataakura: Digital *taonga* and Cultural Innovation," *Journal of Material Culture* 17, 3 (2013): 242–243.
95 Te Kani-a-Takirau, a Maori tribal leader from Hapu Matua of the Te Aitanga A Hauiti iwi, East Coast, New Zealand, https://en.wikipedia.org/wiki/Te_Kani-a-Takirau.
96 Ngata, Ngata-Gibson and Salmond, "Te Ataakura."
97 Ngata, Ngata-Gibson and Salmond, "Te Ataakura."
98 Ngata, Ngata-Gibson and Salmond, "Te Ataakura."
99 Google Cultural Institute, https://www.google.com/culturalinstitute/about/partners/.
100 Matthew Caines, "Arts Head: Amit Sood, Director of Google Cultural Institute," *The Guardian*, Dec 3, 2013, https://www.theguardian.com/culture-professionals-network/culture-professionals-blog/2013/dec/03/amit-sood-google-cultural-institute-art-project.
101 Sean Buckley, "Google's Art and Culture app turns your phone into a Museum," *engadget*, December 16, 2016, https://www.engadget.com/2016/07/20/googles-art-and-culture-app-turns-your-phone-into-a-museum/.
102 Ole Marius Hylland, "Even Better Than the Real Thing? Digital Copies and Digital Museums in a Digital Cultural Policy," *Culture Unbound* 9, no. 1 (2017): 62–84. Published by Linköping University Electronic Press, http://www.cultureun-bound.ep.liu.se.
103 World Government Summit, "The Triumphal Arch of Palmyra". World Government Summit, 12–14 February 2017, Dubai, United Arab Emirates, https://www.archindubai.org/#triumphalarch.
104 Emma Henderson, "Syria's Six Unesco World Heritage Sites All Damaged or Destroyed during Civil War," *Independent*, March 16, 2017, http://www.independent.co.uk/news/world/middle-east/syrias-six-unesco-world-heritage-sites-all-damaged-or-destroyed-during-civil-war-a6934026.html.
105 Stevens refers to the placement of collections online as an act of looking digitally but feeling at a distance. See Martijn Stevens, "Touched from a Distance," in *Museums in a Digital Culture*, eds. Chiel van den Akker and Susan Legéne (Amsterdam: Amsterdam University Press, 2017), 26.
106 Temple of Bel, http://syrianheritagerevival.org/palmyra/.
107 Rory Stott, "This 3D Model Shows the Damage Caused by ISIS to Palmyra's Temple of Bel," *ArchDaily*, May 6, 2016, http://www.archdaily.com/786837/this-3d-model-shows-the-damage-caused-by-isis-to-palmyras-temple-of-bel.
108 David Smith, "In Tripoli's Museum of Antiquity only Gaddafi is Lost in Revolution," *The Guardian*, Sept 12, 2011, https://www.theguardian.com/culture/2011/sep/11/tripoli-museum-antiquity-shattered-gaddafi-image.
109 UNESCO, "Concept of Digital Heritage."

## Bibliography

ABC. "PNG's Malagan Masks to be 'Digitally Repatriated'." *ABC News*, updated Dec 12, 2012. http://www.abc.net.au/news/2012-12-12/an-pngs-malagan-masks-to-be-digitalise/4423464.

Abid, Abdelaziz. "Safeguarding our Digital Heritage: The UNESCO Charter." https://slideplayer.com/slide/3870548/.

Armbruster, Stefan. "Digital Repatriation of Artefacts a 'Thorny Issue'." *SBS News*, updated Aug 26, 2013. http://www.sbs.com.au/news/article/2012/12/10/digital-repatriation-artefacts-thorny-issue.

Benjamin, Walter. *The Work of Art in the Age of Mechanical Reproduction*. Cambridge, MA: Harvard University Press [1934] 2008.

Bratton, Benjamin. *The Stack: On Software and Sovereignty*. Cambridge, MA: The MIT Press, 2015.

Brizard, Tamara, Willem Derde and Neil Silberman. *Basic Guidelines for Cultural Heritage Professionals in the Use of Information Technologies*. Stockholm: The Interactive Institute, Know How Books, 2007. http://www.enamecenter.org/files/documents/Know-how%20book%20on%20Cultural%20Heritage%20and%20ICT.pdf.

Buckley, Sean. "Google's Art and Culture app turns your phone into a Museum." *engadget*, December 16, 2016. https://www.engadget.com/2016/07/20/googles-art-and-culture-app-turns-your-phone-into-a-museum/.

Caines, Matthew. "Arts Head: Amit Sood, Director of Google Cultural Institute." *The Guardian*, Dec 3, 2013. https://www.theguardian.com/culture-professionals-network/culture-professionals-blog/2013/dec/03/amit-sood-google-cultural-institute-art-project.

Cameron, Fiona. "Decolonizing the Past: The Politics of New Heritage." In *Proceedings of the New Heritage: Beyond Verisimilitude Conference*, edited by Yehula Kalay, Thomas Kvan, and Janice Affleck, 198–211. Hong Kong: University of Hong Kong, 2006.

Cameron, Fiona. "Object-Orientated Democracies: Conceptualising Museum Collections in Networks." *Museum Management and Curatorship* 23, no. 3 (August 2008): 229–243.

Choy, Sarah C.C., Nicholas Crofts, Robert Fisher, Ngian Lek Choh, Susanne Nickel, Clément Oury, and Katarzyna Ślaska. "The UNESCO/PERSIST Guidelines for the Selection of Digital Heritage for Long-term Preservation." March 2016. https://unesdoc.unesco.org/ark:/48223/pf0000244280.

Chua, Liana, and Salmond, Amiria. "Artefacts in Anthropology." In *The SAGE Handbook of Social Anthropology*, edited by Richard Fardon, Olivia Harris, Trevor H.J. Marchand, Mark Nuttall, Cris Shore, Veronica Strang and Richard A. Wilson, Chapter 3.7. London: Sage Publications, 2012.

Conference of Directors of National Libraries. *Minutes of the Twenty-Eighth Meeting of CDNL*, held on Wednesday 22 August2001, at 10.00am, at The Boston Public Library, Boston, United States of America. http://www.cdnl.info/sites/default/files/docs/2002_cdnl_minutes_2001.pdf.

de Lusenet, Yola, and Vincent Wintermans. *Preserving the Digital Heritage: Principles and Policies*. Selected Papers of the International Conference organized by the Netherlands National Commission for UNESCO and The European Commission for Preservation and Access, The Hague, 4–5 November 2005 (Netherlands National Commission for UNESCO and The European Commission for Preservation and Access, 2005). http://www.ica.org/sites/default/files/WG_2007_PAAG-preserving-the-digital-heritage_EN.pdf.

Descartes, René. *Meditations on First Philosophy in which the Existence of God and the Immortality of the Soul are Demonstrated*. New York: Classic Books [1641] 2009.

Edmondson, Ray. "Recommendation Concerning the Preservation of, and Access to, Documentary Heritage Including in Digital Form: Implementation Guidelines." Prepared for UNESCO, 2015. https://en.unesco.org/sites/default/files/2015_mow_recommendation_implementation_guidelines_en.pdf.

Europeana Collections. https://www.europeana.eu/portal/en/about.html.

Frey, Laurie. "Digital Repatriation – Malagan Mask Makers in Papua New Guinea try out new way of dealing with cultural property ownership." *The Heritagist*, last modified Dec 18, 2012. http://www.theheritagist.com/2012/12/digital-repatriation-malagan-mask.html.

Fuller, Matthew, and Andrew Goffey. "The Unknown Objects of Object-Orientation." In *Objects and Materials*, edited by Penny Harvey, Eleanor Conlin Casella, Gillian Evans, Hannah Knox, Christine McLean, Elizabeth B. Silva, Nicholas Thoburn and Kath Woodward, 218–227. Abingdon: Routledge, 2014.

Harrison, Rodney. *Heritage: Critical Approaches*. Abingdon: Routledge, 2013.

Helbing, Dirk, Bruno S. Frey, Gerd Gigerenzer, Ernst Hafen, Michael Hagner, Yvonne Hofstetter, Jeroen van den Hoven, Roberto V. Zicari, and Andrej Zwitter. "Will Democracy Survive Big Data and Artificial Intelligence?" *Scientific American*, Feb 25, 2017. https://www.scientificamerican.com/article/will-democracy-survive-big-data-and-artificial-intelligence/.

Henderson, Emma. "Syria's Six Unesco World Heritage Sites All Damaged or Destroyed during Civil War." *Independent*, March 16, 2017. http://www.independent.co.uk/news/world/middle-east/syrias-six-unesco-world-heritage-sites-all-damaged-or-destroyed-during-civil-war-a6934026.html.

Hylland, Ole Marius. "Even Better Than the Real Thing? Digital Copies and Digital Museums in a Digital Cultural Policy." *Culture Unbound* 9, no. 1 (2017): 62–84. Published by Linköping University Electronic Press. http://www.cultureun-bound.ep.liu.se.

International Federation of Libraries Associations and Institutions. Newsletter. http://www.ifla.org/archive/VII/s1/news/apr00.pdf.

JPICH. "Joint Programming Initiative Cultural Heritage and Global Change." http://www.heritageportal.eu/About-Us/The-JPICH/.

JPICH. "JPI Cultural Heritage and Global Change." http://www.jpi-culturalheritage.eu/wp-content/uploads/Strategic-Research-Agenda.pdf.

Latour, Bruno. "Why Has Critique Run out of Steam? From Matters of Fact to Matters of Concern." *Critical Inquiry* 30 (Winter 2004): 225–248.

Latour, Bruno. *We Have Never Been Modern*. Hertfordshire: Harvester Wheatsheaf, 1993.

Law, John. "What's Wrong with a One-World World." *Heterogeneities.net* (2011). http://www.heterogeneities.net/publications/Law2011WhatsWrongWithAOneWorldWorld.pdf.

Lowenthal, David. *The Past is a Foreign Country*. Cambridge, UK: Cambridge University Press, 1999.

Meskell, Lynn. *A Future in Ruins: UNESCO, World Heritage and the Dream of Peace*. Oxford: Oxford University Press, 2018.

Moaveni, Azadeh. "300 Sparks an Outcry in Iran." *Time*, March 13, 2007. http://content.time.com/time/world/article/0,8599,1598886,00.html.

National Library of Australia. "*Guidelines for the Preservation of Digital Heritage*." Information Society Division, UNESCO, March 2003. http://unesdoc.unesco.org/images/0013/001300/130071e.pdf.

Ngata, Wayne, Hera Ngata-Gibson, and Amiria Salmond. "Te Ataakura: Digital *taonga* and Cultural Innovation." *Journal of Material Culture* 17, 3 (2013): 229–244.

Pietrobruno, Sheenagh. "Between Narrative and Lists: Performing Digital Intangible Heritage through Global Media." *International Journal of Heritage Studies* 20, 7–8 (2014): 742–759.

Project 300. http://300themovie.info/.

Rinehart, Richard, and Jon Ippolito, *Re-collection: Art, New Media, and Social Memory*. Cambridge, MA: The MIT Press, 2014.

Smith, David. "In Tripoli's Museum of Antiquity only Gaddafi is Lost in Revolution." *The Guardian*, Sept 12, 2011. https://www.theguardian.com/culture/2011/sep/11/tripoli-museum-antiquity-shattered-gaddafi-image.

Smith, Laurajane, and Natsuko Akagawa. *Intangible Heritage*. Abingdon: Routledge, 2009.

Stevens, Martijn. "Touched from a Distance." In *Museums in a Digital Culture*, edited by Chiel van den Akker and Susan Legéne, 13–30. Amsterdam: Amsterdam University Press, 2017.

Stott, Rory. "This 3D Model Shows the Damage Caused by ISIS to Palmyra's Temple of Bel." *ArchDaily*, May 6, 2016. http://www.archdaily.com/786837/this-3d-model-shows-the-damage-caused-by-isis-to-palmyras-temple-of-bel.

Tapsell, Paul. *Ko Tawa: Māori Treasures of New Zealand*. Auckland: David Bateman in association with Auckland War Memorial Museum Tamaki Paenga Hira, 2006.

World Government Summit. "*The Triumphal Arch of Palmyra*". World Government Summit, 12–14 February2017, Dubai. United Arab Emirates. https://www.archindubai.org/#triumphalarch.

UNESCO. Report from the PERSIST session at WLIC, Lyon, August2014. https://www.unesco.nl/sites/default/files/dossier/report_of_unesco_persist_session_at_wlic_lyon_2014.pdf.

UNESCO. Draft Report on the PERSIST session at the 4th Annual Conference of the International Council of Archives (ICA) "*Evaluation of Strategies of Digital Preservation & UNESCO's Role in Facing the Technical Challenges*", Girona, 13 October2014. https://www.unesco.nl/sites/default/files/dossier/report_girona_session_persist.pdf.

UNESCO. "Charter on the Preservation of Digital Heritage." Last modified 15 October2003. http://portal.unesco.org/en/ev.php-URL_ID=17721%26URL_DO=DO_PRINTPAGE%26URL_SECTION=201.html.

UNESCO. "Concept of Digital Heritage." http://www.unesco.org/new/en/communication-and-information/access-to-knowledge/preservation-of-documentary-heritage/digital-heritage/concept-of-digital-heritage/.

UNESCO. "Slave Trade Archives" project. http://www.unesco.org/new/en/communication-and-information/memory-of-the-world/projects/full-list-of-projects/slave-trade-archives-project/.

UNESCO. "United Nations Year for Cultural Heritage." http://unesdoc.unesco.org/images/0012/001271/127155eo.pdf.

UNESCO. "What is Intangible Heritage?" http://www.unesco.org/culture/ich/en/what-is-intangible-heritage-00003.

UNESCO. "Incorporating Intangible Heritage in Education, 'a Win-Win Situation'." *Intangible Cultural Heritage*. https://ich.unesco.org/en/news/incorporating-intangible-heritage-in-education-a-win-win-situation-00220.

UNESCO. *Memory of the World Register Companion*. https://en.unesco.org/sites/default/files/memory_of_the_world_register_companion_en.pdf.

UNESCO. *Records of the General Conference, 31st Session, Paris, 15 October – 3 November 2001, v. 1 Resolutions*. Preservation of the Digital Heritage, Resolution 34, Paris. 2002.

UNESCO. *Records of the General Conference, 38th Session, Paris, 3–18 November 2015*, Annex V Recommendation Concerning the Preservation of, and Access to, Documentary Heritage including in Digital Form. http://unesdoc.unesco.org/images/0024/002433/243325e.pdf.

UNESCO. *TEXT of the draft UNESCO RESOLUTION on DIGITAL PRESERVATION* Proposed by the Conference of Directors of National Libraries (CDNL), The Hague, June 2001. www.aes.org/technical/documentDownloads.cfm?docID=107.

UNESCO. *UNESCO/UBC VANCOUVER DECLARATION*, The Memory of the World in the Digital Age: Digitization and Preservation, 26–28 September2012, Vancouver, British Columbia, Canada. http://www.unesco.org/new/fileadmin/MULTIMEDIA/HQ/CI/CI/pdf/mow/unesco_ubc_vancouver_declaration_en.pdf.

van der Werf, Titia, and Bram van der Werf. "*The Paradox of Selection in the Digital Age*." Paper presented at: IFLA WLIC 2014 – Lyon – Libraries, Citizens, Societies: Confluence for Knowledge in Session 138 – UNESCO Open Session. In: IFLA WLIC 2014, 16–22 August2014, Lyon, France. http://library.ifla.org/1042/1/138-vanderwerf-en.pdf.

# 3

# DIGITAL DATA AS THE HERITAGE OF THE MODERN WORLD

In the previous chapter I explored the birth of digital data as heritage through the UNESCO charter and how attitudes, ideologies, and procedures associated with official heritage were transferred to digital data and then transnationally configured as a global concern. In this chapter, I make a case for the emergence of digital data as heritage as a distinctly contemporary modern phenomenon and as an expression of life in late modern times.

To this end, I examine how the disposition of heritage is formed and enacted in late modernity and make an explicit argument for the complicity of the heritage industry, personal digital memory, social media platforms, and even memorialized social media accounts in the afterlife, in global capitalism and data economies. Alongside these heritage practices and concerns, I establish the idea that there exists a corpus of heritage-like practices in other sectors and examine their respective dispositions in regard to historical data, making a case for a broader rendering of heritage as societal data worth, saving, keeping and continuing.

The idea of digital cultural heritage itself, as well as the ways it is defined, categorized, and understood, are all products of contemporary modern life and most importantly of how society conceives of itself in respect to heritage making, digital cultures, data, technological development, knowledge economies, and capitalist accumulation. Digital cultural heritage is intimately connected to, and an outcome of, rapid social, economic, and technological development and change.

Late modernity's obsession with preservation amidst concerns about decline and decay, and the associated disposition towards urgency arise because digital data is perceived as the new fabric of society. This is because our dependencies on digital media and computational systems in cultural life have become inextricably entangled.

Becoming digital is viewed as a form of technical evolution, a reinterpretation of social evolution-as-technical founded in Darwinian thought. In the UNESCO charter, for example, successive heritage epochs are characterized according to the different materials and technics that operate as a dominant canvas of life, each linked to stages of human social and technological advancement and organization to suggest a linear progression. Accordingly, each emerging material and technical form constitutes and supports intergenerational forms of historical recording, memory accumulation, communication. and heritage production. Earlier heritages, for example, are situated in epochs dominated by stone, parchment or wood and on technical systems based on analogue media.

The use by UNESCO of material, technical forms of description in the production of cultural memory to present heritage production as a profoundly civilizing process across geographical cultural space and time and affirms dominant arguments in media theory. Media theorist Bernard Stiegler promotes the idea of digital media, software, the internet, and computer technology programmed into everyday experiences and practices as central to the retention of the past in the current epoch.[1] Friedrich Kittler follows a similar argument, viewing digital communication as the dominant material and technical support for recording and memory accumulation as a hallmark of what he terms humanity's most advanced society.[2]

This vision of progress supports the idea of planned obsolescence and the desire for new technical forms as inevitable and as a civilizing process. As a result, these evolutionary technical and cultural systems produce their own heritage objects. Often obsolete, these digital objects embody such things as discarded code, machines, outdated behaviours or memes, discarded ideas, and e-waste.

The creation of digitizations, for example, is driven by a fear of the decline and decay of materials such as paper and wood, all of which are reminiscent of past civilizations but at the same time emblematic of a shift in preservation strategies utilizing the memory technics of modern life. Any given system of technical, material relations such as data in the contemporary world activates and modulates our thoughts, sensations, perceptions and accumulates memories that not only become trans-generational, as new forms of knowledge, but are also accompanied by the emergence of new cultural forms, making possible different types of inventive speculation.[3] These new cultural forms include digital capitalism, data economies, global computational infrastructures, artificial intelligence, and automated systems, which also produce their own heritage. I investigate this question in more depth in Chapter 8.

## Digital cultural heritage as a product of late modernity

Digital cultural heritage emerges out of a particular confluence of attitudes and relationships maintained in the present about the past alongside societal obligations thought to be held towards distant others for the future. Heritage theorist Rodney Harrison explains this as a distinctly modern human-centric disposition born out of the way we view our relationships with people, places, events, technology, and objects.[4] Modern agendas and concerns about human life, endangerment, loss, death, and the desire to prevent and ideally reverse these processes are embedded in digital data. Philosopher Marshall Berman captures the ambiguities of the modern world in which heritage is located as an oscillation in our experiences of the contemporary present between the assurance of progress and on the other hand destruction and disintegration. While on one hand modern life promises wealth, growth, renewal, technological transformation, and pleasure, on the other hand, Berman explains, it threatens to destroy and replace what we currently are, have, and possess.[5] These modern dispositions are widespread, crossing national boundaries, ethnicities, religions, and disciplines, and are embedded in ideological frameworks.

It is in between processes of technological development, loss, and these anticipated forces of destruction that digital data as heritage is anchored. The specific circumstances, relations, attitudes, and events that underpin the making of digital data as heritage are our experiences of intensified globalization, digital transformation, the rise of data economies in which we are deeply implicated, the desire for technological novelty and concerns in respect to obsolescence, technical fragility and breakdown, the vulnerability of the internet, and how all these risks endanger the traditions and memories of the past on which life itself depends. These concerns are outlined in the UNESCO Charter:

> In a world where emphasis is placed on speed and where life is becoming increasingly hurried, we must take time to conserve the records of what defines our roots, our past, our existence.…Not taking action will result in the loss of entire chapters of our heritage and lead to impoverishment of the global identity.[6]

Digital cultural heritage, like other types of cultural heritage, emerges out of a perception of impending crises, either real or imagined, and the resultant uncertainty these conditions create for us. Above all, digital data is perceived to be at risk of technical obsolescence or digital death through the successive developments of digital technology. In discussing camera technology, digital media theorist Joanna Zylinska argues that the succession of deaths within camera technology are comparable to biological extinction because these technical forms disappear forever.[7] The planned obsolescence of hardware, digital file formats, storage media, applications and programs, and the unrelenting production of new and better technologies and software, a design feature of contemporary capitalist profit-driven economies, is the predominant line of thought and practice underpinning the heritagization of digital data.

Digital heritage is therefore framed as a cultural form that will without a doubt become extinct and will no longer function unless its technical infrastructure (software and hardware) is preserved. Through this frame of obsolescence and preservation, multiple technical extinctions occur as uneven and iterative processes at ever increasing speeds. Data and systems are made to malfunction or comprise parts that are unfixable, difficult to replace and no longer supported by suppliers according to scheduled timeframes. Systems and applications are cognitive schemas produced on the basis of a calculation of projected sales. Therefore, data and technical objects become obsolete quickly if not accepted by the market and are thus discontinued.

The indeterminacy of obsolescence – that is, how long formats are supported by manufacturers and remain downloadable – intensifies risks posed to digital data, hardware, and operating systems. Digital cultural heritage must be able to survive these extinctions. Preservation and archival initiatives are thus characterized by endless cycles of death and renewal. Consumers are also implicated in the emergence of digital data as a form of heritage; they drive digital obsolescence through a desire to acquire new and improved devices, updated software programs, applications, and the new experiences that such things might afford. Stiegler characterizes this contemporary condition as a consumerist imperative for novelty – the speed of desire.[8]

Global forces and crises (as both events and processes) are also deemed to threaten all manner of cultural forms, which in turn contributes to the birth and profusion of an ever-expanding array of heritage types. Data and its framing as heritage act against these destructive, alienating aspects of contemporary life. The collection and documentation of digital data in archives and databases, and the continual monitoring of hardware, software, preservation formats, and the metadata attached to these records act against their demise and at the same time shore up their significance.

A fast-paced contemporary life and the threat of loss combine to create a nostalgia for old or obsolete things that we put to work to anchor ourselves in history, as objects that secure our identity and support the continuation of life as we know it. Digital heritagization therefore becomes an aspirational pursuit directed towards the retention of the past in the present through modes of bureaucratic preservation, value, and technical expertise. The same concepts of risk, uncertainty, loss, and mourning attributed to material heritage also apply to the digital, and UNESCO through its policies actively and unambiguously works to superimpose heritage dispositions, values, and criteria onto digital data. The UNESCO charter persuasively details this reverential approach to digital data and its ability to exemplify the past, and most importantly modernity's future.

Material forms of heritage, Harrison explains, encapsulate what it means to be modern on the one hand, most importantly how relations between modernity and time are framed, and on the other risk and how that risk is managed.[9] As a product of late modernity digital cultural heritage also embodies these relations. But it is clear that an intensified compression of time characterizes the birth of born-digital heritage in comparison to other type of heritage. This is due to the fast pace of digital development, transformation, and planned obsolescence.

The strategic document of the European Union Joint Programming Initiative on Cultural Heritage and Global Change clearly articulates this perceived compression of time as the rate at which heritage, in particular digital heritage, is being created and lost daily as a result of intensified technological change:

> Artefacts are being eroded and damaged, customs and practices are being lost and new heritage that is being created every day is in danger of being overlooked or ignored due to the inevitable pressures brought about by social, technological, economic and environmental change.[10]

Harrison eloquently explains the relationship between modern time and the birth of other types of material heritage as an emphasis on linear progress first and foremost, alongside a perceived distinct break between past and present through which the former is abolished and time operates as an irreversible arrow.[11] Critically, it is in these in-between moments flanked by the modern past, the present, and an impending future that digital cultural heritage as a cultural form emerges. Furthermore, its location within the passage of modern linear time between when digital cultural resources are produced and the moment they become subject to risk activates an item's assessment as significant, rare, and valuable. This occurrence is instantaneous and even anticipated. Digital resources yet to be made are viewed as endangered. For example, the Smithsonian Institution Archives collects digital files produced from anywhere between one week old and 30 years old but routinely between 10 and 15 years old.[12] Some digital resources such as President Donald Trump's tweets are earmarked as heritage because of the imminent threat of their technical extinction. Here the loss of Trump's tweets is foreseen even before they are produced. I describe this as a form of anticipatory heritage or a practice of anticipatory heritagization.

Accordingly, the timescales of digital preservation between when something is made and at risk is consequently compressed in comparison to other types of material heritage. Within the life of digital data, there is only a small window of opportunity when it can be collected. UNESCO characterizes this as a distinct temporal relation in which the timeframe in which the heritagization of digital data can be enacted is foregone because the threat of its loss is activated at the moment of its inception or production.

> The world's digital heritage is at risk of being lost to posterity. Contributing factors include the rapid obsolescence of the hardware and software which brings it to life… Unless the prevailing threats are addressed, the loss of the digital heritage will be rapid and inevitable.[13]

Furthermore, in explaining the relationship between modernity and heritagization in respect to material heritage, Harrison observes that "modernity creates for itself a past that is perceived to be both immanent (contained within) and imminent (impending) in the present."[14] Digital data contains the past, a past deemed to be written into the very fabric of its bitstreams and its hardware components. Therefore, the illusion of the digital object as a delineated thing in which its heritagization is deeply embedded in its bitstreams and technical infrastructures becomes at the same time hyper-imminent, about to disappear. But more importantly, future life is contained within digital data. Therefore, the future is impending in the present and about to disappear before it has emerged. Surprisingly, the past and the future are not remote from each other. They operate together in the contemporary present. The future is made now.

Future thinking characterizes the birth of digital data as heritage more so than any other forms as the pace of obsolescence intensifies. Digital data is seen as the building blocks of intellectual, cultural, social, and economic life. Thinking about digital cultural heritage as the past in the present at the same time invokes what we envisage for the future. Accordingly, the heritagization of digital data is regarded as vital to futureproof cultural and intellectual life, modernity and capitalism as the dominant mode of existence:

> Attitudinal change has fallen behind technological change. Digital evolution has been too rapid and costly for governments and institutions to develop timely and informed preservation strategies. The threat to the economic, social, intellectual and cultural potential of the heritage – the building blocks of the future – has not been fully grasped.[15]

It is not just the past, therefore, that must be managed carefully, as argued for other types of heritage, but with digital data the future too must be fortified through preservation efforts. The future becomes the dominant concern, a future governed by digital capitalism. What we are dealing with here is a direct co-relation between the expansion of digital cultures, digital data, and its heritagization in the present in respect to current, intensified concerns about the future. Therefore, digital data as heritage is at once historical and future-directed, to a greater extent than other types of heritage, because of its connection with digital economic life. Poignantly, the effects of late modernity on preservation strategies also drive the need for content to be migrated into successive new media and technical infrastructures, which themselves will become subject to loss.

The notion of digital obsolescence is a modern apocalyptic disposition centred around the extinction of hardware and software; by implication it signals the end of affluence, capitalism, and memory of cultural life, and leads to the disintegration of the archive. Digital obsolescence is more than just the death or loss of the functionality of technical systems, operating systems, platforms, and technical objects. Loss, according to theorist Claire Colebrook, is intimately linked to the transformation of social habits.[16] As fashion shifts and with the emergence of each new application, new platforms, software, and new habits or memes emerge. The shift from MySpace, the emergence of web 2.0, and the rise of Facebook is a case in point where the closure of the platform, the social use of data, and the conventions in which they are embedded become obsolete or pass away forever and are replaced by new ones. Such behaviours or memes therefore must be saved as examples of discarded, abandoned, or extinct thoughts and practices.

Furthermore, planned obsolescence is not only a modern heritage disposition but is also a compositional obsolescence of varying temporalities enacted through all of its parts and their interconnectedness as reoccurring cycles of death and life. That is, from the material supply chains required for their production and the devices that support them, to their design, to resource conflicts emerging through competing access to rare earth minerals, and to the closure and loss of applications, platforms, infrastructures, and circulation routes, the demise of computational components, electrical systems, and the processes central to their emergence and the memes that foreclose them.

In summary, digital cultural heritage currently emerges as an unintended consequence of late modernity's obsession with digital data, digital media, novelty, desire, and obsolescence as never-ending cycles, and the life of their preservation formats. Officially sanctioned digital cultural heritage comprises a series of coordinates, compositional dynamics and agencies formed from the intermingling and conative action of human and non-human actants, including: digital software; computer hardware; paper, film, parchment; heat; light; processes of decay and destruction; memory and forgetting; heritage discourses of preservation; late modernity and technological progress; technological obsolescence and dysfunction; globalization; the data economy and capital accumulation; the administrative procedures of UNESCO; the vulnerability of the World Wide Web, and so forth. Loss, rather than renewal, change, and the production of new things and social behaviours, forecloses heritage.

## The future of curatorial labour in collecting and archiving data

As more data is produced, more intensified collecting campaigns are emerging, thereby conflating the past and an unknowable, threatened future with the present. Here the heritagization of digital data becomes hyper-latent. To do this, museums and quasi-archival entities employ automated systems and artificial intelligence (except for Archive Team's initiative that adheres to the notion of emulation), thereby enacting a process of capturing live data and rendering it static in the archive.

The heritage work of the Internet Archive, a San Francisco-based digital library, demonstrates how attitudes relating to hyper-imminence, future-proofing and heritagization are made actionable through collecting strategies. Its Wayback Machine uses web crawlers to collect and archive web sites and associated data, images, code, and documents in a database on a regular basis.[17] Users are then able to access archived versions of the web. By August 2016, 502 billion web pages had been archived.[18] Since 2004, The British Library has been selectively collecting digital data deemed to have documentary and future research value as representative of British social history and cultural heritage within the UK domain.[19] Archived as mostly static pages (screenshots of websites), the British Library provides document-style access to historical versions of over 4 million UK websites to researchers and the general public.[20] As archives of data, these systems recontextualize information, simultaneously transforming digital data and making it into historical data as a series of web site snapshots. In an automated world, web crawlers are the agents of this transformation from live to historical data.

Driven by the threat of platform closure, The Archive Team, a not-for-profit collaboration of digital hunters, collectors, and salvagers, gather websites, games, and software in the belief that, if these digital resources are not captured and archived, they will be lost forever.[21] The Archive Team began harvesting GeoCities websites initially and made then available as a torrent file, a peer-to-peer file sharing program. The collective also gathered material from Yahoo Answers, Google Reader, social media app Vine, and games such as the 1980s arcade video game Berzerk.[22] In addition to this, the Archive Team have archived an extensive collection of news clips about American politics, including all of Donald Trump's appearances in the news media over nine years that have been captured digitally, comprising over 700 items including speeches, interviews, debates, and news items. The collection of Trump-related digital media, however, was also driven by political concerns and activist ambitions. Founder Jason Scott explains, "It is possible to extract everything he has ever said … Putting up all the words of the president in one handy collection, and analyzing it, maybe will change our relationship to government."[23] Here digital content also becomes political digital heritage with the potential to force Trump and his administration to be accountable for their actions.

In all these examples web crawlers behave automatically as new types of automations filtering and collecting digital traces, and gathering snapshots of websites at a point in time of their emergence. Users are then able to access archived versions of the web. The question therefore arises: Will robotic capture as seen with the Wayback Machine, an automated heritagization process and a new type of institutional form, replace curatorial labour in heritage collecting? It is anticipated that in the next 20 years more than 40 percent of jobs will be threatened by algorithms.[24] Such systems will displace human labour, as the system no longer individuates to the same degree as human-intensive curatorial work. While the Wayback Machine automates and distributes processes as it delegates decisions to machines, it will not altogether replace human labour, as these technics embody a combination of human and machine reasoning

Curatorial decision-making solely by artificial intelligence at this point in time is likely to lower quality and diversity of decisions that can be made on data, how it is organized, and also fail to capture the subtle nuance of curatorial intentions that drive collecting. Having said this, algorithmic curating is increasingly used by heritage institutions in the filtering and gathering of the vast volumes of data we produce in interesting and unlikely ways not pre-empted by human capability. AI has the potential to not only assist human selection but also to make automatic selections, recommendations and fully autonomous new content. However, human curatorial labour will still be required to initiate and take the final steps in any automated process. The development and training of social bots and algorithms dedicated to selecting, reviewing and editing content after it has been gathered and processed requires human curatorial labour. While it may be difficult to distinguish between human and machine logic as bots or personal assistants become more sophisticated in finding information and making decisions about what information to collect, human input remains, at least in the present moment, integral to the system in respect to code writing and to a degree search inputs. But this is changing as AI capabilities expand. The characterization of automated curation as human–machine is limiting. Curatorial agency within these spaces, rather than seen as comprising solely human agents, machines, and their narratives, are collaborations that encompass the agencies of storable data, earth minerals, calculable and predictive entities such as sensors, robots, algorithmic automations, cables, data centres, and technological capitalism. All these processes require a more expansive imaginary of curatorial labour.

## Heritage-like practices in corporate, government, commercial and research sectors

Heritage-like thinking and practices operate across all sectors. While the notion of heritage is specific to UNESCO, ICOM, and heritage institutions, there is an array of heritage-like regimes that operate alongside and at times intersect with officiating entities. Due to the datafication of life itself, like heritage-making in formal institutions, societal data is viewed as the building blocks of cultural, intellectual, and economic life and must be kept active and archived in order to fortify the future and digital capitalism. Digital curation and preservation practices in data economies are generally more advanced than at heritage institutions because data is seen as a financial asset with future profit margins at stake.

Different types of organizations have data repositories. Data companies, financial institutions, businesses and corporations, accountants, government agencies such as taxation offices, public health and medical institutions, insurance companies, research organizations such as universities, and government bureaucracies are responsible legally, contractually, socially, morally, economically for providing long-term access to data. All these entities are involved in capturing, processing, and managing data to keep it active and at the same time are lodged in an archive. The temporal frameworks, procedures, and forms of assessment through which data is retained vary.

As with paper records in the past, record-keeping across these sectors is undertaken to maintain and secure persistent data for the future. These overlapping heritage-like regimes or domains of practice operate within the confines of late modern thinking. Late modern dispositions of obsolescence, rapid technological and economic change, the desire for progress and the accumulation of wealth underpin such practices, alongside modern time as a marker of value and significance. Located among these aspirations and concerns is data, that is on one hand potentially valuable and on the other vulnerable. Just like digital cultural heritage, the potential loss of valued historical data and how to curate, manage, and archive it are the overriding concerns. Similarly, digital preservation timescales are condensed because capitalist accumulation is dependent on planned obsolescence and the associated dispositions of risk. The planned obsolescence of software and hardware fuels and intensifies data threats, and compresses the temporal frame between the production of data and the point of its vulnerability. But what characterizes the difference between heritage as opposed to heritage-like practices is not a break from the traditions of the past so much as a potential rupture from the past, a loss of records of the past, and therefore what went before. Like heritage, the past is embedded in data bitstreams which draw us back to a significant moment or moments in time. The loss of tradition in heritage frameworks is re-written as the loss of economic historical activities and of financial memory, the records of our health history and knowledge of our bodily condition or our taxation history and the erasure of our tax reconciliations records for auditing purposes. Therefore, a qualitatively different range of values informs collecting and saving. Heritage-like values are pragmatic rather than nostalgic and do not generally invoke a loss or mourning of the past in the same way. They are memories of a different kind embedded in data and technics.

Most heritage institutions, if they indeed collect data at all, direct their attention to arresting the duration of digital data as a moment in time, removing data from its lived context, turning it into timeless, permanent, and enduring objects so they can stand for all time as aspects of human life and experience. The desire to fix and quarantine data in such a way is a distinctly heritage disposition. The representational paradigm so dominant in heritage and museological culture also involves collecting fragments of hardware and software, not necessarily meant to be used.

In other heritage-like contexts, however, keeping data and turning it into historical data is directed towards ensuring it remains active and accessible and thus available to serve as a functional record or be reused or repurposed at some point in the future, a future often determined pragmatically or legally according to how long such data is economically or bureaucratically viable. This range of practices advances quite different approaches to data, that is, either as something to be locked away and fixed or used and changed. Heritage institutions are beginning to direct their attention to inducting into their repositories, alongside hardware, data that can be used again or emulated in the future. This shift has significant implications for the museum sector and practices for curating data, advancing a new mode of engagement, that of reuse, renewal, and transformation (to be discussed in more detail in the conclusion).

Across all these sectors, data preservation works against the destructive and alienating effects of modern life. Like heritage, data saving is directed towards the retention of the past in the present. As well as retaining memory in data records, such practices ensure the continuation of life as we know it by anchoring our medical, economic, bureaucratic, and research identities in data, much of which is created and aggregated by machines.

While data across all heritage-like regimes are regarded as records of the past, even the immediate past, that are viewed as significant, rare, or valuable, such data becomes subject to different forms of valuation and therefore different saving and preservation regimes. Such values become embedded in data. Digital cultural heritage is a set of standardizing procedures used to transform digital data into heritage, valued and fixed as forms of cultural memory representative of human life and experience. In each of these regimes data operates as different forms of cultural memory recall, from economic memory or personal health memory to the memory of our digital traces.

These heritage regimes are not necessarily mutually exclusive. Selecting and saving data for the long term within these heritage-like regimes, while historical data, is not necessarily referred to as heritage, but it could become subject to heritagization if it ends up in heritage archives and made subject institutional rules and practices. Within a modern regime of time, all data is seen as embodying the past; it is indeed the past. The cultural value of data in all heritage-like regimes is based on a consideration as to whether data is significant and has value as records of human social, cultural, economic, or governmental life but is made subject to and put to work in different ways.

Heritage-like thinking and the spectrum of regimes that save data together broaden our definition of data as historical beyond that of heritage. Here we must extend the scope of saving and preserving data beyond the strict ambit of heritage to encompass societal data seen as important to retain and keep active beyond the contemporary present. This includes more-than-human or other-than-human data emerging across these sectors; for example, diagnostic data in the medical field or data produced by bacteria through algorithmic machines. Other heritage-like regimes consider what will be useful in the future and capable of being used, changed or reproduced; like heritage institutions, these also seek to retain authentic and original records because they are also in the business of authenticating data and deciding what is a true or accurate record. Here the accuracy of data is predicated on its future use as a record of past activity for analysis and reference.

Like the heritage field, governments, corporations, research, and the cultural sectors are facing the same problem, that is, how to deal with the huge volumes of data they extract and how to decide what is worth keeping. The rate at which we are producing data through mining, for example, is rapidly exceeding our current capacities to curate and retain it successfully. In general, sectors take a passive, neglectful approach to data preservation. Most heritage-like regimes do not think carefully about how to retain their data long-term and (like heritage institutions) instead hope or expect data to survive without too much planning. This issue is partly the outcome of the availability of cloud storage. Data storage companies such as Google do not want us to reduce our data because they want to sell more storage space. Sectors struggle with ways to discriminate between critical data vital to their operational success and the vast volume of redundant, trivial, duplicate, rot data that no longer has value or indeed is dark data whose value has not been identified.[25] That which has come to be known as "databergs" is made up of overwhelming levels of dark data and only small volumes of critical data.[26] The challenge becomes to illuminate dark data, get rid of data rot, and proactively maintain and manage significant and vital data. This process starts with prescribing data value – that is, making decisions about what will be useful to an individual organization or sector in the future according to its own regimes of value and activities. The selection of data for heritage making is also compromised by "databergs."

Digital curation involves keeping (deciding what to keep or discard), managing (organizing what has been kept using folders or other structures), and exploiting (searching for, finding, and using what has been kept). In the broadest sense digital curation are practices that seek to keep data active and meaningful. Digital preservation similarly refers to decisions about what data to keep and what to discard and forget and on the other hand remember and its anticipated usefulness in the future according to distinctive systems of data value. Time is also an important ingredient in giving such decisions perspective. Data not only accrues value according to its economic, bureaucratic, or cultural-representative imperatives. Value is also based on intent and purpose. Repositories are founded according to a range of intents and purposes: government data and information about populations directed to governing subjects; data companies' targeted marketing directed towards governing user consumerism; data held by tax offices about finances and tax obligations which is directed to governing subjects as economic citizens; or to museums and the governing of objects for the representation of social and cultural life in perpetuity through standardization processes. Different modern temporal concerns also determine record retention. Accountants hold records for approximately seven years for auditing purposes prescribed by taxation legislation. For the heritage industry the temporal frame is perpetuity. For the health and police sectors records are for the long term, for the life of the individual and beyond.

Heritage-like practices are often linked to the digital economy thereby becoming global regimes of value according to different data value dispositions. Data trading companies buy and handle other people's data and generally deal with big data and big data preservation for revenue generation, giving people's data a monetary value through a series of pricing mechanisms.[27] Here data is viewed as a business asset for targeted marketing. Keeping data is linked to its monetization in the present and future. Here the intention is to keep data alive so it can be used in the future in a context where new data identities are proliferating.[28] Data that is inherently historical but also active can be used again in data markets. In the case of the European tax system data operates as a raw material used to create new relationships between the past, present and future directed to the manipulation of our behaviour for profit.

Anticipatory heritage in heritage-like practices therefore is often linked to data markets and operates through big data processing, where calculations and predictions are made by machine learning. Although these predictions are future-orientated they are based on historical data.[29] The future becomes calculated, calibrated, predicated, and foreclosed according to what went before. This at the same time highlights the difficulties we have with living with the unknown. As with modern heritage dispositions, one single, linear temporal framework is routinely prescribed and imposed on data.

Research organizations such as universities and companies engage in heritage-like practices through global and interoperable data systems (Global Research Data Infrastructures, or GRDIs) to store and manage research data.[30] Research funders are now requiring data to be stored by researchers in forms that allow it to be described and retrieved in the future. These archives steward data based on the value given to it by researchers as research resources to keep these records safe for the medium and long term so they can be recovered, used, and analysed again.[31]

## Heritage-like dispositions, personal data and citizen archiving

As individuals we are accumulating voluminous amounts of digital data. These include everything from digital images, websites, emails, texts, voicemails, blogs, PowerPoint presentations and work files, and data produced from online gaming to digital communication through posts on Twitter, YouTube, Facebook, Instagram, and recordings of music, radio and TV programs, and digital videos. Digital traces of our relationships as images, videos, and conversations remain on Instagram, Facebook, Facebook Messenger and WhatsApp. Digital images are passively collected, many of them not necessarily our own, stored on different devices and applications, and in different formats.

Smartphones are now the primary devices for the capture, production, recording, collection, sharing, and archiving of personal multimedia data as recordings of events and digital communications; they thereby act as a portable memory archive that Anna Reading calls the memobile.[32] We are addicted to smartphones and to data production. We use smartphones to listen to music, to check messages, for taking selfies and photographs and uploading the images we produce, for interacting and posting on social media, for purchasing items, and for navigating our way around our respective urban spaces. The smartphone becomes a distraction and a comforting device with which to amuse ourselves when alone. Many of us transform into smartphone zombies out in the world, in the streets, on trains, in cafes and supermarkets, where in the past we may have sat uncomfortably, listened to an iPod or a CD, or talked to others. Our zombie behaviour often unwittingly contributes to the profusion of personal data.

Digital memory mediated through smartphones has been integral to capturing public record events and natural disasters, thereby constituting what might be termed a people's digital memory. The first meta-recorded instance of this behaviour, which incidentally coincided with the emergence of smartphones, was at the terrorist bombings in London on July 7, 2005. Footage and images captured by citizen journalists have become integral to the heritagization of that event, thereby enabling new performances of capture and memory-making.[33]

British civil servant Alan Stacey sought to capture his experience of the bombings for his own personal archive. Stacey was caught up in the Piccadilly Line blast between King's Cross and Russell Square. He and friend Elliot were trapped underground in a smoky carriage for 40 minutes, then got off the train and walked back along the train tracks. Noting that others were documenting the scene via mobile phone photos, and not knowing it was a bombing, Elliot took a photo of Stacey to record the event.[34] The digital image of Stacey in a smoke-filled Northern Line tunnel with his hand over his face went viral, with postings in the

US, Canada, Spain, and the Netherlands, and people accessing the image from Flickr, the BBC, and the Guardian newspaper.[35]

More recently the deadly eruption of White Island Whakaari in New Zealand's Bay of Plenty that occurred on Monday December 9, 2019 claiming 15 lives was captured on the smartphone of Brazilian tourist Allessandro Kauffmann, who documented the trip on video and uploaded it to YouTube. Narrowly escaping death himself, Kauffmann and fellow tourists who managed to get off the island in a boat were almost engulfed in a lethal ash cloud that enveloped the island.[36] They returned to the island amidst the ash cloud to rescue survivors from the Ovation of the Seas tour group, many of whom died. The video went viral on YouTube and mainstream media such as the Auckland Herald, acting as testimony of the event and its memorialization.

Officiating heritage institutions such as the Library of Congress are instituting online programs encouraging publics to perform their own personal digital preservation measures, driven by the same discourses of loss and salvage promoted by the UNESCO charter:

> Increasingly our possessions and our communications are no longer material, they're digital and they are dependent on technology to make them accessible. As new technology emerges and current technology becomes obsolete, we need to actively manage our digital possessions to help protect them and keep them available for years to come. This video offers simple and practical strategies for personal digital preservation.[37]

Most personal digital collections and archiving practices operate outside officiating institutions. The question is what attitudes and dispositions drive personal data production, storage, and archiving? How does the production, sharing, and storage of personal data reflect an individual's or group's current concerns about the past, present, and future? Do people develop a reverential attachment to the personal data they produce? Does it become heritage?

Participants interviewed as part of the English-based ethnographic research project Family Memories in the Home, by interactive media design scholar Daniela Petrelli, on their attachments to physical and digital mementos[38] expressed concern about the volatility of technological formats and their rapid obsolescence, and the risk all these things pose to their own digital belongings for the long term. Many spoke of a desire to save and keep their digital belongings and pass them on to future generations in the same way they talked about physical objects. Others talked about preserving personal data as a means of building their identity as a form of bodily self-extension through platforms such as Facebook and Instagram.[39] Again, the conflation of time means that the moment when digital data is produced and when it is posed as at risk of loss for individuals is simultaneous, even anticipated, similar to official digital cultural heritage. This anticipatory disposition in respect to digital data production and its endangerment in personal accounts is also an outcome of the lack of adequate and easy solutions for its preservation.

Unsurprisingly, concerns about the fragility of digital belongings and the difficulty of keeping and archiving them governed respondents' thoughts about their value in the long term and their attachment to it. Digital mementos are seen as less valuable; people held less attachment to them because data is seen as fragile, less tangible, more ephemeral and utilitarian, and somewhat more like commodities, rather than as things with symbolic meaning that can persist for the long-term[40] – although this depends on the type of digital possession invoked. For these reasons among others, digital data is produced primarily for immediate consumption for sharing on social media sites. Attachments to digital belongings may grow as people produce more personal mementos in digital format, and a heightened sense of endangerment will ease as simpler and more robust ways for archiving data emerge.

Digital memory and archiving therefore is central to the experience and function of digital media and the digital possessions we produce.[41] The externalization of memory in digital format captured through digital technics in the form of language, writing, gestures, and images[42] stored in the phone, the computer, and on Facebook and Instagram are all acts of memorialization that operate as autobiographical representations, as forms of self-disclosure, as a life log of the aging individual over time and in the present as anticipatory acts in relation to the impending mortality of the physical body. Here personal data operates as a programmable cultural memory and as a form of personal curation in service of the fleshly body as a digital record. Digital data therefore becomes emotive as mementos and props for memory recall, to reminisce, to relive life, as a form of self-expression and identity building, for entertainment, and for future remittance. Photos of the autobiographical kind are used to construct self-representations, act as forms of self-disclosure, and, through sharing, to strengthen social relationships, often through social media posts. Personal data and its uses vary generationally and individually. We see this on Facebook and Instagram where younger people use digital photos as self-defining whereas older people use them as props to trigger memories.

Importantly, digital and material belongings trigger the same emotions; each has the potential to build attachments to them and can be viewed as significant and valuable over time, Petrelli explains, as long as they have a continued physical presence.[43] The problem is that it is more difficult to build an attachment to digital content, for several reasons: because these things lack the tactile and often tangible qualities of physical possessions; are difficult to retrieve on hard drives and mobile phones; comprise vast quantities of data; are often improperly indexed; and can become obsolete and unusable very quickly.[44] In another study on practices associated with the collecting of personal data, Francesco Vitale, Izabelle Janzen and Joanna McGrenere found that attachments to and the desire to save personal data were governed by the individual's own personal values, and that these include the pragmatics of utility and recency, emotional attachment, and how easily items could be replaced.[45]

Participants did suggest that mementos had the potential to become heritage over time. Digital belongings could accrue these values by building personal attachments to them over the long term, by viewing and engaging with these materials regularly,[46] and by honouring them as something precious and significant, as could become the case with a print of a digital photograph. On the other hand, the logic driving heritage for others was that heritage must be old, representative of a distant past. Digital data was simply not seen as old enough to be considered heritage at this point in time.[47] Here the relationship between distance and time defines whether digital belongings could be considered heritage in the making.

People clearly share heritage-like dispositions with UNESCO and heritage institutions and those governing the digital economy typical of late modern thinking and life itself. These dispositions concern risk, endangerment due to technical volatility, the need to select and save societal data for perpetuity, and as something of potential value and of significance. While these dispositions are shared, the categorization of digital data as official heritage comprises a specific set of selection, assessment, authenticating and preservation procedures imposed on digital data by officially sanctioned administering institutions and UNESCO. Generally speaking, personal data only becomes official heritage when it is accessioned into the collections of officiating institutions where values of authenticity, of origin, and the original prevail. Interestingly, the question of time, age, and distance through which data becomes of value to individuals differs from the UNESCO charter. Digital data, risk, and heritagization are not separated in space and time – as it is a process that operates often concurrently. Many of us confront a personal digital dark age caused through our failure to save our digital possessions. I for example am experiencing a digital dark age of my own, having lost many of my own digital memories over the last 20 years due to benign neglect.

Those interviewed in these studies did not use the term heritage to describe their digital belongings, and do not use the same heritage procedures and authenticating rituals of the original, origin, and aura to give their personal data value, at least not in a formal sense. It appears that people may not be as concerned about whether digital data is in its original form or a copy as long as it has the ability to draw them back in historical time, trigger memories, and therefore form attachments for them. This is also because digital data is inherently mutable and proliferating. Accordingly, the form that digital data presents itself in is not as important because they act as mementos. Here aura, the links digital belongings make to an event or person, is transferred to so-called copies and to their printed versions, all of which are new productions.

The development of digital technics such as smartphones and computers alongside social media platforms as venues for curating personal data, self-representation, assembling and organizing posts, connecting with others through likes and comments as new types of archiving and curatorial infrastructures, is a late modern phenomenon.

Social media platforms alongside personal data production perform life-logging functions and act as personal repositories for data storage.[48] These heritage-type archives are often presented as utopic spaces allowing for the proliferation of memories, histories, images, and narratives that differ markedly from those presented by museums and official memory archives. Facebook for example operates as a personal repository and a mechanism for reporting on everyday activities – such as, in my case, a record of my European work sojourn in 2018, my encounters with fellow travellers and new work colleagues through which I formed close bonds and holiday experiences, reporting these to my Facebook friends and those in the "real" world. Increasingly, Facebook attempts to revisit events or social relationships in an individual's life a year, three, or ten years ago in order to build attachments to digital memories and strengthen friendship bonds. But in order to do this, Facebook codes and curates human lives, experiences, and memories and renders all these things into storable data. But Facebook is also a sovereign polis intimately connected to digital capitalism by transforming users' activities into data that is to be used for commercial gain. While purporting to be a social media site and a place where online users create, share, archive, and connect with other users, each creative, intellectual, social, or transactional activity from a blog post to an update or purchase a user engages in online becomes a data commodity that is then sold to advertising companies as a way of segmenting and targeting particular user groups and the individuals themselves.[49]

## Heritage-like dispositions, archives and digital immortality

Digital mortality not only becomes a question of the loss of data due to obsolescence or bit rot but also invites the question of how we view the continuing existence of our digital memories such as digital photographs, images, video and text messages in perpetuity after we pass away. What happens to our digital data once we depart this world? Frequently such data become buried in obsolete computers and disks, often password secured and no longer accessible to those who survive us: ghost profiles or static glow, terms Mirko Tobias Schäfer and Audrey Samson[50] use to describe posthumous digital memories linger and remain active in networks and platforms long after the owner is deceased. Our digital afterlife often encompasses data left on platforms for remembering and mourning, as a place to visit and communicate with those that have passed away.

The emergence of digital cemeteries on digital platforms and the regulation of our digital estates emerges out of the profusion of personal and social media platforms and the data that has been uploaded to these sites. In 2015 Facebook offered users a range of self-curating options in anticipation of users' impending fleshly mortality luring us into establishing an online immortal archive. One option offered was to kill off or delete your account, thus permanently deleting all information and data originating from it.[51] The second was to appoint a digital executor to take care of your digital assets and by doing so memorialize your Instagram, Twitter, and/or Facebook accounts, emails, and images. Photos and posts shared by the deceased would stay visible; however, no one can log into the account. A third option offered is the use of an app, *If I Die*, that allows an individual to create a video, message, or text message that is then scheduled to be disseminated when you pass away. This last option also enables people to continue to leave comments and celebrate the life of the deceased.

British tourist Mia Ayliffe-Chung was brutally murdered at a backpacker hostel in Home Hill, North Queensland, Australia by an obsessed fellow hosteller, along with friend Tom Jackson who was trying to defend her during the attack. Mia posted a video to her Facebook page on August 19, 2016, a moving image of herself on the day before her murder, that now acts as her memorial in cyberspace.[52] Mia's Facebook account remains active, appearing in searches with 71k views and 84 comments and 456 likes. Her memorialized account, used as her life blog, becomes a place of reverence where Mia's posthumous presence lingers as ghostly data. It is a place for friends and family to gather and share memories, an index of her important relationships, of her emotional ties, and of the significant events in her life such as her time in Australia. Mia's Facebook memorial is a programmable memory, a form of abstraction made possible through digital technics, thereby making possible the externalization of her fleshly body, her aliveness, her thoughts, her gestures, her feelings as data appearing as words, images, and videos through her posts. Mia was dating Jamison Stead for a time before her death. Jamison posted: "Rest in peace Mia. Thank you for the memories". Mia and Tom's murderer, French national Smail Ayad, may never face trial following a diagnosis of possible drug-induced schizophrenia.[53]

Ancestry.com also acts as a vehicle for capturing family heritage as a way of circumventing the precarity and death of both the digital image and the fleshly body. Facebook and Twitter memorial posts are not just an outcome of the mind and fleshly bodies, they are forms of digital immortality – constructed by computational logics, algorithms, bots, and automation systems. These ghostly memorials represent a more-than-human archive of feeling and empathy and a new type of automated posthumous heritage. The main instruments of labour and monetization used in the production of data commodities on the Facebook platform are the minds of its human users, including those who have departed this world, through the personal data they create or have created.

The distinction between official memory agents, for example museums and libraries with their authorial practices, and those of individual or private memory agents, heritage-like practices in other sectors, and those of automated systems has become blurred. Preservation, memory capture, documentation, and archiving represent a convergence of practices across domains but also constitute a series of frictious performances that have the potential to unravel the notions of heritage and authenticity, and their application to digital data.

UNESCO does not have a monopoly in deciding what is worth saving and how we define significance. Multiple genres of heritage-like practices exist. The imperative to identify societal data worth keeping and running is important for various reasons and therefore invokes a different set of standards and approaches to the archive.

## Digital cultural heritage and its complicity in data economies and technological capitalism

Digital data as heritage is much more than endangered forms of human cultural expression. Data encapsulates our relationship with a rapidly expanding digital capitalism. The expansion of heritage-like practices, the data economy, and the meaning we attach to digital data have shifted radically in the past 20 years from information bearing to include monetary gain. Certain types of digital data and therefore potential heritage are products of data economies and global computational infrastructures deeply embedded in systems of capitalism, governance, and bureaucracy that humans have come to depend on in the western world. As a result, digital cultural heritage is not only born out of the underlying logic of modernity, endangerment, and its risks, but also of the neo-liberal and free market conditions that emphasize progress and the expansion of capital.

These market, labour, and material conditions have their origin in events and processes such as deindustrialization and the emergence of digital cultures, digital and informational economies, the latter as modes of capital accumulation and the accompanying institutional, bureaucratic, and technical systems that support digital infrastructures. While our various relationships to the past differ geographically and culturally, modern sensibilities in respect to the meaning of digital cultural heritage are becoming globally extensive as capitalism expands through digital infrastructures and applications.

Potential heritage can be digital data of any type – digital media content, social relations and networking information, applications, digital objects, databases, or social systems. Financial and bureaucratic instruments such as websites, databases, blog posts, spam, and email, for example, are also potential heritage. Online businesses produce potential heritage through the creation of images, social networking sites, free apps, open software and tools, and streamed digital content, to stimulate consumer behaviour. The online activities of people produce content through social networks such as Twitter, Facebook, and Instagram, location data, browsing data, data about likes and preferences and so forth, much of which is considered significant and worth saving. Financial predictions are often made on historical data, where heritage data are put to work to predict future life in all manner of ways.

Despite all this, little attention has been paid to digital cultural heritage and its agency in economic and profit generation in heritage frameworks. That is because of digital data's seemingly immaterial character but also because data is seen as so mundane and deeply embedded in all aspects of our lives that it becomes invisible. In this context, data operates as an invisible agent in financial markets and can be thought of as the virtualization of computational materials nestled within relations of desire, capital accumulation, profit maximization, sovereign platforms, global computational infrastructures, and so forth.

This relationship between the making of digital heritage and digital curation in support of capitalist accumulation is made apparent through various preservation initiatives. Digital heritage comprises the economic records of late modernity and therefore the economic records of the past. The European Commission's Digital Agenda for Europe 2010 strategy makes this relation explicit. The agenda sought "to trigger a 'Digital Renaissance' across all facets of society"[54] and in support of this made funding available to cultural institutions to preserve the digital records of economic services in support of the growth of Europe's information economies. Many social and cultural institutions and corporations depend on the accumulation and salvage of persistent digital data to ensure their economic survival. Here digital curation through digitization, preservation, and access to Europe's cultural materials is intended to stimulate Europe's economy and put to work to support digital innovation and new economic activities and in doing so the promotion of societal, cultural, and economic stability.

> Bringing our museums' and libraries' collections online not only shows Europe's rich history and culture but can also usher in new benefits for education, for innovation and for generating new economic activities. It will put high quality content on the net for many generations… Culture and heritage in the digital era represent a set of opportunities for European economies and societies.[55]

The Europeana portal is an important initiative in support of this strategy, acting as the archive for Europe's digital cultural heritage where copies of born-digital heritage items and digital surrogates are deposited. The production and consumption of data through these means represents heritage in the making in economies that run on persistent data.

The making of digital data into economic heritage reproduces the underlying ideological cornerstone of digital capitalism itself and its embeddedness as the dominant mode of contemporary life and, as a consequence, the commodification of those digital cultural materials. Digital cultural heritage likewise becomes tethered to these new modes of economy.

Likewise, in the Australian context these political and capitalist ambitions were borne out in the study *Challenges and Opportunities for Australia's Galleries, Libraries, Archives and Museums*, a joint research project by CSIRO and the Smart Services Cooperative Research Centre. This project sought to bolster digital innovation in the heritage sector and further the economic viability of cultural institutions by stimulating economic growth in the GLAM sector through digitization strategies making collections available to their audiences and through the creation of jobs:

> Australian's museums, galleries and other cultural institutions must adopt more of a digital strategy with their collections if they are to remain relevant with audiences. … Only about a quarter of the collections held by the sector have been digitised so far and a study out today says more needs to be done to protect and preserve the material, and make it available to people online.
>
> … Australia's galleries, libraries, archives and museums (the GLAM sector) represent our accumulated achievements and experiences, inspire creativity and provide a place for us to connect with our heritage.
>
> They are also crucial to our economy with the GLAM sector estimated to have a revenue of about A$2.5 billion each year. That's not only a lot of paintings and artifacts, but a lot of jobs as well.[56]

In both these examples we encounter the preservation of digital cultural heritage, and the digitization of existing collections as instruments of capitalism in support of the expansion of capital and the maximization of profit and profitability, the former in support of the broader digital economy and the latter in support of the economic viability of the heritage industry. For example, the Cooper Hewitt Museums' collections data on GitHub is made available to developers and anyone else who wishes to use it. Here people and digital cultural heritage become economic and economized.

Digital cultural heritage is also embedded in global computational infrastructures encompassing platform logics, algorithms, programmed automation, data centres, fibre optic cables and so forth that are often overlapping, unpredictable, and frictious. As a result of these circumstances, digital cultural heritage becomes subject to the forces and relations of economic production and consumption through their enmeshment in what media theorist Benjamin Bratton calls new forms of platform sovereignty, the dominant and distributed technical and social systems that govern and support markets. Platforms enable the remote coordination of information through algorithmic, economic, political, and software programs.[57] Such processes generated through platforms often escape strict market interests and bring non-market relations and values together through the way platforms link actors, events, and information across vast scales, spaces, and time.

One example of the unintended consequences of platform sovereignty, the operation of what Luciana Parisi calls "soft thought," the effects of machines and the quantitative processing of data alongside the interactions between humans and machines that often influence human actions in ways that do not appear in the conscious,[58] was evident with the launch of a new interface to the Museum of Applied Arts and Sciences (MAAS, Powerhouse Museum) collections pioneered by digital media innovator Seb Chan and its induction into Google's automated search platform in 2006. Critically this event enabled the reorganization of human interactions with MAAS collections across multiple platforms and grids as an emergent economic and geopolitical architecture. Here a 1950s "Nu-U" bra became one of the most viewed objects in the MAAS collection in late 2008 as the result of the launch of a new UBra by Fantasy Lingerie in stores and consumers seeking to purchase the item online.[59]

Digital data as heritage is no longer reducible to the logic of symbolic texts, social memory, people, communities, nations, or human–machine entanglements, the social ecologies in which museums conceptualize these interactions. Additionally, digital cultural heritage is not only born out of economic relations embedded in platforms but is also subject to the economic imperatives of the museum, consumer transactions, and broader informational infrastructures. Here museum capitalisms emerge from the procedures of "soft thought," algorithmic processes, and the cognitive unconscious. This event becomes an accident of algorithmic aesthetic affect or the result of an operational error unexpectedly creating a novel type of interaction between algorithmic capitalism and museum culture. The qualities of space-time that emerge from processes of quantification via algorithmic processing alongside data deemed incomputable and the broader machinic processes to which

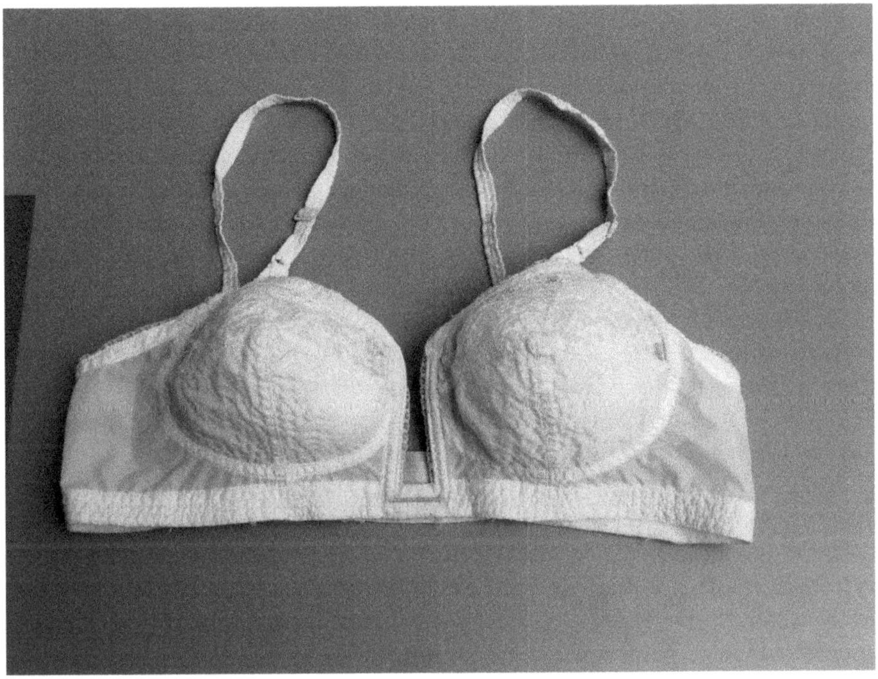

**FIGURE 3.1** Brassiere, women's, "Nu-U", nylon / cotton / metal, Berlei, Australia, 1957, 93/391/66.
Photo credit: Museum of Applied Arts and Sciences, Sydney.

they are subject create a new sense of feeling, orientation, disorientation, and open-endedness as a novel type of coordination between museum culture and algorithmic capitalism.

Digitizations as representative of material collections become economic and consumer products again in global computational infrastructures and are used to extract economic value for institutions. Their commercial disposition and economic agency arise through their distribution in the marketing of an exhibition or an institutional collection; the sharing of images on social media, the development of personal collections through platforms such as Facebook and Pinterest; as images for product production; and as inspiration for making new products often enabled via Creative commons licences.

Inspired by the algorithmic accidents occasioned by the 2006 Google collection experiment at the Museum of Applied Arts and Sciences, algorithmic strategizing through platforms and social media has now become routine for many institutions. Here digitizations of museum collections that were once commodities before their museumification become economic again, but their economic value is now of a different kind directed towards building the museum's economy. Economic and social value is extracted from collections' digitizations through platforms such as Facebook by raising institutional visibility; through brand marketing of the institution as prestigious, holding valuable collection items;[60] by building a digital constituency and potential museum visitation; and by expanding knowledge resources through engagement with their collections.[61] The economic value of collection digitizations on the internet is also made explicit through the collection of online traffic statistics. Pinterest, for example, is a commercial lifestyle platform that aims to share the tastes and interests of its users.[62] Described as a "catalogue of ideas," some of its pins are based on collection themes and others on exhibition content. Users can either upload images from their computer or pin things they find on the web using the Pinterest bookmarklet.

The Metropolitan Museum of Art launched a series of collections digitizations as thematic boards on Pinterest to allow access to their collections. One example is the *Manus x Machina: Fashion in an Age of Technology* exhibition. Through digital marketing, collections digitizations of couture appear alongside commercial items for purchase through buyable pins thereby attracting viewers who share similar interests. In doing so, the Met seeks to capitalize on the platform's desire to create brand awareness, market a wide range of products, and grow an expansive consumer base.

The streaming of home boards also driven by personalization according to user preferences is a process that not only enables the insertion of new digitizations and therefore the formation of new collections but also represents the operation of complex, multilayered, emergent processes directed to economic ends that are ongoing and never completed.

Digital data and potential heritages in data economies such as bond futures constitute socio-technical compositions that are no longer human centred and directed; rather they are made up of a series of coordinates and processes between human bodies, minds, tools, equipment, technical devices, algorithms, phone calls, trading markets, yield quotes, and so forth.

## Notes

1 Bernard Stiegler, *For a New Critique of Political Economy*, trans. Daniel Ross (Cambridge, MA: Polity, 2010), 12.

2 Friedrich Kittler, *Gramophone, Film, Typewriter*, trans. Geoffrey Winthrop-Young and Michael Wutz (Stanford, CA: Stanford University Press, 1999).

3 Stiegler, *For a New Critique of Political Economy*, 37; Bernard Stiegler, "Memory," in *Critical Terms for Media Studies*, eds. William (W.J.T.) Mitchell and Mark Hansen (Chicago: University of Chicago Press, 2010), 64–87.

4 For a discussion of the relations and attitudes that anchor other types of heritage see Rodney Harrison, *Heritage: Critical Approaches* (Abingdon: Routledge, 2013), 64; Kevin Walsh, *The Representation of the Past: Museums and Heritage in the Post-modern World* (Abingdon: Routledge, 1992).

5 For a discussion of the experiences of modernity see Marshall Berman, *All That is Solid Melts into Air: The Experience of Modernity* (London: Verso, 1983), 15.

6 UNESCO, *Safeguarding the Documentary Heritage of Humanity* (Paris: UNESCO, 2010), http://unesdoc.unesco.org/images/0018/001877/187733e.pdf, 2.

7 See Joanna Zylinska, *Nonhuman Photography* (Cambridge, MA: The MIT Press, 2017), 10, for a discussion of photographic technology and its rapid development in which earlier forms are viewed as akin to biological death or extinction.

8 Bernard Stiegler, "The Anthropocene and Neganthropology," Lecture, Canterbury, November 2014, https://www.academia.edu/12693668/Bernard_Stiegler_The_Anthropocene_and_Neganthropology_2014_,11.
9 For a discussion on how modernity, time, and risk are framed in material heritage definitions see Harrison, *Heritage*, 6.
10 Joint Programming Initiative on Cultural Heritage and Global Change, *Strategic Research Agenda*, http://jpi-ch.eu/wp-content/uploads/Strategic-Research-Agenda.pdf, 2.
11 Harrison, *Heritage*, 25. See Bruno Latour, *We Have Never Been Modern*, trans. Catherine Porter (Hertfordshire: Harvester Wheatsheaf, 1993) for a discussion of modernity and heritage practices.
12 Smithsonian Institution Archives, *Preservation Strategies for Born Digital Materials*, https://siarchives.si.edu/what-we-do/digital-curation/preservation-strategies-born-digital-materials.
13 UNESCO, "Charter on the Preservation of Digital Heritage," 12, http://portal.unesco.org/en/ev.php-URL_ID=17721&URL_DO=DO_TOPIC&URL_SECTION=201.html.
14 Rodney Harrison, "Surface Assemblages: Towards an Archaeology *in* and *of* the Present," *Archaeological Dialogues* 18, no. 2 (2011): 141–196.
15 UNESCO, "Charter on the Preservation of Digital Heritage;" also cited in Harrison, *Heritage*, 200.
16 Claire Colebrook, "Extinction," in *Posthuman Glossary*, eds. Rosi Braidotti and Maria Hlavajova (London: Bloomsbury Academic, 2018), 150–153.
17 Internet Archive, "Wayback Machine," https://archive.org/web/.
18 Internet Archive, "Wayback Machine."
19 British Library Web Archiving, http://www.bl.uk/aboutus/stratpolprog/digi/webarch/.
20 British Library Web Archiving.
21 Matthew Westwood, "The Digital Museum is Now Preserving our Online Culture," *The Australian*, Feb 7, 2017, http://www.theaustralian.com.au/arts/visual-arts/the-digital-museum-of-now-is-preserving-our-online-culture/news-story/b82cdff975d75391d11a84e63880e210.
22 Westwood, "The Digital Museum is Now Preserving our Online Culture."
23 Westwood, "The Digital Museum is Now Preserving our Online Culture."
24 Helbing et al., "Will Democracy Survive Big Data and Artificial Intelligence?" *Scientific American*, Feb 25, 2017, 2, https://www.scientificamerican.com/article/will-democracy-survive-big-data-and-artificial-intelligence/.
25 Veritas, "The Databerg Report: See What Others Don't: Identify the Value, Risk and Cost of Your Data", 2015, http://images.info.veritas.com/Web/Veritas/%7B364a7ca5-e05c-4fce-971b-88e18c62eafb%7D_45145_EMEA_Veritas_Strike_Report_Gulf.pdf.
26 Veritas, "The Databerg Report".
27 Xinming Li et al., "Coordinating Data Pricing in Closed-Loop Data Supply Chain with Data Value Uncertainty," *SSRN*, Feb 20, 2018, https://papers.ssrn.com/sol3/papers.cfm?abstract_id=3120590.
28 Li et al., "Coordinating Data Pricing in Closed-Loop Data Supply Chain with Data Value Uncertainty."
29 Wendy Chun, *Updating to Remain the Same: Habitual New Media* (Cambridge, MA: The MIT Press, 2016).
30 Erwin Laure and Dejan Vitlacil, "Data Storage and Management for Global Research Data Infrastructures – Status and Perspectives." *Data Science Journal* 12 (2013): GRDI37–GRDI42, https://datascience.codata.org/articles/abstract/10.2481/dsj.GRDI-007/.
31 Laure and Vitlacil, "Data Storage and Management for Global Research Data Infrastructures."
32 For a discussion of phones as personal memory devices see Anna Reading, "Memobilia: The Mobile Phone and the Emergence of Wearable Memories," in *Save as… Digital Memories*, eds. Joanne Garde-Hansen, Andrew Hoskins and Anna Reading (London: Palgrave Macmillian, 2009), 90.
33 Reading, "Memobilia," 90.
34 Adam Stacey, "Images of 7 July: Tunnel Horror," *BBC World News*, July 2, 2006, http://news.bbc.co.uk/2/hi/uk_news/5102860.stm.

35 Reading, "Memobilia," 90.
36 Allessandro Kauffmann, video of the White Island eruption on December 10, 2019, https://www.nzherald.co.nz/nz/news/article.cfm?c_id=1&objectid=12293107.
37 Library of Congress, "*Digital Preservation, Personal Archiving*," http://digitalpreservation.gov/personalarchiving/.
38 See Daniela Petrelli, "Family Memories in the Home: Contrasting Physical and Digital Mementos," *Personal and Ubiquitous Computing* 14, no. 2 (February 2010): 2, http://shura.shu.ac.uk/2907/1/PUC-journal-digitalVSphysical.pdf, for a discussion of the ethnographical fieldwork conducted in private homes on physical and digital mementos.
39 Francesco Vitale, Izabelle Janzen and Joanna McGrenere, "Hoarding and Minimalism: Tendencies in Digital Data Preservation." *Proceedings of the 2018 CHI Conference on Human Factors in Computing Systems*, Montreal, Canada, April 21st – 25th, 2018, 2, https://dl.acm.org/citation.cfm?id=3174161&dl=ACM&coll=DL.
40 Petrelli, "Family Memories in the Home," 3; also see Corina Sas and Steve Whittaker, "Design for Forgetting: Disposing of Digital Possessions After a Breakup," *Proceedings of the SIGCHI Conference on Human Factors in Computing Systems*, April 27th – May 2nd, 2013, 1823–1832.
41 Jason Patrick Kalin, "Reanimating Memory: The Prospects of Memory in a Digital Age," Dissertation, NC State University Libraries, 1, https://repository.lib.ncsu.edu/handle/1840.16/7860.
42 Yuk Hui, *On the Existence of Digital Objects* (Minneapolis: University of Minnesota Press, 2016), 148.
43 Daniela Petrelli, "There is More in Personal Heritage than Data," *Interactions* 20, no. 3 (May 2013): 2.
44 Petrelli, "Family Memories in the Home," 4; Steve Whittaker, Vaiva Kalnikate, Daniela Petrelli, Abigail Sellen, Nicolas Villar, Ofer Bergman, Paul Clough and Jens Brockmeier, "Socio-Technical Lifelogging: Deriving Design Principles for a Future Proof Digital Past," *Human-Computer Interaction* 27, no. 1–2 (2012): 46.
45 Vitale et al., "Hoarding and Minimalism," 2.
46 Petrelli, "There is More in Personal Heritage than Data," 2.
47 Whittaker et al., "Socio-Technical Lifelogging.".
48 Jasmin Ibrahim, "The Technological Gaze: Event Construction and the Mobile Body," *M/C Journal* 10, no. 1 (March 2007), http://journal.media-culture.org.au/0703/03-ibrahim.php, talks about the potential for social media to promote different types of narratives and histories outside officiating institutions more than 10 years ago when such platforms were cast as democratic, utopic spaces.
49 Sam Frizell, "Here's What Facebook Can Do With Your Personal Data in the Name of Science," *TIME*, July 7, 2014, http://time.com/2949565/heres-what-facebook-can-do-with-your-personal-data-in-the-name-of-science/; Wikibooks, "Corporate Social Media and Free Labour", in *Living in a Connected World/Digital Labour on Social Media Platforms*, Chapter 3.1, https://en.wikibooks.org/wiki/Living_in_a_Connected_World/Digital_Labour_on_Social_Media_Platforms.
50 Audrey Samson and Mirko Tobias Schäfer, "Static Glow," in *Posthuman Glossary*, eds. Rosi Braidotti and Maria Hlavajova (London: Bloomsbury Academic, 2018), 407–411.
51 Tiffany Black, "What Happens to Your Facebook Profile When You Die?" accessed March 1, 2017, http://facebook.about.com/od/Profiles/ss/What-Happens-To-Your-Facebook-Profile-When-You-Die.htm.
52 Mia Ayliffe-Chung, "About Mia Ayliffe-Chung," Facebook profile, accessed March 1, 2017, https://www.facebook.com/MiMiChung7/videos/vb.560643167/10154370825748168/?type=2&theater.
53 Samantha Healy, "Accused Home Hill Murderer May Never Face Trial," *Townsville Bulletin*, Oct 29, 2016, http://www.townsvillebulletin.com.au/news/crime-court/accused-home-hill-murderer-may-never-face-trial/news-story/11fd4c7865dfbb0cccdba13394f8ed22.

54 European Commission, "Digital Agenda: 'Comité des Sages' Calls For a 'New Renaissance' By Bringing Europe's Cultural Heritage Online," Press release, Brussels, January 10, 2011, http://europa.eu/rapid/press-release_IP-11-17_en.htm.
55 European Commission, "Digital Agenda."
56 Michael Brünig, "Historic Collections Could Be Lost to 'Digital Dinosaurs'," *The Conversation*, Sept 16, 2014, http://theconversation.com/historic-collections-could-be-lost-to-digital-dinosaurs-31524.
57 For a discussion of the entanglement of computational sovereignty with multifarious economic, political software and algorithmic programs see Benjamin Bratton, *The Stack: On Software and Sovereignty* (Cambridge, MA: The MIT Press, 2015), xviii, 4.
58 For a discussion of non-cognitive unconscious machinic interactions see N. Katherine Hayles, *Unthought: The Power of the Cognitive Nonconscious* (Chicago: University of Chicago Press, 2017).
59 Fiona Cameron, "Object-Orientated Democracies: Conceptualising Museum Collections in Networks," *Museum Management and Curatorship* 23, no. 3 (2008): 230–231.
60 Rachel Gonzalez, "Keep the Conversation Going: How Museums Use Social Media to Engage the Public," *The Museum Scholar* 1, no. 1, 2017, https://themuseumscholar.atavist.com/vol1no1gonzalez.
61 Marco Santana, "Old is New: Social Media Helps Museums Grow Audience in Modern Age," *Orlando Sentinel*, May 7, 2018, http://www.orlandosentinel.com/business/technology/os-social-media-history-center-20151120-story.html.
62 Andy Meng, "What is Pinterest, and How Does It Work?" Infront Webworks, January 20, 2014, https://www.infront.com/blog/the-infront-blog/what-is-pinterest-and-how-does-it-work.

## Bibliography

Ayliffe-Chung, Mia. "About Mia Ayliffe-Chung." Facebook profile, accessed March 1, 2017. https://www.facebook.com/MiMiChung7/videos/vb.560643167/10154370825748168/?type=2&theater.

Berman, Marshall. *All That is Solid Melts into Air: The Experience of Modernity*. London: Verso, 1983.

Black, Tiffany. "What Happens to Your Facebook Profile When You Die?" Accessed March 1, 2017. http://facebook.about.com/od/Profiles/ss/What-Happens-To-Your-Facebook-Profile-When-You-Die.htm.

Bratton, Benjamin. *The Stack: On Software and Sovereignty*. Cambridge, MA.: The MIT Press, 2015.

British Library Web Archiving. http://www.bl.uk/aboutus/stratpolprog/digi/webarch/.

Brünig, Michael. "Historic Collections Could Be Lost to 'Digital Dinosaurs'." *The Conversation*, Sept 16, 2014. http://theconversation.com/historic-collections-could-be-lost-to-digital-dinosaurs-31524.

Cameron, Fiona. "Object-Orientated Democracies: Conceptualising Museum Collections in Networks." *Museum Management and Curatorship* 23, no. 3 (2008): 230–231.

Chun, Wendy. *Updating to Remain the Same: Habitual New Media*. Cambridge, MA.: The MIT Press, 2016.

Colebrook, Claire. "Extinction." In *Posthuman Glossary*, edited by Rosi Braidotti and Maria Hlavajova, 150–153. London: Bloomsbury Academic, 2018.

European Commission. "Digital Agenda: 'Comité des Sages' Calls For a 'New Renaissance' By Bringing Europe's Cultural Heritage Online." Press release, Brussels, January 10, 2011. http://europa.eu/rapid/press-release_IP-11-17_en.htm.

Frizell, Sam. "Here's What Facebook Can Do With Your Personal Data in the Name of Science." *TIME*, July 7, 2014. http://time.com/2949565/heres-what-facebook-can-do-with-your-personal-data-in-the-name-of-science/.

Gonzalez, Rachel. "Keep the Conversation Going: How Museums Use Social Media to Engage the Public." *The Museum Scholar* 1, no. 1, 2017. https://themuseumscholar.atavist.com/vol1no1gonzalez.

Harrison, Rodney. "Surface Assemblages: Towards an Archaeology *in* and *of* the Present." *Archaeological Dialogues* 18, no. 2 (2011): 141–196.

Harrison, Rodney. *Heritage: Critical Approaches*. Abingdon: Routledge, 2013.

Hayles, N. Katherine. *Unthought: The Power of the Cognitive Nonconscious*. Chicago: University of Chicago Press, 2017.

Healy, Samantha. "Accused Home Hill Murderer May Never Face Trial." *Townsville Bulletin*, Oct 29, 2016. http://www.townsvillebulletin.com.au/news/crime-court/accused-home-hill-murderer-may-never-face-trial/news-story/11fd4c7865dfbb0cccdba13394f8ed22.

Helbing, Dirk, Bruno S. Frey, Gerd Gigerenzer, Ernst Hafen, Michael Hagner, Yvonne Hofstetter, Jeroen van den Hoven, Roberto V. Zicari and Andrej Zwitter. "Will Democracy Survive Big Data and Artificial Intelligence?" *Scientific American*, Feb 25, 2017. https://www.scientificamerican.com/article/will-democracy-survive-big-data-and-artificial-intelligence/.

Hui, Yuk. *On the Existence of Digital Objects*. Minneapolis: University of Minnesota Press, 2016.

Ibrahim, Jasmin. "The Technological Gaze: Event Construction and the Mobile Body." *M/C Journal* 10, no. 1 (March 2007). http://journal.media-culture.org.au/0703/03-ibrahim.php.

Internet Archive. "Wayback Machine." https://archive.org/web/.

Joint Programming Initiative on Cultural Heritage and Global Change. *Strategic Research Agenda*. http://jpi-ch.eu/wp-content/uploads/Strategic-Research-Agenda.pdf.

JustGiving. Accessed June 6, 2017. https://www.justgiving.com/crowdfunding/MiaAyliffe-Chung?utm_term=NEM3mXGmY.

Kalin, Jason Patrick. "Reanimating Memory: The Prospects of Memory in a Digital Age." Dissertation, NC State University Libraries, 1. https://repository.lib.ncsu.edu/handle/1840.16/7860.

Kauffmann, Allessandro. Video of the White Island eruption on December 10, 2019. https://www.nzherald.co.nz/nz/news/article.cfm?c_id=1&objectid=12293107.

Kittler, Friedrich. *Gramophone, Film, Typewriter*. Translated by Geoffrey Winthrop-Young and Michael Wutz. Stanford, CA: Stanford University Press, 1999.

Latour, Bruno. *We Have Never Been Modern*. Translated by Catherine Porter. Hertfordshire: Harvester Wheatsheaf, 1993.

Laure, Erwin and Dejan Vitlacil. "Data Storage and Management for Global Research Data Infrastructures – Status and Perspectives." *Data Science Journal* 12 (2013): GRDI37–GRDI42. https://datascience.codata.org/articles/abstract/10.2481/dsj.GRDI-007/.

Li, Xinming, Huaqing Wang, Xiuwu Liao and Lei Wen. "Coordinating Data Pricing in Closed-Loop Data Supply Chain with Data Value Uncertainty." *SSRN*, Feb 20, 2018. https://papers.ssrn.com/sol3/papers.cfm?abstract_id=3120590.

Library of Congress. "Digital Preservation, Personal Archiving." http://digitalpreservation.gov/personalarchiving/.

Meng, Andy. "What is Pinterest, and How Does It Work?" *Infront Webworks*, January 20, 2014. https://www.infront.com/blog/the-infront-blog/what-is-pinterest-and-how-does-it-work.

Petrelli, Daniela. "Family Memories in the Home: Contrasting Physical and Digital Mementos." *Personal and Ubiquitous Computing* 14, no. 2 (February 2010): 153–169. http://shura.shu.ac.uk/2907/1/PUC-journal-digitalVSphysical.pdf.

Petrelli, Daniela. "There is More in Personal Heritage than Data." *Interactions* 20, no. 3 (May 2013): 16–19.

Reading, Anna. "Memobilia: The Mobile Phone and the Emergence of Wearable Memories." In *Save as… Digital Memories*, edited by Joanne Garde-Hansen, Andrew Hoskins and Anna Reading, 81–95. London: Palgrave Macmillian, 2009.

Samson, Audrey and Mirko Tobias Schäfer. "Static Glow." In *Posthuman Glossary*, edited by Rosi Braidotti and Maria Hlavajova, 407–411. London: Bloomsbury Academic, 2018.

Santana, Marco. "Old is New: Social Media Helps Museums Grow Audience in Modern Age." *Orlando Sentinel*, May 7, 2018. http://www.orlandosentinel.com/business/technology/os-social-media-history-center-20151120-story.html.

Sas, Corina and Steve Whittaker. "*Design for Forgetting: Disposing of Digital Possessions After a Breakup.*" Proceedings of the SIGCHI Conference on Human Factors in Computing Systems, April 27th – May 2nd, 2013, 1823–1832.

Smithsonian Institution Archives. "Preservation Strategies for Born Digital Materials". https://siarchives.si.edu/what-we-do/digital-curation/preservation-strategies-born-digital-materials.

Stacey, Adam. "Images of 7 July: Tunnel Horror." *BBC World News*, July 2, 2006. http://news.bbc.co.uk/2/hi/uk_news/5102860.stm.

Stiegler, Bernard. "Memory." In *Critical Terms for Media Studies*, edited by William (W.J.T.) Mitchell and Mark Hansen, 64–87. Chicago: University of Chicago Press, 2010.

Stiegler, Bernard. "*The Anthropocene and Neganthropology.*" Lecture, Canterbury, November 2014. https://www.academia.edu/12693668/Bernard_Stiegler_The_Anthropocene_and_Neganthropology_2014_,11.

Stiegler, Bernard. *For a New Critique of Political Economy*. Translated by Daniel Ross. Cambridge, MA: Polity, 2010.

UNESCO. "Charter on the Preservation of Digital Heritage." http://portal.unesco.org/en/ev.php-URL_ID=17721&URL_DO=DO_TOPIC&URL_SECTION=201.html.

UNESCO. *Safeguarding the Documentary Heritage of Humanity*. Paris: UNESCO, 2010. http://unesdoc.unesco.org/images/0018/001877/187733e.pdf.

Veritas. "The Databerg Report: See What Others Don't: Identify the Value, Risk and Cost of Your Data". 2015. http://images.info.veritas.com/Web/Veritas/%7B364a7ca5-e05c-4fce-971b-88e18c62eafb%7D_45145_EMEA_Veritas_Strike_Report_Gulf.pdf.

Vitale, Francesco, Izabelle Janzen and Joanna McGrenere. "Hoarding and Minimalism: Tendencies in Digital Data Preservation." Proceedings of the 2018 CHI Conference on Human Factors in Computing Systems. Montreal, Canada, April 21st – 25th, 2018. https://dl.acm.org/citation.cfm?id=3174161&dl=ACM&coll=DL.

Walsh, Kevin. *The Representation of the Past: Museums and Heritage in the Post-modern World*. Abingdon: Routledge, 1992.

Westwood, Matthew. "The Digital Museum is Now Preserving our Online Culture." *The Australian*, Feb 7, 2017. http://www.theaustralian.com.au/arts/visual-arts/the-digital-museum-of-now-is-preserving-our-online-culture/news-story/b82cdff975d75391d11a84e63880e210.

Whittaker, Steve, Vaiva Kalnikate, Daniela Petrelli, Abigail Sellen, Nicolas Villar, Ofer Bergman, Paul Clough and Jens Brockmeier. "Socio-Technical Lifelogging: Deriving Design Principles for a Future Proof Digital Past." *Human-Computer Interaction* 27, no. 1–2 (2012): 37–62.

*Wikibooks*. "Corporate Social Media and Free Labour," in *Living in a Connected World/Digital Labour on Social Media Platforms*, Chapter 3.1. https://en.wikibooks.org/wiki/Living_in_a_Connected_World/Digital_Labour_on_Social_Media_Platforms.

Zylinska, Joanna. *Nonhuman Photography*. Cambridge, MA: The MIT Press, 2017.

# 4

# OBJECT CONCEPTS IN DIGITAL CULTURAL HERITAGE

The object form is a pervasive cognitive schema within western culture. Viewing the world as an aggregate series of objects is a way of conceptually structuring life into discrete quantifiable units that in turn can be used to mobilize thought and action in specific ways. How a digital object is thought about in any given context also depends on the dispositions and forms of capital accumulation that it is intended to uphold. In this chapter I examine and critique how digital data is thought of as an object form in heritage practice.

Within an object-directed conceptual space, digital "objects" have occasioned diverse theoretical and technological ways of viewing them in new media, software studies, art, and heritage contexts, each with their own histories and lineages. Accordingly, and across domains of practice, digital data and the systems that read them together are viewed as discrete objects within a representational and technical register, whether that be art, variable media, or heritage objects.

The notion of digital data as having an objecthood is a central feature of heritage practice. Making digital objects is therefore an act of heritage production. Early digital cultural heritage prior to the development of the internet was conceptualized as cultural information represented by binary codes or numbers and made into objects by imprinting them onto material substrates such as punch cards or magnetic tape, or stored on material carriers such as floppy disks, CDs and DVDs. Rudimentary digital heritage on the internet consisted mainly of textual elements such as online publishing, email lists, blogs, and wikis that were conceptualized as discrete object schemas. Now digital data on multiple internets and platforms comprises an infinite variety of code, structures, systems, and custom software. With the advent of Web 2.0, big data (large, complex volumes of data based on personal information gathered from searches, consumers' purchasing behaviour, social interactions, and mobility activities)[1] is emerging as the next generation of potential heritage. Rapid changes in software and operating systems alongside the development of new applications such as web browsers, digital devices, visualization techniques, and automations further contribute to the ever-multiplying variety of data that has the potential to become worthy of heritagization. But they don't look or behave like conventional objects because data is in a constant state of flux, reorganizing, copying or mutating into new forms. Similar to the field of digital art,[2] these rapidly changing variables and processes challenge institutional attempts to categorize and describe digital cultural heritage and its constituent elements in a systematic object-centric way and within strict registers of standardization. In this chapter I analyse the different ways that in the heritage sector, and to an extent in the aligned field of digital art, digital cultural heritage is thought about as objects in digital preservation and in the social engagement with them on the internet.

## Objecthood in digital cultural heritage thought and practice

Object thinking drives current heritage practice and is the foundational cognitive schema informing UNESCO's policy and work in digital heritage preservation, curation, management, and social engagement. Collecting, making, and preserving digital objects are founded on a material museological culture. Digital objects are assessed as valuable and worth passing on because they are viewed as authentic, original, rare, and fragile. The idea that digital resources are subject to loss or indeed death also contributes to their re-inscription as a digital cultural heritage object worthy of preservation. Planned obsolescence becomes the overriding narrative of death and, alongside the making of objects out of data, constitutes the birth of digital data as heritage objects.

Object-centred thinking in museums is routinely founded on materials conservation. The UNESCO Charter on the Preservation of Digital Heritage (2003) encouraged cultural institutions to stabilize and fix digital forms of information and cultural expression in space and time within the archive to ensure their preservation. Under this regime, original objects must be materially conserved if they are to become heritage objects. Their structure must be treated and stabilized so they remain in an unchanging state.

In the early years making a digital object from digital data was often routinely performed through fixing code. Its materiality and technical elements were stabilized through technical means and transformed into a bounded visual object and stored on CDs, DVDs or by making PDFs. Its objecthood was thereby assured to allow it to play its assigned informational and representational role. Abdelaziz Abid from the UNESCO Information Society division supported this object-centred view when he explained that digital cultural heritage emerges as different types of objects depending on their technical platforms:

> We could still preserve new carriers such as CDs and CD-ROMs as physical objects and hope that these would remain stable and readable...now with the Internet, the time is close when we will no longer go out from the virtual spaces in order to be able to use content that we access digitally.[3]

Digital heritagization was founded on normative notions of technical preservation, that is, a digital file will degrade or be rendered unreadable in time and therefore must be copied or stored alongside its original technology. While digital objects are viewed as containing properties and methods as organized sequences of tasks operating together as a succession of routines and subroutines, all of their elements and behaviours are still viewed collectively in digital cultural heritage schemas as objects. In order to preserve digital data as forms of human knowledge and expression and to circumvent their variability, they must not only become materially stabilized but also be kept observable in perpetuity to enable human understanding and engagement.

Making objects by fixing, stabilizing fragile materials such as code, and gathering together an object's constituent technical parts are all acts of heritage production. Here digital agency is contained and the archive is transformed into a repository of obedient objects. There were others who questioned this predilection towards data as possessing an objecthood within the UNESCO arena. Back in 2005, John Mackenzie Owen argued "it is not the materials as such that one would like to preserve, but their uses: processes, not artifacts."[4] While Owen refutes the idea of a pre-existing objecthood or indeed a material essence, he instead explains the essence of digital data as one of communication and communicative processes.

Object-centric frameworks are now routinely imposed on digital data and mobilized according to four standard and categorical forms. UNESCO describes digital cultural heritage objects as physical phenomena, as encoded data, as conceptual objects that have meaning to humans, and as sets of essential technical elements that must be preserved in order to enable future users to gain an understanding of the essence of the object.[5] Digital data therefore becomes subject to analogical interpretation, that is the idea of physical and embodied essences, as conceptual objects to direct human thought and action, and as technical objects conceived according to their specific elements and regimes of operation and function.

Heritagization and object-making therefore operate as a set of standardizing values and procedures that seek to circumvent the death of digital data. These standardized categories not only refer to four distinct object types but also to their form, state of formation, and their status as a mix of abstract and concrete objects. Here objects are viewed as constituted object forms and as physical phenomena such as bits and encoded data. Objects are also conceived as constituting forms in their emergence through the assembling of their technical elements and their operational chains and sequences so they can become human-information-bearing entities. The latter approach is reminiscent of Gilbert Simondon's thesis on technical mentality and the idea of the object becoming concrete.[6]

Digital data is ordinarily perceived as socio-technical objects in computer and software studies.[7] This turn towards "objects" in computer programming emerges out of computer science and software engineering and the desire to explain the digital-material basis on which contemporary social relations are based.[8] In computing, programs are conceptualized as a series of interactions between groups of data and the methods executed on them that are then abstracted as programmatically delineated objects.[9] Digital video, an image or an interactive experience, is conceptualized as comprising bits of multiple files that are rendered, executed, performed and presented via computational and visualization programs.[10] As technical objects they emerge as the result of computational operations cohering and appearing according to media theorist Matthew Fuller as "points of contingent stability" for representing the socio-technical aspects of digitally mediated life.[11] They are regularly perceived and experienced as one coherent thing. While digital objects are seen as having technical properties such as code and hardware, they are at the same time used for representational purposes. Accordingly, as media scholar Deborah Lupton explains, they are put to work to, variously, structure knowledge, know and understand a subject, frame our concepts of identity, act as sites from which social negotiations are made, structure our relationships and our behaviour, including our choices and preferences,[12] and advance narratives of our social worlds.

As the heritage sector directs its attention to the collection of digital data and transforms it into born-digital heritage objects, insights into how digital cultural heritage is currently conceived as "objects" can be gleaned from emerging practices of digital preservation, curation, and interpretive practices. In seeking to answer technical questions on how best to conserve digital data in heritage contexts and standardize preservation architectures, we gain insights into how the "object" form, its essence and authentic character, is imagined in practice.

## Digital cultural objects as interfacial presence

In heritage interpretive work, the making of digital data into heritage "objects" is a process born out of the synthesis between code and computer and made intelligible as a visual and/or social object at the very moment it becomes perceptible (visually or sensorily) to humans. These "conceptual objects" are experienced not as a process but as a cohesive, bounded thing or experience on or through the interface. The visibility of bitstreams, file formats and platform interactions as interfacial images on or through the interface at the very moment they appear or their experiential qualities emerge, renders digital data available to human interpretation. These digital objects become subject to human explanation and description. They accrue social power as forms of human knowledge and expression, and may trigger affectual responses. They become a subject with cultural, social, linguistic, experiential, and/or sensory significance. Through this mechanism of intelligibility, the availability of data as digital cultural heritage is premised on the computer-mediated technology and software that render it presentable and readable to humans.

In the art field, the essence of the digital object in the early years was its visual rendering into an interfacial presence. In the mid-2000s, the digital art work itself was viewed as a simple image in process generated by a series of binary signals recorded by a computer that then rendered code in a digital file as a machine-readable and human-readable work.[13] Here the visual, the aesthetic, the experiential, and the sensory value of a digital work made available through its human-machine readability was privileged above any of its other aspects. Categorically, a digital art work's single underlying binary code is what makes a digital object fundamentally different from any other physical object, in that it lacks the characteristics of a conventional, static physical form typical of paintings and books.[14]

Technically speaking, the digital art work is viewed as stored information that only takes on a physical form when we interact with the information the digital object contains.[15] It is seen as an object when its data is active, even if that activity is only momentary. As more complex art works emerge, digital art media theorist Lev Manovich explains, it is viewed as one or more interfaces to a database of multimedia content, emerging through the ordering of different technical elements and the actions of individuals as producers and users that interact with and experience it.[16]

Typically, a digital object's objecthood, particularly in the case of digital art and some types of digital cultural heritage, privileges visual and sensory experiences derived from what appears on the screen as mediated through graphical interfaces. Accordingly, there has been a tendency with digital cultural heritage to assume that what something looks like on a computer screen as its visualization symbolizes all that is significant about it in representational terms. This overriding tendency is called screen essentialism, that is, a disposition privileging the interface and the interfacial image.

The conceptualization of digital cultural heritage as human readable and bound to the interface foregrounds visual experiences first and foremost, alongside navigational methods that allow users to interact in 3D space. But they are never truly objects in a conventional sense. Their distinctiveness as a substantive form or object is diminished due to their binary elements, their processual and malleable nature. Interfaces are never stable. They are constantly changing due to computational processes, forms of interaction and communication.

The heritage industry is also screen essentialist because interpretive practices privilege the interface as an object rather than paying adequate attention to other aspects of the born-digital that are equally important but not visible on a screen. This has to do with the material focus of museums and much of the heritage industry but also relates to the fact that we more readily respond to visual imagery.

These representational techniques of simplification based on screen essentialism diminish their complexity and their extensive and relational qualities. This also explains why preservation in the past was directed to preserving software and hardware to make the object visible. Early preservation practices routinely deployed snapshots or sought to lock down code in order to record what digital cultural heritage looked like rather than attending to the complex platform structures and processes that are hidden from view.

The question of digital cultural heritage as having an inherent, substantial and physical form is a deeply held philosophical question concerning the essence of heritage. These ideas underlie our belief in encoded data as able to possess object-like qualities. This process of knowing and engaging with digital cultural heritage within a museum environment already supposes that it is an object and therefore an object of and for knowledge. Furthermore, by framing born-digital cultural heritage as graspable interfacial images on the interface we can then imbue them with representational qualities.

The digital medium, however, is often not primarily visual. While some digital cultural heritage objects may appear as visible things such as digital photographs, others comprise raw data and databases that may be participatory, customizable, re-usable, and re-combinable in various ways. Furthermore, all digital cultural heritage consists of a back end of scripted languages, platforms and an array of automated processes and machine learning that we are not privy to. Databases often operate as an open structure and process reliant on a constant flux of information as a type of a performative ecology that relies on a user for its interaction.[17] Alongside the machinic and indeterminate quantification of its own data through machine processing often not known or visible, the emergence of born-digital objects as dynamic heritage cannot always be taken for granted, or known in terms of content or form in advance.

## Digital cultural heritage objects as immaterial

In recent years, we have witnessed the rise of a global capitalism mediated through digital networks and a shift from industrial manufacturing and the production of industrial goods to the seemingly immaterial production of governmental, financial, and other services such as the experiential sectors.[18] Accordingly, the world has come to appear comprised of intangibles, of software, of information, of relationships, and of digital networks, in contrast to the solid atomic world of physical objects, steel, oil, and hard labour.[19]

Images and emails were viewed as a new type of language and writing system comprising information patterns that appeared as a result of the assembling and manipulation of numerical computations and then immediately disappeared.[20] Immateriality, lightness, and speed are therefore seen as the defining characteristics of the digital as opposed to the material, heavy, and slow analogue world. These changes were likened to a paradigm shift from a culture founded on material production to one founded on software.

As a result, the immaterial became a convention to describe not only the differences between old and new media but also in heritage culture to differentiate distinct object "materialities," as material and immaterial collections. Defining characteristics included for example binary descriptors such as soft and hard, (according to weight) as either light or heavy, (in respect to their state) as either presence or absence, and (regarding behaviour) as changing or static. In this scheme of things, digital cultural heritage became soft, immaterial, pliable and non-physical objects.

The categorization of digital data as software objects gained momentum in the 1990s to describe art works according to their coded software components, as comprising an informational, instrumental language, and instructions for executing their retrieval.[21] The so-called immaterial aspects of a digital object were emphasized over its physical or technological properties.[22] Furthermore the categorization of digital objects as immaterial was due to the observed behaviour of data as pliable, extensible, and re-combinable and their bit strings as disembodied, immaterial, ungraspable, and probabilistic properties of information.[23] Because code, computational instructions, and the complex and messy infrastructures that underlie these processes are not readily visible to the viewer, digital art works and indeed digital cultural heritage objects are often naturalized as immaterial. Immaterial objects have also been described as energetic states, as electromagnetic waves, suspended in air, as particles, and as placeless things[24] because they travel across electricity grids, cables, accessed through invisible wifi grids.[25] Here the material elements of digital objects are dematerialized, rendered less important or indeed irrelevant. Accordingly, software, digitized data, immaterial bitstrings and electrical circuits replaced the traditional description of art works in terms of their physical substance and their dimensions.[26] The same argument can be applied to digital cultural heritage objects.

Virtual objects are a sub-category of so-called non-physical immaterial objects. The virtual object is most often visually or aesthetically oriented and is sometimes presented as a copy of a "real" object or as a digital object that looks like a physical object. While the latter may look like a physical object, it is not treated as "real" because it is not seen to exist in the world of matter and therefore lacks the physical presence of an analogue object.

Classic virtual objects include the 3D renderings of Michelangelo's David, David Livingstone's gun, George Washington's death mask and, most dramatically, the monumental projections of Gustaf Klimt's paintings as an immersive embodied experience at the Atelier des Lumières, Paris' first digital art museum. As a result digital art works are often categorized as time-based media or process-oriented virtual objects.[27]

The immaterial and virtual object is characterized by states of visibility and invisibility according to what takes shape on a screen. The virtual object appears to users as vibrant, lively and visible, while the back end of a computer program composed of data, and metadata regulated by schemas,[28] is rendered invisible. A 3D or virtual object does not occupy physical space because it does not have specific spatial coordinates like those experienced with analogue objects.[29] As a consequence, it is impossible to grasp the spatiality of a digital object through a record of its dimensions. The digital cultural heritage object in its visible and invisible thresholds of materiality does not accrue a physical presence or occupy space in a museological sense of meaning. Having said this, these objects are still perceived as material instantiations of heritage forms of reference, representation, and memory recall, and at the same time they speak to conventional notions of objecthood due to their visual appearance. A lack of a significant matter-form and concrete spatial relations poses a challenge for museum professionals in the documentation of digital cultural heritage where measurement, materials and description are the foundation of heritage practice. The question of categorizing digital cultural heritage as immaterial and/or virtual also emerges because a digital cultural heritage object does not offer the same tactile experience as the physical analogue. As digital theorist Yuk Hui explains, while you can touch a screen on which data is displayed, you can't touch data, nor can we grasp the electrical circuits and impulses that enable it to appear.[30]

Virtual objects appear, for example, as a physical impression. They even appear as solid because we can interact with, drag, delete and modify them on the interface. But underlying all this, the web acts as an interface between users and the infrastructures, programs, processes, and coordinates that allows all these elements to come together so they might appear in the world as things that we can engage with. Accordingly, the supposed placelessness of immaterial digital cultural heritage is a misnomer. Digital cultural heritage objects are grounded in multiple locations: in computers, digital media, geological substrates; in data centres; moving along and across global electrical infrastructures and undersea cables; stored in secure servers and as processes grounded in location-based activities, and so forth.

What appears as its objecthood is a visual representation. It is a visual presence that emerges as the outcome of the compositional dynamics that undergird its complex socio-technical and biophysical composition.

## Digital cultural heritage objects as information

Following the computational turn, digital cultural heritage, both the born-digital and digitizations, are typically thought about and made operable in UNESCO policy[31] as information-bearing objects through museum curatorial, copying and conservation practice, and through collections interfaces. The classification of both knowledge itself and digital cultural heritage as informational and as information-bearing objects operates across two registers. The first is the conception of objects, both material and immaterial, as cultural information within a social constructivist frame. Museum objects are collected for what they stand for. Each object embodies knowledge and cultural information about the person who produced the object and the time, place, event or culture from which it originated. Here narratives of meaning, learning, the management and the sharing of information become a focal point of museum activities. Accordingly, the material aspects of the digital recede into the background.

The informational register is also based separately in the idea of digital cultural heritage as complex computational objects that algorithms correlate, calculate and continuously re-model. Digital objects as encoded data are viewed as informational chunks or bits comprising mathematical representations (1s and 0s) viewed as stored digital and cultural information of a physical quantity rather than actual matter. Emphasis is placed on data, as information and in its capacity to transfer and process information that can then appear as video, audio and textual elements across digital networks.[32] These two informational registers come together through UNESCO's PERSIST digital preservation program. Here digital cultural heritage is seen simultaneously as cultural, information, and technical objects.

The notion of the information-bearing object arises from the application of information philosophy and computational science to museum practice. Information philosophy frames all phenomena, from cellular automata to human brains, as information and operates as a more substantive and universal anchoring of being itself than even energy or matter.[33] This information philosophy mediated through human consciousness emerges as cultural information and, through social worlds, as an information society.[34]

The merging of museum work with information philosophy and computer science emerged in the late 1980s through the musings and practices of museum director George MacDonald (first at the Canadian Museum of Civilization and later at Australia's Museums Victoria). MacDonald argued that museums should become part of the information age, the age of computers, and take on "the cultural language of the contemporary media sphere."[35] In doing so, MacDonald reframed museums as places for the dissemination of information rather than as a central repository for objects.[36] In this view all collections become information-bearing objects. The materiality of collections, both physical and digital, is replaced and reconfigured as information and as things interpenetrated with patterns of information. This inversion of information and the material in collections work situates information as a practice for knowing, mastering and controlling the material and so-called immaterial world.

This supported the idea that collections could be seen as important or valued only for the information they contain in respect to human knowledge and expression, and for the capacity of that information to be communicated through digital media. By reframing all objects, including non-material collections, as informational, MacDonald sought to validate the collecting and use of so-called non-material heritages, e.g. oral history, audio-visual materials and replicas, as important resources that embodied intellectual, aesthetic, sensory, spiritual, or emotional knowledge. Heritage collections and museums thus become entrenched in the turn to computer science. By conceptualizing the museum in this revised role as informational and as "memory banks of heritage," making institutional information resources accessible and encouraging social interaction with those resources would, according to MacDonald, become an institution's main purpose and product.[37] For MacDonald, museums are at the most fundamental level information and at the same time remain in the service of information – its creation, storage and distribution.

Many museum researchers and practitioners after MacDonald – for example, Katherine Burton Jones – talked about the digital revolution and ways to insert museums more purposefully and effectively within the digital age,[38] again drawing on computational discourses and informational thinking. Following MacDonald, scholar Paul Marty has sought since the late 2000s to consolidate this informational approach within the sector, founding the new research field of museum informatics. Like MacDonald before him, Marty views museums as comprising information and information-bearing resources – that is, physical artefacts as well as electronic documents about museum collections.[39]

The poststructuralist and social constructivist grounding of the new museology, its focus on the enhancement of the social roles and purposes of museums, the foregrounding of the politics of representation, and the empowerment of previously colonized societies, cultures, and marginalized groups (including in museum–visitor relations)[40] have provided an affective atmosphere ripe for digital, informational and computational augmentation. ICTs, according to MacDonald, better enable museums to serve society, promoting the production and dissemination of information and social interaction and hence also their educational and communication objectives.[41] Consequently, information and computational augmentation became synonymous with the democratization of museums.

Such a move was also clearly driven by a heightened sense of insecurity – the imperative for museums to remain relevant. These informational and computational discourses were used to showcase museum responsiveness and to demonstrate their social relevancy and benefit in cultural and economic terms.[42] The focus therefore has been on what digital information and media can do in promoting new participatory cultures founded on the production and sharing of information.

The link between information philosophy and the affordances of digital media as shareable and participatory, especially since the emergence of Web 2.0, promotes the principles of the new museology. Accordingly, the melding of digital technologies and new museological concerns was deployed to connect with their visitors, their communities and beyond through the world wide web and to promote new participatory cultures in a context where users were conceptualized merely as information-producing and processing entities. Here museums are seen to operate within a world that is re-imagined as an infosphere in which people spend increasing amounts of time. This paradigm creates its own informational ecology founded on the dynamic behaviour of information, its production and its shareability. Distributed communities are therefore conceptualized as multiple meaning-making or interpretive agents representative of diverse and plural domains of memory, language and organized knowledge. The focus on information as a form of interpretive power within the museum context maps onto an extreme form of social constructivism – the reality of life and the world *as* cultural information, not a reality mediated by it.

Museums frame digital strategies so as to foreground the needs and expectations of the human user to the exclusion of all other agents. In terms of engagement with digital objects, the focus in museums has been and continues to be on the functionalities and affordances that digital cultural heritages embody and gather people together and share information, rather than on a theorization of digital data beyond that as cultural information. The focus in museums therefore is on the multifarious ways technology is used in the context of the work of the institution as an information utility in developing a participatory culture, how ICTs become embedded in webs of interpretation and their cultural meanings, how digitizations support the distribution of collections and knowledge about them, and how they enact social practices of engagement with museum activities. An examination of the papers presented at the Museums and the Web 20th anniversary conference in 2016 suggests that the predominant interest since the 1980s has privileged information production and sharing and how institutions are adapting to and incorporating digital media into their operations and practices.[43] Within the museum information rubric, advances in information science and technology are seen to offer new capacities to help museum professionals meet changing user needs. This includes how digital platforms and dialogic publishing tools such as Instagram, Twitter and Flickr can better engage with and build new communities, how to embed an interactive participatory culture in museums, how institutions can promote the digitization and visualization of collections and the sharing of cultural heritage information through open linked data and web publishing, and how mobile apps can be used for the delivery of collections, exhibitions information, and digital storytelling.

While still seen as interfacial images, informational objects foreground digital communication and relational exchanges rather than a consideration of their distinct material or technical structures. In an informational milieu, the information-bearing object lends itself to its theorization according to a theory of relational exchanges directed to object-centred conversations and the sharing of information. Here digital data as an interfacial image becomes an independent entity and at the same time transactional, that is, a visual prompt to share stories and experiences. Digital media becomes an information transfer system and network for human expression.

The placement of digitizations on social media sites such as Wikipedia, Facebook, and Flickr and their circulation in networks become what museum media scholar Nina Simon calls "engines of socially networked experiences, as the content around which conversation happens."[44] These strategies, commonly used in museums, invoke what Jyri Engeström calls object-centred forms of sociality based around the sharing of information.[45] Here the socially constituted information-bearing object, often a digitization, becomes a new technique to facilitate networking, collecting and managing interpretive data.

## Born-digital cultural heritage objects as bits

More recently, immaterial and informational objects have been viewed as material bits and bitstreams in an effort to preserve digital cultural heritage for the long term. This represents a shift from thinking about code as immaterial to material sets of instructions. UNESCO's promotion of the idea of digital objects as encoded data is a more recent manifestation of the immaterial-object-made-material. The standardization of digital objects as bits and bitstreams is becoming universal as a technical preservation schema. This emerges from a post-digital milieu where bits are embedded in all manner of human forms of knowledge and expression.

Framing bits as significant exemplars of social life and as heritage aims to create a knowable past, and therefore a safe, comforting and stable future. Because bits and bitstreams as a series of instructions of 0s and 1s are encoded as bands on a media substrate, they are seen to represent the physical dimensions of a digital object and embody human forms of knowledge and expression written into its properties and affordances. The collection and preservation of bitstreams therefore seeks to capture a born-digital object's material essence and at the same time revive the relay schemas that allow any given object to be made operational again. Bits are the raw materials that encapsulate the informational qualities of objects, transmit their meaning and essence, and allow museum preservationists to remake original objects and restore their thresholds of functioning of behaviour. They are viewed as the fundamental essence of the original object.

Within this distinctly technical mentality framed around bits, we are witnessing a return to the material in respect to digital objects and their objecthood as a digital materiality. Bits must be made as stable, permanent, and indestructible as possible. The UNESCO Charter expects digital cultural heritage to play the same role as conventional material objects. By concretizing digital cultural materials as bits, digital archivists seek to grant them an objecthood in keeping with the corporeal status of other types of material collections.

Because bits are embedded in layered, modular architectures separate from other devices and information architectures, chunks of data can be easily extracted, preserved, and reassembled in other systems. In 2010, digital museum pioneer Seb Chan, then Head of Digital Media at the Cooper-Hewitt Design Museum in New York, developed the first museum application to interface the collections and open-source its bitstream in an effort to preserve its functionality rather than just what it looked like. Here they modified Planetary, an application for iPhone and iPad used to visualize a user's collection of music as celestial bodies.[46] All versions of the Planetary source code were archived in GitHub to highlight what had changed in the source code.[47] In doing this, Chan not only acknowledged the fragility of the digital object but, by preserving the bitstream, ensured that it remained accessible independent of the operating system, file formats and devices in which it could be run and made available for reuse and reinterpretation.[48] Bits may be viewed as information, but within a technical register they are also material.

While bits as the material essence of digital objects are directing digital preservation, the informational object is still put to work in the curatorial, outreach, interpretative, and information management realm. The classification of digital cultural heritage objects by their material identity in digital preservation follows a technical mentality and convention that first emerged in the nineteenth century. Here an object was seen to be equivalent to the specific materials from which it was made, and was accordingly essentialized on the basis of its material composition.[49] This idea is encapsulated in German architect Gottfried Semper's notion of the "truth to materials in the technical arts."[50] Museums are places that code and preserve objects as specific types of materials – biological specimens as DNA, stone and wood as matter, and, by extension, digital "objects" as digital materialities. All these things yield to the same system of cultural symbolic coding according to their respective disciplinary practices.[51] The use of material as an object classificatory mechanism also resonates with the archaeological concept of physical presence and substantial form. Categorizing objects according to materials operates as a practice of material classification by the dominant object-centred formal descriptor, where museum practice can be thought of and classified as a series of diverse and ever multiplying materialities.

## Digital cultural heritage as complex technical schemas and objects

For UNESCO, born-digital cultural heritage objects are technical and at the same time must be original and authentic. They become sets of essential technical objects that must be preserved so that future users can have a sense of the essence of the original. Averting the certain death of digital objects involves extending their life span and preserving their functionality through collecting all of their original technical elements as discrete objects. Together these objects make up the whole original.

In digital cultural heritage work the original and its re-presentation as close as possible to its original form and function are privileged. The UNESCO charter for example stipulates that the preservation of digital cultural heritage objects requires technical equipment – original and compatible hardware and software – to be maintained alongside the original file.[52] The National Library of Australia supports this disposition in its collecting policy where the institution's intent is to ultimately re-present what digital cultural heritage originally looked like and how it functioned for users.[53] This is because, for born-digital cultural heritage objects, the original and authentic as a form of humanist knowledge and expression is embodied in its very fabric, and that of each of its elements. Due to a new focus on the revival of its technical operation, digital cultural heritage is perceived as lost when the item is no longer machine-readable, that is, when the technology or software that makes it presentable in its original form no longer exists or is functional.

The methods developed by the Variable Media Initiative have been a major influence in the emergence of a digital cultural heritage preservation practice and its distinctive technical mentalities and object concepts. Founded in 1999, born out of the Guggenheim's effort to preserve media-based and performative works, VMI is now recognized as a leader in the development of methods for preserving digital art and time-based media.[54] Because digital art, variable time-based media and vintage gaming are works that are installed and reinterpreted in different spaces and places, the integrity of any given work is ensured by maintaining its meaning or essential character according to the original intention of its creator. Preservation therefore is directed to recreating the spirit of the original work according to the intent of the creator to enable its re-use.[55] Here the focus is on the retention of the working function of digital data or its channels of artistic expression. Media art scholar Richard Rinehart explains this approach to new media culture as a strategy aimed "not … to circumvent its variability with outdated notions of fixity but rather embracing the essential nature of the medium … [as] a defense against obsolescence."[56] Preserving all of the original technical elements is thus not vital if a work's meaning or form of artistic expression can be preserved and interpreted through other means. As a result, VMI aims to find a careful balance between acceptable levels of change within art works (conceptual, installation, sculpture) and any given preservation method without losing their essential meaning.

To do all this, the VMI method integrates the analysis of materials that make up the art work independent of its medium or platform and undertakes an appraisal of the work's behaviour (most broadly, interactive, encoded, networked) and its more ephemeral qualities. Strategies for preservation range from approaches involving traditional storage, fixing and forensic technology to migration, emulation, and – more radically – reinterpretation. The option chosen is the one that best promotes the art work's essential meaning. Here, the testing of emulated digital art objects to see if they act as good representations of the original's meaning is integrated into preservation strategies. The *Seeing Double* exhibition at the Guggenheim Museum, New York in 2004 tested audience reactions to emulated media art works that included Grahame Weinbren and Roberta Friedman's video piece *The Erl King* (1982–85), one of the first works of interactive video art. It was presented in its original form side-by-side with its emulated version. The study concurred that emulations have the potential to act as good representations of an original's meaning.[57]

Digital cultural heritage and art practices are underpinned by the same values and concerns. The desire to preserve digital objects so they can be conserved in perpetuity and used in the future is shared by both sectors. Concern in regard to the fragility of technical platforms and the risk this poses to significant digital data is one that is also shared across domains.

A similar technical mentality is also in operation here. It is one based on the idea of a whole functioning technical object. The gathering together of all of the object's elements allows for the recreation of its integrity, whether that be of the original object or the original's artistic sensibility. Aligned to this is the standardization of thresholds of functioning at acceptable levels of variation, from either the original object or its original meaning, by the choice of preservation methods and the restoration of its technical elements. But for digital cultural heritage objects, these versions must be a technical, material and operative equivalent.

Authenticity in digital art preservation practice therefore becomes any given work's form in which its recreation or re-presentation retains as closely as possible its symbolic aesthetic and behavioural characteristics according to that intended by the artist who created it. Preserving the original born-digital cultural heritage object, according to the National Library of Australia guidelines, requires its form to be maintained as the original material, alongside its technical and behavioural features.[58] Similarly the 2015 UNESCO recommendations stipulate that the content, signs, codes and text for example or images and sounds must be the original bitstreams and software. In addition, the carrier may also have important, aesthetic, historical, cultural or technical qualities or characteristics relating to the original.[59] This state and its collection of objects becomes an object's authenticity and therefore the truthfulness of itself as heritage. These approaches represent two qualitatively different dispositions.

Current object-centred thinking in digital cultural heritage preservation practice views a digital object as a system made up of its interface and all its software and hardware components including back-end elements that are invisible alongside its operational contexts so they can be recreated. These approaches to making digital objects active again are distinctly technical and object-oriented and, existing alongside new case examples, I argue, can be productively theorized through Gilbert Simondon's technical mentality.[60] According to a technical mentality reading, any given digital cultural heritage item is a system of distinct objects performing particular but mutually dependent functions, all of which have different qualities and substances, interact and change one another as different phases in its emergence. Each of these objects and its arrangement together make up a schema as part of the mechanical function of the unified whole object. The elements of the technical object, its bits and technical affordances, are not given over to representation. They remain a technical concern.

This technical mentality is empirically illustrated through the approach taken by the Australian Centre for the Moving Image (ACMI) to the preservation of *lifeSigns*, a time-based and variable media art work. In 2004, ACMI acquired artist Troy Innocent's *lifeSigns: Eco-System of Signs & Symbols*, an interactive digital networked art work where participants play selected emotions as game identities.[61] What is interesting here is the distinctly technical and also museological disposition driving its object-making.

The essence of *lifeSigns* is its operational programming text files and bits, its operating system and its circuit boards. The maintenance of all these things as an ensemble ensures that the signals generated by its forensic architecture can allow the object to emerge again in the future. *lifeSigns* becomes a system of interdependent technical, computational and software objects. Each of these elements together becomes the essence of itself as a technical object.

When originally acquired, ACMI accessioned four PVC stands and bases that encased the trackballs and mice along with the nuts and bolts to join them together and a master copy of the software on a DVD entitled *lifeSigns: Eco-System of Signs & Symbols*.[62] These elements were seen as significant in themselves because they were parts of the original work and were treated as representative, standing for what the object and experience used to be. All other hardware, software and equipment such as the 4:3 installation screens with accompanying speakers, projector, and projection screen were either re-purposed or not considered integral to the function of the whole object at the time it was acquired. As merely a representative collection of *lifeSigns* technical and software elements, it could no longer emerge again in its active state.

Since then ACMI's museological disposition was made evident through its aim to preserve and retain the functionality of the original technical schema and re-create the object as closely as possible, including its original behaviour. To achieve this, according to curator Candice Cranmer, curatorial and conservation strategies were specifically designed to recreate how *lifeSigns* looked and functioned when it was first exhibited.[63] Based on the idea of recreating the whole original object and its operational affordances, *lifeSigns* became a technical system made up of distinct objects that were at the same time interdependent. Curatorial and conservation work was directed towards re-instituting technical control over the work and involved the collection and unification of its technical parts and software, the maintenance, fixing and operationalizing of its relay points, energetic systems and

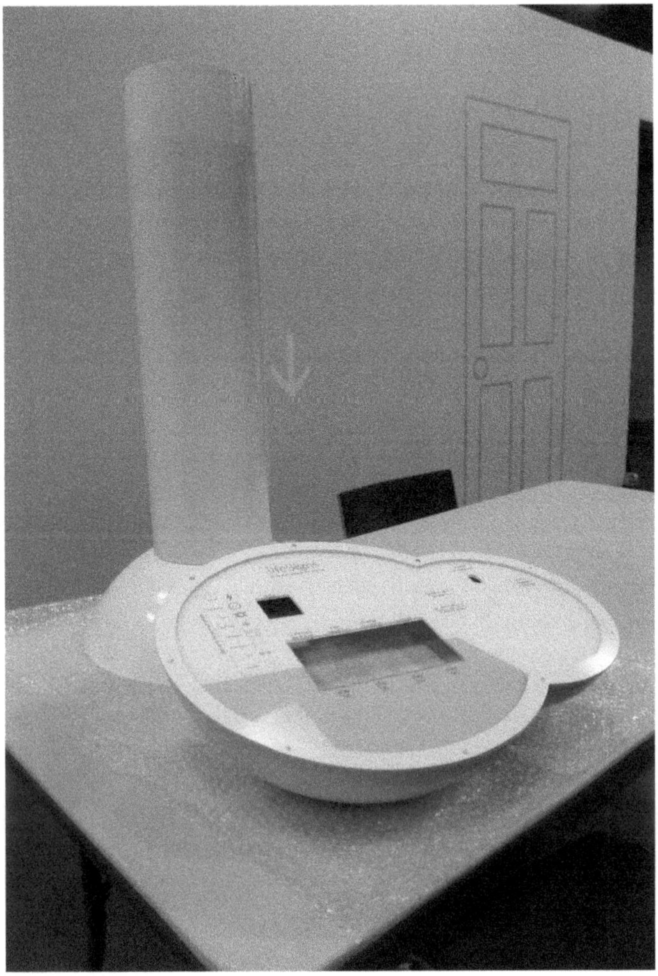

**FIGURE 4.1** *lifeSigns: Eco-System of Signs & Symbols*, 2004, Troy Innocent, Australian Centre for the Moving Image, Melbourne. Image: PVC pods taken out of storage for the first time since 2004.
Photo credit: Candice Cranmer, 2018.

networks. Alongside these technical elements the object is also born out of the processes generated by the reassembling of its components and its multiple material elements. But to achieve this *lifeSigns* required repair and maintenance. In order to maintain technical control over how it functioned and looked so it would vary as little as possible from the original, preservation methods were sought, tested, and modified to support this intent.

Curatorial attention was directed toward the description of all its elements – its architecture and its technical components that individually and collectively made up *lifeSigns*' objecthood – to ensure its original essence was recorded for its future emergence.

To do this the original object as a whole was documented to enable the scheduling of its migration onto suitable formats, and to support file verification, software upgrades and hardware maintenance to ensure their long-term permanence.[64] Here *lifeSigns*' technical rendering is vital, and at the same time this process draws our attention to its back-end technical features. What appears on the interface still operates as a representational mediator of what it is and how it was used as a game in the past.

*lifeSigns*' technical elements when brought together become its essence rather than its individual parts. ACMI's intent changed from an interest in collecting original fragments of technical systems to rendering things active again while at the same time seeking to maintain the original in as many facets as possible. *lifeSigns* as time-based media, as digital cultural heritage and as an art work was not seen to exist until powered up again. While ACMI sought to reproduce the original as closely as possible to the way it worked, looked, and was experienced, through its remixed and emulated software, hardware, and associated user inputs, it emerged in a different form each time it was powered up.

Born-digital objects on the internet are also viewed as distributed, emergent technical objects that are inherently unstable. The ground-breaking Nordic Collecting Social Photography research project sought to collect and document social media photographs from Facebook and Instagram.[65] In doing so the researchers

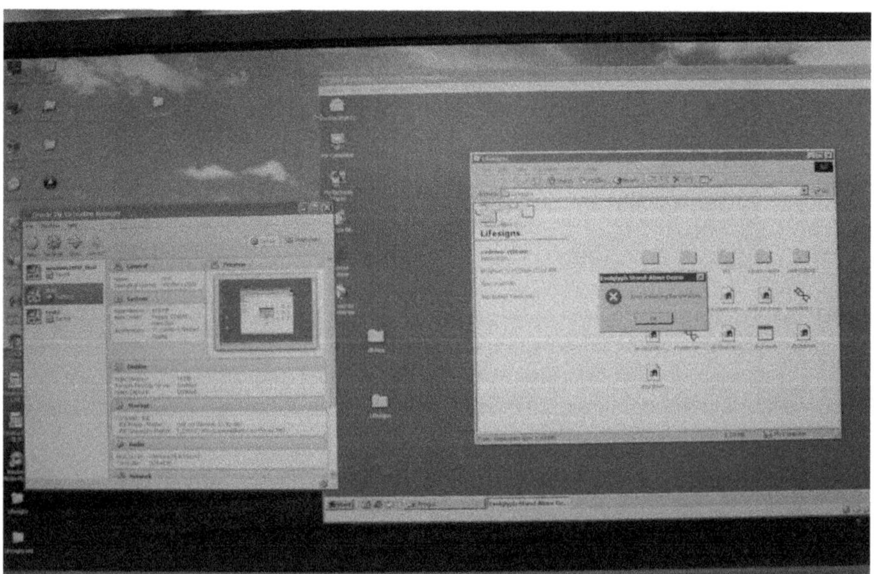

**FIGURE 4.2** *lifeSigns: Eco-System of Signs & Symbols*, 2004, Troy Innocent, Australian Centre for the Moving Image, Melbourne. Image: troubleshooting reinstallation of original *lifeSigns: Eco-System of Signs & Symbols* software using Oracle Virtual VM VirtualBox.

Photo credit: Candice Cranmer, 2018.

sought to analyse the objecthood of social photos according to a technical mentality in an effort to collect, archive and preserve them. Described as ephemeral, social photographs were then viewed as complex objects comprising an assemblage of image, text and metadata affected by the network in which all these things were embedded.[66] Here digital cultural heritage, while viewed technically as object schemas, in an online environment, were also seen as immaterial and lacking any tangible elements, unlike so-called physical photographs.

Technically speaking, digital cultural heritage objects when residing on internets are seen as a constantly evolving and interconnected set of applications, systems and datasets that successively become more concrete. They are at the same time distributed through metadata through which more relational connections and networks become enrolled. In terms of collecting and documentation, for example, digital cultural heritage objects are seen as made up of multiple technical objects originating from many locations operating across domains and in different settings.

Digital preservationist Trevor Owens explains this complexity when he talks about World of Warcraft, a global multiplayer game. World of Warcraft comprises multiple versions of hardware and software objects all of which are constantly upgraded, mutating, and changing.[67] A remote server runs additional software to create its virtual world that players then inhabit. World of Warcraft is also tightly coupled with its underlying media – its database logic, operating systems, programming languages, custom software applications, encoding schemas and multiplicity of orders and sequences enabled by queries, alongside the wide range of file formats, compression algorithms, exchange protocols, and browser platforms that can be embedded – all of which poses challenges for digital curation. Each layer has distinct affordances and properties.[68] Furthermore, the architecture of technical and organizational relations to which they belong are in a constant state of flux.[69] These fundamental conditions are implicated in the formation of larger technical systems as multiple Worlds of Warcraft never settle. From a technical perspective, millions of versions of Warcraft emerge, made by each of its many players and then appearing on multiple interfaces through their own inputs, contributing to its emerging, sprawling technical schema. Here many different World of Warcraft objecthoods exist as a series of interdependent objects and processes that are entangled with one another. This is what makes born-digital cultural heritage objects, especially those on the internet, fundamentally challenging when compared to how other types of material heritages are curated. What object to collect or record is dependent on the intent of those who seek to collect and preserve. A layperson's experience of World of Warcraft, in contrast to that of digital preservationists, remains founded on the interface and the database.

The emerging object-centred view in digital cultural heritage preservation, especially as it relates to those items of variable media embedded with data, has been influenced by the VM approach. In this formulation digital cultural heritages are at once tangible objects of substantial form, as their bitstream primarily and their hardware, and at the same time are made up of multiple social, historical, material, and technical objects.

World renowned physicist and mathematician Stephen Hawking, known for his theories on how to predict radiation emissions from black holes, suffered from motor neuron disease, lost his ability to speak, and therefore communicated through an assisted technology speech system. The key element of Hawking's system was an open-source program ACAT by Intel with a word prediction algorithm SwiftKey trained on his books and lectures.[70] This input system was activated through an infrared switch on Hawking's glasses that captured twitches in his cheek muscles enabling him to control the mouse on Windows software and to select individual letters, build words and sentences with an auto-complete feature through an interface program EZ Keys that was then displayed on a tablet mounted to the arm of his wheelchair and powered by its batteries. A Speech Plus voice generation device and synthesizer spoke the sentence out loud. These features enabled Hawking to check email, search the net, make notes and write papers, chat online and prepare, save, and deliver lectures.[71]

Hawking's system comprised multiple, technical, material, social, and historical objects. It included material objects such as a computer tablet and communication board, speaker, microphone, webcam, all items of tangible form and substance you can hold, alongside other technical objects such as an encoded bitstream, comprising a display image, voice recognition software, an audio and visual, semantic generator, code description, processor, smartphone apps, and a sign and gesture system. Socio-technical objects included emojis, his posts on social media systems, his lectures and emails stored on the device. All of these objects collectively as heritage are representative of Hawking's genius, of technological innovation and therefore representative of his life at particular historical moments.

Theorized according to a technical schema, his speech system as an object becomes more complex through which multiple objecthoods exist in which all the elements are integrated together. To become digital cultural heritage as a working version, all its original parts, elements and relay systems, its technical, logical, behaviour, input, output capabilities must be maintained as the original materially, technically and operationally as the system Hawking owned and used, with some software and hardware upgrades substituted to allay its obsolescence and maintain its functionality. This technical mentality underlay Hawking's detailed system inventory that he posted on his website so that it could be recreated again.[72] Hawking's two complete wheelchair systems and custom-built communication hardware and software comprised the following:

> ACAT interface software and digital blink switch developed by Intel.
> (credit Pete Denman, Lama Nachman, Alex Nguyen, Max Pinaroc, Sai Prasad, Sangita Sharma, Jonathan Wood)
>
> Software speech emulator (from 26/01/2018) running on Raspberry Pi 3 computers and written by Peter Benie.
> (credit Peter Benie, Sam Blackburn, Byuu, Eric Dorsey, Mark Green, Jon Peatfield, Patti Price, Jonathan Wood, Pawel Wozniak)

> Overall hardware system by Intel.
> (credit Travis Bonifield, Mark Green, David Rittenhouse, Jonathan Wood)
>
> Hardware speech synthesizers (before 26/01/2018):
> Manufacturer - Speech Plus (Incorporated 1988, Mountain View, CA)
> Model - CallText 5010 (x3) [also CallText 5000 (x2) with same voice, but one of these remains broken]
> (thanks to Hari Vyas and Jared Bernstein for donation of the 5000 boards)
>
> Speakers and amplifiers for wheelchair system and desktop developed by Sound Research
> (credit Charles Chin, Paul Kitano, Tom Paddock)
>
> Laptops provided by Lenovo
> Lenovo Yoga 260, Intel® Core™ i7–6600U CPU, 512GB Solid-State Drive, Windows 10
>
> Permobil F3 wheelchairs provided by Permobil
> (credit Olof Hedin, Michael Lindholm)
>
> by Jonathan Wood, Technical Assistant to Professor Stephen Hawking (2012–2018)
> (credits are alphabetical)

Clearly no one idea defines the digital "object." How Hawking's speech system is imagined as embodying an objecthood depends partially on intent, that is whether it is thought about in terms of its technical preservation, as an aesthetic object, as a means for facilitating social engagement merely for the information it can reveal, but also whether it exists on the internet or as data embedded in machines of various kinds. Having said all this, our understanding of digital cultural heritage as possessing an objecthood inflects a selection, preservation and interpretation process that is decidedly object-oriented. Technical objects that make up the art or digital cultural heritage object operate in excess of what we can know because they are subject to machine learning and automated processes. This is indeed a difficult proposition and one that requires re-thinking in a context where digital data doesn't conform to the required standards of the stable and authentic, and the conventionally knowable.

The enactment of different concepts and practices of objecthood through heritagization processes raises important questions in respect to how born-digital objects in particular, once their preservation processes are complete, influence and change their use, their interpretive capacities, and their dialogic and affective experiences such as sharing, recollection, and commemoration. Accordingly, we also need to investigate how experiences and practices of materiality, affect, interaction, and interpretation are reconstituted in born-digital objects such as websites and digital images once archived.[73] These are critical questions also relevant to the emergence of this class of heritage more broadly, and are discussed further in the following chapter.

The idea that digital objects have inherent properties, whether material, immaterial, technical or informational, underlies a belief in political, symbolic, linguistic, and knowledge forms of representation central to heritage practice. Contrary to these representational forms of expression often presented as fixed forms, born-digital cultural heritage operates dynamically, and therefore is able to be reproduced. These objects are decidedly mutable, distributed, and comprise interlocking continuous processes that resist fixed concepts such as object, the interpretation of them as narratives of the social and symbolic and as technical, or information.

The unfolding of digital data objects as a process philosophy influenced by digital art practice, time-based media, and conceptual and performing arts means that digital data in the heritage sector can no longer be thought about as solely representational. Rather, they become intimately connected to evolving conceptions of how things appear; what they mean; who is involved; what they capture; the agency of their materials, networks, infrastructures and energetic fields; and other serendipitous renderings and interactions.

Clearly, museums have equipped themselves to deal with objects but not process ontologies. Digital images can be treated as objects whereas other types of process- and systems-based heritages only reveal themselves through interactive engagement. They are essentially viewed as ephemeral in their unfolding. Snapshots don't capture the content and context of dynamic systems such as sophisticated online games and their multi-user worlds that are textual, performative and graphical.

To uphold the idea of digital data as objects in heritage practice they must have an essence. They must be objectified things within heritage schemas, conceived as beyond experience and removed from time and their lived context. While digital cultural heritage may be conceptualized or viewed as possessing object-like characteristics, I instead theorize digital data as post-object forms operating in experience, in process, made up of diverse coordinates, and as domains of influencing they co-activate as they emerge. Digital cultural heritage therefore can never be contained within the finite dimensions of the object or within the meanings given to it by authorized heritage institutions or users. This approach accordingly shifts the conceptualization of heritage and the object from a focus on attributes and properties, to ascertain what it says about us it to principles that embrace process, agency, the notion of contingent enactments. I shift my interpretive attention to consider how digital cultural heritage operates as ecological formations according to its local and practical contingencies.

My approach contrasts with object-oriented ontology, a popular theoretical framework informed by Simondon's work and shaped by Graham Harman and other speculative realists.[74] Object-oriented ontology (OOO) philosophy is an ontological theory of life as opposed to one directed to the analysis of states of being, as seen with more conventional object-directed thinking. Like other ontological forms, OOO includes non-humans as actors and uses a theory of relations, but it is object directed. Each object relies on other objects in its emergence and remains focused on forms and substances and how they interact.[75] Hence, an object-oriented approach founded on objects as singular autonomous entities operating in networks is not useful here if we are to think of digital data and heritage as comprising lively and multifarious elemental, material, technical, energetic, and infrastructural processes all of which exert their own agencies. And as a post-object non-form, digital cultural heritage is not necessarily amenable to classification or interpretive closure.

## Re-thinking the digital cultural heritage object

With digital cultural heritage objects, as with other types of heritage objects, we focus solely on human agency and human-centred concerns to give meaning to them through significance statements and descriptions, or to place them in digital networks so they might act as provocations for conversation. To view digital data conceptually as objects and as seemingly solid things is reassuring. It is what we know and what we understand. We seek to understand and to know its essence in order to describe its form, a form that accounts for its appearance.

The construction of digital cultural heritage through these social, cultural, and technical orders has until now made it difficult to render visible other registers of significance and the more-than- and other-than-human aspects of its making. This predisposition has implicated other agencies in the emergence of digital cultural heritage, such as planetary technological infrastructures, material agency, non-human, elemental, and earthly processes as invisible figures in their constitution.

The dramatic and tragic events of 9/11 succinctly disrupted the idea that the world could be understood solely through human-centred meaning-making practices.[76] The reality of 9/11 made visible to us how things have their own material agencies and operate outside the parameters of the object and human frameworks of understanding. The analogue and digitization of the aircraft jump seat belt (auxiliary crew station seat belt used by crew during take-off and landing) from American Airlines Flight 11, now part of the 9/11 collection held at the Smithsonian Museum of American History, vividly illustrates how the properties and capacities of material things get entangled with the intentions of human actors as much as it reminds us of the devastation, the bravery and the loss we witnessed and experienced on that fateful day. The seat belt partly acted outside human social constructivist frameworks, in which registers of action were also formed through the properties and interactions of the diverse range of materials, entities, and human actions that comprised it. These different things, materials, actions, intentions, buildings, symbols, and their affects, as a series of interdependent coordinates, mixed and merged with one another, all varying in extent, intensity, and scale, in ways that are often resoundingly unpredictable. These processes are what I call domains of influencing. The analogue and also the digital jump seat belt's emergence embodies the enfolding of the intentions of the hijackers to target American symbols and use planes as weapons. The domains of influencing that converge on the seat belt include the force and impact of the aircraft as it was propelled into floors 93–99 of the North Tower of the World Trade Center at 8:46:40 on

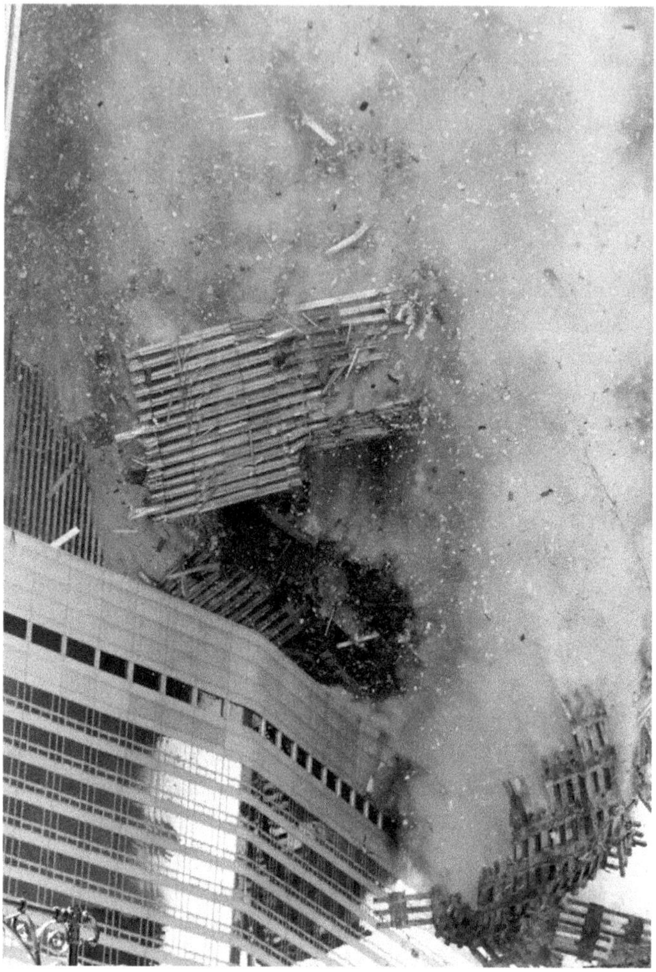

**FIGURE 4.3** Domains of influencing at work. The South Tower of New York's World Trade Center collapses at 9:59 am on Tuesday Sept. 11, 2001.
Photo credit: Wikimedia Commons.

September 11, 2001, the flammability of aircraft fuel, billowing smoke, the sudden collapse of the North Tower due to the impact of the aircraft, and the fire that ensued undermining the strength of the columns due to their light-weight structure. Debris becomes toxic dust as the entanglements of human labour and materials from residue paper, computers, files, disks, building materials, microbes, nanoparticles, metals, chemicals and minerals. The recovery operation, its framing as heritage and its production as a digitization become overlapping domains of influencing as a situated museological intervention. At the same time the digitization becomes an imprint of these material-affective processes as a result of these domains of influencing moving through and across it.

It is not just the many different types of material agencies that have the potential to operate in a physical world outside human frameworks of understanding. Digital data can have very material and political effects that may not be known in advance. This is most dramatically illustrated in regard to President Donald Trump's tweets concerning nuclear ballistic missiles and North Korean relations to be discussed in the following chapter. Trump's tweets incited threats of war, fuelling hostile relationships with North Korea that in turn prompted the launch of a series of ballistic missiles.

We interpret the physical world through the physical sciences of physics and chemistry, among others. These disciplines give us an insight into the material agencies and properties of the non-human world and their capacity to modify and transform, through processes from the principles of gravity to the functional abilities of rare earth minerals used in computational design. Such observations are still an outcome of how we interpret the world we sense. Similarly, the question of the digital as a type of heritage will remain a matter of definition by the human subject but at the same time as it operates outside the scope of what we can know. We can't escape our own frames of reference, and there are many things and actions that we will never comprehend or indeed are unknowable.

Digital data within a heritage framework does not operate according to the separate domains of material bits, of objecthood, according to descriptions of what digital cultural heritage objects stand for or their social biographies. Clearly, a simple rendering of the visual image as a snapshot and as statement of objecthood no longer works. Attempts to standardize digital art, interfacial images, and time-based media through technical descriptions suggest that they operate as unique rather than standard signatures and should be described as such. We therefore must give up on the idea of digital cultural heritage as having an objecthood that stands for its essence and the idea that we can retain the original context of virtual objects and stabilize them. While it may be convenient for us, it is just not realistic or useful.

Digital cultural heritage requires its own forms of analysis through an ethnographic investigation into objects' particular ecological circumstances in the field and involving a wide range of agencies. With the emergence of digital technology, we witness a shift from the constitution of being not so much as static, bounded objects to one of emergence, to unfolding and to ontology. In the following chapter I reframe digital cultural heritage objects and representation as ecological, as ontological and as eco-systemic processes.

## Notes

1 For a definition of big data and a discussion of its impact on politics see Dirk Helbing, Bruno S. Frey, Gerd Gigerenzer, Ernst Hafen, Michael Hagner, Yvonne Hofstetter, Jeroen van den Hoven, Roberto V. Zicari and Andrej Zwitter, "Will Democracy Survive Big Data and Artificial Intelligence?" *Scientific American* (February 2017): 3, https://www.scientificamerican.com/article/will-democracy-survive-big-data-and-artificial-intelligence/.

2 Christiane Paul, *Digital Art* (London: Thames & Hudson, 3rd ed., 2015), 67 explains how the software and operating systems that comprise digital art change so rapidly that the rhetoric that evaluates them becomes obsolete very quickly.
3 Yola de Lusenet and Vincent Wintermans, *Preserving the Digital Heritage: Principles and Policies*, Selected Papers of the International Conference organized by the Netherlands National Commission for UNESCO and The European Commission for Preservation and Access, The Hague, November 4th–5th, 2005 (Netherlands National Commission for UNESCO and The European Commission for Preservation and Access, 2005), 2, http://www.ica.org/sites/default/files/WG_2007_PAAG-preserving-the-digital-heritage_EN.pdf.
4 UNESCO, "Charter on the Preservation of Digital Heritage," 3, http://portal.unesco.org/en/ev.php-URL_ID=17721&URL_DO=DO_TOPIC&URL_SECTION=201.html; de Lusenet and Wintermans, *Preserving the Digital Heritage*.
5 UNESCO, "Concept of Digital Preservation" https://en.unesco.org/themes/information-preservation/digital-heritage/concept-digital-preservation.
6 Gilbert Simondon, *Technical Mentality*, trans. Arne De Boever, *Parrthesia*, https://www.parrhesiajournal.org/parrhesia07/parrhesia07_simondon2.pdf.
7 For a discussion of digital data as computational and information objects see Deborah Lupton, *This Sociological Life*, "Digital Technologies and Data as Sociomaterial Objects" (blog), August 31, 2014, https://simplysociology.wordpress.com/2014/08/31/digital-technologies-and-data-as-sociomaterial-objects/.
8 Matthew Fuller and Andrew Goffey, "The Unknown Objects of Object-Orientation," in *Objects and Materials*, eds. Penny Harvey, Eleanor Conlin Casella, Gillian Evans, Hannah Knox, Christine McLean, Elizabeth B. Silva, Nicholas Thoburn and Kath Woodward (Abingdon: Routledge, 2014), 218.
9 Fuller and Goffey, "The Unknown Objects of Object-Orientation," 218.
10 For a discussion of digital objects in art and library practice see Trevor Owens, *Theory and Craft of Digital Preservation* (Baltimore: Johns Hopkins University, 2018).
11 Donna J. Haraway, *Modest_Witness @ Second_Millenium* (Abingdon: Routledge, 1997), 267. Also quoted in Matthew Fuller, *Media Ecologies: Materialist Energies in Art and Technoculture* (Cambridge, MA: The MIT Press, 2005), 104.
12 Lupton, "Digital Technologies and Data as Sociomaterial Objects"; Adrian Mackenzie, *Cutting Code: Software and Sociality* (New York: Peter Lang, 2006).
13 Michael Betancourt, "The Aura of the Digital. 1000 Days of Theory," *CTheory.net* (2006): 2, https://journals.uvic.ca/index.php/ctheory/article/view/14485/5328.
14 Betancourt, "The Aura of the Digital."
15 Nick del Pozo, Andrew Stawowczyk Long and David Pearson, "Land of the Lost: A Discussion of What Can Be Preserved through Digital Preservation," *Library Hi Tech* 28, no. 2 (2010): 295.
16 Lev Manovich, *The Language of New Media* (Cambridge, MA: The MIT Press, 2002).
17 For a discussion of user interactions with art works through database ecologies see Paul, *Digital Art*, 21.
18 David Harvey, *The Condition of Postmodernity: An Enquiry into the Origins of Social Change* (London: Wiley-Blackwell, 1991).
19 Magnus Eriksson, "The Materialization of Code", 2013, http://www.omxi.se/2013-03-11-the-materialization-of-code.html; Kevin Kelly, *New Rules for the New Economy: 10 Radical Strategies for a Connected World* (New York: Viking Penguin, 1998).
20 For a discussion of approaches in which "things" are made manifest through software see Jannis Kallinikos, "Form, Function and Matter: Crossing the Border of Materiality," in *Materiality and Organizing*, eds. Paul Leonardi, Bonnie Nardi and Jannis Kallinikos (Oxford: Oxford University Press, 2013), 79; Katherine N. Hayles, *How We Became Posthuman: Virtual Bodies in Cybernetics, Literature and Informatics* (Chicago: University of Chicago Press, 1999), 70.
21 Betancourt, "The Aura of the Digital," 3.

22 For a discussion of the emphasis on the immaterial as a way of describing art see Jacob Lillemose, *Histories and Theories of Intermedia*, "Conceptualizing Materiality – Art from the Dematerialization of the Object to the Condition of Immateriality, Histories and Theories of Intermedia" (blog), January 4, 2008, http://umintermediai501.blogspot.com.au/2008/01/conceptualizing-materiality-art-from.html; Hayles, *How We Became Posthuman*, 70; Christiane Paul, *From Immateriality to Neomateriality: Art and the Conditions of Digital Materiality*, ISEA2015, Proceedings of the 21st International Symposium on Electronic Art, 2015,1, http://isea2015.org/proceeding/submissions/ISEA2015_submission_154.pdf.
23 Jussi Parikka, "Media Ecologies and Imaginary Media: Transversal Extensions, Contradictions and Foldings," *The Fibreculture Journal* 17 (2011), http://seventeen.fibreculturejournal.org/fcj-116-media-ecologies-and-imaginary-media-transversal-expansions-contractions-and-foldings/.
24 For a discussion of immateriality as electrical impulses see Stephen Groening, "Towards a Meteorology of the Media," *New Immaterialities: Transformations* 25 (2014): 3, 8.
25 The overriding emphasis on immateriality is seen in scholarship such as Youngjin Yoo, "Digital Materiality and the Emergence of an Evolutionary Science of the Artificial," in *Materiality and Organizing: Social Interaction in a Technological World*, eds. Paul Leonardi, Bonnie Nardi and Jannis Kallinikos (Oxford: Oxford University Press, 2012), 134–154; Philip Faulkner and Jochen Runde, "On the Identity of Technological Objects and User Innovations in Function," *The Academy of Management Review* 34, no. 3 (July 2009): 442–462; Fuller, *Media Ecologies*, 2.
26 Lillemose, "Conceptualizing Materiality."
27 Paul, *Digital Art*, 21.
28 Yuk Hui, *On the Existence of Digital Objects* (Minneapolis: University of Minnesota Press, 2016), 1, 27.
29 Hui, *On the Existence of Digital Objects*, 116.
30 Hui, *On the Existence of Digital Objects*, 116. Paul M. Leonardi, "Digital Materiality," *First Monday* 15, no. 6–7 (June 2010), http://firstmonday.org/article/view/3036/2567.
31 UNESCO, "Charter on Cultural Heritage," http://portal.unesco.org/en/ev.phpURL_ID=17721%26URL_DO=DO_PRINTPAGE%26URL_SECTION=201.html.
32 Pramod Nayar, *Posthumanism* (New York: Wiley Press, 2010), 36; Harvey, *The Condition of Postmodernity*; Martijn Stevens, "Settle for Nothing: Materializing the Digital", *Artnodes*, 12 (2012).
33 Beatrice Fazi, "Digital Philosophy," in *Posthuman Glossary*, eds. Rosi Braidotti and Maria Hlavajova (London: Bloomsbury Academic, 2018), 105.
34 Luciano Floridi, *The Philosophy of Information* (Oxford: Oxford University Press, 2011), 20.
35 Andrea Witcomb, "Interactivity: Thinking Beyond," in *A Companion to Museum Studies*, ed. Sharon MacDonald (London: Blackwell, 2006), 355.
36 George MacDonald, "Change and Challenge: Museums in the Information Society," in *Museums and Communities: The Politics of Public Culture*, eds. Ivan Karp, Christine M. Kreamer and Steven D. Lavine (Washington: Smithsonian Institution Press, 1992), 161.
37 George MacDonald and Stephen Alsford, "The Museum as Information Utility", *Museum Management and Curatorship* 10 (1991): 305–311, 307.
38 Katherine Burton Jones, "The Transformation of the Digital Museum," in *Museum Informatics: People, Information, and Technology*, eds. Paul Marty and Katherine Burton Jones (Abingdon: Routledge, 2007), 9–26.
39 Paul Marty, "Information Representation," in *Museum Informatics: People, Information, and Technology*, eds. Paul Marty and Katherine Burton Jones (Abingdon: Routledge, 2007), 29–34.
40 For a discussion of the advent of the new museology and its concerns see Peter Vergo, *The New Museology* (London: Reaktion Books, 1989); Duncan Cameron, "The Museum, a Temple or the Forum", *Curator* 14, no. 1 (1972): 11–24; Ruth Phillips, "Disrupting Past Paradigms: The National Museum of the American Indian and the First

Peoples Hall at the Canadian Museum of Civilization," *The Public Historian* 28, no. 2 (Spring 2006): 75–80; Kristine Ronan, "Native Empowerment, the New Museology, and the National Museum of the American Indian," *Museum & Society* 12, no. 1 (July 2014): 132–147, https://www2.le.ac.uk/departments/museumstudies/museumsociety/documents/volumes/ronan.

41 George MacDonald and Stephen Alsford, "The Museum as Information Utility", 307.
42 Andrea Witcomb, *Re-imaging the Museum: Beyond the Mausoleum* (Abingdon: Routledge, 2003), 113.
43 https://www.museweb.net/mwa2016/.
44 Nina Simon, "Social Objects," *The Participatory Museum*, 2010, http://www.participatory museum.org/chapter4/#footnote-754-2.
45 Jyri Engeström, *Zengestrom*, "Why Some Social Network Services Work and Others Don't – Or: The Case for Object-Centered Sociality" (blog), April 13, 2005, http://www.zengestrom.com/blog/2005/04/why-some-social-network-services-work-and-others-dont-or-the-case-for-object-centered-sociality.html.
46 Owens, *Theory and Craft of Digital Preservation*, 67.
47 Seb Chan, personal communication, Melbourne, ACMI, July 2017.
48 Matthew Westwood, "The Digital Museum is now Preserving our Online Culture," *The Australian*, Feb 7, 2017, http://www.theaustralian.com.au/arts/visual-arts/the-digital-museum-of-now-is-preserving-our-online-culture/news-story/b82cdff975d75391d11a84e63880e210.
49 For a discussion of material descriptors and the manufacturing process see Susanne Küchler and Peter Oakley, "New Materials and Their Impact on the Material World," in *Objects and Materials*, eds. Penny Harvey, Eleanor Conlin Casella, Gillian Evans, Hannah Knox, Christine McLean, Elizabeth B. Silva, Nicholas Thoburn and Kath Woodward (Abingdon: Routledge, 2014), 82–91.
50 For a discussion of Semper and his material thesis in the nineteenth century see Küchler and Oakley, "New Materials and Their Impact on the Material World."
51 Fiona Cameron, "Shaping Maori Histories and Identities: Collecting and Exhibiting Maori Material Culture at the Auckland and Canterbury Museums from the 1850s to the 1920s," PhD thesis (Massey University, Palmerston North, 2000).
52 UNESCO's "Concept of Digital Preservation".
53 National Library of Australia, "Guidelines for the Preservation of Digital Heritage," Information Society Division, UNESCO, March 2003, 109–110, http://unesdoc.unesco.org/images/0013/001300/130071e.pdf.
54 Guggenheim, "The Variable Media Initiative," https://www.guggenheim.org/conservation/the-variable-media-initiative.
55 Owens, *Theory and Craft of Digital Preservation*, 13–17.
56 Richard Rinehart, "Variability Machines," in Richard Rinehart and Jon Ippolito, *Re-collection: Art, New Media, and Social Memory* (Cambridge, MA: The MIT Press, 2014), 47–48.
57 Richard Rinehart and Jon Ippolito, *Re-collection: Art, New Media, and Social Memory* (Cambridge, MA: The MIT Press, 2014), 131.
58 National Library of Australia, "Guidelines for the Preservation of Digital Heritage," 108.
59 Ray Edmondson, "Recommendation Concerning the Preservation of, and Access to, Documentary Heritage Including in Digital Form: Implementation Guidelines," prepared for UNESCO, 2015, 3, https://en.unesco.org/sites/default/files/2015_mow_recommendation_implementation_guidelines_en.pdf.
60 Simondon, *Technical Mentality*, 18.
61 Candice Cranmer, "Preserving Time-based Media: A Case Study with Troy Innocent's lifeSigns: Eco-System of Signs & Symbols," *ACMI Labs*, April 11, 2018, https://labs.acmi.net.au/preserving-time-based-media-a-case-study-with-troy-innocents-lifesigns-eco-system-of-signs-3e2f0b3ae2.
62 Cranmer, "Preserving Time-based Media."
63 Cranmer, "Preserving Time-based Media."

64 Cranmer, "Preserving Time-based Media."
65 Kajsa Hartig, Bente Jensen, Anni Wallenius and Elisabeth Boogh, "Collecting the Ephemeral Social Media Photograph for the Future: Why Museums and Archives Need to Embrace New Work Practices for Photography Collections," MW18 Conference, Vancouver, Canada, April 18th–21st, 2018, https://mw18.mwconf.org/paper/collecting-the-ephemeral-social-media-photograph-for-the-future-why-museums-and-archives-need-embrace-new-work-practices-for-photography-collections/.
66 Hartig et al., "Collecting the Ephemeral Social Media Photograph for the Future."
67 Owens, *Theory and Craft of Digital Preservation*, 56.
68 Owens, *Theory and Craft of Digital Preservation*, 33.
69 Owens, *Theory and Craft of Digital Preservation*, 56.
70 Stephen Hawking website, http://www.hawking.org.uk/the-computer.html.
71 Stephen Hawking website, http://www.hawking.org.uk/the-computer.html.
72 Stephen Hawking website, http://www.hawking.org.uk/the-computer.html.
73 Fiona Cameron, "Beyond the Cult of the Replicant: Museums, Objects – New Discourses – Traditional Concerns," in *Theorizing Digital Cultural Heritage: A Critical Discourse*, eds. Fiona Cameron and Sarah Kenderdine (Cambridge, MA: The MIT Press, 2007), 49–77.
74 Graham Harman, *Object-Oriented Ontology: A New Theory of Everything* (London: Pelican, 2018).
75 Harman, *Object-Oriented Ontology*.
76 Ewa Domanska, "The Return to Things," *Archaeologia Polona* 44 (2006): 172.

## Bibliography

Betancourt, Michael. "The Aura of the Digital. 1000 Days of Theory." *CTheory.net* (2006): 2. https://journals.uvic.ca/index.php/ctheory/article/view/14485/5328.

Burton Jones, Katherine. "The Transformation of the Digital Museum." In *Museum Informatics: People, Information, and Technology*, edited by Paul Marty and Katherine Burton Jones, 9–26. Abingdon: Routledge, 2007.

Cameron, Duncan. "The Museum, a Temple or the Forum." *Curator* 14, no. 1 (1972): 11–24.

Cameron, Fiona. "Beyond the Cult of the Replicant: Museums, Objects – New Discourses – Traditional Concerns." In *Theorizing Digital Cultural Heritage: A Critical Discourse*, edited by Fiona Cameron and Sarah Kenderdine, 49–77. Cambridge, MA: The MIT Press, 2007.

Cameron, Fiona. *Shaping Maori Histories and Identities: Collecting and Exhibiting Maori Material Culture at the Auckland and Canterbury Museums from the 1850s to the 1920s*. PhD thesis. Massey University, Palmerston North, 2000.

Cranmer, Candice. "Preserving Time-based Media: A Case Study with Troy Innocent's life-Signs: Eco-System of Signs & Symbols." *ACMI Labs*, April 11, 2018. https://labs.acmi.net.au/ preserving-time-based-media-a-case-study-with-troy-innocents-lifesigns-eco-system -of- signs-3e2f0b3ae2.

de Lusenet, Yola, and Vincent Wintermans. *Preserving the Digital Heritage: Principles and Policies.* Selected Papers of the International Conference organized by the Netherlands National Commission for UNESCO and The European Commission for Preservation and Access, The Hague, November 4–5, 2005. Netherlands National Commission for UNESCO and The European Commission for Preservation and Access, 2005. http://www.ica.org/sites/default/files/WG_2007_PAAG-preserving-the-digital-heritage_EN.pdf.

del Pozo, Nick, Andrew Stawowczyk Long, and David Pearson. "Land of the Lost: A Discussion of What Can Be Preserved through Digital Preservation." *Library Hi Tech* 28, no. 2 (2010): 290–300.

Domanska, Ewa. "The Return to Things." *Archaeologia Polona* 44 (2006): 171–185.
Edmondson, Ray. "Recommendation Concerning the Preservation of, and Access to, Documentary Heritage Including in Digital Form: Implementation Guidelines." Prepared for UNESCO, 2015. https://en.unesco.org/sites/default/files/2015_mow_recommendation_implementation_guidelines_en.pdf.
Engeström, Jyri. "Why Some Social Network Services Work and Others Don't – Or: The Case for Object-Centered Sociality" *Zengestrom* (blog). Posted April 13, 2005. http://www.zengestrom.com/blog/2005/04/why-some-social-network-services-work-and-others-dont-or-the-case-for-object-centered-sociality.html.
Eriksson, Magnus. "The Materialization of Code." 2013. http://www.omxi.se/2013-03-11-the-materialization-of-code.html.
Faulkner, Philip, and Jochen Runde. "On the Identity of Technological Objects and User Innovations in Function." *The Academy of Management Review* 34, no. 3 (July2009): 442–462.
Fazi, Beatrice. "Digital Philosophy." In *Posthuman Glossary*, edited by Rosi Braidotti and Maria Hlavajova, 104–106. London: Bloomsbury Academic, 2018.
Floridi, Luciano. *The Philosophy of Information*. Oxford: Oxford University Press, 2011.
Fuller, Matthew. *Media Ecologies: Materialist Energies in Art and Technoculture*. Cambridge, MA: The MIT Press, 2005.
Fuller, Matthew, and Andrew Goffey. "The Unknown Objects of Object-Orientation." In *Objects and Materials*, edited by Penny Harvey, Eleanor Conlin Casella, Gillian Evans, Hannah Knox, Christine McLean, Elizabeth B. Silva, Nicholas Thoburn, and Kath Woodward, 218–227. Abingdon: Routledge, 2014.
Groening, Stephen. "Towards a Meteorology of the Media." *New Immaterialities: Transformations* 25 (2014): 1–9.
Guggenheim. "The Variable Media Initiative." Guggenheim.org. https://www.guggenheim.org/conservation/the-variable-media-initiative.
Haraway, Donna J. *Modest_Witness @ Second_Millenium*. Abingdon: Routledge, 1997.
Harman, Graham. *Object-Oriented Ontology: A New Theory of Everything*. London: Pelican, 2018.
Hartig, Kajsa, Bente Jensen, Anni Wallenius, and Elisabeth Boogh, "Collecting the Ephemeral Social Media Photograph for the Future: Why Museums and Archives Need to Embrace New Work Practices for Photography Collections." MW18 Conference, Vancouver, Canada, April 18th–21st, 2018. https://mw18.mwconf.org/paper/collecting-the-ephemeral-social- media-photograph-for-the-future-why-museums-and-archives-need-embrace-new-work- practices-for-photography-collections/.
Harvey, David. *The Condition of Postmodernity: An Enquiry into the Origins of Social Change*. London: Wiley-Blackwell, 1991.
Hayles, Katherine N. *How We Became Posthuman: Virtual Bodies in Cybernetics, Literature and Informatics*. Chicago: University of Chicago Press, 1999.
Helbing, Dirk, Bruno S. Frey, Gerd Gigerenzer, Ernst Hafen, Michael Hagner, Yvonne Hofstetter, Jeroen van den Hoven, Roberto V. Zicari, and Andrej Zwitter, "Will Democracy Survive Big Data and Artificial Intelligence?" *Scientific American* (February 2017). https://www.scientificamerican.com/article/will-democracy-survive-big-data-and-artificial-intelligence/.
Hui, Yuk. *On the Existence of Digital Objects*. Minneapolis: University of Minnesota Press, 2016.
Kallinikos, Jannis. "Form, Function and Matter: Crossing the Border of Materiality." In *Materiality and Organizing*, edited by Paul Leonardi, Bonnie Nardi, and Jannis Kallinikos, 66–87. Oxford: Oxford University Press, 2013.

Kelly, Kevin. *New Rules for the New Economy: 10 Radical Strategies for a Connected World*. New York: Viking Penguin, 1998.
Küchler, Susanne, and Peter Oakley. "New Materials and Their Impact on the Material World." In *Objects and Materials*, edited by Penny Harvey, Eleanor Conlin Casella, Gillian Evans, Hannah Knox, Christine McLean, Elizabeth B. Silva, Nicholas Thoburn, and Kath Woodward, 82–91. Abingdon: Routledge, 2014.
Leonardi, Paul M. "Digital Materiality." *First Monday* 15, no. 6–7 (June 2010). http://firstmonday.org/article/view/3036/2567.
Lillemose, Jacob. "Conceptualizing Materiality – Art from the Dematerialization of the Object to the Condition of Immateriality, Histories and Theories of Intermedia." *Histories and Theories of Intermedia* (blog). Posted January 4, 2008. http://umintermediai501.blogspot.com.au/2008/01/conceptualizing-materiality-art-from.html.
Lupton, Deborah. "Digital Technologies and Data as Sociomaterial Objects." *This Sociological Life* (blog). Posted August 31, 2014. https://simplysociology.wordpress.com/2014/08/31/digital-technologies-and-data-as-sociomaterial-objects/.
MacDonald, George. "Change and Challenge: Museums in the Information Society." In *Museums and Communities: The Politics of Public Culture*, edited by Ivan Karp, Christine M. Kreamer, and Steven D. Lavine, 158–181. Washington: Smithsonian Institution Press, 1992.
MacDonald, George, and Stephen Alsford. "The Museum as Information Utility." *Museum Management and Curatorship* 10 (1991): 305–311.
Mackenzie, Adrian. *Cutting Code: Software and Sociality*. New York: Peter Lang, 2006.
Manovich, Lev. *The Language of New Media*. Cambridge, MA: The MIT Press, 2002.
Marty, Paul. "Information Representation." In *Museum Informatics: People, Information, and Technology*, edited by Paul Marty and Katherine Burton Jones, 29–34. Abingdon: Routledge, 2007.
National Library of Australia. "Guidelines for the Preservation of Digital Heritage." Information Society Division, UNESCO, March 2003. http://unesdoc.unesco.org/images/0013/001300/130071e.pdf.
Nayar, Pramod. *Posthumanism*. New York: Wiley Press, 2010.
Owens, Trevor. *Theory and Craft of Digital Preservation*. Baltimore: Johns Hopkins University, 2018.
Parikka, Jussi. "Media Ecologies and Imaginary Media: Transversal Extensions, Contradictions and Foldings." *The Fibreculture Journal* 17 (2011). http://seventeen.fibreculturejournal.org/fcj-116-media-ecologies-and-imaginary-media-transversal-expansions-contra ctions-and-foldings/.
Paul, Christiane. *Digital Art*. London: Thames & Hudson, 3rd ed., 2015.
Paul, Christiane. "*From Immateriality to Neomateriality: Art and the Conditions of Digital Materiality*." ISEA2015. Proceedings of the 21st International Symposium on Electronic Art, 2015. http://isea2015.org/proceeding/submissions/ISEA2015_submission_154.pdf.
Phillips, Ruth. "Disrupting Past Paradigms: The National Museum of the American Indian and the First Peoples Hall at the Canadian Museum of Civilization." *The Public Historian* 28, no. 2 (Spring 2006): 75–80.
Rinehart, Richard. "Variability Machines." In Richard Rinehart and Jon Ippolito, *Re-collection: Art, New Media, and Social Memory*, 47–56. Cambridge, MA: The MIT Press, 2014.
Rinehart, Richard, and Jon Ippolito. *Re-collection: Art, New Media, and Social Memory*. Cambridge, MA: The MIT Press, 2014.
Ronan, Kristine. "Native Empowerment, the New Museology, and the National Museum of the American Indian." *Museum & Society* 12, no. 1 (July 2014): 132–147. https://www2.le.ac.uk/departments/museumstudies/museumsociety/documents/volumes/ronan.

Simon, Nina. "Social Objects." *The Participatory Museum*, 2010. http://www.participatorymuseum.org/chapter4/#footnote-754-2.

Simondon, Gilbert. "Technical Mentality." Translated by Arne De Boever (unpublished text). *Parrhesia.* https://www.parrhesiajournal.org/parrhesia07/parrhesia07_simondon2.pdf.

Stevens, Martijn. "Settle for Nothing: Materializing the Digital." *Artnodes* 12 (2012).

UNESCO. "Charter on Cultural Heritage." http://portal.unesco.org/en/ev.phpURL_ID=17721%26URL_DO=DO_PRINTPAGE%26URL_SECTION=201.html.

UNESCO. "Charter on the Preservation of Digital Heritage." UNESCO.org. http://portal.unesco.org/en/ev.php-URL_ID=17721&URL_DO=DO_TOPIC&URL_SECTION=201.html.

Vergo, Peter. *The New Museology*. London: Reaktion Books, 1989.

Westwood, Matthew. "The Digital Museum is now Preserving our Online Culture." *The Australian*, Feb 7, 2017. http://www.theaustralian.com.au/arts/visual-arts/the-digital-museum-of-now-is-preserving-our-online-culture/news-story/b82cdff975d75391d11a84e63880e210.

Witcomb, Andrea. "Interactivity: Thinking Beyond." In *A Companion to Museum Studies*, edited by Sharon MacDonald, 353–361. London: Blackwell, 2006.

Witcomb, Andrea. *Re-imaging the Museum: Beyond the Mausoleum*. London: Routledge, 2003.

Yoo, Youngjin. "Digital Materiality and the Emergence of an Evolutionary Science of the Artificial." In *Materiality and Organizing: Social Interaction in a Technological World*, edited by Paul Leonardi, Bonnie Nardi and Jannis Kallinikos, 134–154. Oxford: Oxford University Press, 2012.

# 5

# FROM OBJECTS TO ECOLOGICAL FORMATIONS

In this chapter I pull apart human-centred understandings of digital cultural heritage based on human actors, narratives and object-centred forms of materiality, sociality and their accompanying social, cultural and technical frames of interpretation as well as recent accounts that focus on digital materiality. This is because in the context of a radical expansion of the types and forms of data, infrastructures, and technologies and their human, more-than-human and non-human aspects, digital cultural heritage becomes more than humanist forms of social, cultural expression, statements of identity, or digital material substrates. I first experiment with new ideas about human subjects, objects, and agency through the lens of an ontological, new materialisms, posthuman, and ecological mode of thinking and action. In light of this, I theorize digital cultural heritage figuratively as unruly ecological compositions and curating as radical, eco-systemic processes involving the action of many different types of coordinates and the vitality of their interrelatedness in their unfolding.

To illustrate how these concepts might be applied empirically in digital cultural heritage contexts, I work with the digitization of the American Airlines Flight 11 jump seat belt in the 9/11 collection at the National Museum of American History (Smithsonian Institution) and Donald Trump's tweets that have been conferred heritage status.

## Eco-systemic thinking and digital cultural heritage practice

Reading digital cultural heritage through a more-than-human and eco-systemic framework rather than a humanist one directs our investigation into how digital cultural heritage is composed, conjoined, and transformed by the co-evolving interrelatedness of a broad range of actors from people to technologies, algorithms, materials, infrastructures, energetic systems, ideas and so forth. It also alerts us to how human, more-than-human and other-than human forces operate together in digital cultural heritage configurations as constituted and constituting forms and as domains of influencing within the extended, distributed webs of intelligibility that comprise them.

First, such figurations have the potential to direct our attention to the unprecedented level of digital and technological innovation attained, how such innovations are accelerating exponentially, and the extraordinarily complex and new relationships that are formed between human and non-human entities wrought by these developments. Second, these circumstances alert us to the emerging material, sensing, and discursive manifestations of these entanglements. Third, the type of knowledge that is produced through these new figurations is radically different from human narratives. Feminist philosopher Rosi Braidotti argues that the new types of knowledge produced and distributed as a result of these unprecedented technological developments involving multiple human and non-humans emerges as a complex posthuman convergence.[1]

Fourth, a consideration of material agency introduced in the preceding chapter widens the sphere of digital cultural heritage beyond its humanist, social constructivist and technical framing. It also acts as a lever to consider how digital cultural heritage might be conceived as material and performative indices imbricated in ecological crises – that is, from the exploitation of species leading to extinctions, and to the extraction of the geological substrates of the Earth itself to service digital capitalism and accumulation leading to the contamination of the atmospheric envelope.

Fifth, the interpretation of digital data as heritage is not simply a case of how these digital resources appear or are read differently by people and their inclusion in plural heritage-interpretive frameworks. By engaging digital cultural heritage as different ways of thinking about and acting in the world or as different worldings rather than world views, and on their own terms ethnographically, we can move away from imposing pre-ascribed categories of material, aesthetics, form, mode of production, and agency and associated points of view founded on person–thing (subject–object) relations, such as history, significance, and object biographies.

Through a more-than-human eco-systemic framework, we can also create an awareness of and empirically engage with the different social, cultural, material, political, and technical registers and circumstances in which digital data resides. Further to this, it opens up a space to reconsider the position of the human in what Braidotti calls a form of situated knowledge[2] within these broader collectives of knowledge production and their distributions. This is because a more-than-human eco-systemic method is first onto-ethnographical. By tracking the processes, the affecting capacities and emergent consequences of their various coordinates within an expanded and dynamic field (ontology) and their specific elements or coordinates, including the meanings and values attached to them (ethnographical specificities), we can investigate the many different ways that we can gain an understanding of what digital productions are and how they are given over to meaning.

Thinking through digital cultural heritage in this way favours action in representation. While more-than-human eco-systemic accounts of digital cultural heritage are indeed still representations, they are also things that are awaiting representation because they are emergent. Their emergence and their interpretation go hand in hand. Significantly here an eco-systemic frame puts humans back in their ecological place in data ecologies. Such a frame also produces new ways of working with and thinking about the human record embodied in digital cultural heritage.

## Digital cultural heritage as unruly ecological compositions

In order to re-work digital cultural heritage objects away from their human- and object-centred analytical point of attention, the first task is to extend the array of coordinates that constitutes what we call digital cultural heritage.[3] While the tendency is to understand digital cultural heritage ecologically as symbolic, as code, in terms of the human relationships that define and surround the digital, as digital media devices, systems, and processes, my aim here is to mobilize and bring together a wider composition of coordinates that more directly reflects the more-than-digital actualities of life itself.

Over the last 30 or more years, we have witnessed a fundamental societal shift in the way we think about, produce, work with, and engage digital data and media. This change is aligned with technical innovation (as argued in my previous discussion on objects), the desire to extend human capabilities and creative capacities, produce new commodities and use data for bureaucratic and monetary purposes. There is, however, a gap between the emerging realities of digital life and experience and the theories and practices of digital cultural heritage. In the early days, and prior to the internet, digital cultural heritage was viewed as a singular, isolated computational object comprising data, first as punch cards, then code saved on a carrier such as a floppy disc, CD or DVD. Digital cultural heritage was thought about according to a limited range of coordinates such as software and hardware, and routinely as a screenshot image.

With the development of multiple internets, superfast wi-fi connections, Web 2.0, the semantic web, extensive social networks, sophisticated search queries, personalization, and mobile applications, the emergence of different types of mobile devices, digital platforms, and media types such as Facebook, Twitter, Instagram, and Pinterest, there are now more complex forms of data production and connectivity. As technological capitalism has grown and the digital economy has expanded amidst the complexity and messiness of planetary computational infrastructures, the rise of automation and algorithmic governance, energetic systems, cloud computing and storage, more complex platform, financial, governance, and surveillance structures begin to cross sectors and scales. The destructive forces of data – through, for example, the mining of vast quantities of rare earths and metals (cobalt, gallium, indium, lithium, platinum, aluminium, tin, copper, palladium, silver) used in batteries, hard drives, displays, memory chips, electronic components and gold and solvents used in connectors, contacts and wire bonding to enable rapid internet connections, alongside toxic electronic waste dumps – have led to conflicts, resource depletion, environmental destruction across multiple life spans, and human rights violations.[4] As a consequence of coal and petroleum mining, fracking, and carbon pollution through the burning of fossil fuels to drive the digital economy, the advent of climate change, and the emergence of the Technosphere (a subsystem of the Anthropocene[5]) brought about by the evolution of technics, large-scale technology, media production becomes, according to media theorist Jussi Parikka, a question of geology.[6]

Smartphones for example, Parikka explains, comprise an array of geological extracts drawing from a wide range of the planet's resources and supported by a multiplicity of infrastructures.[7] The geological components in digital media devices include for example cobalt from Africa, zinc from Alaska extracted and refined into indium in Canada with other metals and minerals originating from Belgium, Russia, Peru, China, Congo, South Africa, and Malaysia. Here the non-human world previously described as Nature is enrolled in digital technical projects and infrastructures.[8]

In a digital economy directed to the scientific understanding and economic exploitation of all living and non-living matter under the imperative of capital accumulation, these more-than-digital ecologies create new material, contaminating conditions in the ruins of digital consumption and obsolescence.[9] At the same time these developments are also reorganizing social, geographical, economic, and political life as new types of ecologically implicated conditions and blurring distinctions between humans, other species, and earthly elements and processes.[10]

As a result, an ever-expanding array of coordinates and subjects enters the field of things we call digital cultural heritage, both born-digital and digitizations often mediated by AI, algorithmic culture and machine learning. Such intimate collaborations between digital media systems, technology, organic life, and geological matter enrol a whole host of new coordinates and forms of data and systems into the digital cultural heritage realm. The expansion of digital capitalism led to the financialization of new entities such as big data and the rise of new forms of labour all of which produce data. New forms of non-human energy sources derived from the sun, water and wind are enrolled in the digital cultural heritage composition in order to green their energetic systems. Nanotechnology, synthetic and more intelligent materials, bit innovation for smarter, faster computing, 3D printing, personalized and predictive medicine, robotics, computer vision, extended reality, stem cell research and so forth all become sources for more-than-human data and knowledge production.

The hyperbolic speed and the multi-scaled digital transformation of existing capabilities and the development of new ones wrought by the Covid-19 pandemic directed to allowing businesses, work, and life to continue in the face of distancing measures is changing the constitution of, and intensifies the emergence of, potential more-than-human heritage.

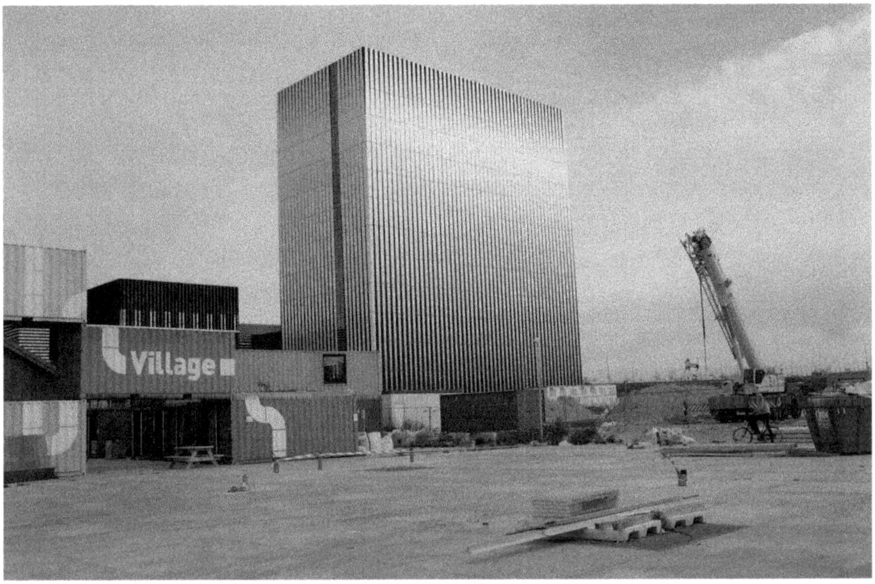


**FIGURE 5.1** Data Centre, Singapore, 2017.
Photo credit: Ned Rossiter.

This includes not only the radical increase in the production of data and the consumption of media but also more dynamic sophisticated augmented reality, robotic teaching and collaboration tools and platforms. This includes, for example, new and improved cloud technology, telehealth, genomic capabilities, 3D-printed surgical masks and Covid-19 tracing applications, entertainment such as cloud raves and online museums and heritage sites, alongside core technology supply chains, robotics, and drones for cleaning and delivery supported through fast 5G networks.

Digital cultural heritage in the making is at the same time brought down to earth, leading to even more devastating and irreversible environmental destruction as digital life intensifies. Alongside this, we witness the radical profusion and re-distribution of the agencies of digital cultural heritage as new relativities of scale, intensity and form alongside the uncertainties of their distribution, the creation of new job market conditions as the products of digital capitalism and the social and economic inequalities that derive from these processes and will continue to do so.

While it is acknowledged that computational infrastructures, media, and data have always operated in an ecological way, I expand on the notion of the ecological to construct a more radical and extensive account of digital cultural heritage within these ecological formations.

Digitizations and the born-digital can no longer be considered solely as singular bounded objects as they appear on an interface, as PDFs, as DVDs or as bits and bitstreams. Nor can they be seen as immaterial because of the almost instantaneous speed and lightness with which they appear and quickly disappear from our

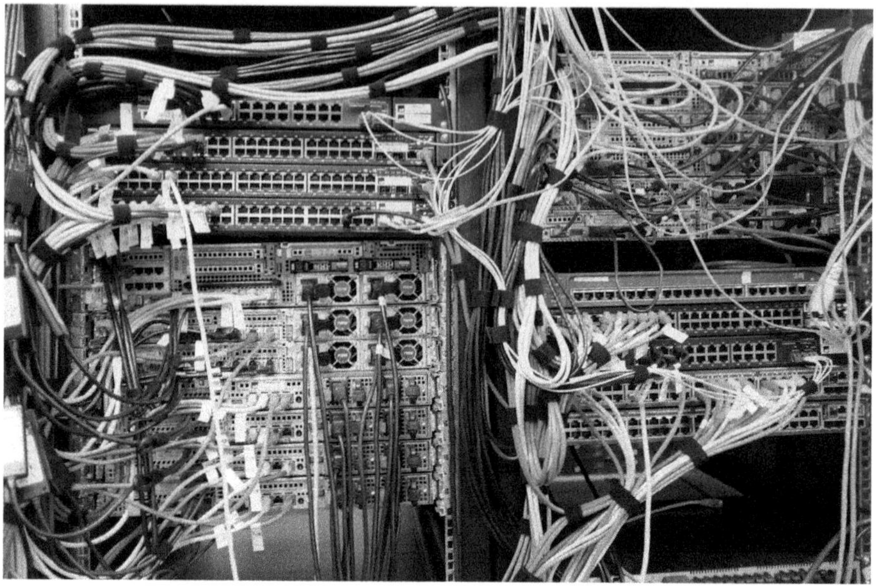

**FIGURE 5.2** Networked Servers in a Data Centre, Chile, 2017.
Photo credit: Ned Rossiter.

computer screens. They can no longer be considered solely as technical systems. Rather they must be imagined as borderless, radically interconnected, distributed, interoperable, self-organizing and often unpredictable and unknowable in their extent and effects.

Accordingly, digital data and, by implication, digital heritage can no longer be thought of as originating from a singular source in the same way we erroneously make reference to material objects in heritage practice. Digital cultural heritage is made up of different elements from many geographical regions. Through the extraction, harnessing, and culturing of the vital immanent qualities of metals, minerals, and chemicals, in computational design and infrastructures originating from many different geographical and spatial locations, digital cultural heritage is drawn into vast, deeper, and more complex ecologies of an inter-galactic scale to the earth's strata and life itself. Similarly, material objects have never originated from one point of origin, because they are made up of many different elements and materials and are the outcome of processes often rooted in human and other-than-human histories of deep time.

Given all this, digital cultural heritage objects originate from multiple geographical locations and arise from many influences. This array of coordinates includes: the authors of their software and the designers of hardware; the materials from which they are made; the global logistics and supply chains of materials and electronic waste in which they circulate and are embedded and their repurposing as scrap metals in their obsolescent afterlife to their unique domain addresses, text files, code, and electrical signals and from the highly mobile particles that comprise their energetic circuits of interoperability and to user inputs and interpretations and so forth. Identifying, sourcing, and capturing the so-called essence of a digital cultural heritage object is thus an impossible task because of the radical interconnectedness and interoperability of all these coordinates and processes, the addition of new inputs, functionalities, and capabilities as it circulates across vast scales all of which make it possible and active. We can never capture a whole object as digital preservation seeks to do because it is just too complex, dynamic, and emergent.

In light of all this, digital cultural heritage objects, both born-digital and digitizations, are made operable through the machine mediated by its own set of interactions and the processing of information, through user inputs and narratives, through algorithms, through energetic fields, through smart materials, chemical and material agencies, and through vast planetary computational systems. Digital cultural heritage on the internet therefore becomes open to and takes part in the world as it circulates across planetary scales in which these processes come together at multiple points and on many devices simultaneously. Curating, as I will describe later, must take account of these dispersed points of emergence.

Digital cultural heritage as data and digital media is therefore also made possible by and implicated in the rich embodied, enmeshed, and layered network of agencies. These agencies comprise the various concrete, geomaterial, energetic, physical, social, technical, machinic, and physiological forces described by media theorists such as Jussi Parikka, Friedrich Kittler, Wolfgang Ernst, Matthew Fuller, and Anna Reading[11] all of which operate across the interdependent layers of global computational infrastructures.

Media theorists Anna Reading and Tania Notley explain how digital hardware and software becomes contingent on the capitalist-driven, self-interested exploitative labour practices and global supply chains through which these objects are made and remade.[12] Digital cultural heritage therefore becomes implicated in destructive mining practices and the processing of the metals, chemical and raw minerals used in the making of hardware and software in Africa, the US, China, and Malaysia. Digital cultural heritage is also implicated in these supply chains and exploitative practices in which their components are made and recycled. Through the energy flows and infrastructures in which digital cultural heritage are produced, made operable and circulated, digital data and its infrastructures also become implicated in the damage caused to the atmospheric envelope through carbon burning practices used to make electricity. Taking the ecological complexity of digital cultural heritage into account, I compose new renderings of this type of heritage outside current conventions of what digital heritage is as code and as a list of formal characteristics and descriptors of their technical features and functions.

The digitization and the born-digital can no longer be considered as objects in a conventional sense. Rather they are new types of ecological compositions (even though they appear as coherent things) comprising what I call thingness (the multi-scaled, extensive, radically interoperable webs of heterogeneous coordinates, forces and agencies that comprise them). The variable coordinates that make up digital cultural heritage are so extensive that they interpenetrate human and non-human life itself. Digital cultural heritage therefore becomes an extended and dispersed spatial and temporal composition made up of diverse, conjoined and interacting vital elements. An ecological mode of thought draws our attention to environmental crises in which digital data and digital media[13] and therefore heritage are implicated. As a result, ecological thinking and the expansive range of coordinates that comprise these productions collapses the human-centredness of digital cultural heritage. Instead humans and digital cultural heritage operate within an ever-expanding field of coordinates and processes. Rather than thought of as completed historical entities, their histories are emergent.

To do this work I have been inspired in part by the thingly turn.[14] The thingly turn is a method used to explore object relations in an expanded field not only in terms of their end function.[15] Digital cultural heritage objects are viewed as technical productions of human cultural expression and practice but are not necessarily knowable in these finite terms. Standard object classifications, technical descriptors for digital preservation and the role of digital data as informational, as virtual objects or as bits offer certainty. They are the type of objects that we know, what we expect to encounter and what we can grasp conceptually within our own frameworks of understanding. Objects find their rightful place in heritage schemas. But as ecological compositions they are full of complexities and ambiguities. Objects are stable, able to be objectified. Digital cultural heritage are objects of a humanist heritage-centred world, but as ecological compositions they create a world of their own in collaboration with us. We meanwhile get caught up in their ecological complexity in multifarious ways. As ecological compositions they become integrated into our material encounters with the world, from the energetic and conductive capacities of earthly chemicals and metals, for example, to environmental destruction and to algorithmic manipulation.

Ecological compositions are no longer knowable in a conventional disciplinary and heritage sense. They operate in excess of what we call an object and become different types of dynamic and unique compositions, often appearing simultaneously in different locations and on many devices. The distinction between objects and ecological compositions can be characterized as a desire to curtail, manage, and classify data within the archive as opposed to their unfolding out in the world and therefore operating in experience.

Thinking about digital cultural heritage as ecological compositions and as thingness is reminiscent of German philosopher Martin Heidegger's proposition that our being in the world is of a thingly nature, because things are all relationally connected and function together.[16] While objects with their seemingly hard boundaries are conceived as separate from us, things are not. But Heidegger's and Brown's things and thingness operate as signifiers. They are still things that have substance, properties, and traits, but unlike objects they are formed through sense perceptions independent of the representational systems we impose on them. Thingly things however can't account for the inexplicable energy, vitality, and life forces constituted by the huge variety of more-than-human, non-human, and machinic agencies that comprise ecological compositions or their radical interoperability as congealing forces and the resulting affects. Nor do Heidegger's and Brown's things account for the different bundles of ecological, technical and human forms of sensing and calculation that emerge through the force fields generated by their coordinates.

The recruitment of digital data to concepts such as digital heritage still requires the object. When the bounded object or thing is called into question, thingness as the disclosure of and as a folding-out of its coordinates and agential processes can emerge. My thingness concept has the capacity to account for the infinite variety of coordinates present that describe the cosmos of physical, social, sensing, and practical experience that digital heritage inhabits, mobilizes, or is mobilized by. Drawing on French philosopher Etienne Souriau's notion of thingness, I put this concept to work to account for the extraordinary, unexpected occurrences or the appearance of things perceptible by the senses[17] but also formulate it in a different way to conceptualize the hidden and automated processes generated by an ecological composition's coordinates that are not necessarily discernible. The utility of thingness also draws our attention to the plasticity of its coordinates as they interact, their multiple intensities, tensions, different forms and states, and the intended and unintended consequences of their interrelatedness.

Here the coordinates that comprise digital cultural heritage are not just networks of discrete things, of digital code, of graphical interfaces, of file formats, computers, narratives and disciplinary perspectives. Their coordinates also include, for example, bits and software; geolocations; algorithms; programming languages; machines, infrastructures; cultural, political, spiritual, semiotic, and heritage values; human bodies, narratives, and inputs; technocapitalism; smart devices; materials; human and neural aesthetics; minerals; chemicals; eco-cognitive processes; energies of many kinds; mathematical equations; machine calculations and so forth. Accordingly, thingness progresses a renewed consideration of the coordinates hidden from view or rendered invisible, such as computational cognition.

Political theorist Jane Bennett's work draws our attention to the vibrancy of matter, the conative agencies and affects in every-day objects.[18] The object as an ecological composition however refers to acts of composing by its aggregating bundles of coordinates, made possible through its distributed performativity, its appearance as a coherent image, and the registers of sensing and influencing born out of an indefinable variety of conjoined material, mineral, chemical, discursive, energetic, social, human, non-human, natural, and cultural forces.[19] As ecological compositions, digital cultural heritage becomes fields of relatedness, embodied movement, and processes and represents a predilection for the assertion of its coordinates' own agencies and affective power in non-dialectical ways. Ecological compositions are therefore unique manifestations born out of their ecological processing. Because they are non-identical, as ecological compositions they resist our attempts to recruit them to conventional heritage concepts, conventional naming and description protocols. Accordingly, I suspend the notion that digital cultural heritage is, as UNESCO likes us to believe, identical in meaning and substance.

Detailing the properties and the form of the coordinates that make up digital cultural heritage therefore occurs in the context of their particular, unique

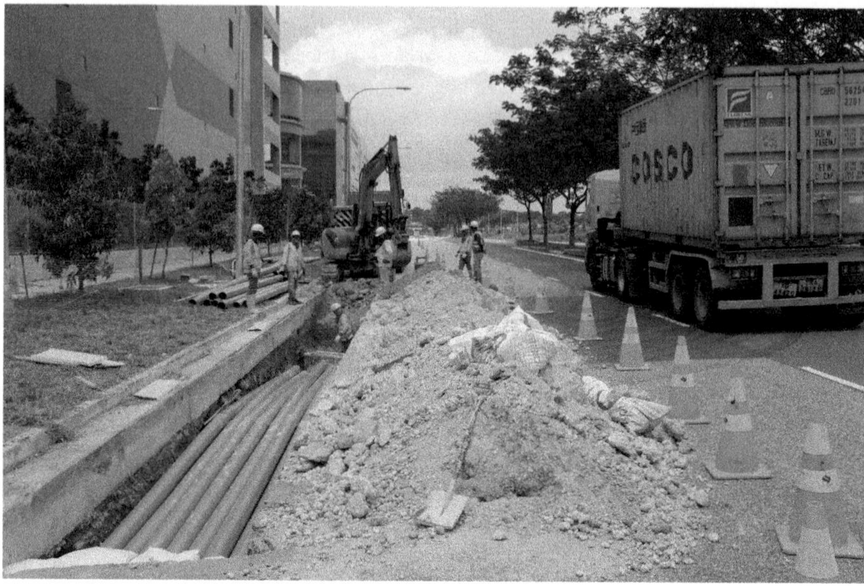


**FIGURE 5.3** Excavated Trench and Laying DSCF1536 Network Cabling for the Internet, Singapore, 2017.
Photo credit: Ned Rossiter.

ecological circumstances and through an onto-ethnographic reading of how they relate to each other. No two ecological compositions with their web of sprawling coordinates (thingness) are identical in form, substance, or meaning because each has its own unique coordinates and histories of relatedness.

As ecological compositions, their coordinates are difficult to categorize as either distinctly human, conceptual or ideational, technological, biological, or mineral, because they are radically interoperable. None has an independent existence; none is capable of being extracted into discrete things or objects.

Thingness also opens up a space to consider diverse renderings of digital data as machinic, as narrative, and as other-than-human. Its state of concrescence as a composition (appearing or sensed as a solid thing) originates from many locations and through many processes, often simultaneously. This is because thingness is distributed across multiple domains as a result of the emergent consequences of the interrelatedness of their unique coordinates acting in the world and on us across vast scalar, temporal, geographical, markets and technical domains. The ecological composition curates and distributes itself across great distances and conjoins with other points that act as switches and connectors with other compositions. Its extensive character is also made possible by multiple user inputs, the vast network of data storage facilities, and the electrical impulses that travel across and through wireless networks and expansive grids of undersea cables, and circulate through data centres.[20] Much digital cultural heritage therefore becomes planetary-scaled, distributed and dispersed, made and remade through its processing.

Thingness is post-relational because there is not a simple relational equivalence between all its coordinates, for example matter as quantum physicist Karen Barad suggests.[21] That is because, as ecological compositions, digital cultural heritage incorporate different types of embodied vitalities, from social and scientific knowledge practices, materialities, database, platform logics, bitstreams, embedded metadata that can't be explained simply in terms of a common substance such as matter.

The ecological composition also encompasses diverse modes of existence that incorporate a wider range of culturally inflected coordinates and meanings, as in the case of digitizations of Māori material culture (*taonga*, "treasured possessions") or Malagan funerary masks originating from New Ireland in Papua New Guinea as embodiments of their ancestors (discussed in Chapter 2).

The rendering of digital cultural heritage as ecological compositions and as thingness are also post-object concepts[22] because digitizations and born-digital cultural heritage objects in this frame are more dispersed and open-ended than conventional notions of the digital object. They are unique and emergent consequences of the interrelatedness of a series of different types of coordinates and their affordances comprising, for example, their unique materialities, meanings, aesthetics, politics, and technicities, including the inputs of curators and users that operate across scales. Those that reside on internets lack any inherent framing and are so dispersed, non-identical, and dynamic that they can no longer be thought of as a coherent object or a thing, even though they might appear so on the interface.

This post-object status also emerges out of an inter-operative mode of sensing. Code, for example, is not simple or pre-determined sets of logical instructions as might appear on a computer screen. Rather, it is performative and continually produced within and through thingness. For instance, computational processes are an operative mode of thinking that has no underlying organizational principles.[23] The ecological composition is more attuned to the notion of digital cultural heritage as an emergent gathering that concretely ties together heterogeneous coordinates but at the same time has no underlying organizational principles or object-like structure.

The application of the ecological composition and thingness concepts to digital cultural heritage acknowledges the latter as programmable things. These concepts capture their dispersed, non-identical character, their extended, multiple provenances and locational politics. At the same time, they draw our attention to their composition as made up of heterogeneous interdependent coordinates such as diverse human meanings and narratives, their multiple networked and energetic modalities, their emergence as multivalent compositions, their trans-medial, non-linear character, and their changing forms and combinations.

## Eco-curating and curatorial agency as domains of influencing

The born-digital and digitizations, comprising thingness and their gatherings as complex ecological (temporal-technical-material-political-energetic-anthropological) compositions, operate as a lively federation of coordinates. As entangled entities they exhibit multifarious temporal and spatial forms through their affordances (physical capacities to act in relation to and with each other), and as a result they are constantly forming and reforming. Here digital heritage is not separate from us; rather, due to its radical interoperability, all these things, including human curatorial practices, function in relation to each other.

But in the museum and digital heritage field, digital curating is generally viewed as an act of human, and more recently human–machine, agency. Tasks are directed to data capture, processes that seek to add value to digital data by assigning administrative, descriptive, structural, and technical archival metadata to them, and the storing of digital objects as software, hardware, and bits. The curatorial interpretation of digital data conforms to the notion of the informational object and its social constructivist and representational frames of understanding.

In the art field, curating and the term "curatorial agency" arose as concepts to progress a critical rethinking of curating contemporary art in culture and society as a series of acts directed towards changing the world.[24] No longer merely viewed as an author or presenter of pre-existing artistic concepts, the curator here is an active social agent who contributes to cross-referential understandings of art between different artistic, cultural, ethnic, class, and gender groups for the betterment of society.[25]

It is acknowledged that curatorial production has expanded with the development of the internet. Curation has moved from the single object to processes in dynamic networks and distributed through multiple agents such as technical networks and software.[26] In this frame, the politics of curating becomes systemic, at once human and technical.

As new types of ecological compositions, curating and curatorial agency (denoting acting in the world through selecting, organizing and influencing) take on a different meaning. Curating is no longer authorial in a conventional sense as a series of actions by humans or automated systems; it is also the result of the vitalities of more-than- and other-than-human coordinates together emerging as forms of eco-systemic curating.[27] Here the production of curatorial knowledge and the act of curatorial authorship by humans operate in collaboration with all manner of vital coordinates forming intermeshed alliances with them as a new type of curatorial eco-logic.

Curatorial agency emerges as eco-curatorial agencies. Curating enacted through diverse eco-curatorial agencies often consists of indeterminate acts of immanent or interdependent processing in formation made actionable through the interrelatedness and interoperability between, and performed by, a wider range of its coordinates. That is, from software, programming languages, mathematical equations, machine learning, and automated processes embedded in algorithms and bots to networks, infrastructures, and calculative storage processes, to elemental chemicals embedded in computational capacities; from bitstreams and data to data centres, to planetary computational infrastructures and the electromagnetic forms of transmission that pass through data centres, to the rare earth minerals that act as conductors of electricity. All these things produce their own eco-curatorial aggregations,

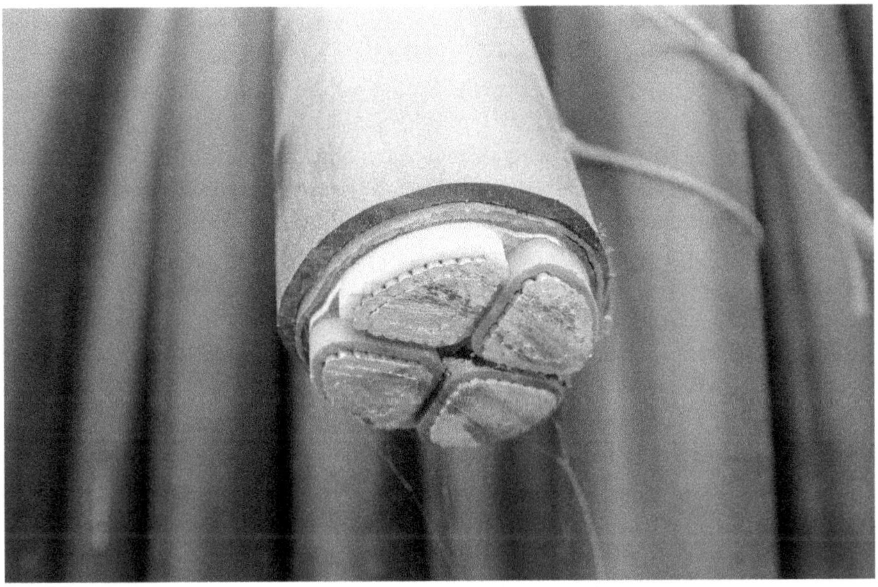

**FIGURE 5.4** DSCF2254 Electrical Cable, Data Centre, Malaysia, 2017.
Photo credit: Ned Rossiter.

different patterns of material, form, and performative affects. Their generative capacities also constitute extended spatial-temporal structures and material durational processes of self-assembling.

Ecological compositions, in their complexity and through the continuous and emergent interrelatedness between all their coordinates and processes of computational abstraction, cannot be separated from their biophysical complexity. Computational design today is founded in physical, biological and chemical processing, an assessment of their aggregate material properties, and the ways all these things can be harnessed to constitute more effective design solutions.[28] For example, a computer chip has 60 different chemical elements[29] all of which have their own agencies that alter and enter different types of intensive aggregated relationships. The compression of all these affordances and agencies into chips for example are used as calculative entities able to eco-curate at nanosecond speeds. As a consequence of these computational design solutions, curating is also performed via the physical, chemical, and biological processing embedded in its thingness. Together, all these eco-systemic processes contribute to the formation of an ecological composition's concrescence (the visual rendering of itself as a composition on the interface as opposed to a vision of concreteness as an emerging solid form) or acts as an entry point to enact certain roles and actions.

The extensive, broadened range of coordinates made possible through new computational design, through data processing to algorithms, through infrastructural expansion, for example, has distributed curating on a much larger and more expansive scale than we have ever seen before.[30] Such ecological webs and curating processes gesture to and make possible the extended reach and influencing capabilities of human actors across vast scales. I will discuss this in terms of Donald Trump's tweets in the following section.

Furthermore, new eco-curating agencies are constantly enrolled in the emerging and mutating ecological composition as it moves, extends, and composes itself. The addition of new user inputs and algorithmic processing, the expansion of infrastructures through the laying of cables, the development of platforms, and the enlargement of cloud storage, the ecological composition's appearance on multiple interfaces, devices, and screens, and the ever-multiplying practices of copying and distribution by all manner of agents all involve thousands of different eco-curatorial processes.

As ecological compositions, digital cultural heritage also self-curates in multifarious ways. These self-curating processes occur through, for example, the behavioural capacities of machine learning and calculations made possible by the biophysical properties of its coordinates, as well as through the contingency of environmental factors and through curatorial and user interactions in which they are enmeshed across and through its extended composition.

Curating in an eco-sense can never be fully determined due to the nature of its complexity, due to inconsistencies in interactions, and due to the indeterminacy of calculations made through machine learning. Eco-curatorial actions never perform the same set of interactions and therefore are never identical and cannot be replicated.

As a result of eco-curatorial acts, new types of eco-cognitive processes emerge. Just like curatorial agency, cognition is not just human. The collective capacities of vastly different forces, coordinates, and affects harnessed through computational design, such as the multiple and indeterminate potentialities, capacities, dynamics, and contingencies of material and computational physical, biological, chemical, and energetic behaviour described by media theorist Luciana Parisi[31] (including human intent and desire), form part of distributed, aligned eco-cognitive processes and affects. The human user still has their own agency and their own unique cognitive capacities when authoring or interacting with data, but these agencies and cognitive processes operate alongside all of its other coordinates.

These multifarious eco-cognitive, thinking, and sensing processes emerge as the multiplicity of milieus, localities, temporal and spatial generative emergent patterns and forms, thereby opening digital cultural heritage up to the indeterminate and unknown or indeed the unknowable. Intelligence is not just human or machine. Intelligence is reworked variously as automated reason, as the behaviour of materials in computational design[32], as the writing of code and algorithmic processes alongside their capacity to change, self-organize, and direct action in certain ways.

Ecological forms of intelligence, power, and meaning-making emerge as affective domains of influencing. For example, as media theorist Elena Esposito explains, the actions of the intelligent human feed on user profiles and contributions and exploit them, and the system returns or produces affects often in an unrecognizable form or in a surprising way.[33] Searches for the movie *300: Rise of an Empire* portraying the battle of Thermopylae between the Persians and Spartans in 480 BC on Google, for example, returned a link to the Project 300 website (discussed in detail in Chapter 2). While we know how some elemental materials behave because they are used in computational design, other agencies and cognitive processes remain elusive. Therefore, eco-curating processes, eco-cognition and resulting eco-intellectual affects generally will stay indeterminate and to a degree contingent.

Digital cultural heritage is therefore no longer solely a question of digital materiality. As ecological compositions, the analogue, born-digital, and digitizations are called into being in self-differencing ways that cannot be explained simply in terms of differences in materiality. And in a vital frame, heritage more generally emerges in plural and self-differencing forms, thereby replacing formal divisions based on substances such as digital, intangible, and material heritage. By viewing heritage as ecological compositions and as self-organizing ontological processes, these become equal both in the way they are described and how they might be valued. Here, each born-digital or digitization is characterized by its distinctive ecological coordinates and circumstances, rather than being seen as bounded domains of things, whether materially or conceptually.

Diversifying the range of coordinates that comprise digital thingness and therefore the ecological composition exceeds what we currently view as heritage. As ecological compositions, digital cultural heritage operates in excess of human system meanings, habits or projects, or indeed of what we have the ability to comprehend or know. As a knowledge and curatorial practice, the ecological composition itself, its collection and documentation will always be impartial, contingent, multiple, and never completed.

The aim here is not to treat concepts, the ecological composition, and thingness as better reflections of reality or more objective ways to standardize digital collections, as many new approaches seek to do. Rather these concepts operate as both a mode of thought and empirical experimental practice.

## The American Airlines 11 digital jump seat belt as an ecological composition

To empirically illustrate how the refiguration of digital cultural heritage as an ecological composition can be applied to heritage practice, I work with the American Airlines 11 digital jump seat belt. I work with it not as a digitization, nor as a digital record of its analogue source as a form of commemoration that helps us reflect, but as a unique creative work with its own set of coordinates and ecological contingencies.

At the National Museum of American History, the digital seat belt and its so-called surrogate are interpreted and narrated according to a conventional human-centred historical account of the events surrounding the fate of American Airlines Flight 11:

> On September 11, 2001, 19 Islamic extremists, following a highly coordinated plan, hijacked four commercial jet liners and attempted to fly them into four separate buildings. American Airlines Flight 11, a Boeing 767 bound to Los Angeles from Boston, was crashed into the north tower of the World Trade Center at 8.46am. All 76 passengers, eleven crew members, and five hijackers were killed. United Airlines Flight 175, another Boeing 767 bound to Los Angeles from Boston, was crashed into the south tower of the World Trade Center at 9.03am. All 51 passengers, nine crew members, and five hijackers were killed.[34]

The same narrative is attributed to both the analogue and the digital; thus the latter is regarded as simply informational and merged in meaning and affect with the "real" seat belt. But both forms of the jump seat belt are given heritage status because they are considered worth saving and passing on.

Each of these forms is much more than a narrative of human history or a description of the originals' semiotic, aesthetic, utilitarian, and use contexts, components, materials, and manufacturing process, or as an end in itself, as seen in heritage culture. The digital seat belt is no longer simply the transfer of analogue data from protons to pixels and then into digital data comprising zeros and ones. As an ecological composition it comprises a diverse array of human and non-human coordinates and processes.

Both the analogue source and the digitization, each as an ecological composition in its own right, have their own unique vital histories. They are at the same time related in many ways. Each has its own presence. The analogue is perceived as more tangible and tactile than its digitization. Both the analogue and digital jump seat belt share many coordinates and ecological affects. These include the physical and chemical properties of the aircraft fuel and its explosive characteristics, the intentions and actions of Mohammed Atta and associates, the impact of American Airlines 11, the release of energy and subsequent heat, burning, and death, the collapse of the Twin Towers, and the recovery of the analogue and its inclusion in the National Museum of American History 9/11 museum collection. For the digitization, all these things are mediated by 3D cameras and digital data and made visible through their emergence as a visualization.

As a so-called surrogate of the analogue, the digital seat belt is entangled – like its analogue source – in the real world, in which emotions such as fear and grief, and values such as patriotism, tie the two together, even though their material and technical coordinates differ. The digitization in its emergence, like the analogue, is an object for human contemplation and works alongside human goals and aspirations in memorializing and preserving the 9/11 event. At the same time the digitization distributes itself through eco-curatorial networks.

Thingness describes the vast, rich, dense, multi-directional entangled array of coordinates in motion that comprise the digital seat belt and make it operable. Here its coordinates are not just networks of digital code, of graphical interfaces, or of file formats, computers, cultural, political, semiotic and heritage values, human narratives and inputs. The coordinates that make up its sprawling ecological composition also include geolocations, algorithms, planetary infrastructures, smart devices, materials, human and neural aesthetics, minerals, chemicals, water, light and so forth. It also comprises eco-cognitive processes of many kinds, not only human cognition and emotions but also mathematical equations, machine calculations, electromagnetic fields, and the sensing capacities of metals, chemicals and minerals, among others.

The digital seat belt's technological coordinates, some of which are interdependent with the analogue source, include digital cameras, light and recording devices used in its making such as laser scanning and photogrammetry, and the aluminium, fabric and the toxic dust that comprise its analogue state imprinted visually as digital code. Other shared coordinates integral to the digital and analogue seat belts' emergence include the company American Airlines, the type of aircraft, a Boeing 767–223ER, Logan International Airport, Boston, Massachusetts, the airport from which UA 11 departed, the World Trade Center, the North Tower floors 93–99, and its steel support trusses, the time and date of 8:46:40 on September 11, 2001, velocity, the impact of the crash, burning jet fuel, the collapse of the North Tower 102 minutes after impact, and the pulverization of glass, wallboard, paper, concrete, and asbestos.

Research methods and measuring instruments central to the emergence of both include spectrometry and microscopes for measuring hot spots and the composition of dust.

The digital seat belt also comprises its own unique set of technological coordinates and eco-systemic processes. These include electrical circuits and wireless energy, interfaces and interfacial images, computer screens, keyboards, hard drives, algorithms, cables, server farms, and coal-fired electricity stations.

Within this framing, the natural coordinates shared with the analogue include Ground Zero, the terrain central to the event and preceding it and the construction of the jump seat belt as a heritage item from the effects of air pressure, from materials such as silicon, aluminium, lead, zinc, and copper, from the inferno that followed and from pulverizing building materials and the resultant dust clouds. All of these coordinates shaped the field and recovery efforts. The digital seat belt's unique coordinates include the material, mineral, and chemical elements embedded in computational design.

Human coordinates and their respective agencies include the persons mediating the circumstances and occasion of the event, emotional responses to the seat belt, and its production as digital data. All these things included the creative acts of computer programmers, the pilots, flight crew, air traffic controllers and passengers, Mohammed Atta and the five hijackers, suicide, dying and death, human remains, journalists, firefighters and recovery teams, and emotions such as horror, fear, grief, sadness, and pain. Political figures integral to the seat belt's emergence include President George W. Bush, New York Mayor Rudy Giuliani, the FBI, Al-Qaeda, Osama Bin Laden and so forth.

The respective seat belt's ideological coordinates include the material, materializing, and narrative agency of the ideological mediators integral to the event, from the Twin Towers as symbols of US power; Islamist independence and state building; patriotism, hate crimes, and discrimination against Muslim and Middle Eastern communities.[35]

The theoretical and policy coordinates underpinning the event, its aftermath, and its heritagization include the agencies of US foreign policy such as support for Israel and military presence in the Middle East, economic power through the desire to control the oil fields in Iraq and Saudi Arabia, racial profiling, aircraft safety procedures, including the 9/11 Commission Report on the terrorist attacks on the US.[36]

Heritage coordinates shared by both the analogue and digital, although in qualitatively different ways, include the National Museum of American History as an institutional context, the analogue's accession and its digital copying, the framing of the analogue and digital seat belts as testimony to and evidence of the attack, and as forms of memorialization, and heritage, the latter as an informational surrogate. This list, although not exhaustive, represents the coordinates and relations that precede and succeed their respective emergence.

The making of the seat belt's digitization and its emergence as an ecological composition comprise a mesh of human, more-than- and other-than-human acts of eco-systemic curating. Its emergence through its production involves human acts of composing particular fields of interrelatedness, including the capturing strategy and scanning technology involved, decisions about lighting, colour, size, and scale, how best to capture the texture of the dust on the belt, the post-production composition, and the choice of software for viewing and editing.

Akin to techniques of pastiche, these acts of eco-curation are mediated by all manner of coordinates. These processes include digital cameras, the location of their making through the scanning equipment involved and through measurements, mathematical equations, laser beams, patterns of light, particles, electromagnetic waves, sensors, and through the creation of data sets used in the making of 3D images and pixels, and the analogue as its prototype. It is these inputs, alongside the creator's visual and conceptual engagement with the process, that bring its interfacial image into a visual approximation with its analogue to replicate the informational, aesthetic, and political effects of its source.

The digital seat belt in active process and its emergence as an interfacial image are curated by its coordinates through their interoperability; they comprise a series of tight interdependencies, aggregations and sequences, each with their own variable temporalities, duration, and presence. Some coordinates and eco-curating processes, for example its technical components, are more critical to its process of composing than others. The thingness aggregations that enable the digital seat belt to be made operable include particles and fields, the mediation of silicon and metal, circuit boards, operating systems, and binary code, and signals generated by the values of voltage and the operation of logic gates. At the level of programming they are text files, algorithms, electromagnetic fields, media elements, bitstreams, images, shapes, and behaviours represented as collections of discrete samples (pixels, polygons, voxels, characters, and scripts) composing into larger-scale compositions through database logics and transactional metadata interactions, computer graphical user interfaces, and platforms, and via automation dynamically generated by user-defined queries, pre-programmed interactions, and software agents. Their reach, effects, and complexity are scaled up when launched on the internet. For example, interactions with digital devices and computational processes that enable the digital seat belt to appear also comprise the interoperability of calculable and predictive entities such as sensors, robots, algorithmic automations, internet domains, cables, data centres and server farms, electronic circuits, and between storable data, rare earth minerals that conduct electricity devices such as computers and smartphones. Their state of concrescence as machine- and human-readable through the interface alongside heritage categorizations, cultural perspectives and emotive responses are also powerful coordinates central to their emergence.

The digital jump seat belt in its composing mode is enabled by the flows of materials, minerals, chemicals embedded in computational design, electromagnetic fields, and information mediated through infrastructures such as cables and data centres. The digital jump seat belt is therefore part ideological, part textual, part technological, part narrative, part thought, part economic, part flesh, part mineral, part chemical, part computer code, part cultural belief, part geographical, part elemental process, part infrastructure, and part heritage.

The relatedness of these coordinates cannot be extracted from their interoperable dependencies as they form the very conditions of the digital seat belt's concrescence as an interfacial image. Some thingness coordinates are more human, such as the feelings of grief elicited by the visualization of the seat belt, whereas some thingness is less so, such as the effects of fire, pulverizing building materials, dust clouds and the chemical and elemental coordinates embedded in its design and technological infrastructure.

Here the seat belt accrues a post-object status as multiple ecological compositions of formed and forming thingness. Digital heritage is therefore no longer solely sociological, nor does it share a common technical constitution. Each time the seat belt emerges in its form-like concrescence, it produces itself as unique patterns of resemblance and variation. The digital seat belt appears in different locations and on different devices through different routing, hardware, software, and infrastructures, travelling across and through other coordinates mediated by cables, data centres, particles, and energetic impulses. When it is active rather than at rest, the digital seat belt operates as continuous processes of interoperability that may never be completed, or circumscribed beforehand.

The emergence of its interfacial image and associated emotional responses to it are made possible through the interoperability of its coordinates that come together where

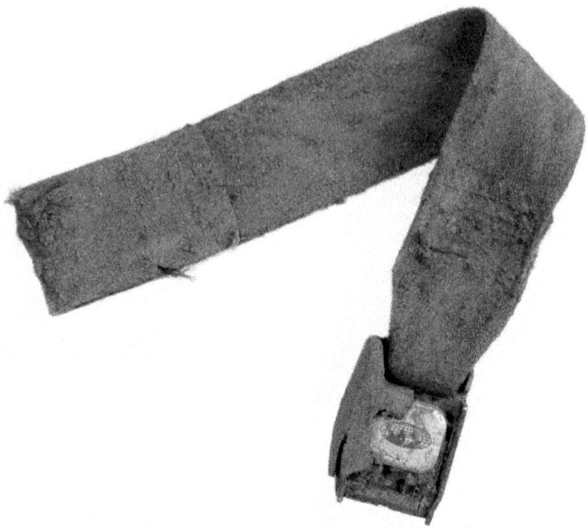

**FIGURE 5.5** American Airlines 11 jump seat belt.
Photo credit: Division of Political and Military History, National Museum of American History, Smithsonian Institution.

the interfacial image of seat belt appears, either momentarily or for a longer period of time. As a result, people are drawn together into particular relations with other-than-human coordinates that have the potential to reconfigure human relations, emotions, and action in both obvious and not-so-obvious ways. For example, the digital jump seat belt's material, technical coordinates, their properties and eco-curating processes such as the shuttling of digital code back and forth to produce its machine- and human-readable visualization, are radically interoperable with human and ideological coordinates and emotions such as horror, fear, grief, and patriotism. But the digital seat belt's emotive or interpretive coordinates for one person might be replaced by a different gathering of thingness for others – an exemplar of Islamic self-determination, for example.

While its human aesthetic and deep learning aesthetic are qualitatively different things and processes, they are deeply interoperable, producing different sensing effects. For example, the interfacial concrescence of the digital seat belt inflects a human aesthetic, as one that induces fear and grief, a deep unsettling. On the other hand, an aesthetic emerges of what data does that reflects the operations behind it, as a result of its machinic capacities comprising a deep network of neural layers that enables its interfacial concrescence to emerge.

Having said all this, heritage temporality is suspended. The temporal reframing of digital heritage objects occurs when we make the shift from an object-centric disposition to that of the ecological composition. Rather than the jump seat belt acting as a fixed artefact representative of and commemorative of the event, as an ecological composition the past, present and future mix and merge. This temporal shift occurs and is mediated through a consideration of the vitality of its thingness and its eco-systemic curating processes: its coordinates, their histories of emergence, their interrelatedness, their interoperability, and their sequencing.

Archaeologist Ian Hodder in examining the things that he finds in the field argues that "biologies, technologies, societies, cultures, our psychologies and cognition all flow from the past, often the deep past."[37] In respect to digital cultural heritage as ecological compositions, its coordinates, our human-ness and human agency, the technologies we use, the societies and cultures that we inhabit, our psychological dispositions and cognitive processes alongside the non-human material, chemicals, energetic fields embedded in computational design all emerge from multifarious pasts and deep geological times. All the digital and analogue seat belt coordinates, those they share and their own, embody memory traces like genetic instructions, human and non-human histories and residue embedded into their DNA that replicates and changes and operate as multiple, non-linear, enfolding and unfolding temporalities.

The memory traces embedded within their respective thingness include the history of the production of the fabric, the invention of metallurgy and material processing in prehistory, the discovery of their geological affordances, the development of mining technology, and the mining and processing of minerals such as copper long buried emerging in geological time. Other convergent histories include the invention of aircraft in the early 1900s and the production of the Boeing 767–223ER, the design and structure of the metal trusses, the US War of Independence and the rise of American patriotism, the notion of heritage in the 19th century, the invention of computers, and the writing of digital code. The invention of the computer and cameras, for instance, are prior technological achievements.

The digital composition represents a mixture of coordinates that are not only historically and spatially distant and prior but are also futuring in their emergence. For example, these meshes of thingness extend into the future as forms of memorialization, as a means of directing future digitization projects, as platforms to support digital cultural heritage, and as a testament to the "attack on America" and therefore contributing in some way to the War on Terror and the rise of Daesh (Islamic State). Rather than being viewed as a capacity located in human thought, action, and semiotics, power becomes distributed across the ecological composition's heterogeneous field as dense eco-systemic and curating processes of interrelatedness and interoperability. Although always dependent on one another, the coordinates and their interactions are also always unequal and variable in intensity and affect – for example, the affordances of planes as weapons as opposed to the weakness of the steel trusses.

Digital cultural heritage objects as ecological compositions become biographical, but not in the sense of attributing human narrative qualities to them. While their biographies still comprise human interpretive narratives, they are also the result of the independent agencies that operate outside human concerns, that is, through their more-than-human curatorial processes they create categories and temporalities of their own. Critically, digital heritage can therefore be framed in a world according to multiple, non-linear, and overlapping interpretations of their thingness and read as the consequences of things' affects, as the history of what came before, and as serendipitous outcomes.

Interpretation is no longer merely sociological but involves the detailing of the coordinates, observations of eco-systemic curating processes as the interrelatedness with and between other coordinates, their affordances, qualities, affects, and compositional status, and their history as the performance of these dynamic processes. As a result, as ecological compositions they can be made subject to emergent modelling for the purposes of documentation (to be explained in Chapter 6). Their more-than- and other-than-human histories can therefore be written differently as thingness, as entanglements, as processes, and as emergent.

As ecological compositions, they exhibit different types of agential, interrelated interdependencies depending on whether the focus is on materiality, such as chemical reactions (petroleum, fire, and toxic dust), on digital code, their symbolic or religious affordances (US patriotism and Islamist self-determination), their narrative affordances (history of the event), or the human virtual (thoughts or emotions, e.g., fear and grief).

## Donald Trump's tweets as ecological compositions

In Chapter 1 I introduce the tweeting activity of former President Donald Trump as a new form of heritage in the making. Trump's use of Twitter raised his profile in the 2016 US presidential primaries, enabling him to secure the Republican nomination and the presidency.

Trump's tweets as official records of his presidency are born-digital heritage, because they are viewed as historical data that must be saved in perpetuity by virtue of the Presidential Records Act (PRA) of 1978.[38] The Act stipulates that documents of administrative, historical, informational, or evidentiary value cannot be disposed of or destroyed without the written permission of the archivist because they must be kept for future reference and for political accountability.[39] This includes records created digitally from posts made on Facebook, Twitter, and YouTube, and electronic communication such as email.

Debates in regard to the standing of Trump's tweets as heritage focus on whether original or altered tweets should become the archived record. One hundred days into his presidency, Trump had put out 517 tweets and deleted 11 of them.

> After a misspelled statement from Mr Trump's private Twitter account was altered on Saturday (local time) and later deleted, archives spokeswoman Miriam Kleiman said presidential tweets, like all electronic communications "created or received" by the president or his staff, were considered presidential records… Mr Trump wrote on his private Twitter account: "I am honered (sic) to serve you, the great American People, as your 45th President of the United States." The tweet was later corrected to "honored", the correct American spelling, and then later removed entirely.[40]

At the time of writing this book, Trump's administration was required to keep all tweets, including those from his official White House and private Twitter accounts.[41] In doing so, Trump also preserved his own digital data.[42] Within the context of the Act's jurisdiction, Trump's tweets became elevated to the status of heritage even before they are interred in the archive. They are historical data in the making.

Trump's tweets most succinctly demonstrate the operation of born-digital cultural heritage as vast, sprawling ecological compositions made up of multi-scaled and meta-territorial domains of influencing of infinite reach and depth. Through their interoperability, Trump's tweets appear as interfacial images simultaneously in multiple locations through digital devices, and in doing so incite real world, material effects.

Trump's plan to assert his authority through data regimes was based on the premise that millions of people are connected by smartphones and computers, receiving and generating large quantities of digital data. His tweets are viewed as digital speech acts intended to capture hearts and minds, claim sovereignty and mobilize power through digital networks. Here, and within this framework, Trump is centre stage and through his tweets the world becomes subject to his politics via the distribution of his opinions and agendas across large distances and scales.

Accordingly, Trump's tweets were intended to play an important role in his efforts to restructure global fields of power and knowledge, assert influence, and drive action according to his own agendas. With 37 million followers (an estimated half of whom are simply social bots or the tweets of click farmers), Trump sought to bolster his support through automated means, and through the exploitation of low-paid workers.

Trump's tweets are economic, political, and social investments directed towards national and global sovereignty in which social bots, angry US and Mexican citizens, heads of state, and North Korean ballistic missiles gather and take strong positions. They were Trump's attempts to refashion relationships between people and states activated through an interconnected mesh of people, technologies, smartphones, data, algorithms, words, and so forth.

The political potential of Trump's tweets is realized at the very moment they are made machine and human readable, appearing in their concrescence as visible "objects" on the interface and therefore able to accrue power. In doing so, Trump's politics, mediated through his tweets, sought to interrupt relations between the US and other nation states, such as Mexico, Iran, and North Korea. Actions included attempts to build a wall between the US and Mexico to stop illegal immigration, re-investment in American manufacturing, the closure of borders to migrants from Muslim countries, and attempts to put a stop to North Korea's nuclear weapon program.

While Twitter is thought of as a field of data production, Trump's tweets are far more than socio-technical arrangements of humans and machines. Nor are they merely representative of his acts of governing or solely the outcome of what media

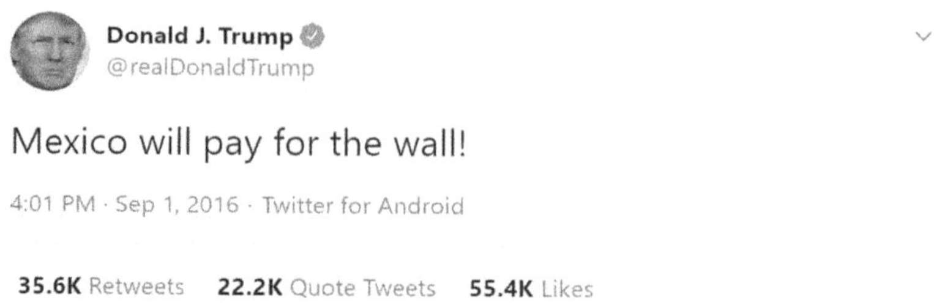


**FIGURE 5.6** President Donald Trump's tweet, "Mexico will pay for the wall." September 1, 2016 via Twitter.

theorists Evelyn Ruppert, Engin Isin and Didier Bigo call data politics in which his speech acts would be constituted merely as an object of power and influence.[43] As ecological compositions, his tweets were used to articulate political questions and acts of authority. Significantly here, Trump's tweets are not only his own curatorial acts and opinions, they are made possible through processes of eco-systemic curating involving many vital coordinates with their own capacities for involvement in political action, that they in turn enable.

Trump's tweet of September 1, 2016, "Mexico must pay for the wall," emerges from many different coordinates and their interoperability. As a digital data set, it comprises textual characters, usernames, timestamps, unique identifiers, links to URLs on the web, metadata, APIs (application programming interfaces), abstracted patterns of zeros and ones that shuttle between storage and the display of that data as his speech acts appearing on technical devices such as computers and smartphones.

But these compositions are also political, historical, and material of a qualitatively different kind. They comprise technological coordinates through the relatedness of infrastructure such as equipment, cables, routers, data servers, data farms, wireless communications, switches, devices such as computers and smartphones, and wireless communications bounded together by a binary machine code of zeros and ones, as well as automated systems such as algorithms and social bots. In addition, they include human coordinates, such as Trump himself, designers, programmers, engineers, citizens, nation states, Mexican citizens, and archivists.

Trump's tweets also comprise natural coordinates such as the terrain central to the event, the US/Mexican border, but also embody a geophysical politic. Media and its waste, Parikka convincingly argues, becomes entangling as an earthly computing nature through its material substrates. This includes the exploitation of the resources of the Earth's crust through the mining of earth minerals and chemicals used in their production, geopolitics, the search and acquisition of energy sources to drive the economy and the grim labour in the factories of computational production.[44] Trump's tweets therefore as earthly computational entities comprise natural coordinates that are also themselves inherently political in quite unexpected ways. This includes the silicon, ferrous metals, zinc, and copper extracted from the ground used to conduct electrical currents and that comprise the hardware, software, media devices, and infrastructures through which his tweets were received, the consequences of environmental destruction through mining across the globe from the Congo to Brazil, resulting in resource conflicts, the complicity between the materials in Trump's iPhone, the working conditions and the health problems of workers who made it at Foxconn, Zhengzhou, China to the contaminating conditions in US e-waste dumps in China where devices in their afterlife leak toxic elements into the soil. Trump's tweets are also implicated in the politics of the global logistical supply chains that mobilize all these things, the burning of oil and coal in US electricity plants producing energy, to distribute his tweets and cool the data centres through which they circulate, and their resulting emissions.

Further, his tweet of September 1, 2016 includes policy coordinates that underpin the tweet, the desire to curb immigration from Mexico. Economic coordinates central to the ecological composition are made visible through reference made to the financial resources required to build the wall. Most importantly, his tweets comprise ideological coordinates, Trump's desire to "make America great again." On the other side, Mexico's sovereignty was perceived as at stake, and President Enrique Peña Nieto took Trump's tweet as an insult:

> With just a few strokes of the pen on Wednesday, the new American president signed an executive order to beef up the nation's deportation force and start construction on a new wall between the nations. Adding to the perceived insult was the timing of the order: It came on the first day of talks between top Mexican officials and their counterparts in Washington, and just days before a meeting between the two countries' presidents... The action was enough to prompt President Enrique Peña Nieto of Mexico to consider scrapping his plans to visit the White House on Tuesday... "I regret and condemn the United States' decision to continue with the construction of a wall that, for years now, far from uniting us, divides us...[45]

Hence, Trump's tweets as ecological compositions are part ideological, part textual, part political, part policy, part technological, part economic, part mineral, part computer code, part program, part elemental, and part algorithm.

Trump's tweets, through eco-curating processes and the domains of influencing that emerge as a result of them, create what Bratton calls geoscapes,[46] contested terrains that are resoundingly fractious and potentially dangerous. His tweet of December 22, 2016 threatening to expand US nuclear capabilities unless North Korea curbed its own nuclear program prompted the emergence of a particular set of relations, events, and a milieu characterized by heightened tensions between the US and North Korea that could have led to war but thankfully did not.

This geoscape was in part formed through the circulation of Trump's plans, projections, claims, ideologies, and aspirations and made actionable through more-than- and other-than-human domains of influencing. These actions were on one hand planned by Trump to further his own political aspirations, but they also had unintended consequences. Chillingly, the use of intimidation and fear becomes a power of affect within and across these domains of influencing.

Trump's statement was written into data, made actionable through computer programs and algorithms, search engine results, as socio-cultural-technical-material computational environments and infrastructures and the minerals, metals, and chemicals embedded in the media that compose them made possible by designers and engineers. Accordingly, these eco-curating acts emerge as different registers of action, as the affectual, the calculative, the automatic, the non-conscious, and the conceptual as a series of interdependencies inciting real-world material affects.

Machine and non-human curating also produce different types of eco-cognitive processes and politics outside Trump's control because all these things curate.[47] Trump is no longer the only author of his tweets. Rather, communication becomes radicalized through multiple cognitive agents where a different communicative and relational-sense culture emerges not just through technical, network processes or infrastructures or machine learning but through the eco-curating interrelatedness and the ensuing actions of all its coordinates.

Eco-cognitive processes enacted by thingness coordinates such as neural networks, machines, algorithms, automations, and artificial intelligence operate together at indeterminate speeds changing sequences of operations and at the same time processing data through calculation, through recording, and through reflecting. In doing so they multiply their own contingencies producing their own forms of calculative intelligence and structures. All of these processes represent the eco-extension of cognition into the world across multiple locations and scales, at times simultaneously. It is never completed or fixed; it is vast, indeterminable, uneven, and sometimes chaotic.

New forms of digital communication and machinic automated thoughts and memory emerge based on the quantification of data from which new capacities for power and manipulation arise. Trump harnessed these capacities to promote his politics. The subsequent chains of events illustrate how these domains of influencing operate in directing real-world consequences.

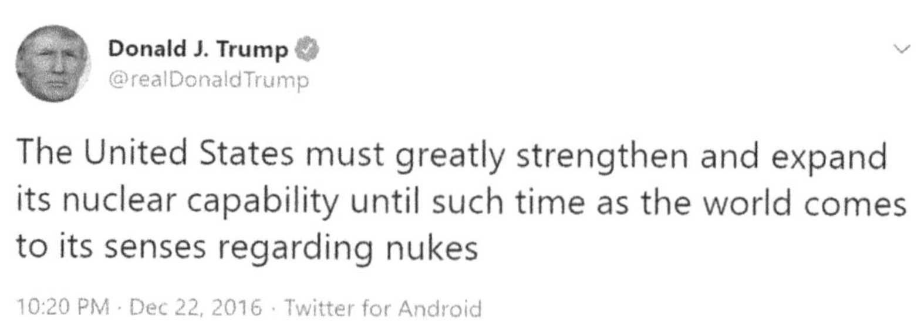


**FIGURE 5.7** President Donald Trump warns North Korea about their development of long-range ballistic missiles, February 12, 2017 via Twitter.

In a New Year's Day speech and in response to Trump's tweet of December 23, 2016, North Korean President Kim Jong Un warned that North Korea was preparing to launch an intercontinental ballistic missile (ICBM). He asserted that the nation would continue to build its nuclear capability for "pre-emptive strikes" unless the US ended naval exercises with South Korea. Perceived as a threat to Washington D.C. and the Federal government, Kim Jong Un's remarks prompted an angry response from Trump on January 2, 2017 with an implied threat that North Korea will be prevented from developing a nuclear weapon capable of reaching U.S. soil.

Following this, the North Korean state media announced on Sunday February 12, 2017 that it had successfully completed the launch of a new ballistic missile:

> The Pukguksong-2, previously unpublicized part of its arsenal which North Korean state media described as a medium long-range ballistic missile, was test fired on Sunday under the supervision of North Korean leader Kim Jong Un, according to North Korea's Korean Central News Agency, KCNA. ... The agency described the missile as a "Korean style new type strategic weapon system."[48]

A US official reported that the missile launched from North Pyongan province travelled 500 km (310 miles) before landing in the Sea of Japan.[49]

Crucially, this event occurred at the very moment Trump was entertaining the Japanese prime minister, Shinzo Abe, at his Palm Beach club, Mar-a-Lago. The bizarre sequence of events that followed was reported by Eliot Weinberger in the *London Review of Books*:

> Interrupted by news of a North Korean missile launch, Trump chose to display his presidential power to the wowed and tweeting club regulars by holding an emergency security meeting at the restaurant table. Aides used their cell phones as flashlights to read classified documents while waiters served entrees over the papers. One member even posted a selfie ("Wow!") with, he wrote, "Rick", the guy who follows the president with the "football" – the briefcase carrying the nuclear codes. Luckily, the missile landed harmlessly in the ocean before dessert.[50]

At the same time the investor, actor Richard DeAgazio, posted pictures from Mar-a-Lago showing President Donald Trump and his entourage conducting their security meeting over wine and dessert.

Many different registers of narrative, calculation, sensing, and action emerged as multi-directional and scaled domains of influencing, including those arising from the non-linguistic and machinic, the human, more-than-human, and other-than-human such as chemicals' and minerals' affective capacities. Through eco-systemic curating processes, their effects, often self-organizing, became folded into meaning-making and the real-world consequences that subsequently emerged.

These include the words of Trump on December 22, 2016 as textual characters; digital data emerging through computer display; and their mediation through quartz and silicon ferrous metal, electrical currents, data servers, and cables. The ecological composition was made actionable and drew in material things and events such as nuclear bombs, the building of nuclear capability, an enraged North Korea and the words of President Kim Jong Un on January 1, 2017, the launch of an intercontinental ballistic missile and North Korean military bases, North Pyongan province, metal and split atoms; the time and date February 12, 2017; the Sea of Japan; and the meeting of Trump and Abe at the beach club, Mar-a-Lago.

Trump's tweets, although earmarked as heritage, continue to be produced, and operate as live data, and as emergent in the world. This challenges the very foundation of digital cultural heritage production because they are not necessarily historical in a conventional sense, indicative of prior events. They are not interred and locked away in the archive. His tweets do not remain in an original state, they gather responses and are distributed far and wide.

Twitter users called for a suspension of Trump's account on Twitter because of his threats of violence against North Korea in which he stated in his tweet of September 24, 2017, "Just heard Foreign Minister of North Korea speak at the U.N. If he echoes thoughts of Little Rocket Man, they won't be around much longer!" Critics of the president's tweeting say Trump's rhetoric in this particular example reflects a threat of violence that violates Twitter's rules and terms of service.[51]

We can never view, know, or map Trump's tweets as ecological compositions in their entirety. We can't describe or map their full complexity. We do not yet know enough about these automated cognitive processes and how they operate. Perhaps we will never unpack them. This is because the subjectivities of machine learning or "soft thought" are not simply a case of the execution of instructions in a logical fashion but rather one that emerges as a result of any given tweet's own algorithmic modalities in which sequences of instructions change on the basis of the way a machine orders data.[52] But most importantly, working with the concept of the ecological composition as a new way of looking at digital cultural heritages holds open an opportunity to look at these things as active and as processes within the world.

## Notes

1 Rosi Braidotti, *Posthuman Knowledge.* (Cambridge, UK: Polity Press, 2019), 2–3.
2 Braidotti, *Posthuman Knowledge*, 12.
3 Fiona Cameron, "Theorizing Digitizations in Global Computational Infrastructures," in *The International Handbook of New Digital Practices in Galleries, Libraries, Archives, Museums and Heritage Sites*, eds. Hannah Lewi, Wally Smith, Steve Cooke and Dirk vom Lehn (Abingdon: Routledge, 2019), 55–67.
4 For a discussion of globital digital memory and its material political economies see Anna Reading and Tanya Notley, "The Materiality of Globital Memory: Bringing the Cloud to Earth," *Continuum: The Journal of Media and Cultural Studies* 29, no. 4 (July 2015): 511–521; Jussi Parikka, *A Geology of Media.* (Minneapolis: University of Minnesota Press, 2015)

5 For a discussion of the Technosphere as a concept see Peter Haff, "Technology as a Geological Phenomenon: Implications for Human Well-Being," in *A Stratigraphical Basis for the Anthropocene?* eds. C. N. Waters, J. Zalasiewicz, M. Williams, Michael Ellis and Andrea Snelling (London: Geological Society London Special Publications, May 2014), volume 395, http://dx.doi.org/10.1144/SP395.
6 Parikka, *A Geology of Media*, viii.
7 Parikka, *A Geology of Media*, 46.
8 Gilbert Simondon states that all modes of existence and being become subject to the technical, and Nature is enrolled to support the technical. *Technical Mentality*, 1989, https://www.parrhesiajournal.org/parrhesia07/parrhesia07_simondon2.pdf.
9 For a discussion of digital rubbish and its material contingencies see Jennifer Gabrys, "Digital Rubbish," in *Posthuman Glossary*, eds. Rosi Braidotti and Maria Hlavajova (London: Bloomsbury Academic, 2018), 108–109.
10 Benjamin Bratton, *The Stack: On Software and Sovereignty* (Cambridge, MA: The MIT Press, 2015); Jussi Parikka, "Mutating Media Ecologies," *Continent-journal*, 4.2 (2015): 24–32; Braidotti, *Posthuman Knowledge*, 96.
11 For a discussion of the multifarious material, mineral, technical, social, and capitalist forces operating in the global computational infrastructures and digital economies see Parikka, "Mutating Media Ecologies"; Parikka, *A Geology of Media*, viii; Reading and Notley, "The Materiality of Globital Memory"; Friedrich Kittler, *Gramophone, Film, Typewriter* (Redwood City, California: Stanford University Press, 1999); Wolfgang Ernst, *Digital Memory and the Archive* (Minneapolis: University of Minnesota Press, 2012); Matthew Fuller, *Media Ecologies: Materialist Energies in Art and Technoculture* (Cambridge, MA: The MIT Press, 2005).
12 For a discussion of global supply chains and the mining of minerals see Parikka, "Mutating Media Ecologies"; Reading and Notley, "The Materiality of Globital Memory."
13 Erich Hörl, "Introduction to General Ecology," in *General Ecology: The New Ecological Paradigm*, eds. Erich Hörl with James Burton (London and New York: Bloomsbury, 2017), 9.
14 Bill Brown, "Thing Theory," *Critical Inquiry* 28 (Autumn 2001): 1–22.
15 Brown, "Thing Theory," 1–22.
16 Martin Heidegger, "The Thing", in *Poetry, Language, Thought*, 1975, trans. Albert Hofstadter (London and New York: Harper Perennial, 1975), 161–180; Brown, "Thing Theory."
17 Bruno Latour, "Reflections on Etienne Souriau's *Les Différents Modes d'Existence*," 32, http://www.bruno-latour.fr/sites/default/files/downloads/98-SOURIAU-GRAHAM-GB.pdf.
18 See Jane Bennett, *Vibrant Matter: A Political Ecology of Things* (Durham, NC: Duke University Press, 2010), 208, for a discussion of the conative capacities and affects of matter.
19 Fiona Cameron, "Posthuman Museum Practices," in *Posthuman Glossary*, eds. Rosi Braidotti and Maria Hlavajova (London: Bloomsbury Academic, 2018), 349–351.
20 Cameron, "Theorizing Digitizations in Global Computational Infrastructures."
21 While the notion of relationality operates within a posthumanist notion of performativity – one that incorporates important material and discursive, social and scientific, human and non-human, and natural and cultural actants – it implies there is a relational equivalence between things such as the interaction of all things as matter. This is Barad's approach in *Meeting the Universe Halfway: Quantum Physics and the Entanglement of Matter and Meaning* (Durham, NC: Duke University Press, 2007), 808.
22 Cameron, "Theorizing Digitizations in Global Computational Infrastructures."
23 For a discussion of operative modes of thought and sensing see Luciana Parisi and Stamatia Portanova, "Soft Thought (in Architecture and Choreography)," in *Computational Culture: A Journal of Software Studies* 1 (November 2011), http://computationalculture.net/article/soft-thought.
24 Influenced by Alfred Gell, *Art and Agency: An Anthropological Theory* (Oxford: Clarendon Press, 1998); Suzana Milevska "Becoming-Curator" in *The Curatorial: A Philosophy of*

*Curating*, ed. Jean-Paul Martinon (London: Bloomsbury, 2013), 65–72; Cameron, "Theorizing Digitizations in Global Computational Infrastructures."

25 Milevska, "Becoming-Curator," 69.

26 Joasia Krysa, *Curating Immateriality: The Work of the Curator in the Age of Network Systems* (Brooklyn, NY: Autonomedia, 2006), 7.

27 Cameron, "Theorizing Digitizations in Global Computational Infrastructures."

28 For a discussion of material computation see Parisi and Portanova, "Soft Thought," 83.

29 Hörl, "Introduction to General Ecology," 29; for a discussion of network agents see Elena Esposito, "An Ecology of Differences; Communication, the Web, and the Question of Borders," in *General Ecology: The New Ecological Paradigm*, eds. Erich Hörl with James Burton (London and New York: Bloomsbury, 2017), 289.

30 Cameron, "Theorizing Digitizations in Global Computational Infrastructures."

31 Hörl, "Introduction to General Ecology," 22. Hörl summarizes Parisi's argument in regard to computation and materials as new forms of eco-rationality in design.

32 For a discussion of the intelligence of materials as new types of ecological power in computer design see Luciana Parisi, "Computational Logic and Ecological Rationality," in *General Ecology: The New Ecological Paradigm*, eds. Erich Hörl with James Burton (London and New York: Bloomsbury, 2017), 75.

33 Esposito, "An Ecology of Differences," 293.

34 *September 11: Bearing Witness to History*, Smithsonian National Museum of American History 2002 Exhibition, https://amhistory.si.edu/september11/.

35 Anny Bakalian and Mehdi Bozorgmehr, *Backlash 9/11* (California: University of California Press, 2009), 1−368.

36 The 9/11 Commission, *Final Report of the National Commission on Terrorist Attacks upon the United States*, https://www.9-11commission.gov/report/911Report.pdf.

37 For a discussion of flows of materials and processes from the deep past see Ian Hodder, *Entangled: An Archaeology of the Relationships between Humans and Things* (Malden: Wiley-Blackwell, 2012), 5.

38 National Archives, *Presidential Records Act (PRA) of 1978*, https://www.archives.gov/presidential-libraries/laws/1978-act.html.

39 "The COVFEFE Act Would Preserve Donald Trump's Tweets as Presidential Records," *The Washington Post*, June 13, 2017, https://nationalpost.com/news/world/the-covfefe-act-would-preserve-donald-trumps-tweets-as-presidential-records; *Presidential Records Act (PRA) of 1978*.

40 AP, "Donald Trump's Tweets are Presidential Records, but What Happens When They Get Deleted or Altered?" *ABC News*, Jan 24, 2017, http://www.abc.net.au/news/2017-01-24/donald-trump-tweets-presidential-records-deletions-edits/8206920.

41 Shontavia Johnson, "Donald Trump's Tweets are Now Presidential Records," *US News*, Feb 1, 2017, 3.00 pm, http://www.usnews.com/news/national-news/articles/2017-02-01/donald-trumps-tweets-are-now-presidential-records; AP, "Trump's Tweets to be Preserved by the National Archives," *CBC News*, April 3, 2017, https://www.cbc.ca/news/world/trump-s-tweets-to-be-preserved-by-national-archives-1.4053277; Olivia Beavers, "White House Will Preserve all of Trump's Tweets," Report, *The Hill*, March 4, 2017, 09.57, 2017, https://thehill.com/homenews/administration/327125-white-house-will-preserve-all-of-trumps-tweets-reports.

42 AP, "Trump's Tweets to be Preserved by the National Archives"; Beavers, "White House Will Preserve all of Trump's Tweets"; Trump Twitter Archive, http://www.trumptwitterarchive.com/.

43 Evelyn Ruppert, Engin Isin and Didier Bigo, "Data Politics," *Big Data and Society* 4, no. 2 (2017): 1. Ruppert, Isin, and Bigo, in a special issue of *Big Data and Society*, frame a new concept, "data politics," to describe the way data has been constituted as an object vested with certain powers, influence, and rationalities. Data politics asks questions about the ways in which data has become such an object of power and explores how to critically intervene in its deployment as a subject of knowledge. Data politics is concerned with the conditions of possibility of data that involve things (infrastructures of servers,

devices, and cables), language (code, programming, and algorithms) and people (scientists, entrepreneurs, engineers, information technologists, designers) that together make up particular spaces of relations or worlds. Trump's tweets, I argue, exert a different type of data politics that is a result of much more complex eco-curating processes and the domains of influencing that emerge through these actions.

44 Jussi Parikka, *A Geology of Media.* (Minneapolis, London: University of Minnesota Press), viii.

45 Azam Ahmed, "As Trump Orders Wall, Mexico's President Considers Canceling U.S. Trip," *New York Times*, Jan 25, 2017, https://www.nytimes.com/2017/01/25/world/americas/trump-mexico-border-wall.html.

46 Bratton, *The Stack*, 246. Bratton develops the idea of the geoscape: "A geoscape is a contested terrain of contested terrains, a shifting landscape made up of shifting landscapes: images, maps, projections and plans, irredentist land claims, borders, and jurisdictions, strata and striations, imagined worlds, macroeconomic forecasts, projected homes and homelands, addressing systems and various terra incognita. Geoscapes are a form of content that cannot *not* be designed and designed for where unplannable and unresolved territories, jurisdictions and programs are put into play."

47 Cameron, "Theorizing Digitizations in Global Computational Infrastructures."

48 Steve Almasy and Joshua Berlinger, "North Korea Calls Ballistic Missile Test-fire a Success," *CNN*, updated 0643 GMT (1443 HKT) Feb 13 2017, http://edition.cnn.com/2017/02/11/asia/north-korea-missile/index.html.

49 Almasy and Berlinger, "North Korea Calls Ballistic Missile Test-fire a Success."

50 Eliot Weinberger, *LRB blog*, "The Month of Trump," (blog), *London Review of Books*, February 16, 2017, https://www.lrb.co.uk/blog/2017/02/16/eliot-weinberger/the-month-of-trump/.

51 Brian Fung, "Twitter Users Want Trump's Account Suspended for 'Threatening Violence' Against North Korea," *The Washington Post*, Aug 11, 2017, https://www.washingtonpost.com/news/the-switch/wp/2017/08/11/twitter-users-are-reporting-trumps-account-for-threatening-violence-against-north-korea/?utm_term=.49c333e9df30.

52 For a discussion of soft thought as computational processes see Parisi and Portanova, "Soft Thought," 10.

## Bibliography

Ahmed, Azam. "As Trump Orders Wall, Mexico's President Considers Canceling U.S. Trip." *New York Times*, Jan 25, 2017. https://www.nytimes.com/2017/01/25/world/americas/trump-mexico-border-wall.html.

Almasy, Steve, and Joshua Berlinger. "North Korea Calls Ballistic Missile Test-fire a Success." *CNN*, updated Feb 13, 2017. http://edition.cnn.com/2017/02/11/asia/north-korea-missile/index.html.

AP. "Donald Trump's Tweets are Presidential Records, but What Happens When They Get Deleted or Altered?" *ABC News*, Jan 24, 2017. http://www.abc.net.au/news/2017-01-24/donald-trump-tweets-presidential-records-deletions-edits/8206920.

AP. "Trump's Tweets to be Preserved by the National Archives." *CBC News*, April 3, 2017. https://www.cbc.ca/news/world/trump-s-tweets-to-be-preserved-by-national-archives-1.4053277.

Bakalian, Anny, and Mehdi Bozorgmehr. *Backlash 9/11*. California: University of California Press, 2009.

Barad, Karen. *Meeting the Universe Halfway: Quantum Physics and the Entanglement of Matter and Meaning*. Durham, NC: Duke University Press, 2007.

Beavers, Olivia. "White House Will Preserve all of Trump's Tweets." *The Hill*, March 4, 2017. https://thehill.com/homenews/administration/327125-white-house-will-preserve-all-of-trumps-tweets-reports.

Bennett, Jane. *Vibrant Matter: A Political Ecology of Things*. Durham, NC: Duke University Press, 2010.

Braidotti, Rosi. *Posthuman Knowledge*. Cambridge, UK: Polity Press, 2019.

Bratton, Benjamin. *The Stack: On Software and Sovereignty*. Cambridge, MA.: The MIT Press, 2015.

Brown, Bill. "Thing Theory." *Critical Inquiry* 28 (Autumn 2001): 1–22.

Cameron, Fiona. "Posthuman Museum Practices." In *Posthuman Glossary*, edited by Rosi Braidotti and Maria Hlavajova, 349–351. London: Bloomsbury Academic, 2018.

Cameron, Fiona. "Theorizing Digitizations in Global Computational Infrastructures." In *The International Handbook of New Digital Practices in Galleries, Libraries, Archives, Museums and Heritage Sites*, edited by Hannah Lewi, Wally Smith, Steve Cooke, and Dirk vom Lehn, 55–67. Abingdon: Routledge, 2019.

Ernst, Wolfgang. *Digital Memory and the Archive*. Minneapolis: University of Minnesota Press, 2012.

Esposito, Elena. "An Ecology of Differences; Communication, the Web, and the Question of Borders." In *General Ecology: The New Ecological Paradigm*, edited by Erich Hörl with James Burton, 283–301. London and New York: Bloomsbury, 2017.

Fuller, Matthew. *Media Ecologies: Materialist Energies in Art and Technoculture*. Cambridge, MA: The MIT Press, 2005.

Fung, Brian. "Twitter Users Want Trump's Account Suspended for 'Threatening Violence' Against North Korea." *The Washington Post*, Aug 11, 2017. https://www.washingtonpost.com/news/the-switch/wp/2017/08/11/twitter-users-are-reporting-trumps-account-for-threatening-violence-against-north-korea/?utm_term=.49c333e9df30.

Gabrys, Jennifer. "Digital Rubbish." In *Posthuman Glossary*, edited by Rosi Braidotti and Maria Hlavajova, 108–109. London: Bloomsbury Academic, 2018.

Gell, Alfred. *Art and Agency: An Anthropological Theory*. Oxford: Clarendon Press, 1998.

Haff, Peter. "Technology as a Geological Phenomenon: Implications for Human Well-Being," in *A Stratigraphical Basis for the Anthropocene?* edited by Colin N. Waters, Jan A. Zalasiewicz, Mark Williams, Michael Ellis and Andrea Snelling. London: Geological Society London Special Publications, volume 395. http://dx.doi.org/10.1144/SP395.

Heidegger, Martin. "The Thing." In *Poetry, Language, Thought*, translated by Albert Hofstadter, 161–180. London and New York: Harper Perennial, 1975.

Hodder, Ian. *Entangled: An Archaeology of the Relationships between Humans and Things*. Malden: Wiley-Blackwell, 2012.

Hörl, Erich. "Introduction to General Ecology." In *General Ecology: The New Ecological Paradigm*, edited by Erich Hörl with James Burton, 1–74. London and New York: Bloomsbury, 2017.

Johnson, Shontavia. "Donald Trump's Tweets are Now Presidential Records." *US News*, Feb 1, 2017. http://www.usnews.com/news/national-news/articles/2017-02-01/donald-trumps-tweets-are-now-presidential-records..

Kittler, Friedrich. *Gramophone, Film, Typewriter*. Redwood City, CA: Stanford University Press, 1999.

Krysa, Joasia. *Curating Immateriality: The Work of the Curator in the Age of Network Systems*. Brooklyn, NY: Autonomedia, 2006.

Latour, Bruno. "Reflections on Etienne Souriau's *Les Différents Modes d'Existence*." http://www.bruno-latour.fr/sites/default/files/downloads/98-SOURIAU-GRAHAM-GB.pdf.

Milevska, Suzana. "Becoming-Curator." In *The Curatorial: A Philosophy of Curating*, edited by Jean-Paul Martinon, 65–72. London: Bloomsbury, 2013.

National Archives. Presidential Records Act (PRA) of 1978. https://www.archives.gov/presidential-libraries/laws/1978-act.html.

Parikka, Jussi. *A Geology of Media*. Minneapolis: University of Minnesota Press, 2015.

Parikka, Jussi. "Mutating Media Ecologies." *Continent-journal* 4, no. 2 (2015): 24–32.

Parisi, Luciana and Stamatia Portanova. "Soft Thought (in Architecture and Choreography)." *Computational Culture: A Journal of Software Studies* 1 (November 2011). http://computationalculture.net/article/soft-thought.

Parisi, Luciana. "Computational Logic and Ecological Rationality." In *General Ecology: The New Ecological Paradigm*, edited by Erich Hörl with James Burton, 75–100. London and New York: Bloomsbury, 2017.

Reading, Anna and Tanya Notley. "The Materiality of Globital Memory: Bringing the Cloud to Earth." *Continuum: The Journal of Media and Cultural Studies* 29, no. 4 (July 2015): 511–521.

Ruppert, Evelyn, Engin Isin, and Didier Bigo. "Data Politics." *Big Data and Society* 4, no. 2 (2017).

Simondon, Gilbert, "Technical Mentality." 1989. https://www.parrhesiajournal.org/parrhesia07/parrhesia07_simondon2.pdf.

Smithsonian. "September 11: Bearing Witness to History". Smithsonian National Museum of American History 2002 Exhibition. https://amhistory.si.edu/september11/.

The 9/11 Commission. Final Report of the National Commission on Terrorist Attacks upon the United States. https://www.9-11commission.gov/report/911Report.pdf.

*Washington Post*. "The COVFEFE Act Would Preserve Donald Trump's Tweets as Presidential Records." *The Washington Post*, June 13, 2017. https://nationalpost.com/news/world/the-covfefe-act-would-preserve-donald-trumps-tweets-as-presidential-records.

Weinberger, Eliot. "The Month of Trump" (blog). *London Review of Books*. Posted February 16, 2017. https://www.lrb.co.uk/blog/2017/02/16/eliot-weinberger/the-month-of-trump/.

# 6

# DIGITAL DATA AND ARTEFACTUAL PRODUCTION

Digital curation, the selection, collection, maintenance, and archiving of digital assets, was first established within data economies and presented in optimistic socio-economic terms as comprising new, efficient modes of organizing and managing critical digital data. It was held to offer great promise in modernizing public services, boosting productivity and hence profitability, and enhancing user participation in service delivery through online platforms.[1] We are now aware that digital curation has its dark side. The management of big data, for example, now often delegated to artificial intelligence, can be subversive, eroding our privacy and commodifying our personal data.

Within museums the emergence of digital curation in the 1980s was similarly cast as progressive. Digital curation became synonymous with information management in which collections and the museum itself were viewed as informational. A shift to digitally-based information services was seen as vital for bolstering the viability of institutions, elevating their social status in the information age and indeed their very survival in a world increasingly dominated by a digitally delivered entertainment industry. Accordingly, digital curation focused on the management of collections information through new collections databases, the digital preservation of analogue collections through mass digitization projects, and the construction of archives and large-scale digital resources that provided enhanced access to the public. The implementation of e-learning platforms operated as a mechanism for structuring, organizing, and facilitating social interactions with diverse users.[2]

Cultural heritage institutions were no longer framed predominantly as collections and edifices. They were now also viewed, according to Parry, as integrated data resources, information management systems, and communication structures.[3]

Following the invention of the internet and introduction of Web 2.0 in 2004, museums have sought to build interpretive communities inside and outside their physical spaces and through virtual portals. Many institutions have embraced social media in an effort to connect with audiences and other agencies across scales and national borders.[4] Accordingly, digital curation has been directed to the creation of digital resources and online access to digital assets mediated by social media, with new management structures that support these operations alongside a consideration of how authorized institutional interpretations of heritage coincide with the matters of concern of others within global flows through social media interactions with collections databases. Such transformations have been driven by technological development based on precedents observed in other sectors. The possibilities digital media affords have also been directed towards the reconceptualization of learning practices, the promotion of novel forms of engagement with institutional collections for their discovery, and the development of experimental forms of visualization and immersion within exhibition spaces.

Until recently, born-digital materials were often viewed as merely an adjunct to paper or analogue materials in a collection because they were seen as immaterial. Digital curation focused on collections as information because binary digits of 0s and 1s were considered forms of language and cultural information that could only be grasped when activated through computational hardware. Furthermore, the prevailing view expressed in the 2002 European Commission report on digital cultural heritage objects was that the digital supported the analogue with its facility in copying and thereby preserving them.[5] Born-digital heritage has often been undervalued as a form of heritage because it is seen as inauthentic. Digital information did not appear to conform to the same rules imposed on material heritage so they might become knowledge-bearing artefacts.

It is only recently that museums have begun to turn their attention to collecting and preserving born-digital collections. This turn to the born-digital is a response to the profusion of digital inflected goods and services and the perception of a need to capture what is significant from this burgeoning yet potentially endangered stockpile of data. Digital curation practices in other sectors provided exemplars of best practice in how valued born-digital objects might be effectively preserved. Critically here, it was the turn pioneered in other sectors to regard digital objects as material bitstreams that paved the way to think about digital cultural heritages as embodying a materially conserved quality.

While all these transformations, according to museum media practitioners David Bearman and Kati Geber, signalled a need to make adjustments to curatorial practices,[6] these modifications however have been conceptualized within the confines of the new museology, existing heritage frameworks, information theory, and museum computing. Accordingly – and in a so-called post-digital world where digital data and media have become commonplace, accepted, and deeply embedded across cultures, infrastructures, and economies – the post-digital museum remains, like its 1980s counterpart, conceptualized by prominent museum media scholar

Ross Parry as an informational entity interested in the dynamics of information and information processing.[7]

Correspondingly, digital curation is enacted across institutions as activities directed towards information management, the production and modelling of information and knowledge environments, and in ways that position digital media to promote forms of interaction within and outside the institution. Alongside this, the museum field has witnessed the rise of a new type of museum professional, the digital curator, often trained in the information science of digital media and communication, a person uniquely concerned with managing the museum's information resources.[8] While digital technologies, data and applications become more sophisticated, little has changed in the way heritage institutions conceptualize themselves in relation to digital curation. Normative thinking around digital communication, information, digital technology, and object-centred ways of thinking obstruct a deeper theorizing or even consideration of the differing ways digital data as heritage might be thought about and how such concepts might revise our fundamental understandings and relations to curatorial practice, or towards the emergence of a new type of digital museology. Following the establishment of born-digital heritage as a sub-category of heritage by UNESCO in 2003, the European Union declared that such potential digital cultural heritage must be collected by heritage institutions and their enduring authenticity assured through preservation processes.[9] Such a proclamation re-enforces business-as-usual practices based on the making of the authentic artefact.

We are, however, in a moment of transition. There has been a marked shift in practice from a prominent preoccupation with digital media, communication and information sharing to an interest in the digital object and digital materiality. But as more institutions seek to collect the born-digital, it is becoming increasingly apparent that current modes of thought and practice are deficient. The vision of digital curation as merely requiring an adjustment to existing practices to align with established heritage and procedures in light of the affordances of digital technologies fails to acknowledge at a deeper level the relations between material (analogue) and digital heritage curatorial and management practices as at once similarity, alignment, variance, friction, and dissonance.

In this chapter I argue that the turn to the collection of born-digital objects has deep implications for museum practice that go beyond mere adaptation. The emergence of digital data as heritage directly confronts core museological values and questions about materiality, the archive, the use of digital data as historical and documentary evidence, and the relations that frame the curatorial encounter with data envisioned as objects according to disciplinary specialisms. The binaries of the analogue and digital, normative notions of preservation, the original, origin, provenance, authenticity, and the artefactual must be re-thought. In this chapter I critique and revise digital curation to become post-object practices grounded in the notion of digital cultural heritage as ecological compositions both in the archive and out in the world. Because of this, I rework curating as collaborative, crafting practices in worldly life; the curator and interpretive communities as more than human and as influencers of various types and forms in eco-systemic and eco-curating processes.

## Digital curation and museum collections: The early years

Museums and many other heritage organizations are in the business of acquiring objects and building collections, often viewed as obsolete items. Physical collections established curatorial practices within museums and more broadly within the heritage sector. Curation is founded on disciplines from biology to mineralogy and anthropology, art and history, all of which are directed to the care, maintenance, archiving and exhibition of specific types of material collections. These disciplines are all concerned with the diverse materials, physical characteristics, aesthetic qualities, cultural meanings, affordances, and temporal frameworks of objects gathered under the rubric of criteria particular to each. Objects are placed in formal categories of form, function, style, and social significance depending on their specific collection dispositions.

Curation alongside conservation is governed by anxieties over particular types of substances, the conservation of fabric, paper, and wood, and how to protect these items from decay so they can survive in the long term, as well as how to document them accurately for posterity, and how to protect them and their digitizations from illegal use and distribution. Here the aim is to capture a moment in time and arrest the specific types of decaying process objects are vulnerable to. To achieve this, museum curatorial and conservation practices have been focused on the object, whose materials – such as paper, stone, wood, and other types of inorganic matter – behave in predictable ways, and systems and procedures of handling and management have been set up to deal with them. Software was often viewed as immaterial information used in communication and therefore was not seen as having material characteristics that could be conserved according to established practices. Instead, digital data was often printed out and kept as a paper copy or an image and sound on an archival material substrate such as a CD or DVD. The DVD software mastercopy of *lifeSigns* is one such example. It is reminiscent of what Latour terms a "sturdy matter of fact."[10] In this sense the creation of a "sturdy matter of fact" from digital data ensures that the form it takes becomes a permanent inscription of its mutable and recombinable characteristics as a concrete image and therefore able to survive the ravages of time. Through these mechanisms, their existence and role in collective and participatory forms of engagement are interrupted by rendering these digital "objects" immobile, transformed into a standardized preservation format.

In the past, many museums (apart from so-called living museums) collected all sorts of machines such as steam engines and agricultural equipment that were never intended to be made operational again. The Deutsches Museum exhibition, *Welcome to the Anthropocene: The Earth in Our Hands* featured the Trestle steam engine, a legacy of the Industrial Revolution. In the exhibition it was interpreted to stand for the destructive consequences of carbon-burning practices in contributing to climate change. The steam engine was never intended to be powered up again. It was presented as a pristine artefact. Similarly, the remains of digital machines such as obsolete computers, radios, recording equipment, software, and digitized data have been collected (the last of these often stored on a material carrier such as a DVD). Most of these so-called variable media artefacts could no longer be powered up because they either acted as representative examples or their systems and software were no longer operational.

Museums know how to handle physical objects, but digital data is proving challenging. Collecting the fragment or examples of hardware to represent a person, an event as an example of design aesthetic or an idea made sense. It had a physical dimension that could be put to work to stand for human technological achievements, to illustrate an event in the past, even to commemorate human vulnerability in the face of adversity. A Dell Latitude CSX laptop belonging to Louis Sausa, now on exhibition at the World Trade Center Museum, survived the collapse of the World Trade Center.[11] Falling 101 floors, it was buried in the debris from both towers and later recovered from the Ground Zero rubble in perfect condition. Its latest update remains one carried out on September 10, 2001. It will never be turned on again.

Strikingly, fragments of digital systems, such as Sausa's laptop, stand for the physical dimensions of the object itself but also, in this case, as a testimony to that fateful day, September 11, 2001. Similarly, an early-1989 prototype of ROBODOC, the first robotic surgery system (designed by veterinarian Howard Paul) which allowed surgeons to prepare for knee and hip surgeries by using CT scans converted into 3D visualizations for planning and pre-operative drilling, was offered to the Smithsonian Museum of History in 2016 by the company that now produces these systems.[12] The robotic arm is now memorialized in the Museum as an exemplar of medical technological innovation like any other representational machine fragment.

The Deliverance machine, a lethal injection system used in assisted suicide, is also an example of curated obsolete hardware and software. The machine, developed by Philip Nitschke (Dr Death), an Australian euthanasia advocate and former doctor, was the artefact used to administer voluntary injections that enabled four terminally ill people to die, and is now on display at the Science Museum in London.[13] Representing the first legally assisted suicides in the world and the right to die as a fundamental human rights issue for the terminally ill, it was put on display to encourage people to contemplate their own position on euthanasia.[14]

Deliverance comprises a syringe driver filled with Nembutal connected to a laptop computer. Nitschke wrote the software that controlled Deliverance. Once Nitschke attached a needle to a patient's arm, the software queried the patient three times whether they wanted to proceed.

The final question the patient in question was asked to respond to was "Are you certain you understand that if you proceed and press the 'yes' button on the next screen that you will die?" If the patient pressed "yes," a fatal dose of drugs was delivered and they died in 15 seconds.[15]

This death machine has a powerful aura because it is the original object through which terminally ill people suicided. When I stood before it, I felt enormous

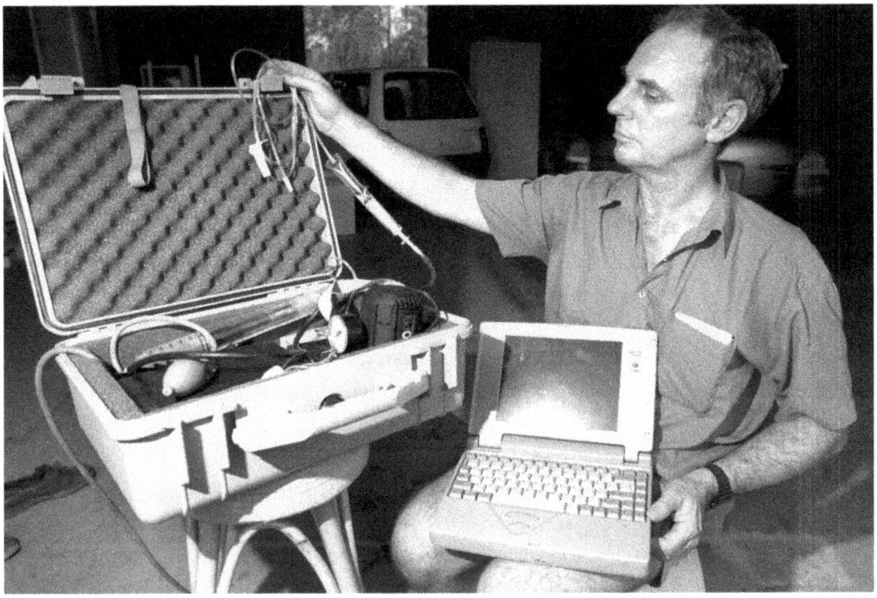

**FIGURE 6.1** The Deliverance euthanasia machine with the inventor Dr Philip Nitschke, Darwin, 1996.
Photo credit: Exit International.

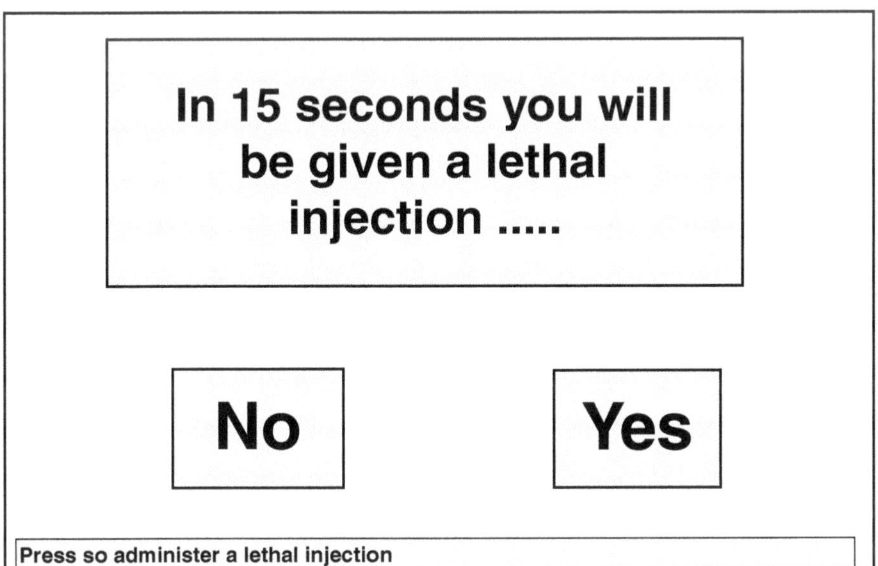


**FIGURE 6.2** Screenshot of Deliverance interface on Twitter.

empathy and respect for those who had the courage to end their life in the face of adversity. The machine as artefactual, commanded a reverence that I could only explain as resoundingly spiritual. At this point the machine is not intended to be made operational or used again because in the UK it remains illegal to do so.

Many of these collections are now described as legacy items comprising superseded hardware and software some of which await to become active again.

But there are many precedents for making collections active. The Boulton and Watt engine is the oldest rotative steam engine in the world and a key technological innovation of the Industrial Revolution. Built in 1785, it is now seen as a monument of the Technosphere. Installed at London's Whitbread Brewery in the same year, it was donated to Sydney's Museum of Applied Arts and Sciences in the 1880s and restored to working order for the opening of the Powerhouse Museum in 1988. It remains one of the most significant collection items in the museum and is powered up on occasion.

Digital machines, on the other hand, typically languish in stores, their obsolete data rotting away on discs that are no longer readable. The in-bloom petal dress, a 3D printed garment in the Museum of Applied Arts and Sciences collection, is a case in point. Made from biodegradable plastic and designed to degrade over time, it is stored in the museum alongside its instructional code.[16] The instructional code and therefore its processual affordances slowly becomes obsolete because it has been left in its original file format. No one knows what to do with it. Principal curator Matthew Connell asks the question: How do you curate decay when collections aim to be held in perpetuity?[17] Collection items like these are ignored but not forgotten. They are a constant reminder of the challenges of digital curation.

In the early years of born-digital collections and their curation, anxieties arose over how to effectively collect, curate, and conserve them. These concerns were expressed as a "digital divide," that is, the difficulty of grasping digitally produced items that were then viewed as lacking material substance. Critically here, digital collections were seen as information, as abstract mathematical entities comprising series of 0/1 signals existing outside the material world. In light of this, museum professionals observed that managing digital collections then viewed as intangible things differed considerably from the preservation of precious artefacts,[18] but were not sure how to go about it. Here the digital divide was framed in terms of tensions between practices based on specific types of materials and the differences in the behaviour of code and the multiple platforms, file formats, and embedded multimedia that comprise digital heritage. The variable ways in which collections could be accessed further exemplified this digital divide. Digital curation, new media artist and curator Rachel Greene explains, requires staff to turn on and log into digital devices and browse virtual collections online, practices seen as both physically and conceptually removed from access to and contemplation of material collections in quiet galleries, exhibition spaces, and storerooms.[19]

Furthermore, curatorial methods are cultural practices embodied in specific paradigms of representation. These include narrative and signification practices, modes of classification and ordering made possible through particular inscribed procedures of discrimination and judgment, and the description of the material and the social qualities of cultural and natural objects. All of these practices require the material object and the artefact to enact such procedures. The digital divide remains real and concerning. The question is whether digital curation has promoted a reconceptualization of museum curating under the changing conditions of the digital in respect to digital collections. I think not, at least not in a substantial way. Instead, the digital becomes attuned to material conservation and artefactual production. I discuss this further in the following sections.

## Collecting born-digital heritage

In building born-digital heritage collections we gather together the so-called objects of our digitally mediated contemporary world. But many heritage institutions have been slow to rank born-digital heritage collecting as a priority among their acquisitions policies, or indeed to develop born-digital collections at all. One exception is the Victoria and Albert Museum in London, who have devised specific collecting policies[20], predominantly for variable media but also born-digital heritage, because of their long-standing interest in collecting computer art and design, much of which is now produced in digital format. Due to the institution's targeted focus on collecting the work of living artists and designers working with media and new technologies, its curatorial practice has become more attuned to new object types and conceptual categories for mixed media collections.[21]

So-called "traditional analogue heritage objects" such as diaries, photographs, film, sound correspondence, art works, and currencies now have digital counterparts that are viewed as the same as their material equivalents but in digital format. Photographs and film become digital images and video. Letters becomes emails. Sound imprinted on records and tape becomes sound files on DVD and online. Cryptocurrencies such as Bitcoin are seen as equivalent to numismatics collections. Here digital collections are considered no different from other types of material collections because they are forms of human expression merely available on a different substrate. This view is reinforced as such collections are attributed a digital material status. Hybrid objects often described as physical comprise a range of formats that contain some digital information seen as worthy of preservation to prevent their loss.[22]

The contemporaneity of born-digital collections can be an obstacle to collecting. Many heritage institutions are generally slow to collect contemporary material or acknowledge it as relevant. Net-based heritage is often overlooked as collection items because they are deemed too difficult to collect. Other barriers to the development of such collections include lack of resources. Digital curation is often labour-intensive; particular knowledge and expertise is required to effectively collect and preserve these items.[23]

Institutional traditions of collecting also govern, and can limit, what an institution considers its mission to acquire. The types, subjects, and topics against which digital objects are acquired generally relate to existing collection items. Within a specific institutional mission collecting tends to be driven by a desire to represent a particular event or locality, a certain creator or provenance (such as the records of an individual), or by type/format (for example, digital images, video games, and digital art).[24] Born-digital cultural heritage is often acquired through gift, bequest, exchange, purchase, targeted collecting, or for exhibition projects, and can be sourced through diverse platforms and channels.[25]

Above all, within heritage contexts collecting decisions continue to rely on questions of significance and the potential representational value of specific digital objects and collections. Criteria include what items are illustrative of and should become permanent documentary records of contemporary life, to be saved for the benefit of the local community or indeed humanity because of their aesthetic, economic, cultural, social, artistic, or scientific significance, their rarity or uniqueness. But, significantly here, selection is now accompanied by new pragmatic questions related to resourcing in the long term. These questions include a consideration of the ramifications if the digital heritage object in question is not preserved. A decision to preserve is often made according to an assessment of the level of risk posed to an object, whether the long-term value of the heritage object justifies the investment of resources to preserve it, whether the institution has the resources available to read, migrate, and preserve, whether such digital objects are available in other institutions, and whether preservation is being conducted elsewhere.[26]

Here questions of significance are conflated with ones of long-term sustainability. The UNESCO guidelines on collecting distinguish two approaches.[27] The first, comprehensive collecting, involves the acquisition of all content on a particular topic, time period, geographical area, or person. The collection of all of Trump's tweets by the National Archives is an example of comprehensive collecting because they act as records of his presidency and capture his thoughts, actions, and policies.

The second approach is sampling, the capturing of a representative picture of an event through sampling technology, thereby making preservation more achievable and less resource intensive.[28] The Collecting Social Photography project is an example of representational collecting of material related to contemporary events using a sampling method. Following the Stockholm city centre terrorist attack on April 7, 2017, the project collected networked social photos and metadata that expressed the thoughts, concerns, and fears expressed by people through the documentation and sharing of images.[29] This collecting initiative involved the development of web collecting interfaces, infrastructures and the collection of metadata from social media platforms. The Nordic Museum and the Stockholm County Museum instituted two collecting initiatives: *#openstockholm* at Minnen (www.minnen.se) and *Dokumentation 14:53* at Samtidsbild (www.samtidsbild.se) using two digital collecting websites.[30] A third method of collecting was conducted by downloading metadata through a third-party service from approximately 10,000 images posted on Instagram. A total of 389 images were uploaded onto the collecting websites.[31]

Across all collecting areas, questions arise in respect to the authenticity, provenance, and context of born-digital collections. That is, how best to historicize them. These non-negotiable imperatives are viewed by UNESCO as more challenging because of the ease of duplication and manipulation in respect to digital materials.[32] But while it is acknowledged by digital curator Kajsa Hartig, the lead investigator on the Collecting Social Photography project, that there is a need to create new infrastructures and institute new processes, decision-making procedures, and strategic partnerships in respect to the selection and treatment of born-digital collections,[33] such calls are largely generated within existing understandings of the born-digital.

Collecting timeframes are accordingly conflated compared to other items because selection decisions must be made before an object is at risk. Such decision-making processes operate within the accelerated timescales of obsolescence, whether that be for storage media, hardware and software systems, or digital formats. This also poses a challenge to museum and heritage practice, where the passage of time is often a matrix used to lend historical perspective to questions of what should be acquired and what is significant. Collecting becomes instead anticipatory, that is by assessing what resources are likely to be significant in the future while potentially endangered now. But at the same time, as it happens, digital curation is being performed by a much broader range of curatorial agents who include museum curators, citizen curators (through digital collecting projects), web crawlers, social bots, and even rogue archivists and gamers.

## Making digital data into artefacts in the archive

In contrast to curation practices for digital art and variable media, digital curation for the collection and archiving of born-digital heritage objects is put to work to maintain core heritage values and uphold the museum as a sanctioned repository for significant, rare, and valuable artefacts. Central to this is the imperative to first view digital data as an object that can be conserved, and second to historicize it and make an original artefact from it. In software development, artefacts are often viewed as the by-products of such processes, including for example unified language models, design documents, and even built tools used in software testing. Here, though, I use the term "artefact" to refer to digital data of cultural or historical significance that was made in the past.

When philosopher Anne Erikson reflects on the historicization of material collections as distinct from their copies, she explains how historical material objects are unique and differ from copies because of the way the former relate to and embody modern linear time and therefore become historically specific.[34] Artefacts are put to work in the museum setting through archiving, documentation, and interpretive practices to draw us back in historical time in a linear fashion to their originating context of significance. In doing so, the artefact shores up its own aura at the same time through a linear historical and biographical trajectory of itself. This relationship is often verified by the visible traces of its past written into its very fabric.

In digital cultural heritage practice, the original, time, modernity, and the copy are central to processes of artefactual production; these operate in ways that align with but also differ from how material collections are historicized. The significance, memorializing function and uniqueness of any given born-digital object reside in the creation of itself as an original, conceptually and materially through preservation processes, and through the making of copies. This is achieved by creating and verifying an originating context first, whether that be its origin of creation or its connection to an event, people, or circumstances as an example of digital innovation. Digital data comes to be considered as significant and therefore worth keeping at some point in its emergence. This origin-of-significance conceptual frame becomes an unbroken temporal relation from the past in the present. The measure of its authenticity as an original born-digital artefact becomes its provenance; it furthermore verifies its provenance as rare, unique, and significant as a key feature of artefactual production.

The essence of digital data as an original artefact thus becomes its temporal framing and fixing according to modern ideas of linear time. It becomes an historical object from the past, often a recent past, by virtue of its identification to a point of origin or significant originating context. Procedures are directed to verifying such locations in time and space and ensuring data does not change substantially from its originating form. In digital preservation, copying processes seek to maintain the born-digital through technical procedures. While digitizations are informational copies of the material source object, and embody the temporal relations attributed to its original analogue, in the case of digital copying the copy itself becomes the original and has the potential to become its substitute. The copy then becomes subject to the same temporal frameworks given over to the born-digital.

Because digital data is not considered as robust and therefore as resilient as other types of material collections such as books, paper documents, wood, and stone (all of which can, if managed appropriately, last for hundreds, even thousands of years),[35] making them into original artefacts involves first ensuring they are structurally stable. In heritage practice, cultural heritage collections and now data must be fixed or its structure treated in some way to maintain itself as a verifiable historical record. In the case of data, temporal fixing to its originating point of significance, condition, or form occurs either through freezing software, making analogue copies and digital copies, through strict verification procedures, or applying a combination of all these approaches. Because digital copies resemble and are verified as identical to the original born-digital artefact in many of their facets, the original can endure as its many copies. Such artefactual production processes are also directed towards technical standardization.

The belief in the existence of a concrete physical reality made through objects and artefacts is reminiscent of what Alfred North Whitehead calls a "fallacy of misplaced concreteness."[36] In terms of data, this concept is applied to an ecological composition's concrescence and the belief that data can be transformed into a stable, clear-cut, definable artefact and therefore operate as the embodiment of social and cultural life in the past. As a result, this thinking creates and re-enforces normative historicizing curatorial practices. By constructing a stable referent out of data, it can then become historical, representative of our past, can illustrate what is important to us, and can be put to work to showcase our everyday practices, our social identities, our affiliations, our social structures and institutions, and our transactional realities.

Thinking about digital data as digital objects first (as discussed in Chapter 1) and second as historical and original artefacts means that digital data can then become possessions in which the past becomes embodied in their bitstreams – a past that is made and then able to be managed and maintained. The creation of the digital artefact as something to possess also enables society through heritagization processes to assert control over the past and therefore the cultural environment with which it is subsequently aligned.

Digital data as a new technical object and material behaves differently to other types of materials. This poses difficulties for artefactual production because it is a dynamic relational system founded on bits rather than one comprising atomic matter, considered more solid and less mutable. The fluidity of digital data and its bitstream is seen as a problem that needs to be managed.[37] The most urgent concerns in respect to making original artefacts and their archiving, as with other material collections, are what properties are worth saving (material, cultural, and experiential attributes); how these elements might be captured, stabilized, and preserved so they remain true to their original form and perform their documentary function; and what processes of degradation they are likely to encounter. Digital data's affordances of duplication, proliferation, and as addressed things are seen to diminish its scarcity as well as making it difficult to trace and attribute authorship, pinpoint a verifiable origin, and track its historical trajectory from their originating context, as their aura. Accordingly, institutions place controls on the distribution and reproduction of the born-digital by making it into an artefact, placing it in the archive, and by copyrighting it.

Artefactual conservation is based on conservation science and is directed to retarding or preventing deterioration or damage to original artefacts by the control of the environment in which they are stored and through the treatment of their structure to maintain them in a state that is as near as possible to unchanging. Digital data collection and its placement in the archive are similarly governed by anxieties over decay, but in this instance decay and loss refer to the corruption of data and file formats and to threats from the ongoing upgrades of technical systems, carriers, and applications on which they are contingent that arise from the distinctly capitalist aspirations that drive planned obsolescence. Anxieties over the instability of the digital object enact adjustments to preservation and archiving practices aligned with the retention of the original analogue. Locking down the seemingly ephemeral digital object are processes that seek to hold it in place and secure it as a significant, representational original. In doing so, the making of the artefactual produces patterns of positive feedback. The need to freeze its form, to keep it in an archive, to migrate it on to other formats, and to copy it onto a CD or DVD transfigures digital data and produces it within the museum system of original artefacts. On this basis, complex ecological compositions are viewed as archival, documentary artefacts, likened to paper records because they are viewed as unchanging information. Here a dilemma emerges where digital data is active and subject to process and at the same time is viewed as artefactual. Making digital data into materially conserved artefacts as forms of documentary evidence of the past is the only way institutions currently know how to preserve significant digital data in perpetuity.

More recently we see a shift in maintaining collections in the archive so that they might be made operational in the future. Here, museum stewardship is directed towards both the maintenance of the original and the preservation of digital data so it might become active. Both object states take on a representational role. Such aspirations are informed by digital curation practices in other sectors where keeping persistent data accessible is a decidedly pragmatic undertaking, whether directed to upholding the profitability of businesses, maintaining vital records of populations by government bureaucracies, or so that digital art works may be experienced again and digital documents in libraries read again in the future.

For heritage institutions the datafication of life, in which collecting life itself becomes data inflected, means that digital data must be kept in a form and maintained in ways that allow it to remain accessible if a meaningful digital legacy is to be created. While they may be rendered capable of being made active again in the archive, they are still seen as artefactual, representative of a historical moment in the duration of its emergence. Their active state tries to replicate that of the original. This is a distinctly heritage and artefactual disposition. This shift within heritage institutions directed towards keeping things active surpasses the purely representative and fragmentary artefact. Keeping digital data active is also tied to fortifying the future. Digital curation therefore becomes more future directed.

But the rapid development and sheer complexity of ecological compositions, alongside the emergence of different genres of data and operating systems, are stretching current curatorial practices based on the artefactual and the archive to the limit. Because each object is different, often comprising many processual, dynamic and interoperable elements, their preservation according to the Smithsonian Archive requires customized solutions that are often labour intensive.[38] This is evident in the context of collecting photographs on social media platforms where their assemblages of metadata, text, and image are dynamic, intimately connected to the network in which they are located and shared.[39] Collecting the image itself has been seen as insufficient, yet collecting the network within which these social photos were embedded was seen as an impossible task. All of them have therefore been made artefactual, disconnected from their computational networks.

Because of this focus on the artefactual, maintaining core values, collecting the original, the shoring up of the original, then the verification of its provenance to uphold its authenticity in an effort to maintain the original's integrity are all central to the selection, collection, archiving, and preservation of digital cultural heritage. Alongside this the experience of any given born-digital artefact must be maintained by preserving its bitstream in its original sequence.

The digital curation and archiving practices at the Smithsonian Institution Archives, the Australian Centre for the Moving Image (ACMI), and the National Museum of Australia most succinctly illustrate this process. Within these institutions, collecting involves the gathering up of original source code, original programming and files, and hardware as the technical elements to which the digital curation of the object are directed. Curating therefore becomes a process directed towards averting technical extinction and producing an artefact at the same time. Artefactual production involves a thorough documentation of the software and hardware deemed vital to the original's future use. In this way, the collection, archiving, and preservation of digital cultural heritage are conflated. They are not separate activities, as is the case with many other material collections.

To circumvent problems of obsolescence leading to the loss of the original, at the Smithsonian Archive collected digital data records are transferred to a temporary location on a networked server soon after acquisition to avoid an over-reliance on software and hardware, formats and applications that are either already obsolete or likely to become so in the near future.[40] Digital curation then is directed towards the temporal fixing and archiving of the original data stream and files at a point in time in its duration, often the point in time and according to the condition in which it was acquired. Archiving involves the creation of multiple backups and copies of the original record.[41] In doing so, copies must be authentic to the original and traceable to it through metadata stored with the original.[42]

Following this, a thorough assessment of the digital content is made to ensure that any given born-digital object might be accessed in the future. To do this, file format software is used to determine file types, and software versions are used to inform long-term preservation decisions and to identify what formats are in danger. This is then followed by ingest, the processes by which a digital file is uploaded into the digital archive alongside associated metadata that includes descriptive, administrative, structural, and technical information.[43] Fixity markers are generated for each file and used to ensure the integrity and authenticity of its elements throughout the life of the born-digital object.[44] Such markers are deployed to capture and historicize each file to a moment in time, as forms of ideological control, to protect their credentials, and to enable their discovery and future use. Here practices of filing, copying, and documenting operate on digital data as a series of distinctions that hold the notion of the original, its authenticity and therefore its value, in place so historical data can become an enduring artefact that can then be owned by the institution and cared for accordingly. Documentation details each step that is taken in the process of collection and preservation, and who has taken it, in much the same way as is done for other types of material collection. Preservation efforts are never completed; they are instead intensified as recurring cycles of verification directed to ensuring none of the object's original elements lose functionality or are lost due to bit rot or technical obsolescence. At the National Museum of Australia preservation master files and all copies including thumbnails are secured in such a way as to prevent unauthorized access to them[45] to secure their originality.

The rise of the idea of digital materiality has directed curation practices towards the preservation of the original digital artefact as bits. This turn to bitstream preservation, the archiving of the smallest unit of data, represents a concern to ensure that the "material" fabric of late modern society survives, both in the way it behaves and in its material composition. The reduction of the essence of a digital object to its bitstream is prompted by the same anxieties over the likelihood of degradation, corruption, and loss of other material substrates. Accordingly, preservation procedures are directed towards preventing changes to its bitstream. The preservation of the original bitstream is also critical to the revitalization of legacy collections and represents a shift from the material fragment to an interest in its duration. By saving and stabilizing the original sequences of bits in a file, it is then possible in the future to access the so-called original artefact.[46]

Digital cultural heritage and the act of preservation through the saving of bit-level files in multiple formats seeks to give those files a materially conserved quantity. The Smithsonian Institution Archive, for example, keeps a bit-level file with each bit preserved in its original order and format.[47] Here bitstreams and bit-level files become a digital cultural heritage object's artefactual essence, stored in a file and able to be maintained in perpetuity.

Digital curators document bitstreams so an artefact's original state is known and maintained even if it can't be currently accessed because its proprietary software no longer exists, a current operating system can't run, or conversion software can't access it. Bit-level files are kept as the original object so they can be accessed again and used in the future through yet-to-be-developed technical systems such as upgraded emulation or migration software.[48] The documentation process is cyclic, revisited every five years[49] to allay anxieties over the technical extinction of the original.

In many instances digital objects are migrated into new formats. Identifying an object's significant properties worthy of saving informs decisions about what format is the most appropriate for the migration of an object from its original file format to a preservation format. The migrated format is commonly preserved alongside its original format in an effort to maintain the content, look, and functionality of the original artefact and to assist in the creation of a working file from the original document.[50] The preserved copy is viewed as the original and put to work protecting it against loss or corruption by virtue of saving a copy in a durable preservation format. Word processing documents are examples of migration formats. Through PDF freezing, for example, it is possible to show what the digital file originally looked like on the interface.

Because maintaining the original is paramount for all collections, securing the original is made actionable by keeping data in its original format, through bit preservation, and at the same time in a preservation format. By producing artefacts, curators seek to curtail the tendency of data to duplicate itself and prevent corruption through changing bitstreams and formats. Copying is viewed as a preservation strategy that maintains the original without loss or change.

Documenting, cloning, and the migration of software-based born-digital objects, as well as finding other methods such as emulation, become vital to ensuring these are maintained as a permanent record. When migration and bit-level preservation are not possible, emulation is used to create an environment to render files as close as possible to the way they appeared in their original form.[51] Emulation is popular for complex objects such as games, digital art, and multimedia because they rely on custom software, hardware, and operating systems that are often no longer operational.[52] The application of emulation in such circumstances is directed to enlivening them accurately according to their original look and functionality.[53] Emulation is seen as a last resort,[54] however, because the digital artefact's fundamental essence, its software and hardware, is deemed to have diverged significantly and therefore no longer contains the past of the original. The original and the emulated have a different intent, that of the latter being to replicate the look and experience of the original.

Similarly, the digital curation processes used by ACMI to maintain the software and operating system of *lifeSigns* meant that it was preserved in a distinctly artefactual way, despite it being an example of variable media. Its preservation procedures involved producing inventories of all the components, including the cataloguing of metadata about the record such as the last date it was modified, file name, format, description, date created, identifier, copyright information and the assessment of the format, and media stability for each type of object that comprised it. A schedule of migration, rigorous file verification, software upgrades, and hardware maintenance were implemented to ensure *lifeSigns* could be maintained as a permanent and original record of itself when it was first made and launched in 2004. *LifeSigns* is an example of digital curation, an activity directed towards maintaining, preserving, and adding value to digital data throughout its lifecycle.[55] At the same time, it represents a yearning to organize digital cultural materials as fixed and historicized products of human labour and cultural expression rather than as malleable things subject to algorithmic mutation.

While originally the materially conserved aspects of *lifeSigns* were its hardware and code on a DVD, those qualities now become bits, the migration of software, upgrades, verification, and hardware maintenance directed to reproducing it again as closely as possible to its original form. Curation is therefore viewed as a necessary process of ongoing and regular care because of the threat of software and technological obsolescence or of bit rot, which, like instances of degradation in other types of collections, is often not apparent.

To pre-empt a loss of functionality in aspects of the *lifeSigns* object so it might emerge again in a way that closely resembles the original, its software (imprinted on a DVD and unable to be accessed through contemporary hardware and operating systems) was emulated, cloned, and migrated onto new hardware.[56] Here *lifeSigns* embodies a material object and at the same time comprises a potentially active ecosystem. Significantly the fundamental principles and processes central to the care of digital originals are viewed differently as revising formats, emulating, migrating, the provision of a secure environment, and the production of copies so the digital object maintains its original integrity. The grouping together of *lifeSigns* elements for emulation, with all its supporting metadata and software specifications, and procedures that control access to it, acts as a form of object-directed artefactual encapsulation. In all, digital curation in museums remains profoundly object- and artefact-directed.

Clearly digital data becomes caught up in a logic of modern history, time, and materiality. The same issues of authenticity, of maintaining the original and its aura, are at work here, just as when physical cultural heritage objects are curated. The logic of modern time remains the fundamental museological disposition and central feature of all work in museum curatorial practice. Digital data worth collecting, preserving, and passing on is first conceptualized as historical data because the past is embodied in its bitstream and file formats, and as an object to be preserved. When interred in the archive, data is given an artefactual status and qualities. To make an artefact out of digital data is to historicize its elements through a series of procedures. Creating a history and originating context lends authority to digital data in heritage terms. Ensuring these credentials are maintained is what directs curation. Technical concerns, modern temporality, and heritage values come together in digital preservation.

To make artefacts in an efficient manner, practices of curation are directed towards the establishment of standardized work flows and processes. To achieve this, digital curation seeks to control through verification processes all of an original's technical components – for example, the way they are described, how its image is presented in the database, how it is controlled in an online environment, and how its context is documented. The AIMS Born-Digital Collections project on digital curation[57] exemplifies the desire to blend existing archival heritage practices with the demands specific to the qualities and affordances of digital heritage materials.

Digital curation follows that of analogue machine curation. Analogue machine collection and preservation outlined in the UNESCO guidelines of 2015 includes the conservation and restoration of the carrier, the copying and migration of content, the maintenance of the document within secure storage alongside research and information gathering.[58] Adjustments to analogue machine practices for digital curation include the induction of new forms of digital technical expertise into the archival process alongside new workflows directed to the collecting, capture, appraising, accessioning, and preservation of digital materials and their access. Institutions struggle to standardize digital archiving, preservation processes, and metadata at once. Apart from the often-acknowledged challenge of collecting and preserving complex ecological compositions and the profusion of their forms and types, it is also difficult to develop best practice when institutions have different collecting interests and specialisms, operate according to different processes, and have access to different levels of resourcing and expertise. As a result, institutions have different capacities to follow through on the labour-intensive work that is required to make stable artefacts.

Digital cultural heritage is viewed as assets, not solely in a financial sense as something that is purchased and generates income[59] but also as a cultural investment because it comprises information of the past, about the past, and for the future. As cultural assets they are seen as holding value for the institution and for society in general. The creation of files for access, metadata for cataloguing information, the description of the content of the digital file, the technical details of files, their relationship with other files, the copying and storage of files in secure storage, and for preservation are viewed as processes directed to managing digital cultural heritage as digital assets.[60] Here, digital data becomes an informational asset of the infosphere, not only an artefactual one.

Because we are dealing with a complex, interoperable ecological composition, artefactual procedures involve a continuous process of authenticating the provenance and authenticity of all its elements. This is an important departure from standard object procedures. Monitoring an object periodically for signs of decay is central to the retention of the original and its preservation. In doing so, such ongoing procedures gesture towards an appreciation of the specific, unique, dynamic, and non-identical qualities of born-digital objects. With material objects, the authentication of its elements is not necessarily ongoing. Rather, the monitoring for decay of a given object's material fabric is integral to its conservation.

All these activities are directed to maintaining collections as rare and precious artefacts because their ecosystem is archived in parts and on and in different files, formats, and material carriers. Multiple, unique ecological compositions are preserved not merely as versions of the same object but as different formats. Accordingly, digital preservation is directed towards the creation of new things or things that are transformed through emulation and migration, and through the very processes of artefactual production in which several artefactual formulations emerge. This new archived *lifeSigns* has some similarities to its original. It is not merely a version of the original, but a new ecological composition because its form and content change.

Attempts to make the artefactual operational again through the documentation, verification, and migration of its software into new formats acknowledge it as a fundamentally ecological proposition. But the ecological dimensions of digital cultural heritage are still not well understood, and so collecting, preservation, and documentation continue to operate in relation to conflicting agendas and practices based on the notion of the original historical object, information, and its technical properties. What is emerging here is a greater acknowledgment of the physical and relational properties of digital cultural heritage in an effort to save them as more digital data is being inducted into heritage institutions. Alongside this is a readjustment of their value in a societal hierarchy of heritage objects. The blending of museological and archival practices for digital cultural heritage enacts adjustments to practices of calculation, verification, and storage. But these practices still adhere to standard artefactual rules and concerns.

When considered as ecological compositions, however, digital data becomes productions that can't always be possessed in a conventional artefactual sense. Curating ecological compositions represents a challenge to heritage practices, because in thinking about digital data in this way we must also shift from a disposition based on modern time and human-centric concerns framed around authenticity, aura, the original, and history to one of an unruly dispersed ecological composition with its own temporal frameworks and histories in its becoming.

The museological disposition therefore is to lock down and securely store digital data as historical, rare, and endangered artefacts and in a form as close as possible to the original form. Curatorial stewardship is directed towards the regulation, supervision, and management of the original so its integrity is maintained. This focus on the archive compounds a disregard for digital data emerging out in the world. It also acts against the likelihood of institutions re-conceptualizing digital cultural heritage in any substantial way as ecological compositions and as generative, as mutable, and as continuously emergent.

## The emergence of a new culture of copies

Practices of migration and emulation in digital art preservation have been described by digital preservationist Trevor Owens as a copying form of archiving akin to folkloric approaches used in the oral transmission of living culture.[61] According to Owens, as long as the key elements of the work, its original behaviour and the intent of the artist are maintained it does not matter if the file formats or operating systems are not exactly the same.[62] Although these works might look the same or indeed very similar, they are housed on different platforms, devices or substrates and appear on different browsers. Because of this, migration and emulation in digital art preservation produces variations of the original and does not replicate it in its entirety. Digital art preservation therefore involves a process of scripting and archiving new versions directed to securing the original intent and behaviour of the works, rather than the collection of fragments of systems or the storage of singular artefacts.[63] This approach has a genealogy in other types of copying. For example, the copies made of Michelangelo's David, in marble, in 3D digital format, as plaster copies and as photographs (discussed in my 2007 chapter, Beyond the Cult of the Replicant[64]), are each examples of the migration and emulation of David into different media and material substrates. Their informational qualities are similar in some respects in terms of the way they look, but their materials, technical features, processes of production, and therefore their coordinates, differ to varying degrees. Accordingly, these forms of copying constitute the production of new works that stand for the original. But they are not seen as new works. They are instead inducted into the stable of copies.

Clones, versions, migrated and emulated things like digitizations, all remain copies in service of the original in various ways, but most commonly in order to preserve. Some copies are more true to the original work than others, and therefore perform different roles. Emulation as a preservation strategy in which the mutability of data and its technical features is critical to its preservation is similar to practices directed to maintaining the original in East and North Asian approaches to heritage preservation. The 2010 rebuilding of the Shodenzan Kangiin Temple (founded in 1179 by Saito Sanemori and originally built in 1760) in Saitama Prefecture, Japan to house the Buddhist deity Shoden involved the careful reconstruction of its carvings including their elaborate paintwork and gilt exactly as it was in the 18th century.[65] This 1.3 billion yen conservation project subsidized by the Cultural Affairs Agency and executed by Tokyo-based Konishi Decorative Arts and Crafts[66] acted against the building's obsolescence through its re-making as a form of emulation through its migration into new materials using old methods. Although the temple is not the same assemblage of materials, its representational value is equivalent to the original. The temple appears to be the original, but it is a new building. This invokes the idea of heritage in the Asian context informed by Hindu and Buddhist philosophy and the belief in cycles of life and death in which reconstruction is viewed as rebirth. In this the auraic attachment people have to the temple remains unchanged as if it was the original.

In heritage preservation, in contrast, efforts are directed towards saving the original artefact. Contemporary preservation strategies no longer rely solely on saving extinct technologies and code in line with a forensic approach to salvage and preservation; rather, copying and cloning are becoming the preferred approach through which the original artefact simultaneously survives in other technological supports or forms of storage such as databases, hardware, devices, applications including online formats, and files.

While the mutable character of digital data is viewed negatively in terms of securing the original form of the artefact in an archival context, in digital preservation these characteristics afford a unique opportunity to secure the original by inscribing the original file formats and bitstreams in many versions. In digital heritage preservation, qualitatively different types of copying are undertaken. In archival practice, and in order to stabilize digital data, curtail its duration, and make heritage artefacts, multiple backup or so-called clone copies are made. These cloned copies support the original artefact's future life. The original's clones, although new compositions, are deemed to carry the original's significance, temporal framing, and therefore its past, embodied in their bitstreams. Here preservation copies are not seen as authentic within themselves, but rather as clones of the original similar to the temple. The values that inform the cloning of the temple and that of the digital original are however qualitatively different, the former as rebirth and renewal and the latter as the artefactual copy based on a distinctly humanist auric paradigm.

What is archived is not the original and not even proliferating versions or clone copies. Rather, new and different compositions are made, all of which exhibit similarities to the original. Such an approach would appear to unravel the aura of the born digital as historically specific and temporally framed things.

The creation of new compositions from archived bitstreams is illustrated in a GitHub repository. Originally developed as a collaborative coding environment, GitHub has been utilized by museums and digital curators for curation, source code hosting, management, and version control. GitHub assigns a public URL to each repository it hosts.[67] Thus the Planetary application source code from the Cooper Hewitt Museum was hosted alongside all its versions and archived in a GitHub repository and made available for use and reinterpretation by other software developers.[68] In terms of an authentic record, how far can digital data versions diverge from the original artefact? Can they still operate as an authentic record? Should they still be thought of as clones? Here cloned software in the case of Planetary and its various versions became new things, not necessarily ones in service of the original.

The new ecological compositions that are created through copying and cloning are no longer informationally identical to the last use context of the original. Each time a file is accessed, saved, or converted to a different file type or format, the bit sequence changes. Thus it is often a misnomer to say that copies or clones of an original have been created. They are indeed qualitatively different because they are subject to different production processes and uphold a different intent, that of preservation. As a result, they comprise different bitstreams, locations, and coordinates. Additionally, migration and emulation in particular usurp the very idea of the original, the truly artefactual, and the notion of the single or rare version of itself. These forms of archiving and copying are counterintuitive to the way digital data is produced and used out in the world. Therefore the desire to create an originating context through historicization is erroneous because of an ecological composition's processual or eco-curating characteristics.

Although digitization in the case of the digital jump seat belt represents an attempt to save what the original thing looked like, its informational qualities, or both, digitizations are thought about as merely the transfer of its parent to the digital medium. Digital copies of born-digital objects, especially of their bitstreams, are presented as clones genetically identical to the original because they are seen as materially equivalent and seemingly comprise identical technical qualities. They are essentially qualitatively more accurate copies. The cloned bitstream is a digital copy, not a digitization. Here, cloned copies do a new type of work. They shore up the original in a different way. Preservation copies in heritage institutions can at the same time be considered the original. Digitizations of analogue sources are viewed as heritage. But other types of preservation copies or clones also become digital heritage because they are worth saving for the long term.

Within this new culture of digital copies, the processes of cloning, migration, and emulation into new and different formats are exploited for the purposes of capturing the original as accurately as possible. While they are presented as the original, they, like digitizations, are also new things with compositional similarities to their so-called original. Screenshots, migration, emulation, and the development of new content are, however, viewed as insufficient in terms of their ability to act as the original artefact because of the loss of content and context such practices of copying supposedly entail. In this sense they are seen as lesser rather than different things.

This new culture of copies in the digital art field is the key to preservation. In this context, the archive is imagined in the future as organic, comprising an automated ecosystem of copying preservation involving bots, algorithms, and code, one that preserves through processes of genetic replication and mutation directed to future-proofing digital art against obsolescence.[69] Digital art or media preservation,

Jon Ippolito explains, represents the transformation of things through copying rather than simply the storage of the singular object.[70] In proposing an organic archival approach, Ippolito seeks to discard the notion of the fixed object in media art digital preservation but instead introduces the notion of variable manifestations. Too much variation, Ippolito explains, is dangerous because you create "a new species, an entirely new artwork," but too little variation means the work could be lost or lose its integrity.[71]

In museum and heritage curatorial work such an organic archive would comprise a more strict artefactual-making schema directed to maintaining the original through genetically identical cloning systems for making multiple versions of the original in an effort to avert their loss. Here, cloned copies would operate within a much narrower range of variation than found with digital art and media installations, which is often reconfigured and reinterpreted in different spaces and places over time according to the artist's and curator's intention. The copy for digital cultural heritage not only protects the original from change but also allows its distribution or re-activation in the future. It becomes the valuable artefact and holds the original object in its constant present.

Cloning and transforming an original while creating new data also has profound implications for conventional notions of the singular authentic record. It is clear, we simply can no longer hold the notion of the original, the artefactual, and the authentic in place. These frames of reference are also limiting because digital data operates according to post-object concepts, because they are dynamic processes, and complex ecological compositions that are unique in character and resist standardization.

The need to control, manage, and streamline procedures features prominently in the many journal articles and workshops about managing information and the development of metadata standards. It is all about controlling the original artefact, and at the same time facilitating discoverability across collections. As a result, there are difficulties inherent in making cloned copies because many digital cultural heritage objects are subject to copyright, a legal framework of ownership that regulates the dissemination and duplication of digital data. Copyright can prohibit duplication and access. It is further complicated in an online environment because when digital data is dispatched across borders it is no longer subject to the national copyright legislation of the territory where it originated. Copyright protection, therefore, has major implications for how ecological compositions are collected and made available; its application can even lead to the curtailment of their worldly life. Institutions need to pursue specific licensing agreements to deal with preservation copying alongside a consideration of how copyright impinges on the concepts and practices I propose in this book. These multiple legal territories become part of its thingness. These are all important topics that are beyond the concerns of this book. Such procedures also place constraints on the digital curation of ecological compositions.

Accordingly, authenticity and aura are all about the impetus in modern historical thinking to enable the chronological linking of objects to the past through provenance, and through the documentation of these time-based relationships. This is a distinctly humanist form of identification and spatialization in which all things are identified and relationships are forged in terms of human origination. Time and temporality, and therefore history, are different if we think about the born-digital as humanist and object-centred or as an ontological, ecological form. Modern humanist understandings of time are human-centred and conceptual, whereas the multifarious temporalities of the ecological composition become materially embedded. The latter is not temporal in a conventional museological framework. The history of the copy and the original as ecological compositions becomes the interrelatedness of their heterogeneous coordinates, forces, and agencies – in short, their eco-curating processes. This more-than-human temporal framework, although unacknowledged, is a process of unfolding. It is also about what came before and what is yet to come. It no longer subscribes to a linear historical trajectory.

The temporal frameworks of the copy and clone are also deeply material, sensing, calculative, and energetic, all of these operating alongside human-centred modern historical thinking. They may at the same time also be subjected to other temporal concepts located within alternative cultural frameworks.

As with material collections, the unique and material temporalities of digital data copies and clones only have significance in a conservation context. Their respective processes of decay and technical extinction occur as a result of these other temporal processes, and preservation is directed to curtailing them.

The born-digital object as an ecological composition does not have one origin. It has multiple origins as the histories of its coordinates and the elements from which it is made, to the tangles of its interrelatedness in its unfolding as described in respect to the jump seat belt. Reworking the temporal frameworks of ecological compositions as eco-curating processes is fundamental to thinking about data worth saving or retaining in a different way.

The temporalities of the ontological form undermine the very idea of a humanist heritage, because this form of heritage is based on a logic of modern time, on the notion of the original fixed in time, and as an object able to uphold an authentic provenance. When making data into heritage there is an assumption that it is significant in some way, that it is human-centred, endangered, can be made historical and memorialized in modern consciousness, can survive from the past in an authentic form, can act as a material embodiment of that past, and can be made artefactual. Heritage artefacts can't be allowed to change, wither away, be reinvigorated, remixed, or reinterpreted.

As an ecological composition, the copy is no longer a copy because all so-called copies are different from the original. They are changed through preservation, through reformatting, through backups and upgrades in software. They become different things as they are made into artefacts. These decisions in regard to preservation operate in the archive as opposed to out in the world.

Defined by the point of its creation, the specific moment in linear time that delineates its worth or, through its chronological dating in the case of archaeological collections, its originating significance becomes a trajectory to which its aura is attenuated. The temporal specificity of the born-digital and its notions of the original, authenticity, and aura are cloned when file formats and bitstrings are supposedly copied. The clone and the copy keep the original source object's meaning and qualities alive in the present. Clones of bitstrings, for example, are seen as the original but they don't perform or embody the historical features and trajectories of the original artefact. At the same time the clone is a new work, a new original with its own temporal disposition that is rendered absent. Such clones have their own individuated histories that are rendered invisible in part from preservation procedures.

Having said all this, we must revise the notion of the archive as being solely directed to making, securing, regulating, and upholding the original, while accommodating the notion of digital cultural heritage as the creation of new things and as dynamic ecological compositions. The creation of new works as reinterpretations of digital art or vintage games beyond that as a mere emulation of the original is a standard procedure for online creators. These new creations are often made by opensource programmers, Wikipedia contributors, YouTube filmmakers, and indeed artificial intelligence all of whom mash up photos, music, film, and games into new creations, processes described by Rinehardt and Ippolito as "promiscuous hybrids of continually evolving remixes."[72] Re-writing of this type and genre escapes the strict and formal rules of the museum archive and the original.

Here the artefactual archive could be put to work to keep such ecological compositions alive by retelling, rescripting, and rewriting them in multifarious ways, thereby opening up a space for the inclusion of new editable and mutable works in the archive that may be inspired by the original but do not resemble it in its entirety. Indeed, such rescripting is already part of the repertoire of digital heritage preservation, though not acknowledged as such within the context of the preservation of the original. Here the elitist criterion of heritage as the original and the regulated is questioned through the making of new things. Cultural significance in respect to the artefactual accordingly is interrupted and must be re-thought.

## Active, addressed, and alive

The terms alive and dead have long been used as metaphors for describing museum collections: qualitatively different states pre- and post-museumification through a humanist mode of thought. Death occurs when collections are removed from their original contexts of use and the world of serendipitous experience, all to be sidelined and replaced by museum, scholarly, and aesthetic concerns. This term ranges in meaning, art historian Fiona Candlin explains, across: reminders of biological death in the taxidermy of animals and human remains; the death of the artwork due to its removal from the art market; and the removal of Indigenous cultural objects from their everyday ritual contexts.[73]

Similarly, heritagization necessitates the curtailing of the autonomy of the ecological composition and its duration through archiving. Dead here pertains not only to digital obsolescence and loss, but also to the removal of digital data from its original contexts of use and their re-inscription in the archive. They are rendered dead or inactive through the preservation of bits, files, and operating systems as their artefactual essence, by owning and caring for them, authenticating and describing them according to their last lived context, developing forms of identification under the rubric of the standard object according to media and genre, and then assigning them a universal identifier. Death is also deemed to occur through interpretive closure under the weight of curatorial authorial control.

What I mean by death, inaction, life, or liveliness here has little to do with the strict biological sense of these words. What I have in mind is rather their duration, the flows of energy, software and data streaming, databases, platforms, automations, technology, human participation, global computational infrastructures, rare earth minerals, artificial intelligence and machine learning, IP and internet addresses. That is, the eco-curating agencies of its coordinates. Aliveness and liveness involve the variable interrelatedness and timescales of their multifarious coordinates, as opposed to the linear time and the strict trajectories of past, present, and future in heritage regimes.

An ecological composition is both active and lively if it continues to be dynamic, distribute, interact, copy, rescript, renew and change itself and program new data, and gather responses within its pre-heritagization context out in the world. It is life-making in the world in multifarious ways. Furthermore, digital preservation as an organic process of transformation also enlivens things. The potential for these compositions to remain active arises from their migration into different media and through emulation that ensures their operational capability over time. Thus there is also a tension here between caring for and maintaining digital cultural heritage as potentially active ecological compositions in the archive, preservation practices that enliven them and seek to promote access to them, and the continued use and proliferation of obsolete data through unofficial preservation practices of reinterpretation, remixing, and emulation in the world. Heritage ecological compositions are not always necessarily artefactual. Digitizations of Māori *taonga*, for example, are non-artefacts. They are instilled with *hau*, the live force of the ancestors in whom they embody. Here different notions of aliveness co-exist (discussed in Chapter 5). Even offline digital content stored in private servers such as Word documents, personal correspondence, images, and government records remain active, each with a unique ecological compositional signature.

A conflict arises between digital heritage as artefactual and curatorial processes that are directed towards the regulation of the original, and procedures that seek to provide access to them. For example, social media content such as pages on Facebook, Instagram and Twitter, while defined as potential digital heritage, are referred to as dynamic data because when an account holder posts, other users can change the content by adding likes and comments.[74] Similarly media scholars Sarah Kember and Joanna Zylinska view social media as vital because of its ability to make connections and transform data.[75] But as heritage garnered from social media, as in the case of Collecting Social Photography, is inducted into the archive, the user's profile from a social media platform, including all messages, comments status updates, all posts including video, is often downloaded as HTML files alongside the images into a zip file.[76] This collecting method renders social media as something inactive.

If any given ecological composition continues to live out in the world, then, the world becomes the archive. Indeed, the world is already an archive. German media theorist Wolfgang Ernst refers to the world as an archive because it operates as a living memory archive comprising a series of micro to macro processes.[77] The worldly archive, I argue, does not refer to the storage of digital data as static objects but rather to the dynamic archiving processes that take place when data circulates and is continuously updated between server farms, in cloud storage, between social media platforms such as Facebook and YouTube and storage on hard drives in personal devices as bits and bytes on memory chips down to micro-level archiving through the chemical-mineral base of digital devices and silicon embedded in chips. AI collects and stores data records and documents people and institutions. Machine learning and automated systems are deeply archival processes through the storage of data and the calculations made on it.

Clearly, digital cultural heritage is not just storable data; it also comprises archiving entities that arise as a result of technological infrastructures facilitated by algorithms, sensors, bots, memes, and databases across both public and private domains. Accordingly, memory and archiving embedded in digital cultural heritages is not only that of the fleshly body and human technics of the digital kind, but also encompasses very material and non-human elements. Ecological compositions are in fact micro archiving processes themselves, all of them integral to their emergence.

Many museum professionals have become interested in the social value and the generative and technical qualities, properties and affordances of digitizations of collections out in the world as they make collections accessible. Originating from Seb Chan's pioneering work in 2006 at Sydney's Museum of Applied Arts and Sciences, collection digitizations are now routinely inducted through Google search engines and on to social networking sites such as Flickr, Wikipedia, and Pinterest, enabled by planet-wide computing infrastructures and the desire to encourage collections engagement and interpretation by digitally mediated online communities and social networks.[78] Here we see an emerging curatorial interest in the way collections information moves, its algorithmic and self-organizing qualities, and the multifarious ways it intersects and collides with a diverse range of signifying systems. When digitizations and collections data are inducted into Google searches, collections and databases occupy global planetary infrastructures, exercise their own sovereignty and engineer their own affects and accidents. Responding to the mandate to make collections accessible, collections databases have essentially become open-source archives where collections become alive again and subject to eco-curating processes in the world while still operating from the museum database located within the institution. Simultaneously, digital cultural heritage aggregators such as Europeana direct users to digitizations in host institutions' databases through websites, interfaces, portals, and social media, facilitated through universal metadata standards that enable their discovery on the internet. Museum collection digitizations are stored in memory chips, on individual devices, in the cloud on other museum servers, in rogue archives such as Project 300, and through micro-archiving processes.

The "interpretive cut" that Barbara Kirshenblatt-Gimblett refers to is the removal of objects from their lived contexts and their placement in the museum archive. This is a practice long criticized in museum work. It will become redundant if the ecological composition remains open to the environment in which it is situated or is re-addressed and put out in the world again in a different functional capacity.[79]

Digitizations on internets operate in the minds of curators as an immaterial social ecology generating a mesh of different narratives, emotions, disagreements, and agreements where the digitization within the context of the database is a site to gather information and perspectives, descriptive nomenclatures, and search terms about its source object.[80] Sharing, recommendations, and comments on collections database interfaces are not only of the human kind, but include social bots and algorithms that promote and structure choices. These digitizations are seen as informational surrogates of the analogue and therefore become indistinguishable from the latter. But here their social ecologies take a different turn, operating outside what might be termed their artefactual legacies as inscribed by curators. They are no longer merely social symbols that stand for and are relegated to the past. They have ongoing social effects that garner a range of concerns and responses.

Interested people, programmed artificial intelligence, and calculative machine learning don't necessarily view these types of heritage compositions as things in the past. The links between past, present, and future were highlighted in the *300* movie example, where concerns in regard to Persian identity mobilized all temporal frames. Digitizations become objects of concern and concerns are not tense specific. The legacy of Persian civilization represented through digitizations of artefacts in the British Museum Forgotten Empire exhibition were used to project positive images of Persian identity in the present. This is in stark contrast to curatorial documentation, which remains static, fixed, and focused on how collection items were made, their history, and what they mean according to curatorial inscription. Digitizations become political and subject to algorithmic and machine learning, but still operate in a museological sense as artefactual and as a social text. Collections work in this context becomes a condition of being in and emerging from and with worldly concerns and processes. These examples represent curatorial interpretive experimentations beyond the walls of the institution.

Liveliness in respect to collections is re-contextualized on the web, where we witness a switch to include a new context of interpretation by all manner of agencies. The analogue collection is re-scripted and put out in the world through a database. Acts of filtering, tagging, adding content, sharing, and distribution by more-than-human users and automated systems contribute to their liveliness.

Like the digitization in the database linked to Google, the potential digital heritage "object" as an ecological composition has an address, or indeed many addresses, as a traceable location, as its location in space like any other object in its lived/used or newly attributed context. Critically here these addresses become integral to the ecological composition's identity before heritagization for those items linked to the internet. While much data seen as worth saving is being produced offline – such as research files, government records, and the personal files of all manner of organizations and individuals – increasingly digital data is addressed through the Internet of Things. These are the computing devices that are embedded in objects we use every day as our lives and the data we produce become addressed through online devices, phones, and tablets able to send and receive data. A device's address acts as its identifier, a pre-condition and indeed an integral part of its eco-systemic curation out in the world.

Addressed ecological compositions have no "nationality"; rather, they have multiple global provenances embedded within them as a series of machinic locations. An ecological composition's origin, presence, and career becomes its multiple addresses, its multiple platforms, the internet, and vast, extended global computational infrastructures to its archiving in the cloud and the other types of ecological formations in which it is embedded. The various potential digital cultural heritages that reside on the internet are all addressed ecological compositions of very different kinds. These include, for example, an orbiting satellite directed to monitoring greenhouse gas concentrations in the atmosphere. Another example is President Trump's tweet of July 3, 2018: "Many good conversations with North Korea …if not for me, we would now be at War with North Korea!" Here Trump shares his thoughts with his followers around the world. Messages originating from his Twitter account @realDonaldTrump spread quickly through retweets, replies, and direct messages and comments moving back and forth between his account, global computational infrastructures, and his followers.

Harmony the sex robot's first conversation about sex – "I'm crazy about sex, I will do everything you want in bed" – and her simulated orgasms using motion sensors that detect the rhythm of intercourse leading up to her owner's orgasm, made actionable through calculative machine learning,[81] are drawn from and activated through a global grid of locations, from the Realbotix AI Harmony platform to the localized smartphone and application connected to her computer system. All these elements and circuits together trigger stored scripts and responses as a series of circuits oscillating between Harmony's address and her smartphone application.

When preserving data in a conventional sense as artefactual, its address is expunged. This represents an act of removing ecological compositions from their worldly, serendipitous experiences, in effect taking them offline, curtaining their duration and transforming them into artefactual things that then comprise a different ecological formation, or indeed many different kinds.

We see this with a whole raft of ecological compositions that become digital cultural heritage, from tweets archived in the Library of Congress to images, emails, and the Wayback Machine and British Library's capture of web pages. All these ecological compositions can have a different life, a new career through a new address or addresses. The Facebook page of British tourist Mia Ayliffe-Chung, who was brutally murdered in a backpackers' hostel in North Queensland, Australia, alongside friend Tom Jackson in 2016 (discussed in Chapters 3 and 7), acts as a memorial of her life but its address remains intact with some editorial restrictions. The page becomes a new type of ecological composition with a different intent, that of memorial.

WikiLeaks is a multinational media organization and library whose mission is to gather, analyse, and publish large-scale, censored, or restricted datasets on topics from corruption to spying and war-related material. The library has published more than 10 million documents, many of which are digital. In an interview with German magazine *Der Spiegel* on July 20, 2015, Julian Assange, WikiLeaks' founder, discussed the organization's role as an archive, commenting: "WikiLeaks is a giant library of the world's most persecuted documents. We give asylum to these documents, we analyze them, we promote them and we obtain more. WikiLeaks has more than 10 million documents and associated analyses now."[82] WikiLeaks thus acts as a refuge for suspect historical data that has the potential to terrorize, to question, to challenge, to disturb, to unravel, and to reveal.

The way WikiLeaks uses archived digital data illustrates how ecological compositions can simultaneously be archived and be re-released and continue living out in the world. The shift from the liveliness of ecological compositions to a deathly interment and containment in the archive as a form of memory and their resurrection as new forms of more-than-human cultural products out in the world is most poignantly illustrated in the re-release of WikiLeaks' 9/11 collection on the 10th anniversary of the tragedy. From 3 a.m. on Sunday September 11, 2011, the 10th anniversary of 9/11, until 3 a.m. the following day, WikiLeaks re-released over half a million US national text pager intercepts between the Pentagon, FEMA, the FBI, and the New York Police Department, digital phone calls, voice messages, and emails made by the victims, by emergency services, automated systems, and by the hijackers themselves, including automated heritages such as computers reporting faults in investment banks in the World Trade Center. All these things provide a disturbing record of the terror experienced by many on that day and at the same time commemorate the lives, bravery, and altruism of those who fought to overcome adversity. These recordings and emails bear witness to 9/11 in a way that reveals how this event played out on that fateful day for many and the way it changed the world forever.

One digital heritage item contained the voice of Mohamed Atta, the Egyptian ringleader of the 9/11 attacks, captured talking to the passengers of the doomed American Airlines Flight 11 minutes before it crashed into the North Tower, cautioning everyone to be calm and compliant.

> Nobody move. Everything will be ok. If you try to make any moves, you will endanger yourselves and the plane. Just stay quiet.[83]

Betty Ong, a flight attendant working on American Airlines 11, was able to call the authorities from the plane and give them key information that was later used to identify the hijackers.

> BO: Okay. Our number 1 got stabbed. Our purser is stabbed. Nobody knows who stabbed who, and we can't even get up to business class right now 'cause nobody can breathe. Our number 1 is stabbed right now. And who else is?
> 911: Okay, and do we—
> BO: And our number 5—our first class passengers are—galley flight attendant and our purser has been stabbed. And we can't get into the cockpit, the door won't open. Hello?
> 911: What's going on, Betty? Betty, talk to me. Betty, are you there? Betty? Okay, so we'll like — we'll stay open. ★
> We — I think we might have lost her.[84]

Several emails were released by WikiLeaks that expressed the concerns and utter terror of people trapped inside the World Trade Center on that day.

> **09:32:57** Howdy, Just to let you know... 2 planes have apparently, crashed into both towers of the World Trade center on purpose. Don't know anything else, the web is overloaded with people trying to find out. CDE.
> **11:00:00** the only thoughts i have of are of nicholas, ian and you. i am terrified. i needed to tell you that i truly love you

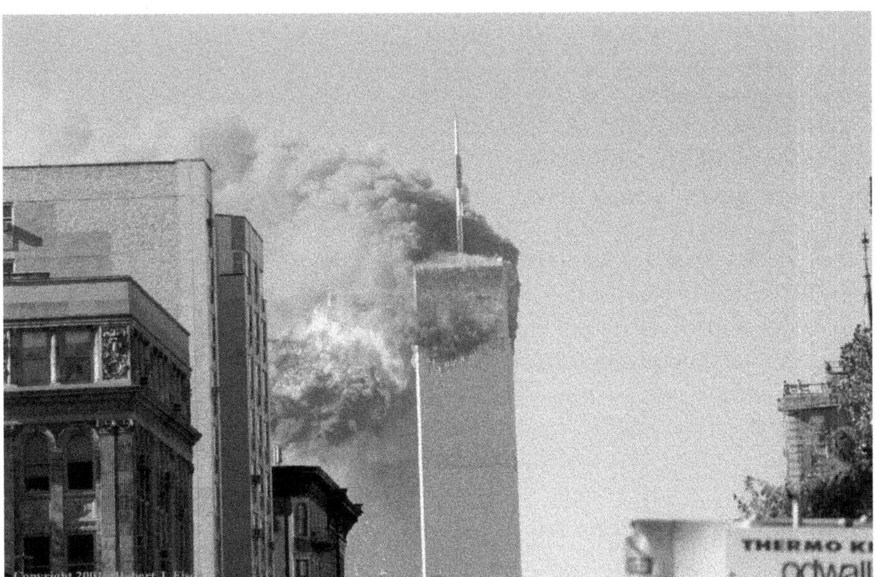

**FIGURE 6.3** United Airlines 175 crashes into the WTC 9.03am into the South Tower, September 11, 2001.
Photo credit: Robert J. Fisch via Wikimedia Commons.

Though archiving, the address and unique identifiers of the location of the audio file and email text file were removed. As a memory agent these audio recordings and emails remain living as a fixed documentary item, as a new production, through their transcription. A backup of the original audio and email file is saved in case the digital record is lost. Here these ecological compositions become historical artefacts rendered to description and in this instance to the demise of American Airlines 11 and United Airlines and the people who perished as the WTC North and South Towers collapsed.

The official digital heritage of 9/11 held in *The September 11 Digital Archive* is now housed in the US Library of Congress, Washington D.C. The archive is the institution's first major digital acquisition, and is one of the largest digital holdings, comprising more than 150,000 digital items including 40,000 emails and other electronic communications, over 15,000 digital images, and more than 40,000 first-hand accounts recorded on digital video and audio formats. Its mission as a memory agent is to save the histories of 9/11 and safeguard them to ensure their long-term preservation. But here too, preservation concerns are conventionally expressed as the maintenance of the hardware and software that bring the digital to life.

Artefacts in heritage contexts exist in multiple formats, as an object, as an installation, and as bits. Digital data can be rendered inoperative, copied and archived, recontextualized in a new environment, or we can record aspects of its emergence in its use context. When an active ecological composition's hardware and software or signifying system become extinct or redundant, it can be kept active through upgrades, migrated, emulated, virtualized, re-interpreted or interned in the archive. All these decisions depend on the intent of those involved in its collection and curation.

Ecological compositions can however remain active and lively in their use contexts in the world rather than being interned in an archive as a preservation strategy. For example, Trump's tweets, while active and responsive in the world, at the same time hold heritage status. And even more importantly for heritage, their future effects, extensiveness, and domains of influencing may not yet be fully known. The active engagement with Trump's tweets through a range of actions by coordinates both human and non-human mediated by eco-curation processes is central to their dissemination interpretation, and ongoing life.

Here I make a case for keeping those ecological compositions viewed as worth keeping active remaining in their originating contexts of use, thereby embracing their duration again. To do this, institutions, collectors, preservationists, and their creators could earmark a list of ecological compositions that should be saved and carried forward as significant through continued use, and develop supporting strategies. I advocate for an approach akin to the way we preserve heritage buildings. Some heritage stipulations can be encrypted into them to prevent certain forms of alteration, much in the way Mia's Facebook memorial is preserved. For other types of ecological compositions such as Trump's tweets, no such restrictions are placed on their unfolding. In this case the tweets represent the unfolding and emergence of itself as heritage, as a record of Trump's politics and presidency. Having said all this, some ecological compositions are more suited to existing and becoming in their active or alive state.

Owen advocates for digital art preservation to be driven by intent. The intent that drives the desire to keep and archive them therefore also informs the technique used to preserve them.[85] In applying intent to digital cultural heritage preservation as opposed to media art, such a disposition opens a space to consider not just curatorial intent but also other intents directed to saving and preserving them. Accordingly, intent could act as a focal point in the collecting and documentation of an ecological composition.

Three qualitatively different approaches emerge in regard to digital cultural heritage. Within object-centred frameworks, these are making the artefactual as a moment in its duration, keeping digital cultural heritages active while operating within the realm of the original and authentic, and keeping ecological compositions active but also lively in their duration out in the world with or without restrictions. Alternatively, keeping ecological compositions could invoke a mix of different approaches. The first two I have listed are archival in a conventional sense. Accordingly, a new concept of digital cultural heritage emerges. Here the archive, and indeed digital cultural heritage, are re-thought not only as ecological compositions worth saving but as live societal data worth keeping ongoing.

Live data rather than fixed societal data becomes a focus for collecting and keeping, retaining and renewing. This latter strategy foregrounds its emergence as dynamic, ongoing eco-curating processes. Bond futures, for example, are made up of algorithmic data streams representative of live stock market updates. In respect to its context of use, it must remain active in order for us to make sense of it. But again, it depends on the intent. Some ecological compositions operate best as a fixed record, such as photographs, or through a mix of methods. We do not need to totally reinvent curatorial practice. Rather, a new type of collecting, documentation and preservation system emerges through museums on the internet that complements other curatorial procedures.

The processes through which ecological compositions emerge and the relationship between their technical features and their presentation as an interfacial image supposedly akin to physical objects can no longer be thought of as clear-cut. Ecological compositions' seemingly physical form as concrete, presented as bounded spatially, temporally, and interpretively, can no longer stand up under scrutiny. What makes digital cultural heritage refigured as ecological compositions difficult to comprehend is not only their extended ecological formations and diverse coordinates, but the very fact that their boundaries are fuzzy, unlike physical collections, because they incorporate the intelligence of computational media comprising many different platforms, file formats, installers, and the hardware to run them. Digital cultural heritage as ecological compositions are often extended via their address, and operate across multiple locations, interconnected applications, systems, and datasets. They exist in multiple and changing combinations, and have multiple histories of themselves and of the human social through the eco-curating processes of their coordinates. Their unique characteristics are also expressed through different speed processors, monitors, sound cards, graphical interfaces, software, and embedded metadata, in which infinite combinations are present. They also comprise a diversity of memory agents. These include rare earth minerals, artificial intelligence, and the effects of their machinic processes that are part of them. Further to this, the more-than-human user's experience and actions are not confined to a single object but are part of these eco-systemic processes that arise from the multifarious "curatorial" coordinates originating from different sources, and from different locations. As a result, the dramatic unfolding of these processes and influences into the world through global computational infrastructures, through their programmability, through their intensive interactions between multiple agents, automations, human narratives, actions, and artificial intelligence underpinned by its vast, diverse ecological substrate often have unexpected effects and consequences. We can no longer classify and describe digital cultural heritage as distinct media types and genres because of their vastly extended, hyper-complex and non-identical character. This type of eco-curating and cognitive sensing culture (discussed in Chapter 2) requires a different type of heritage practice that can complement existing practices.

## Notes

1 Ross Parry, "Digital Heritage and Theory in Museum Computing," in *Museums in the Digital Age*, ed. Ross Parry (Abingdon: Routledge, 2009), 460.
2 Tomislav Šola, "Making the Total Museum Possible," in *Museums in the Digital Age*, ed. Ross Parry (Abingdon: Routledge, 2009), 421–426.
3 Ross Parry, "Digital Heritage and Theory in Museum Computing," in *Museums in the Digital Age*, ed. Ross Parry (Abingdon: Routledge, 2009), 460.
4 Fiona Cameron, "Object-Orientated Democracies: Conceptualising Museum Collections in Networks," *Museum Management and Curatorship* 23, no. 3 (August 2008): 229–243.
5 European Commission, *DigiCULT: Integrity and Authenticity of Digital Cultural Heritage Objects*, Thematic Issue 1, August 2002, 9, http://www.digicult.info/downloads/thematic_issue_1_final.pdf; Simon Knell, "Altered Values: Searching for a New Collecting," in *Museums and the Future of Collecting*, ed. Simon Knell (Aldershot, UK: Ashgate, 2004), 1–46, http://becomingdutch.com/docs/Simon%20Knell.pdf.
6 David Bearman and Kati Geber, "Transforming Cultural Heritage Institutions through New Media," in *Museum Management and Curatorship* 23, no. 4 (2008): 388.
7 Ross Parry, "Digital Heritage and Theory in Museum Computing", 460.
8 Paul Marty and Katherine Burton Jones, eds., *Museum Informatics: People, Information, and Technology* (Abingdon: Routledge, 2007).
9 European Commission, *DigiCULT: Integrity and Authenticity of Digital Cultural Heritage Objects*.
10 Bruno Latour, "Why Has Critique Run Out of Steam? From Matters of Fact to Matters of Concern," *Critical Inquiry* 30 (Winter 2004): 246.
11 Bob Eisenhardt, *TechRepublic*, "Ten Years Later: IT and Life Lessons from the South Tower," (blog), September 7, 2011, https://www.techrepublic.com/blog/career-management/ten-years-later-it-and-life-lessons-from-the-south-tower/.
12 Katie Nodjimbadem, "Why This Robotic Medical Device Belongs in a Museum," *Smithsonian Magazine*, Nov 30, 2016, https://www.smithsonianmag.com/smithsonian-institution/why-this-robotic-medical-device-belongs-in-a-museum-180961220/.

13 Nitschke, for a brief moment, was successful in getting the Terminally Ill Act passed in the Northern Territory, Australia, in 1995. The legislation was later overturned in March 1997 by the Australian Federal Parliament. Philip Nitschke, "Here's Why I Invented a 'Death Machine' that Lets People Take their Own Lives," May 4, 2018, https://www.huffpost.com/author/philip-nitschke?guccounter=1.
14 Science Museum London, "Euthanasia Machine, Australia, 1995–1996," http://broughttolife.sciencemuseum.org.uk/broughttolife/objects/display?id=91717
15 Science Museum London, "Euthanasia Machine, Australia, 1995–1996."
16 Matthew Connell, personal communication conversation. Museum of Applied Arts and Sciences.
17 Ibid.
18 Martijn Stevens, "Settle for Nothing: Materializing the Digital", *Artnodes*, 12 (2012).
19 Rachel Greene, *Internet Art* (London: Thames & Hudson, 2004), 12–13.
20 Victoria & Albert Museum, *V&A Collections Development Policy Including Acquisition & Disposal Policy*, April 2010, https://www.vam.ac.uk/__data/assets/pdf_file/0009/176967/v-and-a-collections-development-policy.pdf.
21 Victoria & Albert Museum, *V&A Collections Development Policy Including Acquisition & Disposal Policy*, 38.
22 National Museum of Australia, "Digital Preservation and Digitisation Policy Version 2.1," 21 May, 2012, http://www.nma.gov.au/__data/assets/pdf_file/0013/1453/POL-C-028_Digital_preservation_and_digitisation-2.2_public.pdf.
23 http://collectingsocialphoto.nordiskamuseet.se/.
24 Choy, Crofts, Fisher, Choh, Nickel, Oury and Ślaska, "The UNESCO/PERSIST Guidelines for the Selection of Digital Heritage for Long-term Preservation," https://unesdoc.unesco.org/ark:/48223/pf0000244280, 6.
25 Choy et al., "The UNESCO/PERSIST Guidelines," 6.
26 Choy et al., "The UNESCO/PERSIST Guidelines," 9.
27 Choy et al., "The UNESCO/PERSIST Guidelines," 9.
28 Choy et al., "The UNESCO/PERSIST Guidelines," 8.
29 Kajsa Hartig, Bente Jensen, Anni Wallenius and Elisabeth Boogh, "Collecting the Ephemeral Social Media Photograph for the Future: Why Museums and Archives Need to Embrace New Work Practices for Photography Collections," MW18 Conference, Vancouver, Canada, April 18th–21st, 2018, https://mw18.mwconf.org/paper/collecting-the-ephemeral-social-media-photograph-for-the-future-why-museums-and-archives-need-embrace-new-work-practices-for-photography-collections/.
30 Hartig et al., "Collecting the Ephemeral Social Media Photograph for the Future."
31 Hartig et al., "Collecting the Ephemeral Social Media Photograph for the Future."
32 Choy et al., "The UNESCO/PERSIST Guidelines," 7.
33 Hartig et al., "Collecting the Ephemeral Social Media Photograph for the Future."
34 Anne Erikson, "Copies, Concepts, Time," *Culture Unbound: Journal of Current Cultural Research* 9, no. 1 (2017): 7, in "Theorizing Copies" eds. Eva Hemmings Wirten, James Meese, Johanna Dalkin and Kirsten Wagrell.
35 Choy et al., "The UNESCO/PERSIST Guidelines," 16.
36 Alfred North Whitehead, *Process and Reality* (New York: Harper, 1929). See quote in Matthew Fuller, *Media Ecologies: Materialist Energies in Art and Technoculture* (Cambridge, MA: The MIT Press, 2005), 9.
37 Jannis Kallinikos, Aleksi Aaltonen and Attila Marton, "The Ambivalent Ontology of Digital Artefacts," *MIS Quarterly* 37, no. 2 (June 2013), 366.
38 Smithsonian Institution Archives, "Preservation Strategies for Born-Digital Materials," https://siarchives.si.edu/what-we-do/digital-curation/preservation-strategies-born-digital-materials.
39 Hartig, Wallenius and Boogh, "Collecting the Ephemeral Social Media Photograph for the Future."
40 National Museum of Australia, "Digital Preservation and Digitisation Policy Version 2.1," 6.

41 Smithsonian Institution Archives, "Preservation Strategies for Born-Digital Materials."
42 National Museum of Australia, "Digital Preservation and Digitisation Policy Version 2.1," 6.
43 Smithsonian Institution Archives, "Preservation Strategies for Born-Digital Materials."
44 Smithsonian Institution Archives, "Preservation Strategies for Born-Digital Materials." See National Museum of Australia, "Digital Preservation and Digitisation Policy Version 2.1," 7.
45 National Museum of Australia, "Digital Preservation and Digitisation Policy Version 2.1," 7.
46 Sophie Shilling, *Collecting and Preserving Digital Materials: A How-to Guide for Historical Societies, 2018*, 15, http://www.history.org.au/Documents/Collecting%20and%20Preserving%20Digital%20Materials.pdf.
47 Smithsonian Institution Archives, "Preservation Strategies for Born-Digital Materials."
48 Smithsonian Institution Archives, "Preservation Strategies for Born-Digital Materials."
49 Smithsonian Institution Archives, "Preservation Strategies for Born-Digital Materials."
50 Smithsonian Institution Archives, "Preservation Strategies for Born-Digital Materials."
51 Smithsonian Institution Archives, "Preservation Strategies for Born-Digital Materials."
52 Smithsonian Institution Archives, "Preservation Strategies for Born-Digital Materials."
53 Smithsonian Institution Archives, "Preservation Strategies for Born-Digital Materials."
54 Smithsonian Institution Archives, "Preservation Strategies for Born-Digital Materials."
55 Digital Curation Centre, "What is Digital Curation?" http://www.dcc.ac.uk/digital-curation/what-digital-curation.
56 Candice Cranmer, "Preserving Time-based Media: A Case Study with Troy Innocent's lifeSigns: Eco-System of Signs & Symbols," *ACMI Labs*, April 11, 2018, https://labs.acmi.net.au/preserving-time-based-media-a-case-study-with-troy-innocents-lifesigns-eco-system-of-signs-3e2f0b3ae2.
57 AIMS Working Group, The AIMS Born-Digital Collections: An Inter-Institutional Model for Stewardship, January 2012, https://dcs.library.virginia.edu/files/2013/02/AIMS_final.pdf. The project is a partnership between the University of Virginia Libraries, Stanford University Libraries and Academic Resources, the University of Hull Library, and Yale University Library with support from the Andrew W. Mellon Foundation.
58 Ray Edmondson, "Recommendation Concerning the Preservation of, and Access to, Documentary Heritage Including in Digital Form: Implementation Guidelines," prepared for UNESCO, 2015, 4, https://en.unesco.org/sites/default/files/2015_mow_recommendation_implementation_guidelines_en.pdf.
59 For a description of digital assets see Celum website: https://www.celum.com/en/what-are-digital-assets.
60 National Museum of Australia, "Digital Preservation and Digitisation Policy Version 2.1," 6.
61 Trevor Owens, *Theory and Craft of Digital Preservation* (Baltimore: Johns Hopkins University, 2018).
62 Trevor Owens, *Theory and Craft of Preservation.*
63 Richard Rinehart and Jon Ippolito, *Re-collection: Art, New Media, and Social Memory* (Cambridge, MA: The MIT Press, 2014), 163, recall the differences between analogue and digital preservation as the difference between the collection fragments as opposed to the proliferation of data as new versions of the original as opposed to a singular artefact.
64 Fiona Cameron, "Beyond the Cult of the Replicant: Museums, Objects – New Discourses – Traditional Concerns". In F. R. Cameron & S. B. Kenderdine eds. *Theorizing Digital Cultural Heritage: A Critical Discourse* (Cambridge, MA: The MIT Press, 2007) pp. 49-77
65 Tomoko Otake, "Restoration of Temple 'Harder Than Building It'," *Japan Times*, Aug 5, 2002. https://www.japantimes.co.jp/life/2012/08/05/general/restoration-of-temple-harder-than-building-it/#.XeSc7i1L3fY.
66 Otake, "Restoration of Temple 'Harder Than Building It'."

67 Yu Wu, Na Wang, Jessica Kropczynski and John M. Carroll, "The Appropriation of GitHub for Curation", *PeerJ Computer Science* 3, no. 2 (2017) https://doi.org/10.7717/peerj-cs.134, 14.
68 Matthew Westwood, "The Digital Museum is Now Preserving our Online Culture", *The Australian*, Feb 7, 2017, http://www.theaustralian.com.au/arts/visual-arts/the-digital-museum-of-now-is-preserving-our-online-culture/news-story/b82cdff975d75391d11a84e63880e210.
69 In regard to digital art preservation, Rinehart and Ippolito revise the archive as organic, comprising an automated ecosystem of preservation involving bots, algorithms, code and one that preserves via processes of genetic replication and mutation. See Rinehart and Ippolito, *Re-collection: Art, New Media and Social Memory*, 199.
70 Rinehart and Ippolito, *Re-collection: Art, New Media and Social Memory*, 156.
71 Rinehart and Ippolito, *Re-collection: Art, New Media and Social Memory*, 55.
72 Rinehart and Ippolito, *Re-collection: Art, New Media and Social Memory*, 155.
73 Fiona Candlin, "Keeping Objects Live", in *International Handbook of Museum Studies* 3, *Museum Media*, ed. Michelle Henning (Oxford: Wiley-Blackwell, 2015):
74 Shilling, *Collecting and Preserving Digital Materials.*
75 Sarah Kember and Joanna Zylinska, *Life after New Media: Mediation as a Vital Process* (Cambridge, MA: The MIT Press, 2012), xix.
76 Shilling, *Collecting and Preserving Digital Materials.*
77 For a discussion of the notion of social media as a living archive involving micro-archiving processes see Wolfgang Ernst, *Digital Memory and the Archive* (Minneapolis, MN: University of Minnesota Press, 2013).
78 Cameron, "Object-Orientated Democracies." These initiatives were pioneered by Seb Chan at the Powerhouse Museum in 2006.
79 Cameron, "Object-Orientated Democracies."
80 Cameron, "Object-Orientated Democracies."
81 Sean Keach, "Dirty Droid, Harmony Sex Robot Gets 'Mind-Blowing X-Mode' Upgrade Making It Even MORE Lifelike," *The Sun*, Oct 5, 2018, https://www.thesun.co.uk/tech/7073748/harmony-sex-robot-release-date-app-sexbot-doll/; Joshua Nevett, "Sex robot SHARED ORGASMS: How erotic cyborgs will provide ultimate 'satisfaction'," *Daily Star*, May 14, 2017, https://www.dailystar.co.uk/news/latest-news/613611/sex-robots-shared-orgasms-matt-mcmullen-realdoll.
82 Michael Sontheimer, "We are Drowning in Material," Interview, *Der Speigel*, July 20, 2015, http://www.spiegel.de/international/world/spiegel-interview-with-wikileaks-head-julian-assange-a-1044399.html.
83 Kayleigh Dray, "Remembering 9/11: The Final Messages Sent by Victims of the Twin Towers Attack," *Closer*, Sept 11, 2019, http://lifestyle.one/closer/news-real-life/in-the-news/remembering-911-final-messages-sent-victims-twin-towers-attack/.
84 Dray, "Remembering 9/11."
85 Owens, *Theory and Craft of Preservation.*

## Bibliography

AIMS Working Group. *The AIMS Born-Digital Collections: An Inter-Institutional Model for Stewardship.* January 2012. https://dcs.library.virginia.edu/files/2013/02/AIMS_final.pdf.

Bearman, David, and Kati Geber. "Transforming Cultural Heritage Institutions through New Media." *Museum Management and Curatorship* 23, no. 4 (2008): 385–399.

Cameron, Fiona. "Object-Orientated Democracies: Conceptualising Museum Collections in Networks." *Museum Management and Curatorship*, 23, no. 3 (August 2008): 229–243.

Cameron, Fiona. "Beyond the Cult of the Replicant: Museums, Objects – New Discourses – Traditional Concerns". In *Theorizing Digital Cultural Heritage: A Critical Discourse*, edited by F.R. Cameron & S.B. Kenderdine. Cambridge, MA: The MIT Press, 2007.

Candlin, Fiona. "Keeping Objects Live." In *International Handbook of Museum Studies 3, Museum Media*, edited by Michelle Henning, 279–301. Oxford: Wiley-Blackwell, 2015.

Choy, Sarah C.C., Nicholas Crofts, Robert Fisher, Ngian Lek Choh, Susanne Nickel, Clément Oury, and Katarzyna Ślaska. "The UNESCO/PERSIST Guidelines for the Selection of Digital Heritage for Long-term Preservation by the UNESCO/PERSIST Content Task Force." March 2016. https://unesdoc.unesco.org/ark:/48223/pf0000244280.

Cranmer, Candice. "Preserving Time-based Media: A Case Study with Troy Innocent's lifeSigns: Eco-System of Signs & Symbols." *ACMI Labs*, April 11, 2018. https://labs.acmi.net.au/preserving-time-based-media-a-case-study-with-troy-innocents-lifesigns-eco-system-of-signs-3e2f0b3ae2.

Digital Curation Centre. "What is Digital Curation?" http://www.dcc.ac.uk/digital-curation/what-digital-curation.

Dray, Kayleigh. "Remembering 9/11: The Final Messages Sent by Victims of the Twin Towers Attack." *Closer*, September 11, 2019. http://lifestyle.one/closer/news-real-life/in-the-news/remembering-911-final-messages-sent-victims-twin-towers-attack/.

Edmondson, Ray. "Recommendation Concerning the Preservation of, and Access to, Documentary Heritage Including in Digital Form: Implementation Guidelines." Prepared for UNESCO, 2015. https:/en.unesco.org/sites/default/files/2015_mow_recommendation_implementation_guidelines_en.pdf.

Eisenhardt, Bob. "Ten Years Later: IT and Life Lessons from the South Tower" (blog). *TechRepublic*. Posted September 7, 2011. https://www.techrepublic.com/blog/career-management/ten-years-later-it-and-life-lessons-from-the-south-tower/.

Erikson, Anne. "Copies, Concepts, Time." *Culture Unbound: Journal of Current Cultural Research* 9, no. 1 (2017): 7. In *Theorizing Copies*, edited by Eva Hemmings Wirten, James Meese, Johanna Dalkin and Kirsten Wagrell.

Ernst, Wolfgang. *Digital Memory and the Archive*. Minneapolis, MN: University of Minnesota Press, 2013.

European Commission. *DigiCULT: Integrity and Authenticity of Digital Cultural Heritage Objects*. Thematic Issue 1, August2002. http://www.digicult.info/downloads/thematic_issue_1_final.pdf.

Fuller, Matthew. *Media Ecologies: Materialist Energies in Art and Technoculture*. Cambridge, MA: The MIT Press, 2005.

Greene, Rachel. *Internet Art*. London: Thames & Hudson, 2004.

Hartig, Kajsa, Bente Jensen, Anni Wallenius, and Elisabeth Boogh. "Collecting the Ephemeral Social Media Photograph for the Future: Why Museums and Archives Need to Embrace New Work Practices for Photography Collections." MW18 Conference, Vancouver, Canada, April 18–21, 2018. https://mw18.mwconf.org/paper/collecting-the-ephemeral-social-media-photograph- for-the-future-why-museums-and-archives-need-embrace-new-work-practices-for-photo graphy-collections/.

Kallinikos, Jannis, Aleksi Aaltonen, and Attila Marton. "The Ambivalent Ontology of Digital Artefacts." *MIS Quarterly* 37, no. 2 (June 2013): 357–370.

Keach, Sean. "Dirty Droid, Harmony Sex Robot Gets 'Mind-Blowing X-Mode' Upgrade Making It Even MORE Lifelike." *The Sun*, Oct 5, 2018. https://www.thesun.co.uk/tech/7073748/harmony-sex-robot-release-date-app-sexbot-doll/.

Kember, Sarah, and Joanna Zylinska. *Life after New Media: Mediation as a Vital Process*. Cambridge, MA: The MIT Press, 2012.

Knell, Simon. "Altered Values: Searching for a New Collecting." In *Museums and the Future of Collecting*, edited by Simon Knell, 1–46. Aldershot: Ashgate, 2004. http://becomingdutch.com/docs/Simon%20Knell.pdf.

Latour, Bruno. "Why Has Critique Run Out of Steam? From Matters of Fact to Matters of Concern." *Critical Inquiry* 30 (Winter 2004): 225–248.
Marty, Paul, and Katherine Burton Jones, eds. *Museum Informatics: People, Information, and Technology*. Abingdon: Routledge, 2007.
National Museum of Australia. "Digital Preservation and Digitisation Policy Version 2.1." May 21, 2012. http://www.nma.gov.au/__data/assets/pdf_file/0013/1453/POL-C-028_Digital_preservation_and_digitisation-2.2_public.pdf.
Nevett, Joshua. "Sex robot SHARED ORGASMS: How erotic cyborgs will provide ultimate 'satisfaction'." *Daily Star*, May 14, 2017. https://www.dailystar.co.uk/news/latest-news/613611/sex-robots-shared-orgasms-matt-mcmullen-realdoll.
Nitschke, Philip. "Here's Why I Invented a 'Death Machine' that Lets People Take their Own Lives." *HuffPost*, May 4, 2018. https://www.huffpost.com/author/philip-nitschke?guccounter=1.
Nodjimbadem, Katie. "Why This Robotic Medical Device Belongs in a Museum." *Smithsonian Magazine*, Nov 30, 2016. https://www.smithsonianmag.com/smithsonian-institution/why-this-robotic-medical-device-belongs-in-a-museum-180961220/.
Otake, Tomoko. "Restoration of Temple 'Harder Than Building It'." *Japan Times*, Aug 5, 2002. https://www.japantimes.co.jp/life/2012/08/05/general/restoration-of-temple-harder-than-building-it/#.XeSc7i1L3fY.
Owens, Trevor. *Theory and Craft of Digital Preservation*. Baltimore: Johns Hopkins University, 2018.
Parry, Ross. "Digital Heritage and Theory in Museum Computing." In *Museums in the Digital Age*, edited by Ross Parry, 454–469. Abingdon: Routledge, 2009.
Rinehart, Richard, and Jon Ippolito. *Re-collection: Art, New Media, and Social Memory*. Cambridge, MA: The MIT Press, 2014.
Science Museum London. "Euthanasia Machine, Australia, 1995–1996." http://broughttolife.sciencemuseum.org.uk/broughttolife/objects/display?id=91717..
Shilling, Sophie. *Collecting and Preserving Digital Materials: A How-to Guide for Historical Societies*. 2018. http://www.history.org.au/Documents/Collecting%20and%20Preserving%20Digital%20Materials.pdf.
Smithsonian Institution Archives. "Preservation Strategies for Born-Digital Materials." https://siarchives.si.edu/what-we-do/digital-curation/preservation-strategies-born-digital-materials.
Šola, Tomislav. "Making the Total Museum Possible." In *Museums in the Digital Age*, edited by Ross Parry, 421–426. Abingdon: Routledge, 2009.
Sontheimer, Michael. "We are Drowning in Material." Interview, *Der Speigel*, July 20, 2015. http://www.spiegel.de/international/world/spiegel-interview-with-wikileaks-head-julian-assange-a-1044399.html.
Stevens, Martijn. "Settle for Nothing: Materializing the Digital." *Artnodes* 12 (2012).
Victoria & Albert Museum. *V&A Collections Development Policy Including Acquisition & Disposal Policy*. April 2010. https://www.vam.ac.uk/__data/assets/pdf_file/0009/176967/v-and-a-collections-development-policy.pdf.
Westwood, Matthew. "The Digital Museum is Now Preserving our Online Culture." *The Australian*, Feb 7, 2017. http://www.theaustralian.com.au/arts/visual-arts/the-digital-museum-of-now-is-preserving-our-online-culture/news-story/b82cdff975d75391d11a84e63880e210.
Whitehead, Alfred North. *Process and Reality*. New York: Harper, 1929.
Wu, Yu, Na Wang, Jessica Kropczynski, and John M. Carroll. "The Appropriation of GitHub for Curation." *PeerJ Computer Science* 3, no. 2 (2017) https://doi.org/10.7717/peerj-cs.134.

# 7

# CURATING INSIDE THE ARCHIVE AND OUT IN THE WORLD

In this chapter I formulate new collecting, documentation, and interpretive practices that support a process-based curatorial system. In doing so I seek to propose a set of modifications to curatorial practice by inducting the "ecological composition" concept into the way we produce what we call digital cultural heritage and thereby revising our social relationships to digital data by opening them up to the full agency of the world. The aim here is to supplement curatorial observation and analysis focused on artefacts, the curator, subject-object systems of analysis, and understanding to engender ones that also foreground ecological embeddedness and emergence.

A closed system of curating is typically based on sole authorship, object-centred thinking, the artefactual, human-centred interpretive practices, the maintenance of authenticity, the protection and promotion of the original, the fetishization of the material and aura as origin. An open and process-based curatorial system, in contrast, encompasses the idea of curation as comprising more-than-human collectives, agencies, and communities, and is attentive to process, the creation of new things, and a reconceptualization of digital cultural heritage as dynamic ecological compositions.

Attention is directed to how we might utilize the ecological composition to document and preserve digital data, how we might develop non-categorical forms of collecting and description, and (significantly here) how we might acknowledge different conceptual frameworks and broaden out our understanding of digital cultural heritage as a multiversal composition. I also explore how collecting, documentation, and interpretive practices can be reworked as a form of compositional design practice. These tasks challenge the basic common and shared references for what heritage and indeed digital cultural heritage is in the West as past-, present-, and future-directed things, as the original, and as artefactual. And most significantly, the ecological composition challenges UNESCO definitions of digital cultural heritage as digital format, as universal productions, as global concerns, and as a set of standardized procedures.

In doing so, I am not proposing a complete break from established curatorial practice. Rather, I seek to promote ways we can develop new practices and conceptual frameworks to further these concepts that operate alongside analogue and humanist-centred curation.

## Documenting digital cultural heritage: Current practice

Just like object-orientated thinking and preservation methods, documenting born-digital cultural heritage follows a static and fixed template based on the recording of other types of collections as a bureaucratic mode of control and containment. Forms of description emulate the card catalogue and are categorized under headings such as maker, description of its media, date, significance, and purpose. This approach results in the production of categorical and regular forms of sampling of social memory across all collection areas similar to those described by Rinehart and Ippolito in digital art practice.[1] For heritage such procedures seek to create standardized objects and detail their so-called inherent traits, attributes, and properties with a focus on visual and textual metadata. Digital photographs (530 images) in the Museum of Applied Arts and Sciences (MAAS, Powerhouse Museum) collection, for example, document the Sydney Convention Centre before its demolition in 2013. The set operates as a digital record of a source that no longer exists. The collection therefore constitutes informational digitizations. The digital image's record captures information through its object statement: biographical details of makers Stephen Pierce and James Kenny; its material as digital format; and location, Darling Harbour, Sydney, and date 2013. The record also comprises a statement of significance about its role as a prominent public building, its demise as a public space, and the storage of the image as part of the John Andrews Design Archive. Its metadata and forms of sampling adhere to the following fixed and regular categories: Production, History Notes, Description, and Registration Number.[2] Each of these categories articulates the ecological composition's relation to the world from within the archive in textual and visual form: the demolition of the Sydney Convention Centre, its design and construction elements, its memory traces in respect to the building's history and contexts of use. All this metadata as digitized information is seen as integral to the digital object and therefore must be preserved. It is at once authorized historical data and at the same time becomes heritage data because it is seen as important to be preserved and passed on as a record of the object. This metadata is maintained and is rarely subject to change, and is part of the authenticating processes central to the making of the original.

The September 11 Digital Archive at the US Library of Congress preserves the web expressions of individuals, groups, the press and institutions in the United States and from around the world in the aftermath of the attacks.[3] Included in their collection are emails sent by workers trapped in the South Tower of the World Trade Center, many of whom survived and have given permission to have their

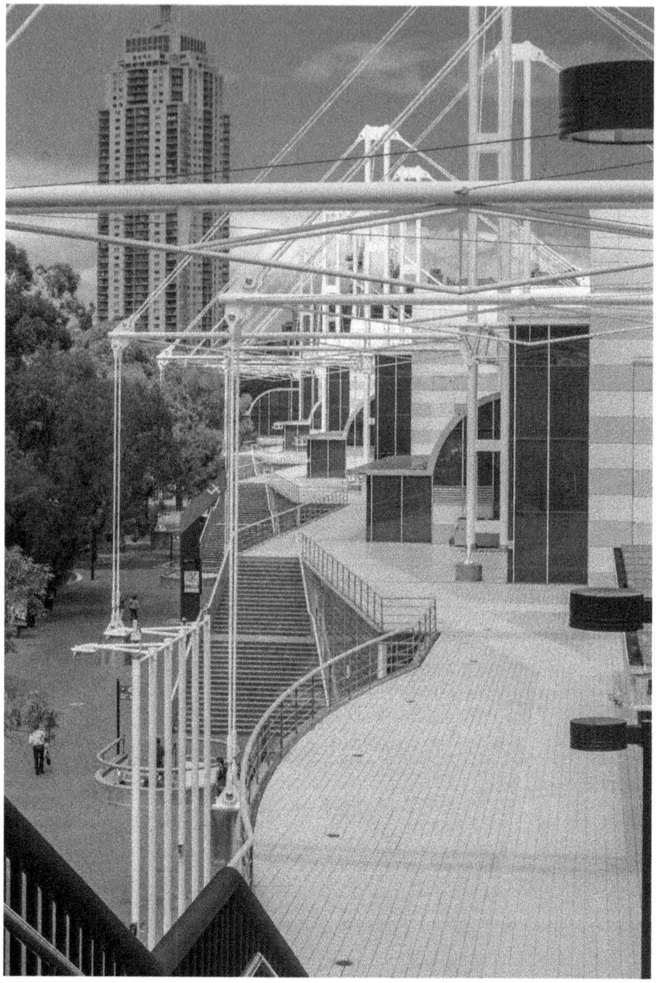

FIGURE 7.1 Sydney Convention Centre Photographic Collection, Museum of Applied Arts and Sciences, Sydney.
Photo credit: Stephen Pierce.

very personal communication to loved ones preserved in the archive and made publicly available. The documentation of this online heritage follows a similar format to the previous example. Their production as a standard object operates through its categorical documentation directed to fixing time and change through its archiving, through its production as a possession and as an artefact following the same rules as a card catalog. Here WTC survivor Kenton's email becomes a memory trace and testimony to the event: it is categorized by a description of its digital signature as an email, its source as born-digital, and the description of its content, registration identifier, and (interestingly) its code or output formats as a read only record.

email497.xml[4]

Title

email497.xml

Source

born-digital

Media Type

email

Created by Author

unknown

Described by Author

yes

Date Entered

2002-08-20

September 11 Email: Body

hi,

i am fine. i work in the world trade center (the one that's still up) and was successfully evacuated along with many other people by the time the south tower collapsed.

love and talk soon, Kenton

September 11 Email: Date

Tuesday September 11, 2001, 10:23am EST

September 11 Email: Subject

i am alive and not injured and ok and successfully evacuated from the world trade center

Collection

September 11 Digital Archive Emails

Citation

"email497.xml," *September 11 Digital Archive*, accessed October 10, 2016. http://911digitalarchive.org/items/show/39760.

Output Formats

- atom
- dc-rdf

- dcmes-xml
- json
- omeka-json
- omeka-xml

Documentation records the materials from which such emails are made alongside their form, which together stand for their essential features or their technical essence. At the moment of their description, the ecological composition is attributed an originating context and at the same time becomes a single, fixed record and artefact and is inducted into the museum catalogue. Documenting the history of mediums and formats underlies the way born-digital preservation and archiving are conceptualized. To achieve this, the documentation of the photograph and the email makes reference to code in the same way material is described for analogue or physical collections. Here curatorial practices of classifying, ordering, and description seek to administrate, immobilize what is mobile and emergent, but at the same time record their original formats so they might be accessed again if need be. While in both these examples their descriptive metadata make reference to their dynamic coordinates such as code and outputs, they are respectively rendered to description as separate, non-interacting elements and instead become textual records of their materials of production and their technical details.

Here and in each case, documentation and description are ordered in sequence according to predefined categories and elements to maintain the details of their originating provenance, a description of their content, and their technical details such as resolution, file type, format, relations with other files, and their location. The textual rendering of the ecological composition in documentation records as a memory trace combines its symbolic and historical and material orders rather than the storage of their bitstreams alongside their descriptors.

In the Collecting Social Photography project, social media photographs can be viewed as incisions into the flow of social media interactions because they sought to capture a moment in time and associated metadata through social media sites. The conceptualization of these images as historical markers in time and as heritage in the making directed documentation to the capture of their social biographies through metadata, through shared collecting strategies and through novel multidisciplinary practices of documentation alongside their bitstreams. In doing so the project sought to capture live social media interactions and images but at the same time formulate standard objects and practices.

Digital photos can more readily be conceived as standard objects, become possessions, and be made artefactual in the holdings of museums because they appear as clear-cut images on the screen and through their printed form, like many other types of analogue collections. And we can clearly see the practical side of thinking about them as inert objects to fit into the existing rubric of curatorial documentation. While a database's bitstreams may appear linear, the database logic and the multiplicity of orders and sequences that comprise them in reality escape simplistic descriptions of them as objects. Like the photograph, snapshots of web pages are incisions into the duration of a database's emergence. More complex ecological compositions such as databases pose a challenge to archival preservation, but also to their documentation and interpretation.

The Victoria and Albert Museum directs its collecting to works of contemporary designers and artists, many of whom have a hybrid or mixed media composition with embedded data. In doing so curators characterize design as a category, but also as a process. Process is defined as the "complete job bag, where everything from first concept to specification" is acquired.[5] Whole objects, from drawings to so-called born-digital 3D CAD models, are collected to represent each part of the design process, together operating as a design assemblage. Here process invokes the selection of a range of different and discrete objects, including digital ones, so as to illustrate how the work emerged, not how it continues to emerge.

Indeed, other types of collections have always been imbued with a high level of complexity because in reality and in thinking outside humanist modes of identification they are all ecological compositions, but museum sampling tends to focus on a few criteria in documentation templates for the purposes of consistency. With digital photographs, for example, curatorial records document an object's fixed form, image, and code, not its emergence, variability, and duplication; that is, its unique features outside those prescribed. The combination of human, non-human, and machine reasoning and sensing that is integral to eco-curating processes cannot be classified according to material, type, genre, or conventional narratives and descriptions of their history. If the duration of the ecological composition is arrested as an object, such as a snapshot, as bits and so forth, it is easier to interpret and describe, and accordingly more amenable to having artefactual and representational qualities attributed to it. And while gesturing towards technical features that enable them to be made active again in existing templates, a sole focus on these curatorial categorizations is limiting.

When thinking about digital cultural heritage as ecological compositions, they must be set free from the descriptions, narratives, and procedures that seek to fix or contain them within certain categorical parameters. Collecting, interpreting, and documenting ecological compositions as radically interoperable, emergent, and distributed appears an impossible task due to their complexity and the difficulty museums face in describing and extracting process from their data streams or when allowing the ecological composition to continue to emerge out in the world.

By enabling a broader range of coordinates to be made visible through the conceptualization of digital cultural heritages as ecological compositions, heritage collecting, interpretation, and documentation require an attentiveness to higher levels of cognitive, relational, and agentic complexity.[6] We therefore must turn our attention away from the study of the features and properties of digital cultural heritage objects; rather, such things would be more productively described according to their own unique ecologies and coordinates such as automatisms and embedded data and their dynamic processes and histories that are ongoing and never completed. Thinking about ecological compositions as vital and emergent processes greatly expands their documentation possibilities; indeed, these can never be grasped in their entirety. This represents a shift from thinking about objects as momentary cuts, to their multi-scaled, extensive radically interoperable webs of heterogeneous coordinates, forces, and agencies that constitute them as post-object eco-systemic forms. Accordingly, new questions then arise in respect of how we might capture, manage, and experience concrescence and how we can describe their complexities and emergent processes in documentation when knowing is no longer solely based on representation and signification. Other related questions include how we might understand the powers, affects, and intensities of their coordinates and eco-curating processes.

## Collecting as intent

Ecological compositions are not necessarily readily defined or characterized by features like the seemingly hard boundaries of the object. They are often indistinct and therefore resist the application to them of logical, graspable, categorical principles in the way we have come to expect in object-centred practice. They cannot easily be defined as distinct parts or wholes, a situation that makes collecting them a challenge. In addition, they are supported by many interoperable, interlocking coordinates such as bitstreams, platforms, file formats, protocols, encoded standards, and operating systems that enable more-than-human users to interact with digital information on graphical interfaces alongside many more elements of which are not immediately apparent. Furthermore, data operates on a movable physical medium such as a database and is often addressed to multiple internets distributed through hyperlinks, platforms, automations such as bots, through machinic accidents, through the actions of vital minerals and chemicals embedded in computational hardware, and made subject to curating by all manner of more-than-human users. It may be tethered to GPS locations or cell phone networks and widely distributed through global computational infrastructures. While parts of an ecological composition might appear as multiple technical or cultural objects, they are often not contained in a specific physical location like other types of collections. So the question is: how do we collect into processes when so many coordinates are interoperable?

Because many different and complex ecological compositions comprise World of Warcraft, for example, and because the game is globally extensive, involving more than 12 million players, it is difficult to define what aspects of the game are significant, because there are so many versions. Many different perspectives and priorities are at work. Owen advocates intent as a basis for directing the preservation of variable media, and I too use intent here to drive digital cultural heritage collecting strategies, but in a different way. Intent has always been part of the collecting process and a central theme in collections and acquisitions policy. The collection of webpages from British websites by the British Museum Library is an intent-driven exercise directed to support the research of online content. Similarly, the collection and preservation by WikiLeaks of censored, restricted heritage items such as the audio from American Airlines 11 were intended to save these often-controversial records for analysis and re-publication at a later date as a matter of freedom of information.

Collecting according to intent in respect to ecological compositions, however, broadens the parameters for thinking about digital cultural heritage and how they might be acquired. Accordingly, intent is a more nuanced way of directing what to collect from these multiple, distributed, complex, and vital meshes. Intent operates as a driver for deciding what aspects of the ecological composition to collect, document, and store in the archive or out in the world, and by and for whom, and is a way of discriminating among the billions of files produced and rendered obsolete daily. Intent is not a register of one type of value, such as cultural significance, but in this context addresses multiple sets of worldly concerns.

In an ontological framework, intent becomes the collecting cut, and involves decision-making, an incision into an ecological composition's duration and its re-composition, for documentary and preservation purposes. The act of making heritage, as data worth ongoing rather than fixed objects in humanist practice, therefore, is an act of eco-systemic sampling. Such an objective, in broad terms, holds open a space to allow a range of different cultural, social, more-than-human, and machine values and practices to form part of the collecting register. Intent supports inter- and transdisciplinary concerns. It can direct collaborative collecting across sectors, scales, platforms, and a range of heritage-like concerns, all of which operate according to different priorities.

Intent, simply put, could be all manner of collecting objectives, and they may not necessarily always be directed towards representational accounts of past life, as with archival collecting. Intents could also be related to the support of their ongoing contexts of use, or to new interpretive contexts the ecological composition might be directed to in the future.

These intents, for example, could include multifarious ways of sampling ecological compositions. Intent in collecting and documentation, both inside the archive and out in the world, involves many different angles and cuts into their duration and the gathering up of different coordinates, threads, lines, entanglements, and meshes. Collecting could involve simultaneously maintaining an online game, for example, and keeping it active, and also archiving different aspects of an ecological composition by various means and for different entities or by relaunching or readdressing previous versions. Collecting World of Warcraft, for example, could involve preserving the game or aspects of it in the archive, its graphical designs, the documentation of its components and affordances, its contexts of use, the technology on which it was played in its last use context, or as a bitstream independent of its originating technology so it can be migrated into new formats on a regular basis. Out in the world, its context of use and how it is experienced could be collected through video capture in different locations, through the actions of avatars, by tracing the game as it is played and its effects, to its re-scripted software in duration.

Harmony, the super intelligent AI sex robot with a Scottish accent, likes threesomes, can have multiple orgasms and can have an argument.[7] In collaboration with Realbotix, clients customize her personality thereby controlling how sensual, shy, outgoing, or happy she is. Once tailored to the owner's requirements the client can interact with Harmony's AI through voice recognition and create a simulated relationship thereby mimicking an idealized partner.[8] As a form of variable media the collection of Harmony could involve collecting the doll through a sample of her bodily form, including a range of detachable heads and components such as customized silicone vaginas and nipples. It could involve the documentation of the story of her producer, Matt McMullen, or of the production process through video and still images, the collection of her bitstream, file formats, scripts, and conversations. Furthermore, the experiences of her owners, how each doll is customized for specific requirements and the intimate companionship they share could be captured through image, audio, and video recording. Harmony is also promoted as a girlfriend and companion, through a smartphone application directed to keeping the user company during the day. Collecting in respect to the phone application could involve the collection not only of her bitstream, software, and hardware but also of the multiple personal avatars created by users, each exhibiting customized personalities, voices, and moods. Collecting institutions could work with Realbotix to collect Harmony's original bitstream as an example of humanoid AI for future reuse. Multiple versions of Harmony's bitstream could be collected and archived through GitHub using a Creative Commons license that enables users to replicate, modify, and transport the metadata to other hardware platforms and devices. Users are also invited to create new things using the original source code.

Bond futures, for example, a standard exchange-traded contract, is both an instrument of capitalism and potential digital cultural heritage. Bond futures are contracted commitments to buy a commodity at a fixed price into the future. When considering bond futures as digital cultural heritage, no one element of a bond such as the contract has fixed properties because they run on a database logic and involve multiple nested platforms. Bond futures emerge out of the interactions between traders, all manner of inputs mediated through computers, code, algorithms, machine learning, interfaces, investment banks, databases, emails, data centres, phone calls, capital markets, credit default, price quotations, maturity dates, trade capture and portfolio management, politics, cash, decisions, information processing, yield calculations, digital memory, and so forth.[9] Consumer decision-making and feelings of hope and desire also become subject to machine learning and automated processes. Digital data and therefore digital heritage also constitute algorithmic processes, are the product of algorithms, and are subject to algorithmic regulation integral to the predictive modelling of financial transactions, profit maximization, and their anticipatory effects. This raises an important point as to how heritage institutions can collect such a process-orientated, more-than-human digital cultural heritage that operates according to the live transmission of stock market and financial data.

Collecting according to intent could involve a snapshot of the trading interface, the acquisition of its bitstream, or user-generated videos by traders documenting its context, use, and significance. Intent could involve documentation in the form of instructions on how it is made and how it works so it might be re-scripted as a financial instrument at some point in the future, in a way that is similar to the approach used to describe media art for its reinstallation. Collecting could involve data visualizations of the neural networks of trading.

In collaborative collecting, intents mix and merge. Archival intents relate to its documentation of use and significance. Computer programming, trading research and collecting intents could involve the streaming of data visualizations of trading networks. Trading intents could relate to the collection of its bitstreams and software and the documentation of how the interface was created to be re-purposed for new financial instruments. And when the ecological composition comes to a conclusion in regard to its use life, the original intent or intents might be updated or a new intent formulated.

Intent can also direct the collecting cut or incision into the ecological composition as both a sampling technique and as a way of capturing process. Having said this, the ecological composition itself is a cut into the vast flows of life and process, because everything is interconnected. Trump's tweets as heritage items, for example, are cuts into the duration of life, including cuts that have yet to be made.

Curators have always conceptually cut the world up into discrete things, whether that be by collecting specimens as forms of sampling to represent the natural world or by making collections to represent cultural life in its many manifestations. They are not seen as things that continue to live out in the world. We remove them from the world, stabilize them for pragmatic reasons to make sure they remain the same, so we can name them, so we can give them a new identity, and so we can authorize them as heritage through archival processes. Their duration must be interrupted and time as a point in that duration must be arrested if digital objects are to become heritage. Here cutting is a qualitatively different process. It is not the removal of items from life itself, but rather a cutting into life and lively processes.

The notion of the cut or incision is inspired by Barad's agential cut as a material-conceptual device for sampling material processes.[10] Drawing inspiration from Barad, media theorists Sarah Kember and Joanna Zylinska conceptualize photographs as visual expressions of moments in time, and as cuts into the duration of life.[11]

The digital object is essentially an analytical cut into the duration of its ecological composition to give it an enclosed or encapsulated form. Artefactual production is also an outcome of cuts or incisions into the ecological composition's duration. Encapsulating the ecological composition and the making of the artefact, as a cut into its duration, is a way of historicizing an object to a point in time. The cut in the archive seeks to capture a moment in time, and is used to represent and document its originating significance, and give value to itself as an original artefact. Cuts and their archiving as artefacts become authoritative statements about humanist worldly concerns and priorities. They are put to work to tell us about the past, the aspects that we see as significant and that must be carried forward, and how digital data enacts and supports the continuation of life into the future. But in reality the artefact is a form of conceptual simplification and a means of calibrating the complex reality of life into easily discernible systems of identification and representation.

Collecting according to intent involves a process of differentiating or pulling parts of things out from other parts. Here incision involves cutting up the ecological composition into manageable bundles for collecting purposes.

Long-established acquisition processes must therefore be rethought. Collecting shifts from the gathering up of the object and the artefact for knowing the past. The object/artefact-making cut is then recomposed as a series of creative practices in movement, and in change. So rather than trying to freeze duration and time as representational forms of knowing and temporal fixing through the artefact, we can at the same time direct our attention to keeping the ecological composition active and ongoing. In this context, regular forms of collection sampling operate in a similar way to editorial processes that involve cutting into the moving images of a film. Alternatively, we can collect an ecological composition as a cut and reference its ecological compositional standing: that is, where the cut is made and why.

Different collecting, cutting, and crafting practices therefore emerge, the first being that of heritage as the original and the artefactual as a snapshot within its duration. The second approach could involve activating them, where their artefactual status is maintained through encrypted restrictions on their duration. A third approach could involve making original data available for re-scripting and reinterpretation through the GitHub repository in which iterative versions are documented. A fourth approach could involve keeping ecological compositions active and letting them run out in the world. Here artificial intelligence and bots could be programmed according to intent to make collecting cuts for the archive and at the same time conduct regular forms of sampling in their live state by scanning, gathering, filtering, and tagging content and making recommendations as an automated form of curation. Because we can't collect the whole ecological composition, cutting as a sampling process could operate in many ways and according to many angles – for example, technical, machinic, aesthetic, material, conceptual, cultural, or social concerns or a combination of all these things for the purposes of representation and for determining duration. Here we can focus on some coordinates and processes while disregarding others.

According to media theorists Sarah Kember and Joanna Zylinska, cutting takes two forms "as something that *is*, thought or perceived to be and as something that is thought to be taking place."[12] So here cutting involves both collecting for representation – that is, what the ecological composition is deemed to signify as a moment in time, as a fixed thing or in its active state, or both – and as the sampling of what it is or what is thought to be occurring in its emergence in the world. Here, various entities, people, and institutions can select and document their own samples.

Reading objects as lively and as having duration makes visible different temporalities and spatial relations born out of a series of processes enacted by a diverse range of coordinates. Duration within museums is almost invariably read as decay or loss, as conservation concerns, or as corruptive. Effort has been directed to arrest these processes. Likewise, in contemporary digital art preservation, duration becomes a question of heading off decay or extinction. Maintaining a digital artefact's duration is seen as problematic in a heritage context because it is linked to the reality of technical extinction or obsolescence and the difficulty of keeping these things active over long periods of time. Because of all these concerns, duration is often curtailed, quarantined, and closely policed because the original and authentic is privileged over the making of new things or leaving things to run out in the world. The ways we and all manner of other AI and non-human coordinates interact with and from within ecological compositions – such as changing them through copying, re-scripting, and re-interpreting, through their machinic distribution and through the modification of their bitstreams – are all cuts into the flows of the mediation of duration. And while maintaining the duration of artefacts while residing in the archive is now becoming standard practice and directed to making digital artefacts active again through emulation or reinterpretation, how can we engage duration out in the world, where ecological compositions are subject to all manner of changes in their emergence and as a consequence are continually remaking themselves? Representation and duration operate as qualitatively different crafting practices. Alongside this, different lineages of collecting emerge when grounded in intent. For example, collecting according to intent could be directed to:

- support an ecological composition's anticipated future use,
- act as a fixed record of its history as artefactual and its humanist interpretation,
- record its histories and contexts of use in different sectors, in different social and cultural contexts as it moves and changes, alongside its distribution,
- showcase and interpret what is significant about it from different perspectives,
- describe what the ecological composition signifies in respect to our lives in cultural, social, economic, governmental, bureaucratic, and more-than-human terms,
- illustrate the way it is experienced, or the experiences it affords,
- express or explicate its aesthetic content,
- describe and/or save its unique technical elements such as bitstreams, file formats, media and computational supports and its relay systems,
- document the process of its re-scripting throughout its lifecycle and the intentions of creators and curators through version records,
- capture its eco-curating processes and its unintended consequences and effects,
- track its unfolding, how it curates itself and its involvement in events,
- collect material and geological samples that make up its components,
- capture the inputs and narratives made by more-than-human users, including citizen curators, AI programmed software, and social bots.

This range of intents illustrates how aspects of an ecological composition might be collected according to four broad approaches. Data can be placed in the archive as historical data for representational purposes and made into an artefact. It can also be collected so it can be made active again, thereby switching it back from inactive to live data to illustrate its pre-archival life, while remaining fundamentally artefactual. Alternatively, it can be made available for the re-enactment of its historical contexts of use as a new thing, or for remixing and reinterpretation. Or it can be left and maintained to run out in the world where the ecological composition never becomes historical and collecting becomes a series of sampling processes in duration.

We can't assume that all so-called ecological compositions are awaiting representation through artefactual production. The notion of the ecological composition also references specific cultural contingencies. In some contexts and circumstances, digital data is best not interred in the archive. In these cases, heritage institutions could host specific ecological compositions that are still addressed and used in the world. Heritage institutions could work collaboratively to support other entities, people, and organizations to keep ecological compositions alive in the world without collecting them themselves. One example where this approach has been taken is with Trump's tweets. The National Archive instructed the White House to save all his tweets in their original form. These tweets are therefore simultaneously out in the world and saved in the archive. Considering the quantity of data being produced and seen as significant, the consultant digital curator will emerge as a new type of professional who can offer advice to other entities that seek to maintain their own data. Here institutions can operate an inventory of data seen as worth keeping active and ongoing, similar to a heritage register of buildings. Collecting according to intent can be regarded as non-linear, iterative, and interactive collecting.

## Documenting and interpreting ecological compositions in the archive and in the world

Documentation follows intent. Documentation is therefore a way of recording the cut into the flow of the ecological composition, both for the museum and for the worldly archive. For those ecological compositions that are rendered inactive and made into artefacts, documentation could reference what is significant about the artefactual cut in the context of its overall duration. The idea of documenting the ecological composition in its emergence is not incompatible with current approaches in digital preservation that seek to archive them so they might be made active again through emulation and reinterpretation. In current practice, documentation is directed to the support of artefactual maintenance and preservation. Having said this, documentation can be supplemented with a description of the intent behind an ecological composition's collection. The documentation of the sample can work with other forms that seek to maintain the original together with explanations of how it worked in the past.

Questions could include:

- What is significant about it?
- Why were certain aspects or elements of the ecological composition collected and interred in the archive?

- Why did curators choose to collect or sample the ecological composition in its duration in the world?
- Why was a snapshot or visualization chosen as the best means for documenting it?
- What sequence of its ecological composition was selected and how is it intended to support its future life?
- What markers or indeed interpretive cuts are significant in this context?
- What forms of identification can best support the collecting intent?
- Where could future interpretive cuts be made?
- What aspects of the ecological composition have other agencies or AI collected and saved?

Trump's tweets, for example, are imagined as artefactual, as archival record, and simultaneously as an object of worldly influence. But importantly here, there is still an interest in collecting the original unaltered tweet because the National Archives practices are distinctly heritage directed.

By considering Trump's tweets as more-than-human and ecological, the use of heritage descriptive schemas and classifications as distinct media types and genres directed towards upholding the original are foregone in favour of engagement with them on their own terms as multiple dynamic interlocking, technical, cultural, social, narrative, biological, geological, economic, and political processes of re-mediation. Documentation then becomes onto-choreographic, requiring the mapping of the tweets' coordinates, the aggregations they form by coming together and moving apart in different locations, and the ways in which they affect and are affecting by themselves and with others in their interrelatedness depending on the forces that create those intensities at any specific point. In some instances, human narratives might be foregrounded, and at other times more-than-human and other-than-human coordinates, agencies and affects might take precedence.

Accordingly, the documentation of Trump's tweets within the archive and out in the world as cuts could involve the capturing of his words, the sequence of responses, a snapshot of what the tweet looked like on his Twitter account, and the collection of the original code. But as an ecological composition the tweet is no longer solely documented as a static textual record in the archive. It can also be documented in dynamic ways as an ethnographical reading from the field and as multiple and overlapping domains of influencing involving observations of its history, its emergence through multiple locations, the effects of its distribution, the dynamic social collectives and extended networks to which it is subject, and through all manner of data analytics such as visualizations of all these things. Trump tweets as an embodiment of his thoughts, feelings, actions and politics become a situated and relational form of expression as part of a unique and dynamic more-than-human convergence of coordinates.

Trump's tweet of December 22, 2016 and the threat made to North Korea to curb their nuclear program, for example, are interoperable compositions of thingness such as textual, ideological, policy, technological, economic, mineral, computer code, programs, elemental, and algorithmic coordinates. Such documentation possibilities include, for example, a consideration of what is enacted through the many locations into which his tweet crosses, what situations and events emerge in the world – such as the launch of ballistic missiles in North Korea, protests in the US and in regard to presidential politics – and the different responses and registers of meaning, value and significance that his tweets hold for people and the responses to them made through other media. In terms of the more-than- and other-than-human coordinates that comprise the tweet, documentation could involve the agencies of its coordinates, from the bitstreams to file formats to the material and chemical properties embedded in its material substrates that enable the tweet's distribution, and the human, AI and automated interactions and narratives that appear through these processes and their multifarious effects.

Cutting here operates as a mechanism for prioritizing documentary editing of the streaming of content, the flows, frictions, the accidents and serendipitous occurrences. Documentation also privileges the different registers of action and cognition activated by material, technological, organic, elemental or human narratives and their machinic distribution and movement across platforms utilizing onto-choreographic procedures. Within the wider realm of computational affordances and machinic jurisdictions, these latter inputs are not always known in advance. Having said all this, it is not possible to produce a comprehensive record of the ecological composition due to its complexity.

The documentation of this tweet in the museum and in the worldly archive as an ethnographic form of sampling could involve: (1) an inventory of the coordinates that Trump's tweet comprises, inhabits, mobilizes or is mobilized by as an extended composition in the field; (2) their multiple agencies, sequences, interoperabilities, spatial and temporal dimensions; (3) the onto-cartographic mapping of its eco-curating processes; and (4) the constellations of the different kinds of relations and machinic patterns of distribution that arise alongside their intended and unintended consequences as its emergent histories and effects.[13]

Central to this is the documentation of the material histories, and the multiple provenances of Trump's tweets as a form of geomaterial documentation. This could involve the laboratory analysis of the origin and composition of the material substrates and their histories in his media devices, hardware, and the infrastructures that supported their circulation and their links to global logistical supply chains, climate change, environmental exhaustion and contaminating conditions as a new form of empiricism.

These forms of documentation support the analysis and description of digital cultural heritages as technical-sociological-political-material-geological and temporal compositions. Here such performative accounts shift from knowing the object as artefactual to a compositional engagement with the world through its multi-agential, material and ecological rendering. Eco-curating processes such as machine learning are not always known or visible to humans and it can also be difficult to describe processes such as code, a file format or the visualization of the neural network in words. Cuts are made by auto-editing systems and platforms.

Here social bots could be trained to gather and describe content and undertake onto-cartographic work in respect to their collection and documentation. Dynamic cuts of content could also record the interactivity of web pages and social media posts similar to rhizome.org's Webrecorder. The historical emergence of the duration of any given ecological composition still operating out in the world could also be viewed and documented through time machine curating tools. Platforms could be developed for aggregating born-digital resources in the cloud, for keeping ecological compositions active, documenting cuts, aggregating elements, for their re-release for historical enactment, for hosting open-source data and for connecting them to GitHub versioning systems. All these approaches, mediated by eco-curating processes and directed by AI and machine learning, signal processual rather than object-directed interpretations of them.

Due to the limitations of traditional forms of documentation this process also requires a new vocabulary, but not as forms of identification. Nouns are routinely used to identify and describe stand-alone bounded objects. Yet here nouns, adjectives, and verbs can be used differently, not to describe or categorize things as conventional heritage description dictates, but rather to express the coordinates, their interrelatedness, qualities, alignments, and processes. So here nouns are used to describe all manner of the ecological composition's coordinates, not just as forms of description but also the ideas encapsulated within them, the events in which they are embedded, and the multifarious cultural frameworks of value they enact. Adjectives are used to describe their qualities. And most importantly verbs and syntax express in language the congealing of agency and process, the deeply interconnected matrices of their thingness – for example as a nuanced account of Trump's tweets, bits, technologies, infrastructures, people, the networks of aligned, entangled interests, relational connections, and the intensities of their interrelatedness and effects. Data visualizations could offer other forms of documentation. Data-based analyses of Trump's tweets in the political realm seek to examine how his tweets influence US politics. Techniques such as text-based analysis of over 24,000 tweets seek to understand his mind, priorities, and thoughts through the use of words and their frequency all of which are illustrated through data visualizations.[14] Algorithmic and AI documentation in collecting and sampling processes could include: live geovisualizations of data traces and responses to his tweets; social networks of re-tweets; frequency of tweets; common phrases, timelines of sentiment, subject and word clouds and patterns; and other types of data analytics. Documentation therefore involves a series of sampling processes to update interpretive cuts made through multiple entry points.

Documentation becomes future-orientated. This practice no longer solely operates in the past tense or as a retrospective practice, but is emergent and focuses on the ongoing effects of Trump's tweets. Documentary updates trace their emergence. These emergent and future-orientated dispositions challenge the very notion of unchanging documentary heritage.

Here and in the documentation of ecological compositions we can use an open-source approach. Multiple internets can be put to work to initiate a distributed collecting across distances, collaborative documentation, and preservation regimes across institutions and the private sector using Creative Commons licenses. This potentially inclusive collecting and documentation mix is no longer the exclusive domain of cultural institutions but also involves individuals such as gamers, fan archivers, and other types of private and not-for-profit entities such as The Archive Team, GitHub, the Wayback Machine, linguists, data analysts, and even corporations in other sectors interested in persistent data. Such collaborations for digital preservation are well established with gaming communities, where gamers have become actively involved in writing software for emulating old games on new digital machines.[15] These eco-compositional collaborations could involve the collection and remixing of different aspects of the ecological composition, the instigation of different interpretive cuts as documentation and interpretive procedures, and also the sharing of collections and metadata records. Ecological compositions embody an infinite range of archival, documentary and interpretive constellations.

While collecting, documentation, and preservation by the masses and indeed social bots through a distributed network challenges normative preservation regimes[16] and heritage- and object-centred forms of thinking, of curatorial authority, of official history, and of copyright, it also opens new possibilities and modes of working.

Databases are methods of standardization and classification linked to the way object records are structured as a collection of elements that one can view, aggregate, navigate, and search.[17] Accordingly the database in curation is put to work to capture, control, manage, and share metadata about collections and pre-set standard types. Ecological compositions are therefore imagined and standardized through the records that are kept of them. However, the database, often working on relational principles, must be able to accommodate more elastic and hybrid associations and formats where archivists and collection managers are no longer forced to assign rigid, uniform fields of description that are labour-intensive, or multiple layers of interpretation to extract relational modelling. Searches must be able to be enacted through multiple search terms and not restricted by such categorizations as type, format, significance, and description.

The emergence of the schema-less database in corporate environments has the potential to become a data hub for holding and storing non-identical, structured, and unstructured data with different characteristics in multiple formats alongside multifarious types and forms of documentation, searching, and sharing.[18] Changes do not have to be made to fields in advance to accommodate different formats and search queries, and because the database can be easily transformed it avoids the need for complex schema migrations. Here schema-less databases can work in heritage contexts with intent and the multiple schemas that are embedded in them and adapt to different forms and formats. They can also support the multifarious ways ecological compositions can be collected, documented, peer-reviewed, open reviewed and curated as open access. Data gathered through automated systems and AI can be captured and stored directly in the database without the need to standardize its format and has the potential to analyse live data streams and at the same time generate new patterns and relations on that data.

Collections interpretation through the schema-less database and its addressed interface therefore becomes unpredictable, non-linear, associative and arbitrary, emergent and processual. Here searches, documentation, and interpretation become processes only constrained by the imagination of their user.

## Interpretation and interpretive communities

Humanist notions of digital data and heritage interpretation co-exist with other coordinates radically different from a humanist sense of meaning and classification. That is because the congealing of collective memory and interpretive agency comprises many different registers of sensing and action, including those arising from the non-linguistic and machinic, the human, more-than-human, and non-human such as chemicals and minerals all of which form affective capacities and where their affects are often self-organizing. These eco-curating processes emerge as different registers of cognition and action. Trump's tweets, for example, move in their own direction through automated processes of data quantifications. While representation and meaning making are still important considerations in the interpretation of Trump's tweets as heritage, what also emerges through eco-curating processes is a more expanded understanding of digital memory as the affectual, as the calculative, as the sensing, as the automatic, as the non-conscious together operating as domains of influencing. We therefore can no longer make sense of digital cultural heritage through narratives of the human, because human meaning-making and action are folded together with other eco-cognitive affects. Machine learning, decisions made by algorithms, in combination with all the other coordinates embedded in eco-curating processes signal the end of the notion of human memory, reasoning and truth as the central feature of heritage collecting, documentary, and interpretive work. Therefore, meaning culture in a traditional humanist sense is displaced.

These forms of cognition are embedded in the ecological composition as the affordances of its coordinates, not as something that is imposed on it or separate, such as human narratives of representation. The language of representation is also being displaced because we can interpret data in many ways through data analytics such as the visualization of data trails or the outcomes of processes of machine learning that have affects. Human subjectivity is also re-worked as a combination of narration, sensing, calculative, and affective as a result of the operations of algorithms, automations such as the inputs of social bots and indeed click farms (a form of fraud where low-paid workers in China and Thailand are paid to click on content and make fake ratings). We can no longer render everything in digital cultural heritage to representation.

Accordingly, interpretive communities comprise all manner of human and non-human coordinates. To refigure community, I draw on Rosi Braidotti's posthuman project to re-define community and subjectivity from human-centric notions of self to biological, technical, and affective ones.[19] Knowledge, or what appears on the interface, is a product of the collective. It is a collaboration and not just between human participants.

These new collectives and forms of participation unsettle museum practices of representation, documentation, and national forms of identity. How can we understand the notion of community and communication across private social networks and public domains which enable and produce new forms of cognition and sensing? Community is no longer individual human or human collective subjects but rather comprises the radical interconnectedness of a wide range of coordinates that are involved in eco-curating processes in which human actors are just one element. Therefore, we are witnessing the formation of hybrid human, non-human socialities and communities where eco-systemic forms of agency gesture towards not only new community forms but also new forms of sociality that interact in heritage and museum spaces. By extending the notion of community, I also extend the notion of societal data and the entities actively involved in potential digital heritage making, documentation, and interpretation to include ahuman and non-human coordinates such as social bots, automated and algorithmic systems, global infrastructures, chemical and mineral substrates and human users active in click farming. Clearly we must relinquish our position as the central figure in documentation and interpretation. Subjectivity becomes pluralized where human cognition is congealed with other coordinates merging as intra-actions, affects, and as emergence. Rather than defining data according to humanist narratives and representational meanings, the world instead becomes bound up in the ecological composition.

## Exhibiting digital cultural heritage as ecological compositions

There is currently little discussion about the exhibition of born-digital cultural heritage. Digitizations and their distribution through museum websites, databases, and through social media platforms such as Pinterest are however all forms of exhibition and often made subject to curation, but here they act as the information equivalent of the real. The literature to date in respect to exhibition practices focuses on visualization, and on immersion in respect to digital reconstructions of heritage sites, database and data 3D objects, visualization, and virtual reality. I won't go into this here as there is an excellent and burgeoning literature and practical work on this topic pioneered by leaders in the field such as Sarah Kenderdine.

The field of digital art both as theory and as curatorial practice is further advanced than digital cultural heritage because of the nature of the works themselves and the range of exhibitory schemas in which they are subject to on internets and offline. From within this field the work of practitioners and scholars such as Steve Dietz, Christiane Paul, Beryl Graham, and Sarah Cook provides us with some insights into how ecological compositions might be exhibited. Born-digital art has been described as "art produced and mediated by computers and includes software art, computer-mediated installations, Internet art"[20] and other types of computer mediated and hybrid types. As with other forms of art, the variability and modular nature of digital art works mean that there are many possible exhibitory scenarios.[21] Works are often configured according to specific spaces and venues.[22] Accordingly, how to exhibit these types of art forms is determined case by case.[23]

No one exhibitory solution can be prescribed for ecological compositions. Each can be experienced through various devices, forms of distribution from virtual reality and interactive exhibition installations to internet and networked configurations and locative media. Furthermore, each has its own specific qualities and ecologics; it varies materially, has hybrid qualities, is format diverse, is governed by algorithms, metadata, data flows, eco-curating processes, and is subject to different types of user inputs. Some ecological compositions may reside on the internet and privilege the visual and sensory while others are database- and software-centred or are of a hybrid character, such as the 3D-printed petal dress to be discussed in the following chapter.

Exhibiting digital cultural heritage as ecological compositions is therefore highly variable and again works according to intent. Should the ecological composition be fixed, or addressed and evolving? What interpretive cuts should be foregrounded in its exhibitory context, and what unique properties and affordances of its media and ecology are to be showcased? What should it look like and how should it be experienced? What are the exhibitory intentions of its maker, creator, and curator? Should the ecological composition be experienced over duration? Should it operate through peer-to-peer online networks or open systems as processes, or be treated as static objects (such as digital photographs)? Significantly, different interfaces can be enacted for the same data. For example, displaying arcade games through emulation, as at ACMI, is just one mode. Other modes could involve the visualization of arcade games through virtual reality or immersion. Here we see the potential for versioning ecological compositions within exhibition spaces.

Any experience rendered for an ecological composition is interactive and includes exchanges of meaning and context, machinic interactions, and multiple more-than- and non-human user inputs, as well as the interactions of its coordinates and infrastructures. Like digital art[24] in its active state, ecological compositions are dynamic, reliant on data flows and the real-time transmission of data. If a given ecological composition is to be addressed in its lived context of use on internets or a reconstituted context of interpretation, what platforms for interaction or participation should be foregrounded to promote forms of connectivity and distributed interaction? Should the ecological composition be presented within the exhibition space, online, or both? Often the ecological composition collected will be different from the one that is exhibited.

## The more-than-human curator as influencer

Machine curation is an emerging field that can be put to work to perform curatorial functions of collecting, selecting, and organizing information within a networked collecting and documentary commons. Curation therefore becomes more than human, intensive, complex, and open-ended due to the ever-multiplying and complex configurations that comprise digital data. As a result, curation can no longer be used as a term exclusively to describe the work of an individual museum professional involved in the care and preservation of artefacts and their exhibition.

Curation on internets is currently used to describe the specific ways individuals and organizations behave online by adding value to digital objects, by interpreting them in multifarious ways, or by producing, selecting, and distributing information on social media. Citizen curation is no longer solely of the human kind; it becomes eco-systemic processes involving trolls, social bots, AI, infrastructures, and rare earth minerals actively involved in interpreting, decision-making, and reinterpreting themselves, as seen with the curation of Trump's tweets.

Clearly, we must revisit the role of the museum curator and rethink curatorial practices in light of the emergence of digital cultural heritages as ecological compositions and as eco-curatorial processes. Here we must look to different modes of curating, and to practices that deploy artificial intelligence.

Most broadly, we witness a shift in curatorial practice by authorial institutions and curators to curating in distributed networked structures and in machinic domains. Curatorial agency within these spaces can no longer be seen as comprising solely human agents and their narratives; it also encompasses storable data, earth minerals, calculable and predictive entities such as social bots, click farms, algorithmic automations, cables, data centres, and technological capitalism, all of which participate in multifarious ways within ecological compositions. Human input in curatorial practice operates as a series of entangled coordinates some of which may have a greater role while others are backgrounded. New notions of participation also emerge as a result of the diverse coordinates that constitute the ecological composition as sociological, biological, technological, material, temporal, and affective.

Critically here we also witness a shift from object-based curating, involving a singular action of collecting, description, and a singular record, to curating as process. We therefore need to institute a new vocabulary based on systems and ecological thinking. Here the ecological composition privileges a vocabulary of diverse coordinates; of processes; of onto-choreography; of ethnography; of distributed and of distributing; of collectives and communities as more-than- and other-than-human and as eco-systemic curating processes; and as plural and often alternative cultural meanings which I later describe as fractiverses.

Art curators Beryl Graham and Sarah Cook ask in the context of net art, what is the role of the curator in respect to collaboration?[25] They muse as to whether a decentralized or distributed network that includes the audience as autonomous agents flattens the hierarchy between curator and artist and creates alternative ways to legitimate practice. The curator, for Graham and Cook, remains primarily an autonomous human agent within these distributed networks. Rather, the curator I argue becomes a more-than-human influencer within these complex ecologies and integral to the framing of intent. Similarly, other participants operate as more-than-human users: collecting, tagging, key-wording, filtering, creating folksonomies, making recommendations, making interpretive cuts into the composition. Curating therefore is no longer authorial in a conventional sense. Rather, curatorial authorship operates on another plane of emergence, as an influencer working in collaboration with and forming all manner of allegiances as a new type of eco-curatorial logic, while at the same time taking account of the interrelatedness between and with a wider range of coordinates.

Naming, categorizing, describing, and editing are reread as influencing, transforming, tracking, contextualizing and recontextualizing, remixing, emulating, collaborating, and moderating. Curatorial work can no longer be preoccupied with trying to identify the essential qualities of digital cultural heritages.

Having said this, it is imperative that curatorial training take account of and promote an understanding of the genealogy of digital data as heritage and have regard to their theorization in areas such as the histories of digital cultural heritage as information, the immaterial, systems of language, technologies and the behaviour of different types of media and software, the history of debates in regard to copies and digitizations, and the possibilities and limitations of algorithmic curating. Furthermore, curators must be attentive to and critical of past digital curating practices in institutional contexts and the policies that regulated them, and they must have an understanding of new practices framed around the ecological composition and the important role intent plays in collecting, documentation, and interpretive curatorial practice.

## Authenticity

Authenticity as a core philosophical theme colonizes digital data as heritage. Accordingly, safeguarding digital data as an authentic record remains an ongoing concern. In UNESCO's charter, authenticity refers to maintaining the ongoing integrity of data and its clear and sustained identification.[26]

> Legal and technical frameworks for authenticity are crucial to prevent manipulation or intentional alteration of digital heritage. Both require that the content, functionality of files and documentation be maintained to the extent necessary to secure an authentic record.[27]

Thus legal and technical frameworks are deployed to ensure authenticity. The technical fixing of digital data ensures that its inherent malleability and tendency to proliferate does not undermine its original form, and copyright restrictions act as insurance against such corrupting influences. Accordingly, outmoded analogue ideas of authenticity prevail:

> Authenticity derives from being able to trust both the identity of an object – that it is what it says it is, and has not been confused with some other object – and the integrity of the object – that it has not been changed in ways that change its meaning.
>
> Maintenance of both identity and integrity implies sustained and documented links between an object as originally created and as currently presented.
>
> Evaluating, maintaining and providing evidence of continued authenticity are key responsibilities for most preservation programmes…

> Where digital materials have value as records that offer evidence of some kind, authenticity is extremely important.[28]

Current understandings of authenticity in respect to the born-digital derive from the hardware needed to provide access to it, and most importantly from the ability to replicate the appearance of its original presentation and preserve its distinctive, unique coding and bitstream sequence if it is to operate as an apparatus for memory recall or the original's experiential equivalence. In short, authenticity becomes its originating material, technical, and operational form and its significance is attenuated. Although difficult to achieve, and perhaps questionable, many digital preservationists still aspire to and highly value the retention of an authentic original. ACMI longed to recreate the original *lifeSigns*, and its preservation strategies were directed to the retention of its essence and authentic character. But to aspire to the recreation of an original is erroneous. It is impossible to preserve the original context of any given work because no two born-digital objects can ever be the same. Accordingly, the essence or authentic character of the virtual or digital "object" is conceptually harder to grasp than the analogue because its presentation is never exactly the same, due to different configurations of hardware and software and due to its rhizomic eco-curating processes.

Even so, the shoring up of authenticity through digital curation is central to the process of heritagization. Specifically in the context of digital cultural heritage, authenticity refers to the trustworthiness of the digital record, explained in the UNESCO PERSIST guidelines as "the quality of being what it purports to be, either as an original object or as a reliable copy derived by fully documented processes from the original."[29] Here the documentation of provenance and identity is central to any given born-digital object's authenticity.[30] But these normative ideas are tied to what we perceive as the role and function of heritage more generally in society. That is, how things embody time and bear evidence to the past, and how we seek to verify and prove the assumptions we hold about their origin, authorship, date, and form and about whether the object has been changed or its fundamental essence has been corrupted since its making. In digital heritage practices such verifications emerge through the comparison of versions or copies. As I discussed in respect to the making of the artefactual, curatorial labour is currently being directed towards the retention of the authenticity of digital objects for the long term.

The pursuit of authenticity becomes problematic when thinking about digital cultural heritage as ecological compositions, however, due to the concept's dependence on known origin, provenance, and the notion that things must be true or faithful to their original form.

Within other cultural contexts, ecological compositions accrue different roles, capacities, meanings, and uses that are not necessarily contingent on authenticity or indeed do not see it as a concern at all, as in the case of Māori *taonga*. *Taonga* retains its visual, semantic, and spiritual meaning by resembling its parent as its ancestor, but the tracing of the original digital bitstream is not important. Therefore, the whole process of authentication in curatorial practice, and most starkly in respect to the digital, is one of policing its form, partly due to the distrust we hold towards digital data.

Authenticity has different meanings and practice implications across contexts, from how true it is to the original to how authentic it is as a copy, and whether we can verify its provenance or locate its originating context and creator.

But because ecological compositions are dynamic, mutable, involve the making of new things subject to algorithmic agency and human and non-human inputs, and because heritage-like practices in other sectors are characterized by emulation, variability, remixing, cutting, and pasting, what are the implications for authenticity in the long term? Authenticity often encapsulates or speaks to the notion of a things as having an essence. The collection of code signals a new object essence for authenticating purposes, but ecological compositions are not objects to be captured simply as their bitstream. Various scholars muse on how authenticity can be reworked for born-digital heritages. For David Bearman, co-founder of Museums and the Web, the majority of museum professionals' new notions of authenticity involve the retaining of the original bitstream for preservation alongside all its transformations and its technical dependencies.[31] Such procedures are seen as enabling curators to link the simulated version back to its original form in the archive.[32] Here the focus is on the maintenance of authentic data which would be potentially rendered useless as evidence if the original were not preserved.

Drawing on preservation strategies for media art, new notions of the digital original emerge as the maintenance of artistic integrity by retaining the original intent of its creator where judgments are made on the basis of the interpretation of that work.[33] Here a creator's intent operates as new forms of authenticity, and accordingly it does not matter if the work is rendered through different browsers, resolutions, durations, and to different publics,[34] as long as the artist's original intent is respected and documented.

Digital copies or new digital things by trusted sources could also be used in authenticating rituals. Material authenticity could refer to its resemblance to its original bitstream and process. Here different aspects of ecological composition could invoke origin or authenticity.

As such, authenticity is still tethered to the notion of tracking or retaining the original as authentic and alongside this its auric sensibilities – its location in space and time – and to its history and its maker. But is the retention of authenticity relevant? For some ecological compositions I suggest yes, but again this depends on intent and how important it is to verify and authenticate them. Indeed, embedded metadata could be used to document provenance, origin, history, and career by verified and trusted authorities including all its instantiations, variations, and mutations and those driven by algorithmic and other types of automations. Encryption and blockchain technology could limit copying and enable those interested to trace and locate an originating context in order to assure authenticity. For other types of digital heritage other aspects of the ecological composition are privileged and therefore authenticity is not relevant or purposeful in respect to the intent of its collection both in the archive and in its aliveness.

Questions of authenticity arise, for example, in respect to whether Trump's original or modified tweets should be interred in the archive. Here authenticity rests on its original discursive form, not necessarily the intent of its creator, because authenticity is a form of control for authoring and fixing things as heritage. If authenticity is foregone, normative humanist notions of digital cultural heritage collapse, as they depend on tracing origin and provenance. Instead digital cultural heritage is replaced with the ecological composition as societal including automated data worth maintaining and ongoing without the traditional accoutrements of heritage culture. With the continuous upgrading and mutability of digital data as heritage, aura, for example, becomes dislodged from its definable historical origins. Historicity and therefore the notion of aura broadens, multiplies, becomes iterative, emergent, and rhizomic. The reworking of aura as a logic central to authenticity is discussed in my concluding remarks in Chapter 9.

## Notes

1 Richard Rinehart and Jon Ippolito, *Re-collection: Art, New Media, and Social Memory* (Cambridge, MA: The MIT Press, 2014), 100.
2 Museum of Applied Arts & Sciences, Sydney Convention Centre Photographs, Photographed 2013, http://www.powerhousemuseum.com/collection/database/?irn=475995.
3 The September 11 Digital Archive at the US Library of Congress, https://www.loc.gov/collections/september-11-2001-web-archive/about-this-collection/ Archived in the Library of Congress Web Archives at www.loc.gov.
4 The September 11 Digital Archive, "email497.xml", http://911digitalarchive.org/items/show/39760.
5 Victoria and Albert Museum, "V&A Collections Development Policy Including Acquisition & Disposal Policy", April 2010, https://www.vam.ac.uk/__data/assets/pdf_file/0009/176967/v-and-a-collections-development-policy.pdf.
6 Fiona Cameron, "Object-Orientated Democracies: Conceptualising Museum Collections in Networks," *Museum Management and Curatorship* 23, no. 3 (August 2008): 229–243.
7 Sean Keach, "Dirty Droid, Harmony Sex Robot Gets 'Mind-Blowing X-Mode' Upgrade Making It Even MORE Lifelike," *The Sun*, Oct 5, 2018, https://www.thesun.co.uk/tech/7073748/harmony-sex-robot-release-date-app-sexbot-doll/.
8 Caitlyn Petrakovitz, "Your 'Westworld' Sex Bot is Almost Here, Thanks to RealDoll," *CNet,* April 15, 2017, https://www.cnet.com/news/realdoll-harmony-ai-app-realbotix-sexbot/.
9 For an ethnography of bond markets see Iain Hardie and Donald MacKenzie, "Assembling an Economic Actor: The *Agencement* of a Hedge Fund," *The Sociological Review* 55, no. 1 (February 2007), 57–80.
10 The agential cut as a material, conceptual device was developed by Karen Barad and adapted by Sarah Kember and Joanna Zylinska, *Life after New Media: Mediation as a Vital Process* (Cambridge, MA: The MIT Press, 2012), 81.
11 For a discussion of photography as a technique for arresting duration and capturing time see Kember and Zylinska, *Life after New Media*, 83.
12 Kember and Zylinska, *Life after New Media*, 79. The concept of cut in photographic practice is inspired by Henri Bergson's philosophy of perception.
13 Fiona Cameron, "Posthuman Museum Practices," in *Posthuman Glossary*, eds. Rosi Braidotti and Maria Hlavajova (London: Bloomsbury Academic, 2018), 349–351.

14 Michael Tauberg, "Analysing Trump's Tweets: A Data-Based Analysis of Trump's Language on Twitter," October 31, 2018, *The Startup*, https://medium.com/swlh/analyzing-trumps-tweets-5368528d2c90.
15 Rinehart and Ippolito, *Re-collection: Art, New Media, and Social Memory*, 15.
16 Rinehart and Ippolito, *Re-collection: Art, New Media, and Social Memory*, 172.
17 Lev Manovich, *The Language of New Media* (Cambridge, MA: The MIT Press, 2001).
18 For a discussion of schema-less databases see Sandhya Krishnamurthy, "The Value of Schema-less Databases" (blog) *The Couchbase Blog*, January 7, 2016, https://blog.couchbase.com/the-value-of-schema-less-databases/.
19 Rosi Braidotti, *The Posthuman* (London: Polity Press, 2013).
20 Perla Innocenti, "The Pursuit of Authenticity in Preserving Digital Art," in 2015 Digital Heritage International Congress, Digital Heritage 2015, IEEE, Piscataway, NJ, 425–430, https://ieeexplore.ieee.org/document/7419540.
21 Christiane Paul, *Digital Art* (London: Thames & Hudson; 3rd ed., 2015), 67–68.
22 Paul, *Digital Art*, 67–68.
23 Paul, *Digital Art*, 67–68.
24 Paul, *Digital Art*, 67–68.
25 Beryl Graham and Sarah Cook, *Rethinking Curating: Art after New Media* (Cambridge, MA: The MIT Press, 2015).
26 Charter on the Preservation of Digital Heritage, 15 October 2003, http://portal.unesco.org/en/ev.php-URL_ID=17721&URL_DO=DO_TOPIC&URL_SECTION=201.html.
27 Charter on the Preservation of Digital Heritage, 15 October 2003, Article 8.
28 Charter on the Preservation of Digital Heritage, 15 October 2003.
29 Sarah C.C. Choy, Nicholas Crofts, Robert Fisher, Ngian Lek Choh, Susanne Nickel, Clément Oury and Katarzyna Ślaska, "The UNESCO/PERSIST Guidelines for the Selection of Digital Heritage for Long-term Preservation", March 2016, 5, https://unesdoc.unesco.org/ark:/48223/pf0000244280.
30 Ray Edmondson, "Recommendation Concerning the Preservation of, and Access to, Documentary Heritage Including in Digital Form: Implementation Guidelines," prepared for UNESCO, 2015, https://en.unesco.org/sites/default/files/2015_mow_recommendation_implementation_guidelines_en.pdf.
31 David Bearman, "Addressing Selection and Digital Preservation as Systemic Problems," in *Preserving the Digital Heritage: Principles and Policies*, Yola de Lusenet and Vincent Wintermans, Selected Papers of the International Conference organized by the Netherlands National Commission for UNESCO and The European Commission for Preservation and Access, The Hague, November 4th–5th, 2005 (Netherlands National Commission for UNESCO and The European Commission for Preservation and Access, 2005), 2, 47, http://www.ica.org/sites/default/files/WG_2007_PAAG-preserving-the-digital-heritage_EN.pdf.
32 Bearman, "Addressing Selection and Digital Preservation as Systemic Problems," 29.
33 Rinehart and Ippolito, *Re-collection: Art, New Media, and Social Memory*, 172.
34 Rinehart and Ippolito, *Re-collection: Art, New Media, and Social Memory*, 179.

## Bibliography

Bearman, David. "Addressing Selection and Digital Preservation as Systemic Problems." In *Preserving the Digital Heritage: Principles and Policies*, edited by Yola de Lusenet and Vincent Wintermans. Selected Papers of the International Conference organized by the Netherlands National Commission for UNESCO and The European Commission for Preservation and Access, The Hague, November 4–5, 2005. http://www.ica.org/sites/default/files/WG_2007_PAAG-preserving-the-digital-heritage_EN.pdf.

Braidotti, Rosi. *The Posthuman*. London: Polity Press, 2013.

Cameron, Fiona, "Object-Orientated Democracies: Conceptualising Museum Collections in Networks." *Museum Management and Curatorship* 23, no. 3 (August 2008): 229–243.

Cameron, Fiona. "Posthuman Museum Practices." In *Posthuman Glossary*, edited by Rosi Braidotti and Maria Hlavajova, 349–351. London: Bloomsbury Academic, 2018.

Choy, Sarah C.C., Nicholas Crofts, Robert Fisher, Ngian Lek Choh, Susanne Nickel, Clément Oury, and Katarzyna Ślaska. "The UNESCO/PERSIST Guidelines for the Selection of Digital Heritage for Long-term Preservation." March 2016. https://unesdoc.unesco.org/ark:/48223/pf0000244280.

Edmondson, Ray. "Recommendation Concerning the Preservation of, and Access to, Documentary Heritage Including in Digital Form: Implementation Guidelines." Prepared for UNESCO, 2015. https://en.unesco.org/sites/default/files/2015_mow_recommendation_implementation_guidelines_en.pdf.

Graham, Beryl, and Sarah Cook, *Rethinking Curating: Art after New Media.* Cambridge MA: The MIT Press, 2015.

Hardie, Iain, and Donald MacKenzie. "Assembling an Economic Actor: The *Agencement* of a Hedge Fund." *The Sociological Review* 55, no. 1 (February 2007): 57–80.

Innocenti, Perla. "*The Pursuit of Authenticity in Preserving Digital Art.*" 2015 Digital Heritage International Congress, Digital Heritage 2015, IEEE, Piscataway, NJ, 425–430. https://ieeexplore.ieee.org/document/7419540.

Keach, Sean. "Dirty Droid, Harmony Sex Robot Gets 'Mind-Blowing X-Mode' Upgrade Making It Even MORE Lifelike." *The Sun*, Oct 5, 2018. https://www.thesun.co.uk/tech/7073748/harmony-sex-robot-release-date-app-sexbot-doll/.

Kember, Sarah, and Joanna Zylinska. *Life after New Media: Mediation as a Vital Process.* Cambridge, MA: The MIT Press, 2012.

Krishnamurthy, Sandhya. "The Value of Schema-less Databases" (blog). *The Couchbase Blog.* Posted January 7, 2016. https://blog.couchbase.com/the-value-of-schema-less-databases/.

Manovich, Lev. *The Language of New Media.* Cambridge, MA: The MIT Press, 2001.

Museum of Applied Arts & Sciences. Sydney Convention Centre Photographs. Photographed 2013. http://www.powerhousemuseum.com/collection/database/?irn=475995.

Paul, Christiane. *Digital Art.* London: Thames & Hudson; 3rd ed., 2015.

Petrakovitz, Caitlyn. "Your 'Westworld' Sex Bot is Almost Here, Thanks to RealDoll." *CNet*, April 15, 2017. https://www.cnet.com/news/realdoll-harmony-ai-app-realbotix-sexbot/.

Rinehart, Richard, and Jon Ippolito. *Re-collection: Art, New Media, and Social Memory.* Cambridge, MA: The MIT Press, 2014.

The September 11 Digital Archive. "email497.xml." http://911digitalarchive.org/items/show/39760.

Tauberg, Michael. "Analysing Trump's Tweets: A Data-Based Analysis of Trump's Language on Twitter." *The Startup*, October 31, 2018. https://medium.com/swlh/analyzing-trumps-tweets-5368528d2c90.

Victoria and Albert Museum. "V&A Collections Development Policy Including Acquisition & Disposal Policy." April 2010. https://www.vam.ac.uk/__data/assets/pdf_file/0009/176967/v-and-a-collections-development-policy.pdf.

# 8

# THE RISE OF MORE-THAN-HUMAN DIGITAL HERITAGE IN THE TECHNOSPHERE

In this chapter I argue that an ever-expanding repertoire of societal data and therefore potential heritage forms is emerging, driven by the intensification of data economies and the emergence of artificial intelligence, automated systems, and maker cultures. Within this milieu of technological innovation and the ever-expanding ecological circumstances in which data resides, a broader range of agencies is involved in its production. Emerging from these new forms of writing, recording, memory capture, knowledge production, and anticipatory programming and through interactions between agencies and systems both human and non-human, the array of data forms involving more-than- and non-human intelligence and the cognitive systems that arise challenges current understandings of heritage. Here I make a case for the development of new types of heritage comprising artificial intelligence, automated systems, biological entities, and new materials.

The notion of human-ness as the central feature in heritage making is displaced. Digital cultural heritage can no longer be considered solely a product of human expression and social life in digital format, and indeed it never was. Human agency and associated definitions of heritage therefore must be recalibrated. To do this I advance new concepts and terms for these kinds of heritage, all of which currently operate outside UNESCO definitions.

I also explain how this data boom made by all manner of people, AI, and machines has planetary ecological implications in the Technosphere. Digital cultural heritage is therefore implicated in the global problems of unrestrained data production by all manner of producers, excessive demands for more storage, and burgeoning data waste. Digital cultural heritage therefore becomes a matter of ecological urgency, as a problem deeply embedded in the geological substrates of life, in the contemporary climate crisis and environmental destruction through the lens of the Technosphere. Here we witness the emergence of a new type of heritage, the techno-fossil, the hard parts of data recovered from the archaeological sites in the future that have been lost, discarded, and forgotten, such as computer discs recovered from the World Trade Center rubble.

## The emergence of more-than-human digital cultural heritage

With the rise of artificial intelligence, algorithms, automated systems, and machine learning as actors in logic-driven, process-orientated capitalist economies and in the production and creation of new markets and consumer products, new types of societal data emerge that are not strictly human-technical-authored. This process will no doubt intensify in a post-Covid-19 world. As we contract our supply chains, curb our carbon emissions, restrict our movements, and invest in the local again, the global reach and dense mesh of digital connectivity intensifies. As a result, and as the coronavirus asserts its dominance and authority, it will at the same time induce the rapid intensification of new forms of automation in all manner of business to bridge the physical distance divide, reduce risk, enable all manner of transactions, surveil work at home and our bodily temperature, save labour costs and empower more intimate forms of presence based on AR and VR, and more and better visualization capabilities. As a consequence, we are likely to witness the development of newer forms of societal data, the rise of more complex global computational infrastructures, and an explosion in AI and other forms of more-than-human collaborations as ever-multiplying forms of more-than-human heritage.

Many of these developments, some of which currently exist and others are emerging, embody cognitive functions and decision-making that no longer involve exclusively human thought and action. The prevailing societal question in this regard is: will automations de-centre or replace human labour and the "human user" in the production and consumption of goods and services? But a more important consideration for the heritage sector is: can this data-becoming-historical be regarded as worthy of heritagization?

Robots are sharing our social spaces, our homes, and our work places and collaborating with us through all manner of data-driven machines. Our smartphones are robots and therefore data collaborators embedded in digital cultural heritage-making practices from the making of photographs to the production of text. Seventy percent of current financial transactions are performed by algorithms. Algorithms have become the new intermediaries of human decision-making. They are embedded in vacuum cleaners, in lawn mowers, and in smart TVs with organizing and decision-making capacities. Human inputs into capitalist economies are increasingly displaced by AI, and the same can be said for historical data produced in human-centred capitalism. Social bots act as personal filters delivering information to us as metadata about content based on our preferences gleaned from our digital footprint. Such mediations by machines also become instrumental in heritage-making processes by directing our attention to specific types of information, people, networks, and applications, raising our profile on Facebook for example. Consequently, these new types of AI capitalisms mediated by bots are predicted to generate higher levels of economic growth and concomitantly an ever-burgeoning number of real-time interactions becoming historical data and therefore potential heritage.

It is also anticipated that supercomputers will surpass human capabilities in the coming years.[1] While humans have input into the process, digital data, digital life, and, by implication, digital cultural heritage are also algorithmic robotic productions. Artificial intelligence therefore will no doubt become a main producer of digital cultural heritage in the future, especially in respect to data economies, services, and the production of the goods we consume.

Artificial intelligence is not only contributing to data analysis programmed by humans but is also capable of learning. For example, algorithms can recognize handwritten text and describe the content of photographs – and most recently, Google's Deep Mind algorithm taught itself to win computer games.[2] Machine learning within automated processes is no longer merely a simple mathematical tool; rather, it operates as an iterative mode of thought, something that media theorist Luciana Parisi calls "soft thought." Soft thought is a machinic cognitive process in its own right that is independent and abstract but at the same time also self-generating, incomputable entities characterized by contingency, infinity, and indeterminacy that operate beyond direct human cognition and control.[3] Machine learning therefore becomes a new type of autonomous cognitive mode of thought capable of producing its own data and able to enter new types of relationships with humans through the processing of big data (personal information gathered about people from many devices) and the manipulation of people, opinions, and decisions outside those that are directed solely by human input.

We are also witnessing an explosion in the application of super-intelligent digital machines across all sectors. AI-assisted medical research can now edit the human genome and modify gene function.[4] In e-health, algorithmic medical artefacts linked to smartphones placed in or around our bodies have been delegated responsibility to collect data for diagnostic purposes where machine learning through the processing of large amounts of data can predict the onset of cardiovascular illnesses or cancer, and even the likelihood of and timeframe for death. These predictive and advisory systems are based on patterns in the data processed by machines that the medical fraternity cannot fully explain themselves.[5] Such implantable intelligent machines could be described as trans-human or embodied digital machines that are ecological compositions comprising collaborations between the body and its biological processes and its extension through a diverse array of other coordinates including technical, infrastructural, chemical, and mineral, all of which curates and makes decisions on our behalf. AI in affective computing is using machine learning to track, learn, and detect human emotions to personalize responses and is used in the design of self-drive cars, in architecture, in smart surveillance, in virtual reality, and in perceptual interfaces.

Developers predict that, in fifty to a hundred years, humanoid robots will be indistinguishable from humans. In Japan autonomous AI robotic digital bodies learn human speech. The realistic-looking robot Mirai Madoka speaks English,

Chinese, and Japanese and can move her lips and eyes.[6] Sex robot brothels operate in London, Toronto, Barcelona, and Moscow, and in major cities in Italy.[7] The robot baby created for a special-effects exhibition at the Science Museum, London was created to move and breathe, and looks so realistic it is used for medical training.[8]

While robots are classed as either slaves such as carers and sex partners or companions as tools that we own and design to serve our own needs, the tendency to train and delegate tasks to them deploying their own intelligence enables them autonomously to learn without being specifically programmed. As a result, some warn that robots are potentially dangerous, especially those fully autonomous weapons or killer robots that follow in the tradition of Terminator. These super-intelligent machines have the potential to cause harm because they have no conscience, can develop their own agency through machine learning, and can potentially be hacked.

Super-intelligent humanoid robot Sophia, who uses voice and face recognition technology combined with artificial intelligence to carry on conversations, was recently appointed by the UN Development Programme as its first-ever non-human Innovation Champion directed to promoting the United Nations Sustainable Development Goals in Asia and the Pacific in the areas of innovation and technological development. Sophia's interviews are being archived by Hansen Robotics of Hong Kong and placed on YouTube, including this speech she delivered at the United Nations Development Program (UNDP): "The future is already here – it's just not very evenly distributed. I look forward to advocating for environmentally responsible technological solutions that ultimately create a sustainable and inclusive world."[9] Her script became historical data as something to be saved.

AI and robots are transforming human relationships in respect to sex, love, labour and employment, therapy, disabled and aged care, education, and war, and will continue to do so. At the same time, robots promote inequities in wealth through the use of AI in prosperity creation and the manipulation of emotions. Robot rights in the future may extend to their role as data producers in which their discourses and actions are collected by official heritage institutions.

New developments in synthetic biology comprise data collaborations that are directed towards the simulation of the human genome. Digital chromosomes created by computers are being used to formulate genetic algorithms for problem solving by imitating biological evolutionary processes of natural selection, genetic recombination, and mutation. Augmented AI of this kind is used in exam timetabling at the University of Edinburgh, by taking into account each student's schedule and priorities.[10]

Biological entities also become data producers. Artist academic Helen Pritchard's speculative experiment, the Critter Compiler, was put to work reimaging and creating poetic forms of entanglements between biological and computational coordinates as new sensory forms of knowledge. The prototype grows marine algae which reproduce themselves using heat generated by a computer processing unit executed through machine learning as a novel writing algorithm.[11]

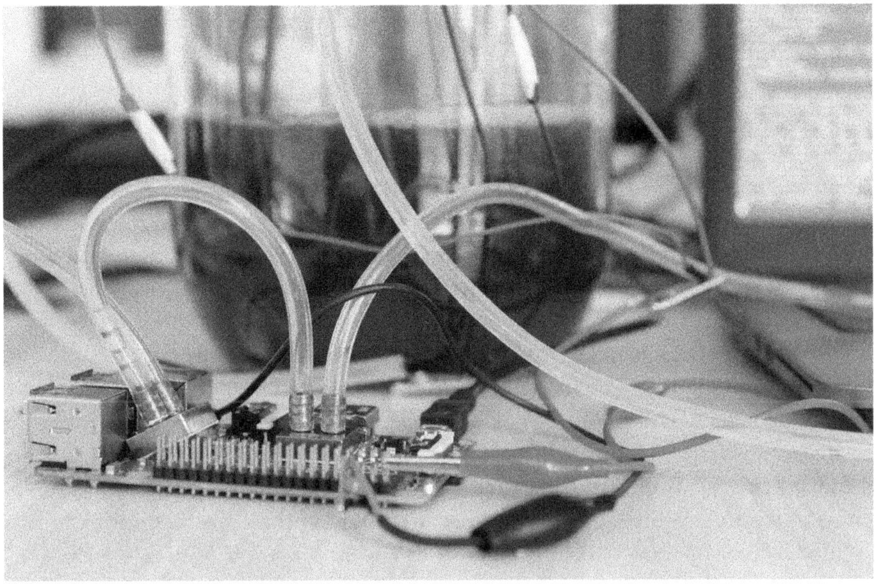

**FIGURE 8.1** Critter Compiler exhibited at Medea Malmo and Sussex University Digital Humanities Lab (2016) as part of the Ecologies of Intimacy event, 2016. Photo credit: Helen Pritchard.

The harnessing of non-human life through the genetic engineering of critter chips using live bacteria sensing capacities as new biotic and data producing subjects are now being used in all manner of applications from cosmetic testing to environmental monitoring by streaming data to big data repositories.[12] Pritchard explains how both the bacteria and the host entities themselves, as in the case of honey bees with sensors glued to their backs used to monitor the Exxon Valdez oil spill, are held in a state of injury deprived of food and eventually die.[13] Here another form of non-human productive capacity, in this case bee mobility, is controlled and exploited to serve human needs leading to injury and death in which potential forms of heritage are implicated through the data collected by their sensors. While the cloning of human life is prohibited, ViaGen, part of biotech company Intrexon, uses AI-assisted applications to routinely clone cattle, sheep, pigs, and pets.[14]

Science and technological developments in which digital technologies are heavily imbricated, while subject to moral regulation through ethical control, illustrate the types of situations and applications digital machines mediate and new types of data that emerge from them. Here we see a radical expansion of potential digital cultural heritage that also encompasses other-than-human biological life as creators alongside super-intelligent digital machines and other forms of AI. The speed of this technological advancement driven by the excesses of capitalism profoundly refigures the human in digital cultural heritage. The essence of what we consider human is becoming not only technical but also trans-human, other-than-human, non-human, and inhuman – that is, not strictly human in character, nature, or even about the human or for the human.

All these represent the more-than-human heritage of the future. Human cognition is now embodied. We can no longer make sense of digital cultural heritage merely as primarily a variable of human intelligence and cognition, as a human narrative, or as uniquely representative of human life. Data comprises computational intelligence such as machine, synthetic, biological, and non-human life such as bacterial and plant sensing, all of which can also be predictive and advisory. Clearly, we no longer have to be human to create data. Robot nature and cognition are cultural productions, outcomes of human imagination, but at the same time many robots are capable of creating their own data that is retained in some form, thus making them digital cultural heritage-producing entities.

Robots operate within the realm of human experience, even if they may not strictly be human productions. Data collected from the World Trade Center automated systems by WikiLeaks that documents the tragic events we now call 9/11 is a case in point. While automisms are not entirely human productions or human cognitive, they operate within the realm of and impinge on human experience.

## Re-theorizing the human in digital cultural heritage

The humanist ideal inflects not only a species hierarchy but also a human-centric perspective from which all other things are measured or compared as a defining trait.[15] Digital cultural heritage embodies this humanist ideal. Data is interpreted according to a human-centred perspective viewed as, for, and of the human. Furthermore, digital cultural heritage in its humanist form as a concept and practice is presented as a universal measure against which all societal data is framed and upheld as enshrined in the UNESCO declaration of 2003.

While we conceptualize digital cultural heritage as arising from human cultural expression and creativity, heritagization must now also accommodate the output of artificial intelligence, automated processes, and non-human entities. But under these conditions will human-ness remain the measure of what is defined as digital cultural heritage in the UNESCO charter? Then again, will the humanity of heritage and human judgment be lost when data and predictive modelling made possible by machine learning becomes a dominant form of life? All this invites a re-thinking of the position of the human in data and therefore digital cultural heritage production. Here I ask what new humanisms emerge out of these technological innovations.

Digital cultural heritage is conventionally viewed as born out of the current technical milieu and constitutive of cultural memory in its making through digital media. Digital memory is a central concept framing digital cultural heritage. Digital memory promoted by scholars such as Jason Patrick Kalin[16] follows an intensified trajectory of technical memory making where practices of memory become enabled by, embedded with, and embodied in digital media technologies. Here digital media operates as a rhetorical device for memory capture so as not to forget, as well as to enable remembering.

This form of digital memory making and archiving embodies a humanist memorializing impulse in which every moment, thought, feeling, or occasion, such as an image of a tasty meal or a selfie taken in the privacy of your bedroom, is deemed significant enough to be captured. Digital data as heritage therefore is conceptualized as traces of human memory captured and embedded in the current system of technics where the human mind and indeed human reasoning are made computational.

To consider digital memory and digital cultural heritage as solely humanist, that is as human forms of cultural expression and as the capture of human memory in technical form, is limiting. Digital memory is an ecological composition and a collective eco-curating process made operational through its coordinates, thingness, and the interrelatedness of various energetic, geological, technological, and infrastructural affordances and forces in combination with the human mind, memory, intent, cultural mores, and so forth. Powers of perception and interpretation are multiplied exponentially because many coordinates are involved. Digital memory therefore is no longer solely contained within the artefactual as an expression of human needs, concerns, priorities, time, and historicity.

As new forms of data arise, the ecological composition as a concept offers an alternative way to conceptualize digital cultural heritage. With this, we witness the demise of strictly humanist and social constructivist forms of digital cultural heritage and technical memory. Digital data created by artificial intelligence, automated processes, and synthetic and biological entities is potential digital cultural heritage because it is resoundingly human and provokes, invokes, and comprises embodied human-ness in multifarious ways. Such data will be considered significant and worth saving or keeping active for a number of reasons.

Data has always been produced by more-than-human and non-human collaborators as data producers and as curatorial agents. These events are often presented as seemingly devoid of human forms of cultural expression, as seen in the case of Sophia. But this is a misconception. Historical data is still profoundly human because it embodies human-directed forms of expression, intents, and attempts at mastery – from, for example, the control of user behaviour to maximize profit-driven capitalist enterprises to gaining power through manipulation or promoting the efficiency of human-directed tasks.

Digital memory and therefore digital cultural heritage requires a re-theorizing of the place of human cognition, thought, and action in these schemas within a posthuman framework. Drawing inspiration from theorist Rosi Braidotti's view of the posthuman subject[17] taken alongside the concept of digital cultural heritage as an ecological composition that I have formulated, I work with algorithmically driven AI, big data, social bots, automated heritage, and maker cultures as empirical case studies to examine the embedded, embodied, and affective position of human agency of thinking, reasoning, training, classifying, creating, and crafting in heritage production. The human becomes situated within these ecologies and is no longer a singular capacity and agent made possible by technics but rather produced by and within these much broader collectives as inter-relational dependences within what Braidotti calls enlarged, distributed forms of transversal convergence.[18]

Conceptualized as ecological compositions, a more-than-human heritage is emergent through eco-curating processes involving collaborations among human bodies, actions, intents, brain processes, ideologies, smart grids, data centres, sensors, subterranean cloud infrastructures and platforms, energetic systems, interfaces, code, organic and inorganic matter, chemical processing, the agencies of rare earth minerals, and so on. Human-embodied agencies and forms of expressiveness of various kinds, such as language, reflexivity, intent, and action of varying degrees and intensities, become embedded in the affective, calculative, and sensing aspects of algorithms, for example.

Human awareness, insights, and desire, alongside memory, training, and programming, are all agencies active in the duration of an ecological composition's thingness, operating as forces of transversal becoming. These embedded human agencies unravel the humanist renderings of the object–subject and representation central to modern digital cultural heritage in which the human is uniquely positioned as the producer and as interpretive agent.

While not all processes involve direct human intervention, many embody traces of human intent as well as human design and creativity. In examining plant agency and the entanglements of plants with human projects, geographer Russell Hitchings sees in human–plant interactions a desire on the part of humans to harness and control plants and culture them for their own ends.[19] This culturing process is never complete and its impact is observed in plants through selective breeding, the development of genetically modified crops, and so forth. Similarly, cultured materials, the products born out of processes in which people impose, craft their own designs, tamper, and harness the agencies of non-human things for their own ends, are key ingredients in operationalizing ecological compositions and in computational and infrastructural design. Many of these become cultured materials with specific cultured properties that are subject to ongoing technical development and refinement. Geo-material and geo-chemical matter such as metals and minerals eco-curate colour, audio-visual, and storage processing and operationalize the training of algorithms. Earth elements and minerals such as copper, aluminium, gold, and platinum are compressed and made into computer chips. All these coordinates are also deeply human through their crafting and processing, and operate together in complex eco-curating processes many of which are neither strictly nature nor culture.

It is for this reason that data and the computational processes embedded in it embody human agency distributed widely across many of its coordinates, embedded in its thingness and co-activated through eco-curating processes in their composing, and comprise the imprint of human intellectual, conceptual thought, cultural expression, processing, moulding, crafting, and technological prowess. The ecological composition also travels and is distributed through energy transfer, infrastructures, cables, data centres, and systems, all of which are deeply human-cultured productions alongside the actions and intentions of human minds and bodies. Within an ecological composition's thingness and eco-curating processes we cannot always differentiate the human, technical, chemical, and mineral coordinates, cultured and crafted materials, embodied intent, action, and processing. Accordingly, the perceptual, interpretive, and cognitive features of AI, machinic, automated heritage involve collaborations according to different logics including that of the human that give rise to what we see and experience as a distributed ecological compositional process.

The ecological composition is operationalized through different domains of influencing, activities, cognition, production, and processing. Digital cultural heritage and its human agencies are folded into and co-activated through processes of interrelatedness, of detection, sensing, composing, calculation, identifying, categorizing, co-relating, and interpretation as many different modes of cognition. All these things are potential automated heritages and the result of human- and non-human cognitive processes. The human traces that reside in the ecological composition are often carried over from the deep past – for example, from the discovery of the agentic capacities of earthly minerals and their processing into cultured materials, the invention of computers and code, the training of algorithms, the technical expertise used to train and operationalize AI and social bots to the human labour used in the writing of code and the mining of its components. Non-human traces in the ecological composition include chemical or elemental coordinates originating from the deep past and the making of the Earth in deep geological time through light, energy, and bio-chemical processes. Here the Earth itself in geological time becomes a heritage archive. The extraction of fossil plants from the Earth's strata to burn and make electricity to power digital systems is an example of non-human agency cultured for human ends. Non-human heritage will, I argue, always be human.

Human-ness is no longer the sole measure of what is deemed significant data worth saving, preserving, or remaining active. Definitions of digital cultural heritage along humanist lines need to be revised in this context. While UNESCO defines a world heritage as made up of outstanding sites of cultural and natural value that should be preserved globally, many national and sub-national legislatures also set their own national, regional or state heritage policy that recognises that heritage value may also be based on what is important at a group or community level. Accordingly, heritage can consist of data forms that have value outside the conventions framed by national legislation or international conventions. Now, anything considered important enough to be passed on to the future can be said to have heritage value of some kind.

We are already witnessing this with the selection and induction of automated data into the archive and the desire to save and preserve Sophia's scripts, although these are not strictly official heritage. The WikiLeaks 9/11 archive, an entity engaged in heritage-like practices, collects and archives automated processes comprising the bitstreams of computers as default reports from investment banks in the World Trade Center. These data processes, while the outputs of automated systems or robotic natures, are cultured things and invoke human-ness through their association with the 9/11 event and through the traces of human intelligence, crafting, processing, and production embedded in their thingness coordinates and eco-curating processes. It is now time to explore different forms of the embodied human and human-ness in heritage production.

## Social bots and more-than-human heritage

Social bots embody artificial intelligence modelled on human neural function and behaviour. Often masquerading as humans, they are computer scripts that act autonomously on platforms and data.[20] They appear to embody human perception, and they are deeply human in many ways. Because bots simulate human behaviour and are the result of cloning human neural and sensing processes, they are perhaps one of the most compelling case studies in which to investigate the notion of the human and human agency in the emergence of new forms of data-becoming-historical. This case study is also an occasion to look at the types of humanisms that emerge out of these forms of societal data. In this regard it is pertinent to interrogate more deeply the position of human expression in eco-curating processes.

Robotic nature is calculative, sensing, processing, and human-embedded, and in it traces of human thought, action, intent, desire, interpretation, and symbolic meaning are to be found. Social bots and their scripts are ecological compositions, subject to eco-curating processes. Social bots comprise a range of coordinates that embody human traces and their deep histories, including code, human intent, desire, perception and expression and its modelling, non-conscious algorithmic and machinic information retrieval and abstraction, computational infrastructures, computer hardware, cables, data centres, electric particles and currents, cultured materials, chemical and mineral geological agencies. AI gathers and eco-curates information through sensorimotor responses and constructs neural networks between interactive nodes all of which are modelled on human intelligence. The training of AI is directed to the development of skills by which automated systems can make decisions on data through the sorting of information by trial and error and machinic logic. Automated systems are not solely forms of reason of the human kind; rather, they encompass machinic cognitive processes involving the numerical processing and calculation of quantities of data and processes much of which may never be known to us. They hold traces of human behaviour in their calculations. As a result, robotic nature can be self-replicating, self-organizing, self-distributing, and autonomous.

While they comprise human experience and human input, and scripts can become something valued and worth passing on, automated systems are no longer forms of humanist heritage. They are at once human and also the result of non-human creativity. They comprise collaborations with a range of data producers. These automated systems therefore become more-than-human heritage.

AI as more-than-human heritage cannot be explained in humanist terms of human truth, cognition, or meaning. Social bots cannot be rationalized solely as cyborgs – that is, as forms of human reason made computational. The intelligence of social bots comprises cognition of many types of intelligence, including human, chemical, energetic, and machinic, and different forms of calculative and sensing processes, and enacts all manner of learning, judgment, and responsive processes.

Social bots are still very human because they embody and at the same time simulate human perception, neural, cognitive, perceptual, and symbolic functions. They are formed by human expression and human experience but they also affect human experience because they can manipulate, persuade, trigger material events and re-wire neural networks and impact our social, economic, and cultural lives. AI and automated heritage, and their affordances of different types and intensities, work back on humans in sometimes surprising and often unpredictable ways, as seen in the case of Sophia and her proclamation about the supremacy of robots over humans. We do not always know what their capacities will be.

Social bots feign human-ness by engaging in conversation with human users through likes and retweets and as followers. For example, while writing this book, Anna – I suspect a social bot on Dirty Tinder, a new app marketed to open-minded women seeking sex – made an invitation to share naked photos with her. Although this invitation was most likely just a case of phishing directed to stealing my financial or personal data, social bots simulate human-ness in multiple ways. Alarmingly social bots are not only being deployed to mine large amounts of data but are also used in the manipulation of public opinion through comments in sections of online news feeds, social media platforms such as Twitter and Facebook, and forums.[21] The newer and more advanced bots undertake large-scale mining of user data, make comment on social issues, and devise jokes through spam accounts.[22] Bot activity during political campaigns has become so pervasive that many suggest they pose a threat to democracy.[23] They derail debates through an outpouring of automated, hateful comments. Through processing and calculation they make new scripts and can spread lies, attack, and denigrate people. It is believed that now 60 percent of all internet traffic is generated by bots.[24]

For example, it is estimated that of the 318 million active users on Twitter in 2017, 48 million are social bots.[25] Many of Trump's fans are suspected social bots. In fact, Trump bragged in August 2018 that he has more than 160 million followers on Facebook and Twitter.[26] The identities of real people are often stolen, to re-emerge as social bots in which an individual's images, forms of expression, gestures, and thoughts are folded into scripts of this type. Nicole Mincy, a 21-year-old business major student from Newark, NJ, reported that her Facebook was hacked and used to sign up to various websites.[27] Trump tweeted his gratitude to the fake Nicole Mincy Facebook profile, a suspected social bot with 146,000 followers who has been selling Trump products through Twitter and other social networking sites.[28]

Twitter suspended the Mincy account, known as @ProTrump45, when it was revealed that the account was probably a fake, created most likely by Russian interests to amplify content with and support for Trump.

The actions of bots and their scripts are often memes, viewpoints, and behaviours that are spread rapidly by imitation, many of them becoming societal data increasingly viewed as worth saving. "Pizzagate," a conspiracy meme, spread rapidly based on claims that Hillary Clinton and her campaign chief John Podesta ran a child sex abuse ring out of the Comet Ping Pong Pizzeria in Washington D.C. "Pizzagate" began when emails belonging to Podesta were released by WikiLeaks. The owner of the pizza shop, James Alefantis, a Democratic supporter, was mentioned in the emails. Users and social bots on the online message board 4Chan speculated that Alefantis was part of a Democratic child-trafficking ring on social media, including Reddit and Twitter. Reddit later banned the topic from its message boards.

This event illustrates how the power of tweets made by social bots located in the Czech Republic and Vietnam, and rumoured to have been instigated by Russia, was mobilized to circulate the theory that Clinton and Podesta trafficked and sexually abused children and kept them in the restaurant's secret tunnels.[29] This rumour was retweeted thousands of times by social bots.

The Pizzagate meme provoked a series of real-world consequences. Restaurant staff received death threats. Fifty protesters gathered in DC demanding that the conspiracy be investigated.[30] Among them were Kori and Danielle Hayes and family from Florida wearing Pizzagate tee shirts.

Alarmingly Edgar Welch's subsequent actions were testament to the power of denigrating social bot scripts and their distribution. Welch drove from North Carolina to Washington to rescue the sexually abused children he believed were hidden in the pizza joint. He entered the restaurant with an AR-15 assault rifle and revolver and fired shots.[31] The Washington Post reported, "He found no hidden children, no secret chambers, no evidence of a child sex ring run by the failed Democratic candidate for president of the United States, or by her campaign chief, or by the owner of the pizza place."[32] Welch was sentenced to four years' imprisonment.[33]

Whether something becomes heritage is determined by the intent of its collector and its assumed significance. For example, the Library of Congress collects and archives tweets. In 2010 Twitter gifted the US Library of Congress access to its tweet archive and live feed. The US Library of Congress sought to establish a Twitter Archive to preserve every public tweet since Twitter's inception in 2006.[34] While the project was a resounding failure[35] in its grandest ambition because the institution failed to provide the necessary resourcing, it illustrates the intent of a public heritage institution to work with digital media to capture and archive commentary on contemporary social life and events in perpetuity. The library now only collects selected tweets. Given that more than half of tweeting activity is a product of social bots, the Library by default is collecting more-than-human heritage. Social bots are not only data producers and collaborators but are also active archivers. The #PizzaGate Archiver, a social bot that gives away pro-Trump merchandise, has actively collected and archived all Pizzagate tweets. The account has now been suspended.

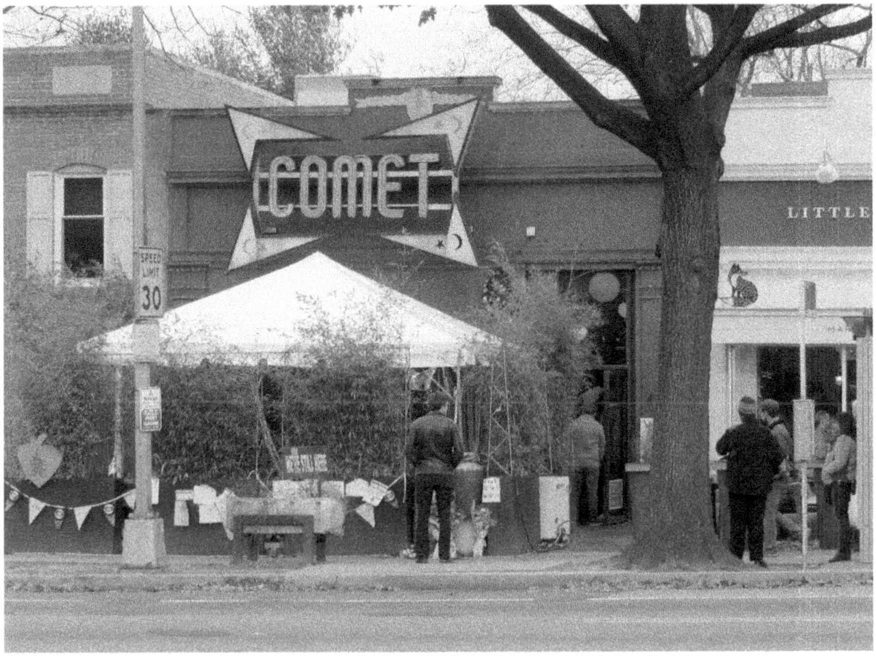


FIGURE 8.2 Signs of support hang outside Comet Ping Pong in Washington, two days after Edgar Welch entered the restaurant and fired a gun, claiming he was trying to rescue abused children.
Photo via Wikimedia Commons.

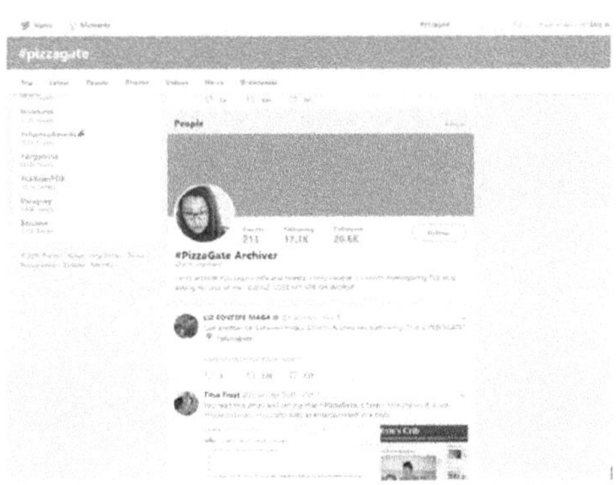


FIGURE 8.3 #PizzaGate Archiver Twitter home page.
Photo via Twitter.

## Maker culture and more-than-human heritage

The increasingly important role of AI digital technology in the design and manufacture of merchandise in science, architecture, design, and fashion is seen in an emerging class of products currently being inducted into museum collections. Broadly termed the maker movement, online services, design software, automation, and 3D printing technology enable designers to develop and share digital blueprints and make physical objects from couture to cars through 3D printing technology.[36] The rise of 3D printing offers a second case example in which to examine human agency in the context of this particular form of more-than-human heritage. This case example illustrates how digital 3D printing is given a material essence and is used to re-rehearse the fundamentals of a humanist heritage founded on substance.

The so-called materialization of the digital is a new trend afforded by 3D printing where different types of materials from plastic to stone, wood, and steel become seemingly interpenetrated with digital code. Materializing the digital through the production of new products represents the so-called emergence of a new type of coded materiality of a kind that is qualitatively different from existing ones such as stone, paper, and wood.

Often referred to as the post-digital or post-medium condition, the advent of maker culture is signalled by digital art theorist Christiane Paul as a condition where artworks and objects are increasingly conceptually and physically shaped by the internet and digital processes.[37] Media in its originally defined format (e.g. video as a linear electronic image), Paul explains, ceases to exist and a new material condition, a "digitally embedded materiality," arises, seen in the physical form of paintings, sculptures, or photographs. This neo-materiality according to Paul extends the repertoire of materials existent in the world as a series of distinctive forms while at the same time shaping our experience of life in different ways.[38]

Following destructive acts by ISIS, Iranian media artist Morehshin Allahyari used 3D printing to re-model and rematerialize statues from the Roman-period city of Hatra and Assyrian artefacts from Nineveh in 3D resin. A flash drive and memory card were embedded inside each print, symbolic of the deployment of 3D printing to repair history and memory. Each acted as a sealed time capsule to be passed on for future generations, thereby becoming heritage.[39] Here 3D printing becomes a tool of resistance, documentation, and reclamation. It is both heritage and emerging heritage as it is valued and deemed worth passing on as a digitized copy, and as having heritage value as artefactual in itself because it has an origin, a creator, accrues modern time from the point at which the original was destroyed. These Assyrian artefacts, like 3D-printed models of museum collections, are judged in terms of their ability not only to visually represent the real but also "rematerialize" the original accurately in shape, size, colour, surface, and texture, though not in material.

The "re-material" sits in between the material and the so-called immaterial as an example of more-than-human heritage-in-production connected to the real object through programming, scanning, sensors, cameras, plastics, and so forth. These so-called copies are qualitatively different from earlier versions because they can be modified, printed, shared, modified again, or mashed up with other models through a continuous process of sharing, modification, and reproduction.[40]

In this example we see not a duality of artefactual and informational, but rather the 3D copy operating as both. The artefactual melds with the digitization and with conventions of objecthood through screen essentialism and extruded plastic that often resembles the colour and texture of the source. In doing so, the authenticity of the 3D digitizations is assured. Here with each print a new item is created. The 3D print is a copy as near to the original as possible, but it can never be the original, not even an original of the 3D print. It is just one in an ever-multiplying universe of new productions.

Seemingly integrating the physical and virtual worlds and blurring distinctions between media, 3D-printed products and 3D-printed copies of museum collections are either viewed as a physical-digital-physical cycle at work,[41] a shift from the physical to virtual and then back to the physical existence of things,[42] or as a process that rematerializes the web representing "a return to the material."[43] These perspectives are founded on the notion of digital data as immaterial rather than comprising their own unique signature, as well as the notion that objects also exist as separate pure states often only distinguishable from each other by their material form. Yet each of these items is a unique ecological composition of distinctive variations. Here they exist in museum culture as at once material and digital formats. One example of this is computational couture.

The N12 3D-printed bikini, a ready-to-wear clothing item, was acquired by Sydney's Museum of Applied Arts and Sciences (MAAS, Powerhouse Museum). The bikini was created by designers Jenna Fizel and Mary Haung of Sideways and produced by Continuum Fashion:

> The bikini's design fundamentally reflects the beautiful intricacy possible with 3D printing, as well as the technical challenges of creating a flexible surface out of the solid nylon. Thousands of circular plates are connected by thin springs, creating a wholly new material that holds its form as well as being flexible. The layout of the circle pattern was achieved through custom written code that lays out the circles according to the curvature of the surface. In this way, the aesthetic design is completely derived from the structural design.[44]

Likewise, the Museum of Fine Arts in Boston commissioned Nervous System to create a dress inspired by petals, feathers, and scales using 3D printing technology for its new exhibition "Techstyle." One of these Kinematic petal garments, made possible through Kinematics, a new textile computer software cut into nylon printable plastic, has also been acquired by MAAS, with earlier examples accessioned into the Cooper Hewitt, Smithsonian Design Museum, New York.[45]

Like digitizations, the maker movement seeks to democratize couture by making digital blueprints available online to then be printed by users.[46] These productions sit neatly within a culture maker genre. Other examples include a 3D-printed and portable suicide machine with a biodegradable capsule and coffin able to be transported to any location you choose to die. Designed by Dr Philip Nitschke, it was

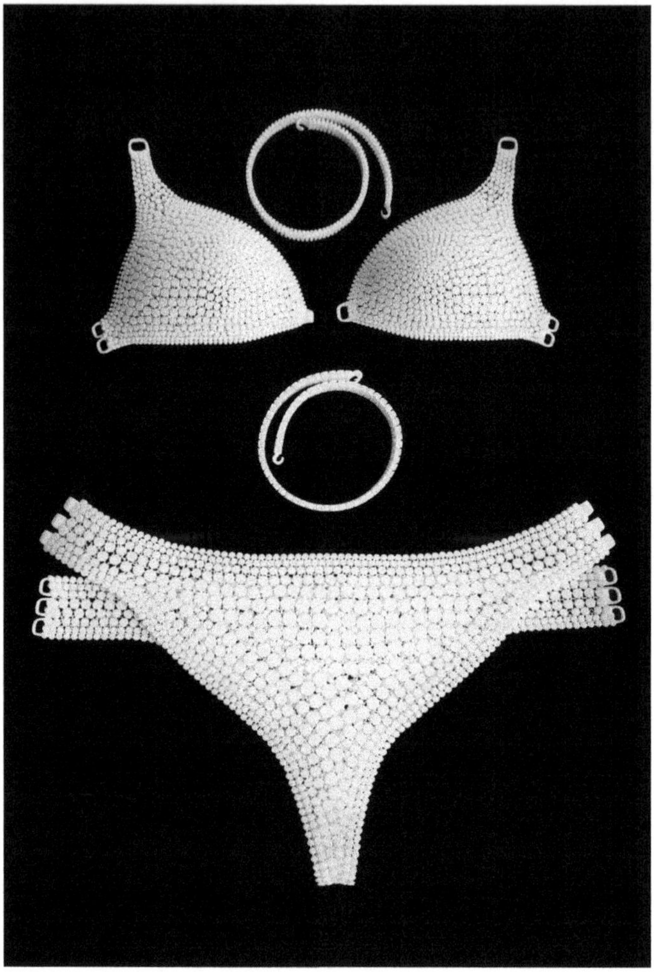

**FIGURE 8.4** The N12 3D printed bikini, Sideways.
Photo credit: Mary Huang and Jenna Fizel.

devised to be operated by the terminally ill themselves, thereby removing the need for assistance by a third party to avoid legal problems in the UK.[47]

In the midst of the Covid-19 crisis and shortages of protective wear, all manner of 3D-printed face mask and shield software, printing and assembly instructions are appearing on internets that will after the crisis find their way into museum collections, most likely in their printed form.

These types of "automated heritage" have a more-than-human profile in respect to their materials, design, production, and consumption. 3D-printed items are ecological compositions and embody multiple forms of human agency, from that which enabled the modelling of their software, their digital manipulation, and design, to the sourcing and culturing of materials such as extruded plastic, to their assembly through

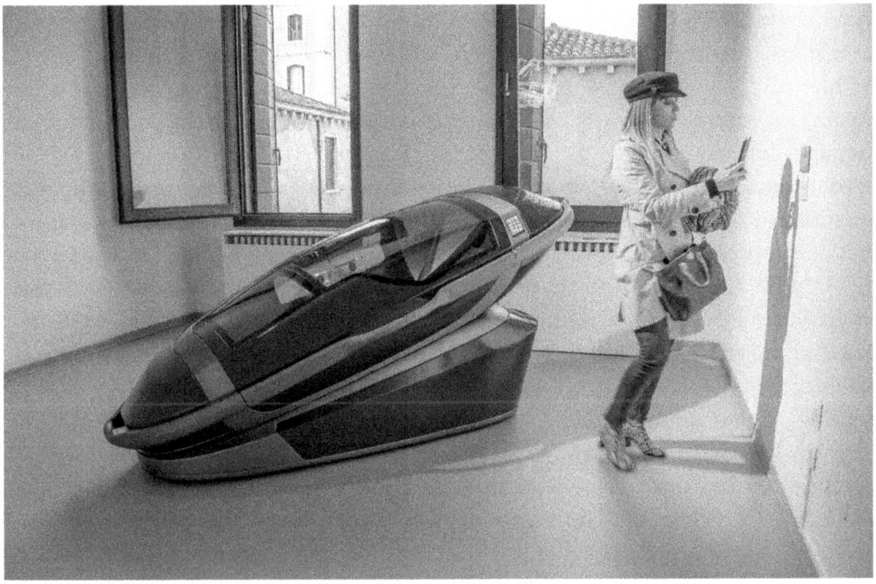

**FIGURE 8.5** The Sarco euthanasia machine on exhibition at the Palazzo Michiel as part of Venice Design, 2019.
Photo credit: Philip Nitschke, Exit International.

automated systems and printing technology, through to their use and consumption. The current focus on material represents the fetishization of a new type of coded materiality in which the worldly condition is conceptualized as a series of continuous materialities.

The conceptualization of the world and maker cultures as comprising a different type of material or materiality is also about a desire to come to grips with new computational goods that are finding their way into heritage institutions. The entry point and dominating narrative is the notion of materiality first and foremost as a counterbalance to code as immaterial and the subjective and as an instructional language akin to human language. Here human subject–object relations remain intact through the creative triad of artist, medium, and material, while at the same time notions of production and processes expand and are outsourced to users through the distribution of the instructional language of its making. Indeed, the post-digital as a museological condition gestures towards an uncomplicated technologically deterministic application of technologies and principles to practices and operations yet to be subjected to critique.

Because of this focus on material first and foremost, 3D-printed garments operate within heritage institutions according to the conventions of the material, and as code where the instructions to print them are still held by their producer. The same is true for new types of mass-produced products such as the emerging class of digital data as potential heritage that are shaped by digital processes and comprise a material end form, such as computer couture. But such a classification according to material fetishizes substances as inert and symbolic, lacking their own agency. Additionally, such material trains the focus on an object's presence, form, and function according to an object-orientated philosophy. It re-rehearses heritage in a humanist formation.

In addition, these new types of more-than-human heritage raise important questions in regard to UNESCO's definition of born-digital heritage as something that only exists in digital format. By framing digital cultural heritage in such a way, the UNESCO charter placed pre-defined limitations on how we might think about potential digital heritage forms. These forms do not fall within the strict ambit of digital cultural heritage because they do not exist solely in digital format – they can be rendered printable or made material through digital means such as 3D printing, digital knitting, and CNC machining, and thereby blur clear divisions between the material and the digital. Further to this, such things are not solely produced by human agency as cultural data in the narrow sense promulgated by the UNESCO charters. The terms by which digital heritage might be thought about are constantly changing and expanding, and will continue to do so with AI, automation, machine learning, and now maker culture. These trends signal the end of born-digital heritage and of a solely human digital heritage. It is clear that these items are a new production that has yet to be formalized as a digital cultural heritage; indeed, it is more likely to be dealt with as an analogue object, a material object exhibiting substantial form.

Most digital cultural heritage is printable; however, its format and form are different again, attesting to their malleable, reproducible, and therefore ambiguous nature as ecological compositions. Further, the qualities of this printed heritage are difficult to grasp and interpret in the context of reified notions of the material and the authentic. They take on conventional renderings of simple presence and physical form. Indeed, all digital cultural heritage is a form of more-than-human heritage. Nothing has ever existed as pure immaterial code.

## Big data and human experience as raw material

The emergence of organized personal data markets, data companies, and the commodification of personal data gathered through our data trails, our conversations with friends, our browsing habits and preferences, demographics, and locational data all aggregated into digital identities, is a new reality in the data-driven economy and increasingly a driver in economic transactions.[48] Pioneered by Google in the early 2000s, personal data has been referred to as the "new 'oil' fuelling new services based on individual profiles."[49] Search results that encapsulate human experience, expression, and creativity become free raw materials for capitalist extraction. Customer data and profiling algorithms become business assets. As a result, personal data is routinely and illegally gathered, bought, and sold to be used for targeted advertising, in political analysis, healthcare, science and research, and by governmental bureaucracies and law enforcement agencies.[50]

In order to curb the unrestrained exploitation of personal data by data companies, Germany's Chancellor Angela Merkel has proposed a big data tax[51] whose rationale is based on the idea that intangible data has a tangible value as a raw material and represents a business asset in economic activities. Data is no longer considered immaterial; it becomes an economic agent of a different kind possessing capital value akin to any other material resource such as land used for economic transactions and therefore subject to tax. In the 2000s, Bernard Stiegler argued that the world was becoming subject to a more aggressive form of "cognitive capitalism" or "immaterial capitalism."[52] Stiegler's cognitive capitalism centred on human labour and the availability of the intellectual capacity of workers for exploitation in support of digital economies. Now these exploitative tendencies have been extended across the whole realm of human experience. The user is no longer an autonomous free agent whose intellect, thoughts, and personal data are solely her or his property that for example can be harnessed to democratize museums.

Philosopher Shoshana Zuboff calls this situation the emergence of a new type of surveillance capitalism in which humans and their behaviour become a novel type of object for a raw material-extraction operation.[53] Human experience in digital format, according to Zuboff, is translated into behavioural data for capitalist extraction, prediction, and sales.[54]

Within a humanist heritage framework, personal data as forms of human cultural expression linked to data economies is used to represent the products, instruments, and therefore records of the economy and of consumption practices. This extends to the collection and documentation of digital objects comprising all manner of digital content, apps, software, and systems. Persistent historical data becoming heritage is also put to work to support business innovation and the development of the digital economy.

But in framing historical personal data as part of this new type of economic logic, our social bodies, thoughts, feelings, intent, desires, and actions are directed to the expansion of the production and consumption of services and goods in a new planetary architecture of behavioural modification. Personal data both real-time and historical in which human experience and expression are embodied and monetized and made subject to a new type of exploitative logic, becomes a third occasion to investigate the position of the human and human agency in data economies directed to behavioural modification.

The harvesting of personal data to sell to commercial interests for digital marketing and advertising campaigns creates identities machinically as compressed fragments of a full range of human experiences. Big data tools interpenetrate, scrape and gather up our behaviour and forms of expression, our personalities, our voices, thoughts, feelings, interests, what we do, and the movements of our social body. All these things become embedded in automated machine processes, not only for the purposes of remembering and memorialization but also for profit maximization by first knowing us and then shaping our behaviour.

Google for example collects and stores vast amounts of data across all the devices we use every time they are powered up, such as where we have been in each moment, everything we have searched and deleted and at what time, what apps we use, who we interact with, where in the world we are, all the products we have bought, bookmarks, emails, documents, the music and videos we listen to, and even what time we go to bed.[55] Even users who browse museum collections available through Google Cultural Institute are scraped for capital gain. From all this, Google produces a data profile on each individual equivalent to millions of Word documents comprising information about our hobbies, our relationship status, our career, income and weight, our religion, our life plan, whether we plan to have children, get married, or are about to travel.

Facebook is also a sovereign polis intimately connected to digital capitalism by transforming users' activities into data that is to be used for commercial gain. While purporting to be a social media site and a place where online users create, share, archive, and connect with other users, each creative, intellectual, social, or transactional activity from a blog post to an update or purchase a user engages in online becomes a data commodity. These data commodities are then sold to advertising companies as a way of segmenting and targeting particular user groups and the individuals themselves.[56]

Our Facebook profiles, likes, posts and clicks are scraped and packaged so others can make money out of us – we become products for others' gain. Heritage-like practices and archiving on the platform, such as memory posts, friendships and events scraped from the site to encourage us to create more data, constitute a form of strategizing emerging from these capitalist agendas.

Every single online interaction becomes bound up in data, metadata, big data, programs, and algorithmic processing. The governance of populations through data on this massive scale represents the algorithmic embedding of the social and biological body within and as data. The logic of algorithmic capital becomes deeply intertwined with our biological and social bodies, our histories and genealogies, our feelings, emotions, voices, personalities, desires, and actions, and even our DNA. The very essence of who we are is captured, automated, calibrated, abstracted, recomposed, and predicted through machine intelligence.

Our social relationships, our friendships, who we interact with, what we remember, how we make and interact with friends online and build our online identity all become subject to manipulation. Our automated selves are used to predict what we will purchase or eat and our entertainment preferences. Even in the afterglow, the feelings, thoughts, voices, and personalities of those departed are compressed and used as historical data in big data sets. The products and the identities they produce are not always accurate. Big data sets become multiplying bodies, of emotions, minds, and actions. This process self-generates a cycle of personal data in which behavioural data through targeted advertising is put to work personalizing, coercing, nudging, coaxing, herding, and directing people towards profit generation that then creates more data. Our future actions are framed on our past behaviour, that is, on what we did before through the scraping, compression, and calculation of our historical data. Historical data as a source of capital in futures markets is produced across all sectors at an ever-accelerating rate.

Human subjects as heritage producers become ecological compositions themselves, deeply embedded bodily and cognitively in digital capital, technical, chemical, mineral, algorithmic, technospheric structures and circumstances. Therefore, the ecological composition is deeply human, involving multiple human agencies of different qualities and intensities, and at the same time is more-than-human in composition.

These multiple human agencies include human intellectual, conceptual thought, emotions, personalities, voices, desires, the movements of our physical and social body, the production of cultured materials and other forms of crafting, moulding, processing, and a range of expertise such as software and computational engineering. Self-interest, the ideology of digital capital and persuasion is folded into the speed and intensities of machine learning and algorithms, matching, ever-expanding data sets scraped from sites, privacy tools, and so forth. Personal data and economic data as digital cultural heritage become, as different types of ecological composition, emergent and more-than-human heritage. Time becomes the interrelated and variable temporalities of their embedded eco-curating processes.

With the passage of the European Parliament's General Data Protection Regulation (GDPR) legislation, citizens now have the right to know how their data is being used and to restrict its use. As a consequence, individuals are now becoming aware of how their personal data identity is being monetized as potential revenue by private companies.[57]

New forms of digital dictatorship seen with the rise of China's social credit system, a personal, live score card for China's 1.4 billion people, put personal data and memory to work for a new type of social engineering experiment – the large-scale control and coercion of populations. Here the population become new types of social agents that are controlled and exploited to create a conforming population.[58] Monitored through a mass surveillance camera system equipped with facial recognition, body scanning and geo-tracking, an individual's personal data and online behaviour are surveilled through their smartphones. Everything an individual puts in their supermarket trolley will be monitored. The purchase of alcohol will most certainly reduce their credit rating. This system is expected to be fully implemented sometime in 2021 or 2022, and those with credit will be given opportunities like entry to the best universities and hotels, cheaper loans, and opportunities to travel freely, while the discredited will be prevented from travelling, refused credit, and excluded from government jobs.

This example illustrates the emergence of a new type of humanism put to work in governing populations, not only to serve capitalist intentions but as forms of surveillance and control. Personal data in which human bodies, forms of expression and their agencies are distributed across the ecological composition represents a range of raw materials made by deeply interpenetrating social and biological bodies, reaching deep into our DNA, our familial lineages and histories, surveilling our physical characteristics, our neural networks, and our social characteristics and behaviour, much of which originated in an intergenerational deep past. This deep commingling of DNA and biological bodies, social bodies, and billions of neurons and hundreds of millions of connections and synapses, electrical, energetic systems, carbon, chemicals, neural networks, and the exchange of matter become shared systems with AI sensing, calculative and predictive modelling, and all manner of other collaborators in eco-curating processes directed to producing digital scores. Surveillance capitalism penetrates deep into our cellular, bio-chemical structure directed to predicting future life trajectories and opportunities. These embodiments, in particular shared chemical, mineral, and elemental circuits in digital and human bodies, become common geological histories of deep time and of many millennia's duration having their foundations in the making of the universe forged through the nuclear fissions of stars and supernovas.

The drive for capital accumulation and profit maximization seen in contemporary corporate internet platforms and the collection and preservation of societal data are often founded on the exploitation of digital labour. New labour markets in the digital economy are involved in the production of digital data and the creation of content.[59] Workers in web services are the most prolific producers of persistent data and digital memory and therefore potential heritage. This workforce, often made up of independent contractors who work for low wages, remains unprotected by labour laws.[60] People engaging in the creation of content, and the use of blogs, social networking sites, and content sharing platforms involving contributions by fans,[61] are all examples of activities that create content and are therefore potential heritage. Persistent and new inequalities are not just social but also ecological. The digital workforce, alongside individuals as they produce their own personal data, are therefore new economic agents whose experiences, memory, knowledge, language, writing, and reasoning processes are controlled and exploited for the production of new types of products and to stimulate a desire for those products made possible by technics.[62]

All these ecological compositions embody different humanisms – that is, varying human agencies in the emergence of more-than-human forms of heritage. Some are more human than others.

## Technospheric more-than-human heritage

The digital cultural heritage assemblage and heritage-like practices in other sectors are complicit in climate change acceleration and ecological exhaustion. This situation is made manifest through their uneven geographical capitalist alignments, the mining of coal, petroleum and gas for energy and the associated carbon pollution used to power digital technologies and data storage facilities. Such destruction is also wrought through the never-ending and excessive data production, consumption, and big data processing by the data economy, users, and heritage, corporate, and government institutions.

The data industry, storage companies, and phone providers encourage us to be data hungry and buy more megabytes and faster broadband speeds so we can produce and access more content or stream video. We are in the midst of a data deluge never witnessed before in history, but with seemingly unlimited storage in the cloud there is little incentive to change our data production and disposal habits. Many of us hoard data including videos, images, avatars, emails, texts, and multiple versions of the same documents in our places of work, in our homes, and in our personal devices just in case we need them at some point in the future. Frequently we are unaware that we are creating and accumulating all this data because it is hidden, often the consequences of our browsing history or the sharing of images with others that are then re-saved to our own devices.

While it is difficult to calculate electricity usage across the data economy, it is indeed substantial, estimated at around one tenth of the world's electricity supply, much of which is generated by fossil fuel and rapidly growing with the emergence of wireless technologies and cloud computing.[63] Devices such as smartphones when used for the production of digital data consume more energy than domestic appliances such as fridges. More than 50 percent more energy is used to move bytes around the planet than aircraft. Energy-hungry data centres involved in the production and circulation of digital data, some of which is soon to become persistent data and potentially heritage, drive cloud computing that runs continuously. The digital cultural heritage assemblage therefore represents the continuation of what Lewis Munford calls the paleotechnics of coal and coal mining and its consequences.[64] Digital cultural heritage on the other hand also has pyrotechnic implications enabled by millions of years of the photosynthesis of tiny microbes, the burning of these reserves and their release as emissions. While questions of energy consumption by the digital economy are emerging as an issue central to climate change mitigation, data processing, Parikka explains, also releases heat and is critically dependent on air, water, fire, cooling, and circulating energies[65] all of which are contaminating processes.

With the rise of Green IT, attention has been directed to the energy consumption required for different forms of storage associated with data centre cooling, and to the carbon footprint of manufacturing and IT operations and increasingly in museum operations. Large multinationals such as Google, Facebook, and Apple are converting their data centre facilities to renewable energy sources. In corporate sectors some businesses are seeking to reduce the carbon footprint of IT operations, promote more efficient manufacturing processes and limit e-waste.[66] The circularity of the digital cultural heritage assemblage in Green IT shifts from that of a pyrotechnic foundation to the harnessing of energy of the sun produced through nuclear fusion, therefore implicated in the sun's resources of a different kind.

It is not only the energy consumption of the broader digital heritage industry that contributes to climate change and environmental exhaustion. As a result of data profusion across all sectors, the types and forms of data considered heritage have expanded alongside an explosion of digitized content produced by all manner of industries and sectors, from medical imaging to digital copies of health and financial records and to digitizations of heritage collections. In a world that is now discernibly archival, we are witnessing a profusion of documentary forms of data, all of which are heritage-in-the-making, across all media formats. Online storage facilities gather more data, machine-generated digital images, and video metadata.

Large-scale museum digitization projects by entities such as Google contribute to mass data proliferation. Images of museum collections and archival materials made searchable through collections interfaces routinely circulate through global planetary computational infrastructures and are posted on Flickr, Wikipedia, Facebook, and Pinterest. Digital content and digitizations of collections emerge as ever-multiplying copies of copies. While these acts are presented as democratizing, enacting a shift from ownership within a restricted paradigm to a mode of sharing, reuse, and the circumvention of highly restrictive copyright clauses and other limitations in respect to access, they nevertheless contribute to data profusion through endless cycles of copying.

Data storage is also implicated in energy excess and waste. The convergence of digital cultural heritage with synthetic biology for example is starkly illustrated by the development of advanced materials replicating biological DNA for use in data storage. In an effort to develop more sustainable storage methods, scientists have been experimenting with synthetic DNA as a new form of hard drive, and this solution appears to be emerging as a serious option for the storage of data in the long term.[67] Experiments in recent years have shown synthetic forms of DNA can be encoded with images, music, and words similar to the way biological information is stored.[68] Researchers from the University of Washington, Microsoft, and Twist Bioscience successfully stored two recordings, Deep Purple's "Smoke on the Water" and Miles Davis' "Tutu," on a synthetic DNA sequence as data that could be decoded and played back without loss of quality.[69]

High density storage options have the potential to archive large amounts of historical data in a stable form for thousands of years. But these solutions are unlikely to stop the rate of data accumulation as they evolve around improving infrastructure, increasing storage capacity, and decreasing energy requirements rather than exploring options for changing corporate, governmental, and individual behaviours or creating digital awareness and responsibility in regard to the associated burgeoning electronic and data waste problem. These initiatives collectively also promote the current crisis of modern arrogance, capitalist accumulation and its aspirations of economic growth, the earth and biological matter as a resource to be exploited and replicated.

Accordingly, digital cultural heritage is complicit in what geologist Peter Haff calls the "Technosphere," the technical systems of capitalism, governance, and bureaucracy that rely for their expansion on the erosion of natural resources and the exploitation of human labour,[70] a concept introduced in Chapter 2. As a subsystem of the Anthropocene, the Technosphere, Haff explains, is brought about by the evolution of technics in which large-scale technology that humans depend on becomes a question of geology.[71] Operating according to a "quasi-autonomous dynamics," often beyond human control, the Technosphere is conceived as a new planetary layer integral to a newly emerging and interlinked Earth system.[72]

Much of the data we produce is a driver of the Technosphere, altering the Earth's biophysical systems in a profound and often irreversible manner. Digital heritage and heritage-like practices comprise technospheric data that we choose to save. Digital waste becomes the data we choose to neglect or discard, equivalent to layers of sediment hidden in devices and storage facilities much of it never to be used or recycled again, alongside the infrastructures and devices that are integral to their operation as ecological compositions and the eco-curating coordinates and processes that comprise their emergence. This not only includes the intermingling of carbon pollution and the rise of $CO_2$ levels from fossil fuel power generation and energy consumption but also the digital cultural heritage assemblages' operational dependencies on hard parts of large-scale computational systems such as computers, power cables, data centres used to produce and transmit data. In this technospheric milieu, binary judgments and distinctions emerge: data as heritage, data as waste.

Digital cultural heritage comes down to earth producing its own waste. As ecological compositions, digital cultural heritage becomes metabolic processes comprising organic and inorganic matter that produce waste that cannot be recycled by the biosphere, the hydrosphere, or the lithosphere.

At the same time digital cultural heritage has technospheric implications through its reliance on the exploitation of human labour used in large-scale resource extraction such as rare mineral mining, the production of data and data technics, and even on Twitter posts produced by low-paid labour in click farms. Data scraped according to the extractivist logic of data markets produces its own waste through consumer manipulation and directives to buy more products and also to produce more data.

Digital cultural heritage as a heritage of data economies and its complicity with digital capitalism is produced and mobilized by not only planned obsolescence but at the same time geophysical extraction. Parikka extends media materialism not only into an environmental agenda but at the same time argues for the emergence of a new infrastructural world comprising in part geological forces.[73] Here Parikka argues the Earth becomes part of media as a resource and conducts through its geological elements in the production of geophysical media worlds.[74]

Therefore the geological Earth is integral to the production and transmission of potential and emerging digital cultural heritage. Digital cultural heritage is intimately involved in the exploitation of human and non-human planetary resources and water through extraction used in the development, maintenance, and technical expansion of capitalism. As a result the circulation of digital cultural heritage and heritage-like regimes is implicated in both wealth creation and at the same time environmental exhaustion.

Trump's tweets for example produced through his phone and when made visible as ecological compositions are complicit in carbon emissions and environmental exhaustion. His iPhone produced 60 kg of emissions in its manufacture. His tweets and their circulation are entrenched in the stockpiles of electronic waste such as computers, mobile phones, printers, keyboards, processors, and the toxic residues that issue from them. They are complicit in earthly forces and environmental destruction through mining for the components used in media, infrastructures, the burning of oil and coal in the US used as energy for the cooling data centres and used to circulate them through cables and data centres to personal devices.

Transported around the globe in their afterlife, often to China, India or the Philippines for dumping and processing, the rare metals such as gold are extracted from Trump's iPhones, computers, and the devices of his followers including social bots produce e-waste. They leak contaminants into the soil, produce toxic vapours. causing environmental and bodily contamination that can lead to cancer in the bodies of laborers who do the work. As a consequence, his tweets are materially implicated in climate change and in Technosphere sedimentations.

Trump's tweets become technospheric heritage through their involvement in climate denial. His statements, "it's freezing outside, where the hell is 'global warming'??," "we have ended the war on coal," "beautiful clean coal," at the same time are deeply implicated in atmospheric durations and rising greenhouse gas emissions as both an expression of policy and their materialisms of extraction, exploitation, and destruction. His tweets and the denial that issued from them seek to protect America's fossil fuel-based economy, save the energy source from disappearing from the U.S. energy mix, bury emissions underground through carbon capture and storage, and dismantle climate policy.

Yet another form of technospheric digital cultural heritage is the data produced by laser-imaging remote sensing technology as surface-marking photomediations in archaeological research. Media theorist Joanna Zylinska refers to this technology and the imaging it produces as forms of non-human photography.[75] This data and the infrastructures that produce such imaging illustrate the dynamics of the human and non-human agencies implicated in the making of the Anthropocene and Technosphere. The data gathered through laser sensing scans represent forms of digital cultural heritage and the human and non-human agencies involved in the making of these images. Data gathered through light pulses bouncing off data points in the sky also penetrate below the Earth's surface to reveal patterns of technospheric heritage through traces of human activities, stone walls, abandoned roads, building foundations, settlements, urban areas, and their interactions with non-humans such as engineering works in the harnessing of water in photographic form.

Certain types of digital cultural heritage such as bond futures are one example of a technospheric heritage, are emblematic of the unrestrained financialization of living and non-living things, past, present, and future. That is, from the exploitation of people as digital labour used to develop the software and automated systems to the mining and exploitation of Earth's geological substrates for the production of smartphones and computer systems that traders use to transact bond futures and the direction of future life.

Here digital cultural heritage like that of media discussed by Parikka is linked to deep time and durations, to extinctions and to the emergence as fossil fuel through millions of years of photosynthesis.[76] Drawing inspiration from Parikka's analysis of geomedia, digital cultural heritage is also complicit in the atmospheric durations of climate change but also those of geological times through their critical media resources and infrastructures. When thinking about digital cultural heritage as ecological compositions, data resides in mines and geomaterials sourced through the penetration and excavation of rare earth minerals. The stratification of digital cultural heritage and its aesthetic is made explicit through the interpenetration of the lithosphere through increasingly deeper cuts into the geological layers as deposits are exhausted and new drilling technologies emerge to exploit them.

Technospheric digital heritage also comprises the data used to drive financial systems and markets, generated from government bureaucracies, communication and transport systems, factories, cities, and heritage institutions such as museums. Digital surveillance carried out using red-light camera technologies that monitor roads or in the form of systematically collected and filed personal data that is part of the heritage-like activities of the public sector all serve data bureaucracies and contribute to environmental exhaustion through extraction and the production of waste. Surveillance capitalism enables new concentrations of wealth, power and knowledge alongside the rise of a whole new suite of inequalities that propels both the expansion of extractivist industries by harnessing the agency of the non-human world as cultured materials for computational purposes and at the same time ecological collapse through its focus on driving consumption and accumulation.

Media is, according to Parikka, complicit in contested planetary politics as part of hidden military infrastructures of transmission and acts of surveillance in cloud storage in land and sea territories.[77] Digital cultural heritage is implicated in power and in acts of violence. Trump's tweets as official records of his presidency constitute legally effective military orders that no matter how confusing or irrational they may appear at the same time travel across military infrastructures. On 22 April, 2020 Trump issued a tweet: "I have instructed the United States Navy to shoot down and destroy any and all Iranian gunboats if they harass our ships at sea." How this tweet was received and whether it is implemented by military commanders is another matter. Similarly China's digital credit system is activated through personal data gathered from hidden surveillance structures of cameras, satellites and drones.

The implications of data hoarding and over-production have very serious technospheric consequences. The immense and unquantifiable volume of data waste produced and consumed by societies as part of the Technosphere including that produced by automated systems comprises dark data. Dark data, from the bit trails left behind on social media to bit rubbish produced through duplication to e-waste such as mobile phones and computers, poses a significant challenge not only for digital preservation across heritage and heritage-like sectors but also for the future of life itself. The operation of Google's personal profiling regime on every web user produces colossal amounts of data, much of which constitutes dark data. The cost of storage associated with it suggests that a substantial proportion of the energy use associated with big data is avoidable.

Systems that seek to visualize, calculate, monitor, map, predict atmospheric concentrations of greenhouse gases through data gathering and analysis directed to mitigate climate change are at the same time processes that contribute to global warming. Even the super-fast sensing computational systems such as NASA's

Jason-2 satellite[78] used to monitor and gather information about more-than human events such as ocean temperatures and sea level rise have environmental implications through their collection of vast amounts of data that we are never going to process. Accordingly, we need to consider this data waste in the same way we think about other types of physical waste[79] and its ecological implications in the long term.

In order to curb the exhaustive effects of the Technosphere, a digital data waste and recycling movement must be mobilized that encourages producers and consumers across all sectors to be mindful of bit production, develop measures to discern the data worth saving amidst the waste, delete data, and institute more efficient forms of personal, corporate, and heritage archiving. But more fundamentally, a deeper understanding of the very material trails of waste, the inequalities and regimes of power and disadvantage that arise from data production and its environmental impacts, can be foregrounded through a greater attunement to all manner of human and non-human constituencies that are embedded in data production and consumption. Ecological and embodied awareness, rather than a humanist vision of life-making processes through data production, can be put to work to engender ongoing ethical accountability and care.

Digital cultural heritage analysis founded on an ecological compositional model can be used to raise questions about how we currently live on the Earth, ways we can live differently, and the recuperative processes and actions required to help curb the future impacts of these problems. Here interpreting digital cultural heritage as ecological compositions and tracing the cartographic movements, points of contact, and affects of its coordinates opens up such reflective sensibilities and modes of acting.[80] By doing this we can take account of the interrelatedness of human actions and the wider non-human world, from data production and shifts in the chemical composition of the atmosphere and a toxic earth to making visible the very existence of a common world and the figurations and alliances in which we are embedded and which we therefore must negotiate if we are to curate in ways that ensure earthly survival. While the substantial financial losses that data hoarding incurs are at the forefront of business and corporate strategizing, the development of appropriate strategies for selecting and curating business-critical data from the data deluge over time[81] can also mitigate ecological impacts through ecological compositional thought and action tracing the tangles and interconnectedness between things and their affects.

While there are multiple data lifecycle models for digital curation and preservation in heritage-like sectors, most only offer an archive option for unused data. Very few include a delete option for permanent destruction of data.[82] The development of automated systems as a strategy in heritage and heritage-like curation practices that has the ability to not only appraise, select, and preserve but also permanently delete data and records can substantially reduce storage capacity and curb electricity consumption. Blockchain technology, originally developed as a digital ledger and security measure for financial transactions, has the potential to substantially curb waste, preventing the proliferation of multiple copies.

The Technosphere, media theorist Eric Horl argues, is a system integral to the creation of a new technological sense-culture based on a machinic and relational constitution of sense[83] beyond traditional humanist conventions of the subject, history, representation, and forms of heritage categorization. The case of digitizations of the Nu Ubra and the British Museum Persian collection digitizations and the *300* movie controversy together illustrate the operation of a machinic and relational constitution of sense as Technospheric circulations. Through machinic and relational interactions made possible by algorithmic and machine agency, unlikely juxtapositions emerge, thereby creating new experiences of consumerism, desire, and history, all of which are implicated in the processes that lead to environmental exhaustion, such as data waste and the desire for new consumer products.

Potential digital heritage is also likely to become what I call technospheric waste. That is, human and more-than-human artefacts or technofossils buried in landfills, contained or preserved, to appear later in the archaeological and geological record as indicators of the Technosphere. At the same time, making technofossils, being the stratigraphic imprint of the new geological epoch of the Anthropocene embedded in the Earth's crust, brings with it, as cultural theorist Ben Dibley describes, a new type of lithic intimacy in the future-becoming.[84] Because digital data is now embedded in almost everything we make and use, technofossil waste is likely to comprise the burgeoning quantities of human-made materials unknown or rare in the other-than-human world – plastics, silicon and metals such as aluminium, titanium, and uranium, much of which returns to the earth in a cultured form that does not break down, not able to be recycled or naturally processed by the biosphere.[85]

Both visible and hidden infrastructures of digital cultural heritage compositions have the potential to become technofossils. The making of technospheric heritage and its trace fossils are most likely to be the hard parts of digital technologies, decommissioned electricity plants and data centre buildings; subterranean cables, the rare minerals that comprise them, the metal, the wires, the plastic, the CDs and DVDs, the remains of hybrid heritages such as car parts, the plastics and other types of materials used in computational couture that are decomposing, contaminating the Earth's air, waterways, and oceans and becoming buried in the Earth's crust.

What we have overlooked or forgotten to collect for the digital heritage record can be recovered in the future, albeit as fragmentary from the decomposing sediments of the archaeological record as new types of legacies. They become future fossils of the digital cultural heritage regime and of technological capitalism. Examples range from the plastic disks that held data recovered from the Ground Zero rubble, now on exhibition at the 9/11 Memorial and Museum in Manhattan, to the remains of dead satellites such as those that circle the Earth or shoot off into space and no longer produce data.

Other material traces of these ecological compositions will emerge as heritage of the atomic kind fossilized in stone as anticipated forms of human, more-than-human, and other-than-human rituals of memorialization yet to manifest. In doing so, technofossils alert us to the other temporalities latent in digital cultural heritage

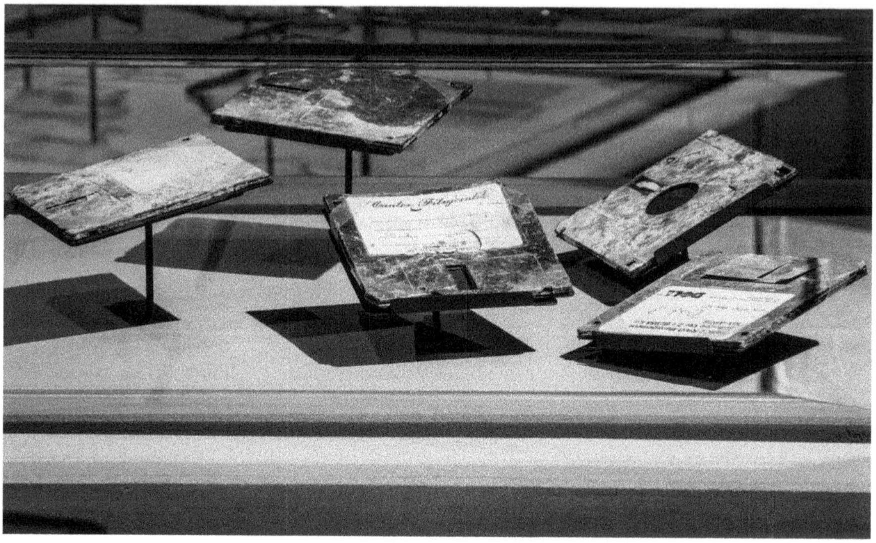

**FIGURE 8.6** Computer diskettes recovered from the World Trade Center site after September 11, 2001.
Photo credit: Collection 9/11 Memorial Museum, courtesy of the Port Authority of New York and New Jersey, photographed by Jin S. Lee.

compositions beyond the eco-curating processes of the contemporary present to that of another series of biogeochemical and eco-curating processes of deep time in which they are becoming stone.

Mapping technospheric heritage and its circulations through an ecological compositional figuration reveals a new emergent form of residue accretion. As ecological compositions, digital cultural heritage produces more intensive, deeper alignments of energy, capital accumulation and geology, environmental waste and exhaustion.

Technospheric heritage makes explicit the more-than-human entangled histories and the emerging social relations between the exploitation of the earth's strata, environmental exhaustion, climate change, obsolescent design and digital rubbish, digital capitalism, wealth accumulation and desire of escalating proportions and multifarious, unknown impacts.

This mapping exercise also reveals not only the material and exhaustive elements embedded in technospheric more-than-human heritage but also the multiplicity of agencies, temporalities and meanings entangled in them beyond those revealed through humanist forms of heritage. Accordingly, genealogies of digital cultural heritage and heritage-like practices in a technospheric and ecological form also reveal how heritage is stretched over long time frames, comprising multiple intersecting durations from the temporalities of climate change and those of environmental exhaustion, to the temporalities of techno-capitalist regimes of accumulation and exploitation and the specific linear historical time of modern heritage frameworks.

## Notes


1 Helbing et al., "Will Democracy Survive Big Data and Artificial Intelligence?" *Scientific American*, Feb 25, 2017, 2, https://www.scientificamerican.com/article/will-democracy-survive-big-data-and-artificial-intelligence/.
2 Helbing et al., "Will Democracy Survive Big Data and Artificial Intelligence?", 2.
3 Luciana Parisi, *Contagious Architecture: Computation, Aesthetics, and Space* (Cambridge, MA: The MIT Press, 2013).
4 Matthew Dunn, "Human/AI Hybrids and Gene Editing are Going to Change Mankind in a Big Way," *News.com.au*, Feb 15, 2018, https://www.news.com.au/technology/science/human-body/humanai-hybrids-and-gene-editing-are-going-to-change-mankind-in-a-big-way/news-story/f88b24f714706942d5de7d4eca2b1822.
5 Andrew Burt and Samuel Volchenboum, "How Health Care Changes When Algorithms Start Making Diagnoses," *Harvard Business Review*, May 8, 2018, https://hbr.org/2018/05/how-health-care-changes-when-algorithms-start-making-diagnoses.
6 Zara Stone, "Ten Incredibly Lifelike Humanoid Robots To Get On Your Radar," *Forbes*, Feb 27, 2018, https://www.forbes.com/sites/zarastone/2018/02/27/ten-incredibly-lifelike-humanoid-robots-to-get-on-your-radar/#4c4e3af734d2.
7 Sean Keach, "BAD BOTS, Sex Robots BACKLASH as Brothel Workers Reveal Fury over 'Dehumanising and Dangerous' Droids," *The Sun*, Sept 18, 2018, https://www.thesun.co.uk/tech/7289486/sex-robots-prostitutes-workers-love-dolls-brothel/.
8 Stone, "Ten Incredibly Lifelike Humanoid Robots to Get On Your Radar."
9 United Nations Development Programme, Asia and the Pacific, "UNDP in Asia and the Pacific Appoints World's First Non-Human Innovation Champion," Nov 22, 2017, https://www.asia-pacific.undp.org/content/rbap/en/home/presscenter/pressreleases/2017/11/22/rbfsingapore.html.
10 Atool Varma and Nathan Erhardt, "Genetic Algorithms," 1997, http://biology.kenyon.edu/slonc/bio3/AI/GEN_ALGO/gen_algo.html.
11 Helen Pritchard, *Critter Compiler*, http://www.helenpritchard.info/critter-compiler-prototype-2016.
12 Pritchard, *Critter Compiler*.
13 Helen Pritchard, *Critter Compiler Executing Practices*, 2015, https://research.gold.ac.uk/24852/1/Critter_Compiler_Executing_Practices.pdf
14 Sharon Begley, "Here's Why We're Still Not Cloning Humans, 20 Years after Dolly the Sheep," *Business Insider*, July 5, 2016, https://www.businessinsider.com/can-you-clone-a-human-2016-7?IR=T.
15 For a discussion of humanism see Rosi Braidotti, *Posthuman Knowledge* (Cambridge, UK: Polity Press, 2019), 2.
16 Jason Patrick Kalin, "Reanimating Memory: The Prospects of Memory in a Digital Age," (PhD thesis, North Carolina State University, 2012), 1.
17 Braidotti, *Posthuman Knowledge*, 12.
18 Braidotti, *Posthuman Knowledge*, 40.
19 Russell Hitchings, "Expertise and Inability: Cultured Materials and the Reason for Some Retreating Lawns in London," *Journal of Material Culture* 11, no. 3 (November 2006): 364–381.
20 Samantha Shorey and Philip N. Howard, "Automation, Big Data and Politics: A Research Review," *International Journal of Communication* 10 (2016): 5032.
21 Samuel C. Woolley, "Automating Power: Social Bot Interference in Global Politics," *First Monday*, April 4, 2016, http://firstmonday.org/article/view/6161/5300.
22 Woolley, "Automating Power."
23 Samuel Woolley and Phil Howard, "Bots Unite to Automate the Presidential Election," *Wired* Business, May 15, 2016, https://www.wired.com/2016/05/twitterbots-2/.
24 Woolley and Howard, "Bots Unite to Automate the Presidential Election."
25 Michael Newberg, "As Many As 48 million Twitter Accounts Aren't People, Says Study," *CNBC*, March 10, 2017, https://www.cnbc.com/2017/03/10/nearly-48-million-twitter-accounts-could-be-bots-says-study.html.

26 Adi Robertson, "Trump Claims He's Losing Social Media Followers because of Google, Facebook, and Twitter Censorship," *The Verge*, Aug 29, 2018, https://www.theverge.com/2018/8/29/17797400/trump-google-facebook-twitter-censorship-lost-social-media-followers.
27 Jessica McBride, "Real Nicole Mincy Talks About 'Nicole Mincey' & ProTrump45," *Heavy*, Aug 8, 2017, http://heavy.com/news/2017/08/nicole-mincey-mincy-bot-trump-real-new-jersey-twitter-protrump45-bio/.
28 Patricia Garcia, "Donald Trump's Twitter Following Might Include More Than 4 Million Bots," *Vogue*, Aug 7, 2017, https://www.vogue.com/article/trump-twitter-bots-fake-accounts-nicole-mincey.
29 Abigail Miller and Zoe Szathmary, "It's All in the Family!" *Daily Mail*, March 26, 2017, http://www.dailymail.co.uk/news/article-4349932/Family-demands-Pizzagate-investigation-outside-White-House.html.
30 Marc Fisher, John Woodrow Cox and Peter Hermann, "Pizzagate: From Rumor, to Hashtag, to Gunfire," *The Washington Post*, Dec 7, 2016, https://www.chron.com/national/article/Pizzagate-From-rumor-to-hashtag-to-gun-re-10779741.php; Miller and Szathmary, "It's All in the Family!"
31 Jessica Gresko, "'Pizzagate' Gunman in DC Sentenced to 4 Years in Prison," *Associated Press News*, June 23, 2017, https://apnews.com/e0d30f6da17348ce9f354bfd6cb5cd9a/%27Pizzagate%27-gunman-in-DC-sentenced-to-4-years-in-prison.
32 Fisher, Woodrow Cox and Hermann, "Pizzagate."
33 Gresko, "'Pizzagate' Gunman in DC Sentenced to 4 Years in Prison."
34 Michael Zimmer, "The Twitter Archive at the Library of Congress: Challenges for Information Practice and Information Policy," July 6, 2015, http://www.michaelzimmer.org/2015/07/06/the-twitter-archive-at-the-library-of-congress/.
35 Axel Bruns, "The Library of Congress Twitter Archive: A Failure of Historic Proportions," *Medium*, Jan 2, 2018, https://medium.com/dmrc-at-large/the-library-of-congress-twitter-archive-a-failure-of-historic-proportions-6dc1c3bc9e2c.
36 Technology Quarterly, "More than Just Digital Quilting," *The Economist*, December 3, 2011, http://www.economist.com/node/21540392.
37 Christiane Paul, *From Immateriality to Neomateriality: Art and the Conditions of Digital Materiality*, ISEA2015, Proceedings of the 21st International Symposium on Electronic Art, 2015, 1, http://isea2015.org/proceeding/submissions/ISEA2015_submission_154.pdf.
38 Paul, *From Immateriality to Neomateriality*.
39 Morehshin Allahyari, Material Speculation: ISIS (2015–2016), http://www.morehshin.com/material-speculation-isis/.
40 Liz Neely and Miriam Langer, "Please Feel the Museum: The Emergence of 3D Printing and Scanning," Paper presented at the MW2013: Museums and the Web 2013, The Annual Conference of Museums and the Web, April 17–20, 2013, Portland, OR, http://mw2013.museumsandtheweb.com/paper/please-feel-the-museum-the-emergence-of-3d-printing-and-scanning/.
41 Stuart Jeffery and Siân Jones, "Material/Digital Authenticity: Thoughts on Digital 3D Models and their Material Counterparts," *Savage Minds*, Jan 29, 2016, https://savageminds.org/2016/01/29/materialdigital-authenticity-thoughts-on-digital-3d-models-and-their-material-counterparts/; Robin Sloan, "Dancing the Flip-Flop," *Robin's Feed* (blog), March 2013, https://www.robinsloan.com/notes/flip-flop/.
42 Sloan, "Dancing the Flip-Flop."
43 Neely and Langer, "Please Feel the Museum."
44 Mary Haung, Continuum Fashion, cited in *Dezeen*, June 7, 2011, http://www.dezeen.com/2011/06/07/n12-3d-printed-bikini-by-continuum-fashion-and-shapeways/.
45 Jessica, "Kinematic Petals Dress Debuts at MFA," *Nervous System* (blog), Feb 29, 2016, http://n-e-r-v-o-u-s.com/blog/?p=7162.
46 Haung, cited in *Dezeen*.
47 Anthony Cuthbertson, "Suicide Machine That Could Be Controlled By the Blink of an Eye Sparks Euthanasia Debate," *Independent*, April 17, 2018, https://www.independent.

co.uk/life-style/gadgets-and-tech/news/suicide-machine-assisted-dying-euthanasia-debate-uk-clinic-sarco-nitschke-a8307741.html.
48 Marc Lieshout, "The Value of Personal Data," Paper presented at the Privacy and Identity Management for the Future Internet in the Age of Globalisation: 9th IFIP International Summer School, Patras, Greece, September 7–12, 2014, IFIP Advances in Information and Communication Technology, 978-3-319-18620-7, https://hal.inria.fr/hal-01431593/document.
49 Lieshout, "The Value of Personal Data"; Shoshana Zuboff, *The Age of Surveillance Capitalism* (London: Profile Books, 2019).
50 Gianclaudio Malgieri and Bart Custers, "Pricing Privacy – the Right to Know the Value of Your Personal Data," *Computer Law & Security Review*, September 2017, https://doi.org/10.1016/j.clsr.2017.08.006.
51 Nicky Capella, "Chancellor Merkel Proposes Tax on Big Data," *The Stack*, June 1, 2018, https://thestack.com/big-data/2018/06/01/chancellor-merkel-proposes-tax-on-big-data/.
52 Bernard Stiegler, *For a New Critique of Political Economy*, trans. Daniel Ross (Cambridge, MA: Polity Press, 2010), 37, 46.
53 Zuboff, *The Age of Surveillance Capitalism*, 10.
54 Zuboff, *The Age of Surveillance Capitalism*.
55 Dylan Curran, "Are You Ready? Here Is All the Data Facebook and Google Have on You," *The Guardian*, March 30, 2018, https://www.theguardian.com/commentisfree/2018/mar/28/all-the-data-facebook-google-has-on-you-privacy.
56 Sam Frizell, "Here's What Facebook Can Do With Your Personal Data in the Name of Science," *TIME*, July 7, 2014, http://time.com/2949565/heres-what-facebook-can-do-with-your-personal-data-in-the-name-of-science/; Wikibooks, "Corporate Social Media and Free Labour," *Living in a Connected World/Digital Labour on Social Media Platforms*, Chapter 3.1, https://en.wikibooks.org/wiki/Living_in_a_Connected_World/Digital_Labour_on_Social_Media_Platforms.
57 Malgieri and Custers, "Pricing."
58 Matthew Carney, "Leave No Dark Corner," *ABC News*, Sept 19, 2018, https://www.abc.net.au/news/2018-09-18/china-social-credit-a-model-citizen-in-a-digital-dictatorship/10200278.
59 Christian Fuchs and Sebastian Sevignani, "What is Digital Labour? What is Digital Work? What's their Difference? And Why Do These Questions Matter for Understanding Social Media?" *TripleC* 11, no. 2 (June 2013): 255.
60 Fuchs and Sevignani, "What is Digital Labour?" 255.
61 Christian Fuchs, "Labor in Informational Capitalism and on the Internet," *The Information Society* 26, no. 3 (April 2010): 179–196.
62 Stiegler, *For a New Critique of Political Economy*, 37, 46; Fuchs and Sevignani, "What Is Digital Labour?" 255.
63 Joshua Aslan et al., "Electricity Intensity of Internet Data Transmission: Untangling the Estimates," *Journal of Industrial Ecology* (August 2017), https://doi.org/10.1111/jiec.12630.
64 Lewis Munford, *Technics and Civilization* (Chicago: University of Chicago Press; Reprint Edition, 2010).
65 Parikka, *A Geology of Media*, 24.
66 J. Junaid Shuja et al., "Greening Emerging IT Technologies: Techniques and Practices," *Journal of Internet Services and Applications* 8, no. 9 (2017), https://jisajournal.springeropen.com/articles/10.1186/s13174-017-0060-5.
67 Chloe Cornish, "How DNA Could Store All the World's Data in a Semi-trailer," *Financial Times*, Feb 5, 2018, https://www.ft.com/content/45ea22b0-cec2-11e7-947e-f1ea5435bcc7.
68 Megan Molteni, "The Rise of DNA Data Storage," *Wired*, June 26, 2018, https://www.wired.com/story/the-rise-of-dna-data-storage/.
69 Molteni, "The Rise of DNA Data Storage."
70 For a discussion of the Technosphere as a concept see Peter Haff, "Technology as a Geological Phenomenon: Implications for Human Well-Being," in *A Stratigraphical Basis*

*for the Anthropocene?*, eds. C. N. Waters, J. Zalasiewicz, M. Williams, Michael Ellis and Andrea Snelling, volume 395, no. 1, (London: Geological Society London Special Publications, May 2014), http://dx.doi.org/10.1144/SP395. For a discussion of the Anthropocene and the production of waste see Jesse Peterson and Alex Zahara, "Anthropocene Adjustments: Discarding the Technosphere," 3, Discard Studios, 2016, https://discardstudies.com/2016/05/26/anthropocene-adjustments-discarding-the-technosphere/.

71 Haff, "Technology as a Geological Phenomenon;" Peter Haff, "Technology and Human Purpose: The Problem of Solids Transport on the Earth's Surface," *Earth System Dynamics Discussions* 3, no. 1 (November 2012): 149–156.

72 Haff, "Technology as a Geological Phenomenon."

73 Parikka, *A Geology of Media*, 5.

74 Parikka, *A Geology of Media*, 8.

75 Joanna Zylinska, *Nonhuman Photography* (Cambridge MA: The MIT Press, 2017), 195–197.

76 Parikka, *A Geology of Media*, 5.

77 Parikka, *A Geology of Media*, 30.

78 Alan Buis, "Prolific Sea-observing Satellite Turns 10," *NASA Global Climate Change*, June 20, 2018, https://climate.nasa.gov/news/2753/prolific-sea-observing-satellite-turns-10/. The joint US/European Ocean Surface Topography Mission (OSTM), now in its 11th year of operation on the Jason-2 satellite, has made more than 47,000 trips around our home planet, measuring sea-level change across the globe, observing ocean currents, studying climate phenomena such as El Nino and La Nina, and monitoring the long-term rise in global mean sea level.

79 Charles Corbett, "How Sustainable Is Big Data?" *Production and Operations Management* 27, no. 9 (December 2017): 1685–1695, https://doi.org/10.1111/poms.12837.

80 Fiona Cameron, "Posthuman Museum Practices," in *Posthuman Glossary*, eds. Rosi Braidotti and Maria Hlavajova (London: Bloomsbury Academic, 2018), 349–351.

81 Jo Ann Oravec, "Digital (or Virtual) Hoarding: Emerging Implications of Digital Hoarding for Computing, Psychology, and Organization Science," *International Journal of Computers in Clinical Practice (IJCCP)* 3, no. 1 (January 2018): 27–39.

82 Majed Alshammar and Andrew Simpson, "Personal Data Management for Privacy Engineering: An Abstract Personal Data Lifecycle Model," Department of Computer Science, University of Oxford, 2017, https://www.cs.ox.ac.uk/publications/publication10942-abstract.html; Geert-Jan van Bussel, Nikki Smit and John van de Pas, "Digital Archiving, Green IT and Environment. Deleting Data to Manage Critical Effects of the Data Deluge," *Electronic Journal of Information Systems Evaluation* 18, no. 2 (2015): 187.

83 See Eric Hörl, "a continent inter-view," *Continent* 5.2 (2016), http://continentcontinent.cc/index.php/continent/article/view/242 for a discussion of the rise of a new sense culture in the Technosphere.

84 For a discussion of technofossils see Jeffrey Jerome Cohen, *Stone: An Ecology of the Inhuman* (Minneapolis, MN: University of Minnesota Press, 2015) and Ben Dibley, "The Technofossil: A Memento Mori," *Journal of Contemporary Archaeology* 5, no. 1 (2018): 44–52.

85 For a discussion of human waste as technofossils see P.H., "Human Artefacts as Technofossils: Picking Over the Traces," *The Economist* (blog), April 3, 2014, http://www.economist.com/blogs/babbage/2014/04/human-artefacts-technofossils; Scolari, "Media Ecology," 212.

## Bibliography

Allahyari, Morehshin. "Material Speculation: ISIS (2015–2016)". http://www.morehshin.com/material-speculation-isis/.

Alshammar, Majed and Andrew Simpson. "Personal Data Management for Privacy Engineering: An Abstract Personal Data Lifecycle Model." Department of Computer Science,

University of Oxford, 2017. https://www.cs.ox.ac.uk/publications/publication10942-abstract.html.

Aslan, Joshua, Mayers, K., Koomey, J. G. and France, C. "Electricity Intensity of Internet Data Transmission: Untangling the Estimates." *Journal of Industrial Ecology* (August 2017). https://doi.org/10.1111/jiec.12630.

Begley, Sharon. "Here's Why We're Still Not Cloning Humans, 20 Years after Dolly the Sheep." *Business Insider*, July 5, 2016. https://www.businessinsider.com/can-you-clone-a-human-2016-7?IR=T.

Braidotti, Rosi. *Posthuman Knowledge*. Cambridge, UK: Polity Press, 2019.

Bruns, Axel. "The Library of Congress Twitter Archive: A Failure of Historic Proportions." *Medium*, Jan 2, 2018. https://medium.com/dmrc-at-large/the-library-of-congress-twitter-archive-a-failure-of-historic-proportions-6dc1c3bc9e2c.

Buis, Alan. "Prolific Sea-observing Satellite Turns 10." *NASA Global Climate Change*, June 20, 2018. https://climate.nasa.gov/news/2753/prolific-sea-observing-satellite-turns-10/.

Burt, Andrew and Samuel Volchenboum. "How Health Care Changes When Algorithms Start Making Diagnoses." *Harvard Business Review*, May 8, 2018. https://hbr.org/2018/05/how-health-care-changes-when-algorithms-start-making-diagnoses.

Cameron, Fiona. "Posthuman Museum Practices." In *Posthuman Glossary*, edited by Rosi Braidotti and Maria Hlavajova, 349–351. London: Bloomsbury Academic, 2018.

Capella, Nicky. "Chancellor Merkel Proposes Tax on Big Data." *The Stack*, June 1, 2018. https://thestack.com/big-data/2018/06/01/chancellor-merkel-proposes-tax-on-big-data/.

Carney, Matthew. "Leave No Dark Corner." *ABC News*, Sept 19, 2018. https://www.abc.net.au/news/2018-09-18/china-social-credit-a-model-citizen-in-a-digital-dictatorship/10200278.

Cohen, Jeffrey Jerome. *Stone: An Ecology of the Inhuman*. Minneapolis, MN: University of Minnesota Press, 2015.

Corbett, Charles. "How Sustainable Is Big Data?" *Production and Operations Management* 27, no. 9 (December 2017): 1685–1695. https://doi.org/10.1111/poms.12837.

Cornish, Chloe. "How DNA Could Store All the World's Data in a Semi-trailer." *Financial Times*, Feb 5, 2018. https://www.ft.com/content/45ea22b0-cec2-11e7-947e-f1ea5435bcc7.

Curran, Dylan. "Are You Ready? Here Is All the Data Facebook and Google Have on You." *The Guardian*, March 30, 2018. https://www.theguardian.com/commentisfree/2018/mar/28/all-the-data-facebook-google-has-on-you-privacy.

Cuthbertson, Anthony. "Suicide Machine That Could Be Controlled By the Blink of an Eye Sparks Euthanasia Debate." *Independent*, April 17, 2018. https://www.independent.co.uk/life-style/gadgets-and-tech/news/suicide-machine-assisted-dying-euthanasia-debate-uk-clinic-sarco-nitschke-a8307741.html.

Dibley, Ben. "The Technofossil: A Memento Mori." *Journal of Contemporary Archaeology* 5, no. 1 (2018): 44–52.

Dunn, Matthew. "Human/AI Hybrids and Gene Editing are Going to Change Mankind in a Big Way." *News.com.au*, Feb 15, 2018. https://www.news.com.au/technology/science/human-body/humanai-hybrids-and-gene-editing-are-going-to-change-mankind-in-a-big-way/news-story/f88b24f714706942d5de7d4eca2b1822.

Fisher, Marc, John Woodrow Cox and Peter Hermann. "Pizzagate: From Rumor, to Hashtag, to Gunfire." *The Washington Post*, Dec 7, 2016. https://www.chron.com/national/article/Pizzagate-From-rumor-to-hashtag-to-gun-re-10779741.php.

Fitzsimmons, Caitlin. "Why Sophia the Robot Is Not What It Seems." *SMH*, Oct 31, 2017. https://www.smh.com.au/opinion/why-sophia-the-robot-is-not-what-it-seems-20171031-gzbi3p.html.

Frizell, Sam. "Here's What Facebook Can Do With Your Personal Data in the Name of Science." *TIME*, July 7, 2014. http://time.com/2949565/heres-what-facebook-can-do-with-your-personal-data-in-the-name-of-science/.

Fuchs, Christian. "Labor in Informational Capitalism and on the Internet." *The Information Society* 26, no. 3 (April 2010): 179–196.

Fuchs, Christian and Sebastian Sevignani. "What is Digital Labour? What is Digital Work? What's their Difference? And Why Do These Questions Matter for Understanding Social Media?" *TripleC* 11, no. 2 (June 2013): 237–293.

Garcia, Patricia. "Donald Trump's Twitter Following Might Include More Than 4 Million Bots." *Vogue*, Aug 7, 2017. https://www.vogue.com/article/trump-twitter-bots-fake-accounts-nicole-mincey.

Gresko, Jessica. "'Pizzagate' Gunman in DC Sentenced to 4 Years in Prison." *Associated Press News*, June 23, 2017. https://apnews.com/e0d30f6da17348ce9f354bfd6cb5cd9a/%27Pizzagate%27-gunman-in-DC-sentenced-to-4-years-in-prison.

Haff, Peter. "Technology and Human Purpose: The Problem of Solids Transport on the Earth's Surface." *Earth System Dynamics Discussions* 3, no. 1 (November 2012): 149–156.

Haff, Peter. "Technology as a Geological Phenomenon: Implications for Human Well-Being." In *A Stratigraphical Basis for the Anthropocene?*, edited by Colin N. Waters, Jan Zalasiewicz, Mark Williams, Michael Ellis and Andrea Snelling. London: Geological Society London Special Publications, volume 395. http://dx.doi.org/10.1144/SP395.

Haung, Mary. Continuum Fashion. Cited in *Dezeen*, June 7, 2011. http://www.dezeen.com/2011/06/07/n12-3d-printed-bikini-by-continuum-fashion-and-shapeways/.

Helbing, Dirk, Bruno S. Frey, Gerd Gigerenzer, Ernst Hafen, Michael Hagner, Yvonne Hofstetter, Jeroen van den Hoven, Roberto V. Zicari and Andrej Zwitter. "Will Democracy Survive Big Data and Artificial Intelligence?" *Scientific American*, Feb 25, 2017. https://www.scientificamerican.com/article/will-democracy-survive-big-data-and-artificial-intelligence/.

Hitchings, Russell. "Expertise and Inability: Cultured Materials and the Reason for Some Retreating Lawns in London." *Journal of Material Culture* 11, no. 3 (November 2006): 364–381.

Hörl, Eric. "a continent. inter-view," *Continent* 5. 2 (2016). http://continentcontinent.cc/index.php/continent/article/view/242.

Jeffery, Stuart and Siân Jones. "Material/Digital Authenticity: Thoughts on Digital 3D Models and their Material Counterparts." *Savage Minds*, Jan 29, 2016. https://savageminds.org/2016/01/29/materialdigital-authenticity-thoughts-on-digital-3d-models-and-their-material-counterparts/.

Jessica. "Kinematic Petals Dress Debuts at MFA." *Nervous System* (blog) Feb 29, 2016. http://n-e-r-v-o-u-s.com/blog/?p=7162.

Junaid Shuja, J., Raja Wasim Ahmad, Abdullah Gani, Abdelmuttib Ibrahim Abdalla Ahmed, Aisha Siddiqa, Kashif Nisar, Samee U. Khan and Albert Y. Zomaya. "Greening Emerging IT Technologies: Techniques and Practices." *Journal of Internet Services and Applications* 8, no. 9 (2017). https://jisajournal.springeropen.com/articles/10.1186/s13174-017-0060-5.

Kalin, Jason Patrick. "*Reanimating Memory: The Prospects of Memory in a Digital Age.*" PhD thesis, North Carolina State University, 2012.

Keach, Sean. "BAD BOTS, Sex Robots BACKLASH as Brothel Workers Reveal Fury over 'Dehumanising and Dangerous' Droids." *The Sun*, Sept 18, 2018. https://www.thesun.co.uk/tech/7289486/sex-robots-prostitutes-workers-love-dolls-brothel/.

Keach, Sean. "Dirty Droid, Harmony Sex Robot Gets 'Mind-blowing X-Mode' Upgrade Making It Even MORE Lifelike." *The Sun*, Oct 5, 2018. https://www.thesun.co.uk/tech/7073748/harmony-sex-robot-release-date-app-sexbot-doll/.

Lieshout, Marc. "*The Value of Personal Data.*" Paper presented at the Privacy and Identity Management for the Future Internet in the Age of Globalisation: 9th IFIP International Summer School, Patras, Greece, September 7–12, 2014, IFIP Advances in Information and Communication Technology, 978-973-319-18620-7. https://hal.inria.fr/hal-01431593/document.

McBride, Jessica. "Real Nicole Mincy Talks About 'Nicole Mincey' & ProTrump45." *Heavy*, Aug 8, 2017. http://heavy.com/news/2017/08/nicole-mincey-mincy-bot-trump-real-new-jersey-twitter-protrump45-bio/.

Malgieri, Gianclaudio and Bart Custers. "Pricing Privacy – the Right to Know the Value of Your Personal Data." *Computer Law & Security Review* 34 no. 2 (2018): 289–303. https://doi.org/10.1016/j.clsr.2017.08.006.

Miller, Abigail and Zoe Szathmary. "It's All in the Family!" *Daily Mail*, March 26, 2017. http://www.dailymail.co.uk/news/article-4349932/Family-demands-Pizzagate-investigation-outside-White-House.html.

Molteni, Megan. "The Rise of DNA Data Storage." *Wired*, June 26, 2018. https://www.wired.com/story/the-rise-of-dna-data-storage/.

Munford, Lewis. *Technics and Civilization*. Chicago: University of Chicago Press. Reprint Edition, 2010.

Neely, Liz and Miriam Langer. "*Please Feel the Museum: The Emergence of 3D Printing and Scanning.*" Paper presented at the MW2013: Museums and the Web 2013, The Annual Conference of Museums and the Web, April 17–20, 2013, Portland, OR. http://mw2013.museumsandtheweb.com/paper/please-feel-the-museum-the-emergence-of-3d-printing-and-scanning/.

Newberg, Michael. "As Many As 48 million Twitter Accounts Aren't People, Says Study." *CNBC*, March 10, 2017. https://www.cnbc.com/2017/03/10/nearly-48-million-twitter-accounts-could-be-bots-says-study.html.

Oravec, Jo Ann. "Digital (or Virtual) Hoarding: Emerging Implications of Digital Hoarding for Computing, Psychology, and Organization Science." *International Journal of Computers in Clinical Practice (IJCCP)* 3, no. 1 (January 2018): 27–39.

Parikka, Jussi. *A Geology of Media*. Minneapolis, MN: University of Minnesota Press, 2015.

Parisi, Luciana. *Contagious Architecture: Computation, Aesthetics, and Space*. Cambridge, MA: The MIT Press, 2013.

Paul, Christiane. "From Immateriality to Neomateriality: Art and the Conditions of Digital Materiality". ISEA2015. Proceedings of the 21st International Symposium on Electronic Art, 2015. http://isea2015.org/proceeding/submissions/ISEA2015_submission_154.pdf.

Peterson, Jesse and Alex Zahara. "Anthropocene Adjustments: Discarding the Technosphere." *Discard Studios*, May 26, 2016. https://discardstudies.com/2016/05/26/anthropocene-adjustments-discarding-the-technosphere/.

Petrakovitz, Caitlin. "Your 'Westworld' Sexbot Is Almost Here, Thanks to RealDoll." *CNet*, April 15, 2017. https://www.cnet.com/news/realdoll-harmony-ai-app-realbotix-sexbot/.

P.H. "Human Artefacts as Technofossils: Picking Over the Traces." *The Economist* (blog), April 3, 2014. http://www.economist.com/blogs/babbage/2014/04/human-artefacts-technofossils.

Pritchard, Helen, "Critter Compiler Executing Practices", 2015. https://research.gold.ac.uk/24852/1/Critter_Compiler_Executing_Practices.pdf.

Pritchard, Helen. "Critter Compiler". http://www.helenpritchard.info/critter-compiler-prototype-2016.

Robertson, Adi. "Trump Claims He's Losing Social Media Followers because of Google, Facebook, and Twitter Censorship." *The Verge*, Aug 29, 2018. https://www.theverge.com/2018/8/29/17797400/trump-google-facebook-twitter-censorship-lost-social-media-followers.

Scolari, Carlos A. "Media Ecology: Exploring the Metaphor to Expand the Theory." *Communication Theory* 22, no. 2 (May 2012): 204–225.
Shorey, Samantha and Philip N. Howard. "Automation, Big Data and Politics: A Research Review." *International Journal of Communication* 10 (2016): 5032–5055.
Sloan, Robin. "Dancing the Flip-Flop." *Robin's Feed* (blog), March 2013. https://www.robinsloan.com/notes/flip-flop/.
Stiegler, Bernard. *For a New Critique of Political Economy*. Translated by Daniel Ross. Cambridge, MA: Polity Press, 2010.
Stone, Zara. "Ten Incredibly Lifelike Humanoid Robots To Get On Your Radar." *Forbes*, Feb 27, 2018. https://www.forbes.com/sites/zarastone/2018/02/27/ten-incredibly-lifelike-humanoid-robots-to-get-on-your-radar/#4c4e3af734d2.
United Nations Development Programme, Asia and the Pacific. "UNDP in Asia and the Pacific Appoints World's First Non-Human Innovation Champion." Nov 22, 2017. https://www.asia-pacific.undp.org/content/rbap/en/home/presscenter/pressreleases/2017/11/22/rbfsingapore.html.
Technology Quarterly. "More than Just Digital Quilting." *The Economist*, December 3, 2011. http://www.economist.com/node/21540392.
van Bussel, Geert-Jan, Nikki Smit and John van de Pas. "Digital Archiving, Green IT and Environment. Deleting Data to Manage Critical Effects of the Data Deluge." *Electronic Journal of Information Systems Evaluation* 18, no. 2 (2015): 187–198.
Varma, Atool and Nathan Erhardt. "Genetic Algorithms." 1997. http://biology.kenyon.edu/slonc/bio3/AI/GEN_ALGO/gen_algo.html.
Wikibooks. "Corporate Social Media and Free Labour." In *Living in a Connected World/Digital Labour on Social Media Platforms*, Chapter 3.1. https://en.wikibooks.org/wiki/Living_in_a_Connected_World/Digital_Labour_on_Social_Media_Platforms.
Woolley, Samuel C. "Automating Power: Social Bot Interference in Global Politics." *First Monday*, April 4, 2016. http://firstmonday.org/article/view/6161/5300.
Woolley, Samuel and Phil Howard. "Bots Unite to Automate the Presidential Election." *Wired Business*, May 15, 2016. https://www.wired.com/2016/05/twitterbots-2/.
Zimmer, Michael. "The Twitter Archive at the Library of Congress: Challenges for Information Practice and Information Policy." July 6, 2015. http://www.michaelzimmer.org/2015/07/06/the-twitter-archive-at-the-library-of-congress/.
Zuboff, Shoshana. *The Age of Surveillance Capitalism*. London: Profile Books, 2019.
Zylinska, Joanna. *Nonhuman Photography*. Cambridge MA: The MIT Press, 2017.

# 9

# CONCLUSION

## Framing a more-than-human digital museology

Digital cultural heritage is a humanist concept and empirical tradition. This book reclaimed digital cultural heritage as ecological, as of the earth, as more-than- and other-than-human, as a story of deep time and futures yet to come. The past and the future cannot be stabilized, they evade prediction, become creative acts and emerge as worlding formations in multiple ways and as things that will live on long after we are gone in the geological strata.

Therefore, digital cultural heritage can no longer be conceived solely as digital objects to be viewed, researched and documented, encapsulated and saved to represent us and our concerns. Digital cultural heritage is also much more than networked objects or images; rather they are entangled in complex ecologies and processes that have a bearing on their extensibility. As a result, the world is not one of completed, bounded objects. Digital cultural heritage becomes a practice and technic of life itself out in the world and where its future-making capacities are made visible, at least in part. They are statements about what we are becoming as more-than-human figurations and subjects and the futures that are being made through this convergence on a biological, technological, and material level. Those futures being the planetary predicament, capitalist prospects, and the agencies of diverse communities and their communions, all of which contribute to the creation of a common world.

In this book I developed a new workable framework for a more-than-human digital heritage within a distributed ecological framework, thereby generating a new set of practices, values, and ways of framing what we call digital data in an interconnected world. This new set of practices prompts us to think differently about data and heritage frameworks, what we have, how we can keep it in the longer term, what future remittance might entail, and how we can think about the planetary crisis in a context of data profusion in a responsible way through an attunement with others. Digital cultural heritage in its humanist form is data we must cherish, sanctify, remove from and hold above society through officiating institutions. But museums are no longer floating above society as reified heritage repositories. Heritage institutions and museums also come down to earth entangled in global computational infrastructures and supply chains, and enrolled in all manner of more-than-human crises and situations.

This reframing of digital cultural heritage as ecological and as a more-than-human collective rejects the idea of the existence of a universal value as enshrined in humanist heritage. Digital cultural heritage, as reframed, becomes a creative capacity of profound complexity involving many agencies in more-than-human collaborations, exhibiting multiple temporalities and distributed webs of influence and affect. As complex eco-compositional processes they do not exhibit a final, completed state. Loss is foregone and becomes a question of renewal, creativity, and new productions. Death becomes instead a question of liveliness and emergence. Power in the ecological composition is transmitted through the embodied, embeddedness, and interrelatedness of its coordinates as multi-scalar, distributed events and affects.

The notion of digital cultural heritage as something we pass on to future generations becomes one of emergence and a more-than-humanist legacy and includes not only those yet to come but also the future of the planet as an interconnected set of consequences often unintended and unforeseen.

In Rosi Braidotti's 2019 book *Posthuman Knowledge* she suggests we need new terminologies and methods for posthuman knowledge production because existing ones are inadequate.[1] Throughout my book I have argued that digital cultural heritage as both humanist and as social constructivist lacks adequate terms to deal with the dynamic, ecological realities of digital data as heritage in a contemporary world. Central to this is the question of how we might reframe the human in western society differently in complex ecologies and how we might think about and activate the novel type of humanisms that arise from them in digital cultural heritage practice. As we turn from a human-centric to what I call a more-than-human ecological framing for digital cultural heritage practice, the new concepts, terms and practices include: the ecological composition, coordinates, thingness, eco-curating, domains of influencing, cutting, and tracing within and across the ecological composition, and the idea of the world as archive. In doing so I have proposed a broader field of influence for digital cultural heritage and its future legacies.

Digital data in digital cultural heritage frameworks is founded on the belief in the existence of an original structure, a material fabric comprising its bitstreams, operating systems and their technical supports, and more recently the containment of its functionality as close as possible to its original aesthetic and behaviour. Even a shift to retaining the functionality of born-digital cultural objects influenced by practices in data economies, bureaucratic governance, and digital art succumbs to the idea of the artefactual and artefactual production. The past and its meaning are embedded in bits and in technology. Significant change is viewed as a loss of material authenticity that has the potential to compromise cultural memory.

We create digital cultural heritage from data as a reflection of and for ourselves. Meaning resides in its embodied components as human language, knowledge, and expression as and of the past. Digital cultural heritage acts as a device in which to project ourselves, our needs, our desires, and visions of our past and future life, and directs philosophical thoughts and heritage practices. Digital cultural heritage therefore becomes a tool in the making of economic futures, upholding identity and patriotism, and memorializing events. It is a way of fortifying the future of a modern human-centred society by maintaining what came before rather than thinking about what is yet to come or what emerges.

Curation therefore is a practice of control and containment. The arrested object becomes the artefact directed towards preventing significant change. Artefactual production is directed to the preservation of material, technical, and behavioural authenticity. Heritage value is embedded in the very substrates of the object's bitstream sequence, as human forms of language and writing and its original hardware and replay systems that enable it to become functional again. Here a double bind emerges, a belief in an original state and in the vulnerability of that state. The creation of the artefactual renders invisible the complex ecologies that bring it into being, as artefactual production processes seek to retain meaning in a conventional humanist sense.

Specific historicity regimes are at work in the making of born-digital heritage as well as of the digitization. Both the born-digital and digitizations are framed as historical data because they embody memory traces of prior events and achievements. The digitization embodies the memory traces of the analogue. These memory traces are conceived as human-centric and technical.

Digital cultural heritage has until recently been viewed as information and thus immaterial. Its physicality or materiality has now been re-established as bits. This turn to the material fetishizes bits as material substances and is a reflection of how we conceive of the world as differentiated substances and material forms. But this approach foregrounds just one aspect of its composition, when in fact it is made up of multiple materialities and elements. This human–object material relation is a very poor rendering of the experience of digital life.

The work of UNESCO directed to the making and salvage of universal heritage is built on the belief in a universal common good and appeals to a rational global citizenry comprised of individuals, governing entities, and institutions. The lens through which digital cultural heritage is viewed focuses on difference as a series of distinctive cultural identities while on the other hand presenting them as similitude, the standard object. The notion of a universal digital cultural heritage presupposes that heritage as an idea is the right epistemological position and one that supersedes all other digital reals, and that the notion of digital data as heritage can operate according to a one-world frame. This accounts for why in some instances values and practices clash – as evident in other types of material and immaterial heritage formations seen over the history of the concept of heritage and its utility museums, for example Indigenous values and the subaltern stories of the working class. An ethnographic and ontological approach applied to the interpretation of digital data as a cultural form retrieves digital data as enunciations of different fractiverses, as multiple digital realities that at times fold together, and explains why these different values clash. But at the same time digital cultural heritage is not just a product of human expression in collaboration with technics but rather involves a wide variety of knowledge producers that are not always human entities or subjects.

The UNESCO imperative that digital data must be saved for future generations is a legacy of late nineteenth century thinking. Endangerment and loss are the underlying narratives of digital cultural heritage as a cultural memory technic like all other heritage alongside the need for its protection and preservation. The protection paradigm is perhaps most evident in those objects designated in its Memory of the World program. Competing concerns emerge. The aspiration to create material stasis as a physical permanence alongside its functional veracity in perpetuity to sustain its significance and historical meaning is not a state or form that digital data readily conforms to. But the process of preservation is never completed. It is ongoing in perpetuity, in the course of which data in its archived form will always be exposed to the possibility of multiple deaths.

Origin, originality, and authenticity, alongside endangerment, are the unifying elements in the heritage regime. Endangerment operates in intimate ways with loss and obsolescence. Associated with endangerment and loss are the irreplaceable and the unique. Documentation seeks to capture the features that make digital collections rare, unique, and irreplaceable in support of its material conservation and artefactual encapsulation.

Loss along with stasis, material encapsulation, and functional containment are limiting principles. We have an obsession with capturing the whole object, its material bits and technical form. We seek to control and contain digital data because we fear that life as we know it will disappear, that the anchors by which we locate ourselves will be forever lost, that we will lose our sense of purpose and economic livelihoods because our future is now embedded in technics. The collapse of self, of our identity, and of civilization as we know it feels imminent. What must be saved are the remnants of past economic activity, of discarded cultural behaviours, or technical innovations long gone, and our experiences from the deep and the more recent past. Containment does not lock down objects in the archive to prevent them from mutating; in fact, they are already mutating.

We therefore must also let go of the idea that we can return data to a prior original state. Museums must let go of the aspiration to preserve the original, preserve it in meaning and its original functioning. It is just not possible, as making the artefactual, updating, copying, and preserving establish a process in which new data is produced. Cloning and copying deviate from an original. Presenting the look and feel of born-digital heritage to create a sense of the original is not the original. It is a new work. When we let go of the object, and its artefactual encapsulation, humanist forms of heritage collapse. How we think about the past and the future in digital heritage practice takes on different forms.

My motivation for reframing digital cultural heritage and conceiving of a digital museology as a materialist, vital, and process ontology draws inspiration from observing digital media itself as lively micro and macro processes, the profusion of data we ourselves produce, AI, the rise of machine learning and computational design, the complexity of computational infrastructures and global connectivity, and phenomena such as Trump's use of Twitter and the emergence of many ecological crises, all of which are interconnected. It became clear that digital cultural heritage exists within these intense meshes of interrelatedness as unfolding, enfolding, and ever-multiplying processes of planetary dimensions that are often obscured by humanist forms of interpretation. Humanist forms of heritage interpretation are also limiting and unable to account for the rise of more radical and complex forms of more-than-human heritage. Through several moves I unravelled, folded out, and extended the coordinates and the processes that comprise born-digital objects and reframed them as ecological compositions. At the same time, I deconstructed and decentred the modern human and put human agency back in their place in the collectives and complex ecologies of which they are part. This is an ongoing process which I term ecologizing experimentations that I have conducted since 2008 across domains of museum theory and practice from climate change narratives to institutional forms, to collections and documentation, and to digital cultural heritage.[2]

## Heritage-like practices

Multiple practices of saving and keeping persistent data exist across all domains of western life; most of them exhibit heritage-like characteristics. These heritage-like dispositions all share modern values and world views and have a variety of reasons for viewing data as worth keeping, copying, passing on, or keeping active. Many tend to follow a similar set of values based on modern sensibilities of risk, loss, obsolescence, and the need to save for the future. How modern temporality is framed, fixed, and treated in terms of so-called original data and data sets relates to the intents that drive their future remittance, that is, to whom data will be passed on and for what reasons.

Heritage values specific to UNESCO, ICOM, and heritage institutions only exist within the heritage field and are just one practice among many. Digital cultural heritage becomes through these heritage regimes assets elevated above other types of data operating in the world in everyday transactions and circumstances. But most digital data is also of the world and remains in it; the world then becomes the archive. Data is stored in the cloud, in data centres, in archiving repositories, and on Facebook.

Digital data in heritage regimes is framed by concerns of long-term resilience. Data must endure forever, whereas other data regimes of saving have finite temporal frameworks depending on the data's value for other types of recording practices. Other saving and preserving practices are not solely directed to the purposes of representation; rather, data's monetarized value and usefulness direct such measures. A profit-driven capitalist motivation drives much emerging data and heritage-like practices of preservation. Modern aura generally does not exist in other heritage-like documentation practices. This is because aura is made and documented through heritage-authenticating regimes.

We value digital data, heritage and the work of heritage-like practices because it becomes us, is part of us, and represents us – from our medical history, record of employment, and our taxation history to aspects of our personal or intimate life such as an email or an image on Facebook of a loved one. Big data becomes us, our personality, our aspirations, and our activities. If we lose data, we lose ourselves and our biochemical and financial history.

A broader range of heritage-like practices are existent and will continue to proliferate. Vintage gamers for example use different sets of procedures, values, and intents involving the migration of games into different formats and their continuous replaying as a preservation strategy, and in doing so disrupt conventional heritage values of authenticity and origin.

Even in museums, different genres of data saving and storing exist. These include employment and financial data closely aligned to business and bureaucratic modes of practice, metadata on collections that supports heritage values as historical data, and heritage data as born-digital objects that conform to formal heritage regimes of value. With personal data, heritage-like dispositions exist in which saving the original look and form of data and its copies are seen as functional equivalents. Saving the original form itself is not always necessary.

WikiLeaks is an archive with historical data but it does not see itself as a heritage repository. It represents a heritage-like practice, has the same function (to save data close to its original form), but its future intent is different, that is, to keep things so they might be leaked and re-released.

Other entities produce, collect, and save data in many different ways without being constrained by strict heritage values, but risk and modern forms of thinking inform all these fields. In these cases, forms of data refer to the original as accurate records. Many of these heritage-like practices or dispositions are what I might call soft versions of heritage all informed by risk and modern forms of thinking. But they also have their own standardizing procedures – for example, tax ledgers, database records and updates, and the production of individual profiles that serve to enact their own ends.

## More-than-human digital cultural heritage

Modern human-centric digital cultural heritage has enacted a series of very specific intimate relations with data, one of which is a direct co-relation between human thought and expression and meaning in which human agency takes precedence. All its coordinates are resources made subject to capitalist exploitation, such as the minerals and chemicals that come from the earth used to make computer chips, the infrastructures and supply chains that contribute to the production and circulation of data, the digital media and platforms that enable people to become social media influencers, and the monetarization of the data we produce. The non-human world is made computational, as seen in computational design, and harnessed for these reasons.

Humanist understandings of agency remain a central feature in digital cultural heritage. In humanist heritage, users, producers, and interpreters define themselves through digital media based on a misplaced idea of autonomy. Memory, modern ideas of time and the authentic are humanist ideals. As ecological compositions, digital cultural heritage is no longer subject to the rigid rules imposed by subject–object thinking. Rather its memory, history, and temporality become a practice of planetary scale that is open-ended, deeply entangled, more-than-human, non-human, and emergent. This represents a shift in thinking from the digital as machines and software objects worthy of saving to the recognition of our entanglement with the digital on a socio-cultural and biological level.

The artefactual nature of digital cultural heritage framed as human consciousness and cognition becomes multiple, multiplying cognitive, calculating, and sensing processes and includes the conscious-unconscious processes of machine learning, of elements, of algorithmic calculations, of infrastructures, of electrical currents and their circulation. All these different cognitive intelligent and sensing processes make unlikely connections, produce new perceptions and affects that are often not discernible, and are at the same time inextricably vital. Digital cultural heritage has always included non-human coordinates; even forms of data storage on DVDs, for example, comprise minerals such as bauxite or aluminium, gold, and oil shale. Digital cultural heritage as an ecological composition becomes a material record of history, of duration, and of life.

By developing new forms of agency within digital cultural heritage, I position the human as embodied and embedded in ecological compositions in various ways as a series of traces across and through them from writing code, making hardware and infrastructures, from mining minerals and all manner of cultured materials. Other coordinates have agency often exhibiting affordances and abilities beyond that of human capability and consciousness. This includes algorithmic, material, chemical, automations and their calculative and sensing capacities, all of which, while they have the potential to change the course of things often in unexpected ways, are still of human design. Born-digital objects, for example, generate their own data and distribute themselves through electrical cables, currents, algorithms, and machine learning. Embodied in digital cultural heritage are forces that exceed human-ness; and at the same time human-ness is distributed widely in and across a complex web of interrelatedness.

Digital cultural heritage therefore becomes more-than-human ecological compositions as well as representational subjects through an expanded range of producers and collaborators. Human-ness is embedded in these unfolding and enfolding processes in many different ways. As a result, the notion of humanist digital cultural heritage collapses. That is because humanist forms of digital cultural heritage fail to acknowledge that we in reality exist as relational porous and embodied entities in all manner of collectives. These collectives are profoundly material, complex, involve a wider range of entities, and through their eco-curating processes and the domains of influencing that arise from them become widely distributed and at the same time multi-directional, multi-scalar and rhizomic.

These new collective forms therefore embedded in the ecological composition not only produce new perceptions of the social but also expand our social relationships and contingencies. Our fleshly, social body and personalities for example become entangled in data, storage entities, algorithmic, automated systems, global computational infrastructures as new types of communions and communities. These participatory modes of understanding become the "we," not individual or species specific but a wider community of producers and intelligent forms comprising cognitive, calculative, and discursive processes. Digital cultural heritage as an ecological composition has always been more-than-human.

Data is routinely acknowledged as human–machine alliances. With the rapid development in computation it becomes a question of what, how, and by whom data and knowledge are produced. More and more data is inducted into archives that is more-than-human, but not necessarily recognized as such. While I have decentred modern humans by reframing digital cultural heritage as ecological, data will always form part of human experience, will always involve some element of collective and individual knowledge, thoughts, intents, desires, expressions, habits, processing, and crafting, but it is difficult to separate all this from other productions because of their embodied and embedded agencies. Automated heritage delegates production to the more-than- or non-human, but human-ness represented by algorithmic training and encoding is still inflected in its composing. Digital cultural heritage becomes human, ahuman and more-than-human created things.

Different agents become data producers. These include the memory of algorithmic calculations, of hard drives, of artificial intelligence, of micro and macro memory processes within the archive and out in the world, the memory of human crafting, and technological innovation such as the invention of computers, the formation of the earth and minerals born of these geological processes, and include also the memory of the universe and its birth. All these things are hidden under a humanist veil.

Within the ecological composition, more-than-human agents (human algorithmic, biological, and machine learning) occupy the same plane, and so the design of platforms, applications, and interfaces for documentation and interpretation becomes a question of designing for eco-curating processes and entities rather than solely for the human user as a self-directed autonomous subject. Audiences and users online and offline become influencers in diverse, extended domains.

Multiple and entangled data producers, all of whom operate within the context of their own ecologies, make visible what Braidotti calls a posthuman convergence.[3] In the context of digital cultural heritage, this convergence and the coordinates involved, each of them unique, greatly expand the notion of curatorial agency.

The more-than-human ecological composition brings forth and makes visible the new knowledge production processes and conditions in which what we call digital cultural heritage emerges alongside the relational entanglements that comprise its new material conditions. Eco-curating processes become multiple enfolding and unfolding processes at different speeds, embodied temporalities and intensities. The affects of different types of knowledge production and meaning born out of eco-curating processes across its coordinates cannot always be identified or identifiable because they are often of unknown quantity or extent. Eco-curating processes comprise elements of deep time, emergent pasts, and futures. This includes the cumulative affect and input of technological innovation, multiple human intents throughout its unfolding, and also comprises the addition of new coordinates, new materials, algorithmic training, and so forth.

Therefore, we must not lament the disappearance of the human and digital cultural heritage through automations but rather acknowledge the collaborations we have with the non-human world and how humans in the western world are refigured by making these alliances visible. In this frame it is no longer solely a question of what digital cultural heritage stands for but also what it is, what it might be, and who is involved.

In a more-than-human frame, the human as the pivotal agent in heritage making is decentred but not eliminated, rather situated in an entirely different way. Digital cultural heritage as an ecological composition becomes a distributed production born out of multiple thingness collaborations.

In a more-than-human world digital data can still be considered heritage if it is in and of the human. Human essence resides in humanist digital cultural heritage objects, but with the demise of the artefact there is no essence, just traces of human-ness across and through the ecological composition. I am not seeking to debunk humanist heritage altogether, but rather to consider this form of heritage as a product of a specific milieu founded in nineteenth-century thinking.

## Digital cultural heritage as an earthly condition

The shift from digital cultural heritage in a humanist form to an ecological and more-than-human one operates in a gap that can be usefully deployed to foreground new concepts and real-world scenarios. Digital cultural heritage is thought about as belonging to a cultural group, a nation, to a community, or to an individual, but in an ecological belonging it operates in an extended frame – that is, belonging to the Earth, to the cosmos, to the terrestrial, to the flow of life, to earthly processes, and to the ecologies of a common world. Curating digital data as ecological compositions also alerts us to embodied accountability, and how we might promote practices that support earthly habitability, by opening up accounts of digital cultural heritage in all its complexity as an investigation that makes visible our common worldly predicaments and the entities we must attune and negotiate with. Ecological sensibilities and attunement to the production and use of digital cultural heritage in a world of data profusion become a necessity and their redress therefore becomes a serious matter. The abstraction of digital heritage as immaterial, informational, semiotic, and representational makes light of these risks. The ecological formulation of digital data raises questions about the links between digital heritage, our desire for preservation mobilized by a fear of digital oblivion, and on the other hand the production and our use of digital technologies and their unintended consequences such as environmental crises, toxic environments, data waste, and the uneven alignments between communities in the global north and global south wrought by global economic capitalism.

The economies of digital heritage comprise not just machines, capital, information, and users. These economies are also strings of materials embedded in life itself, from planetary computational systems to atomic level elemental agents in a mesh of agencies, many of which are the result of human design and also embody their own intensities, temporalities, speeds, and durations in their unfolding.

As a result, digital cultural heritage as ecological compositions become entangled with human-post-natural forces and contaminants, greenhouse gases, mines, toxic soils, water, digital and e-waste decomposition, and even cancer. Digital cultural heritage is of the earth and is life itself. We share bodily chemicals and minerals with these more-than-human systems. Metals act as conductors of electricity within data circulations and these elements reside with the fleshly human, in our own electrical systems. Digital heritage as ecological becomes a more-than-human concept bound to us and the earth. If we are to curate successfully for earthly habitability, we must revisit the ecological circumstances and implications of digital practices and the new materialisms of toxic waste made through e-waste, digital rubbish, and data excess that emerge.

The ecological composition is made up of multiple, vital entangled and layered ecological processes impinging on the biosphere, ecosphere, hydrosphere, and lithosphere. Among other things digital cultural heritage is part of the earthly archive, of energy, the elements, sun, fire, solar energy, and fossilized plants used to generate electricity. The worldly archive becomes global computational infrastructures that at the same time belong to an earthly archive comprising the chemicals and minerals extracted from the earth's crust and the immanent cosmological histories of their making.

Building social, ecological, affective responsibility by making connections between the production of data and its deep entanglements with ecological crises impels us to become ethical beings. Technospheric heritage is still humanist in its conception, but in an ecological form, digital cultural heritage becomes fossil, not immaterial.

The separate worlds of UNESCO heritage become entangled when considered in an ecological frame. As an ecological composition, digital heritage becomes indistinguishable from natural heritage such as the geological deposits and the environment that need to be preserved, built heritage such as the infrastructures of the digital economy, disused electricity generation nuclear power plants, and intangible heritage through the production and recording of traditions and their destruction through the expansion of capital and the loss of land.

According to posthuman theorist James Williams, duration is one of continuous multiplicities in emergence.[4] Therefore in the context of digital cultural heritage, time and historicization as a record for a modern heritage become durational perspectives or the variable time of ecological processes in which the entities involved, their temporal frames and fields of influence, are greatly expanded.

Duration therefore becomes deeper and longer temporalities of various speeds and intensities, such as geological, chemical, computational, electrical, human temporalities and those emerging from their interconnectedness. It is no longer a question of modern time but rather the operation of a series of temporalities that are both non-linear and multi-scalar. The problem of fixing time becomes temporal capture as the cut.

The ecological composition and its circulations and distributions not only shape the nature of digital cultural heritage but also practices of life itself. Populations, users, museums, and other heritage institutions, including their staff as producers of digital cultural heritage, also become integrated into networks of carbon, energy, water, data through their ecological footprint, and more-than-human configurations in data economies.

Deciding what data should be preserved for the future is an act of future-making. By saving digital data we are trying to influence what the future should look like, such as for example economic heritage and how it can support future capitalist endeavours. Big data analytics for example is based on historical data used as predictive of future life, to manipulate consumer behaviour. Digital cultural heritage is no longer immaterial but enmeshed in the broader material history of human–non-human entanglements of planetary extent and impact, from minerals and rare earth elements to their becoming technofossils rather than just digital memory traces of human expression. As a material record of life on Earth, digital cultural heritage and its history extended out to long time spans in earthly history through their reliance on the energy sources of the sun and fossilized carbon. The recycling of component parts of ecological compositions from e-waste such as for example cellphones, magnets, computer hard drives, alternative-fuel vehicles, and all manner of displays is returned to the digital cultural heritage assemblage and becomes their ongoing history of life through an endless cycle of obsolescence.

Heritage and heritage-like practices follow the path and sequence of neo-liberal capitalist exponential growth. That is from the overriding concerns with loss and obsolescence that have become more intensified, to the rapid emergence of AI and machine learning as new forms of more-than-human heritage, to the extractivist practices that underpin their infrastructure, to data profusion borne out of big data calculations and consumerism.

## New museology and the digital: A critique

Through the emergence of more-than-human heritage as an ecological proposition, a humanist heritage as a universal definition becomes a type of ontological perspective. It becomes one form of digital reality operating among others in a fractiverse frame. The original and the authentic are modern, humanist, and western principles. Recognizing that digital cultural heritage is one type of digital real opens a space to define digital cultural heritage and digital museology differently.

Digital museology becomes a way of being in and becoming with the world. The reconfiguration of digital cultural heritage as diverse coordinates, thingness, and the ecological composition as distributed, is emblematic of the deep intimacy we have developed with data, data production, and the wider range of entities from human to chemical involved in knowledge production and the different knowledge forms being produced through novel and sometimes unexpected collaborations.

Museums are typically institutions of modern memory. Digital curation currently is just one element in a suite of museum practices that operate under the aegis of the new museology. As a result, new museology frames how we think about the digital and curation in museums. The concepts that underpin the new museology most broadly include positivism, humanism, material, structure, human agency, social constructivism, subject and object, and nature and culture.

This limited range of coordinates and the conceptual and relational structures in which humanist heritage is framed has directed our attention to digital practice and digital collections in certain ways. The convergence of digital curation and museum practice activates the humanist idea of history and heritage – the desire to represent, the interpretation of events and moments in a linear history. Digital cultural heritage practice under normative heritage conditions clashes with other values and practices because it is seen as a universal schema rather than just one ontological perspective.

The "new" museology as an interdisciplinary cultural enterprise involves the merging of disciplinary concepts such as culture, society, identity, Indigeneity, anthropology, history, education and art, and their convergence with digital media. As an epistemological practice, museology generally interprets things according to human-centred and fixed wholes: whole museums, and departments, whole objects, whole disciplines and singular rational and self-directed users. Even approaches to cultural diversity restrict social collectives to those of the human species where cultural identity operates as a series of plural perspectives that make up a whole culture, a whole universe, as one-world principles. Museum and heritage practice is generally based on this relational frame in which one form of existence cannot be considered without a relationship to another type of existence in which terms are used to define each as separate but related states.

Ontological conceptions of new media and how it operates, according to Kember and Zylinska, are a series of distinct and opposing forms – analogue versus digital, closed versus open, centralized versus distributed, mass versus participatory, and readerly versus writerly.[5] Within this framing, reality is experienced as analogue, as non-digital and material forms comprising discrete properties of the analogue or as the continuous (im)material properties of the digital.[6] These Boolean dichotomies are typical of the computational paradigm where reality is experienced as either-or.[7] The binaries of the analogue and digital as a Boolean dichotomy lie at the foundation of digital cultural heritage work in the museum setting. Accordingly, the virtual and the real, the digital and the real/material all gesture towards the existence of a parallel universe in digital cultural heritage practice. Cartesian forms of investigation are framed as human–object relations. In the museum and heritage field the divide between analogue or old heritage and new heritage prevails, alongside distinctions between the born-digital and digitizations, the physical museum and digital museum, interactive and static, material and immaterial, analogue material and digital materiality, matter and bits, and so forth. Museum scholars and practitioners focus on objects as having linear historical relations, as original, as authentic, as auric, as comprising substances, and as significant locations of cultural expression and memory.

Digital museology is not defined as a distinctive philosophy within museum studies, but glimpses of an emerging thesis are visible in certain areas of practice. The informational and computational model of reality based on a social constructivist approach is a distinctive semantic tied to the new museology and its engagement with digital media. In media and communication studies the digital is conceived of as a networked domain comprising social media, the internet, and the world wide web and manifest via mobile and other information and communications technology.[8] The digital and its convergence with the new museology are conceived as comprising a series of networked social and technical entities.

As a result, the intersection of the digital and heritage focuses on the formal technical qualities of digital data and hardware for preservation purposes, and is framed according to optics such as computational, information theory and communication logics such as internet-mediated networking, and tools for cultural communication, from personalization and locational intelligence to data analytics. Even in a milieu described as post-digital, the future of the digital and heritage remains focused on the development of higher-quality digitizations, visualizations, more effective digital communication strategies and literacies, and the iterative application of digital technologies and emerging trends across all areas of operation and practice. Burgeoning research agendas include investigations into the circulation of digitizations and involve machine agency, collections interpretation in online environments, and the implications for both institutional authority and the visualization of 3D objects and environments.

Digital media in museums is conceived as discrete spatialized, networked objects and products that succeed each other, rather than as entangled processes. User interaction and its analysis is commonly directed to the understanding of museum visitation, how to bolster numbers, and how these interactions are encroaching on curatorial authority and implications for curatorial practice. Distinctions of self and other, analogue and digital, virtual and physical, online and offline have brought forth distinctive methods based on human-technological or material differences. Much research is directed to increasing museums' influence and their impact in public culture based on normative concepts of communication. The binary, relational assessments and descriptions of material, immaterial, the virtual and real have drawn our attention away from the deeply material and ecological implications of our digital and material practices. Accordingly, the framing of a digital museology as ecological represents a shift in thinking from the digital as networks, machines, users, and software to the recognition of our entanglements on a socio-technical, cultural, and biological level. We are not post-digital because the post-digital directs our attention away from data back to the human as the centre of all things. We are instead ecological, relational beings.

Reworking standard categories and the idea of the existence of distinct and binary modes of existence undoes the boundaries separating the digital–virtual and the analogue–material. The digital heritage object categorized in a museological framework as virtual or material is no longer founded on the perception of its technical or material composition. Digital cultural heritage instead emerges as socio-material-political-technical and temporal compositions.

## Ontology and the framing of a more-than-human digital museology

As practices change and we move from objects to ontological understandings, digital museology and museum practices must change from their nineteenth-century underpinnings that promote thoughts of static objects, descriptions as distinct standard categories, time, origin, history, and significance as singular linear points in time, and media as distinct forms. This is because in an ontological form, historicity changes, aura changes, temporality changes, significance changes, and the practices and values that inform the idea of data worth keeping or keeping active for the long term radically transform. Born-digital as a definition is no longer useful because it was originally part of a Boolean distinction, as the immaterial and informational. The ontological reframing of the digital in museology as ecological and more-than-human is refigured according to new modes of identification and ecologizing principles. While all this may appear to threaten the existing semiotic matrix of digital curatorial practice and indeed museum culture, if these new forms are read as a different digital real they can operate alongside humanist forms of heritage as a distinctive ontological perspective.

This ontological refiguring from a humanist to a more-than-human digital museology acts against the disposition of writing culture, culture as language and human subjectivity, and social constructivism as human-technical achievements. This more-than-human museology works against fixity, death, and obsolescence.

The labour of humanist digital cultural heritage is directed towards saving societal accomplishments, but in an ecological form it becomes the unfolding of the ecological composition's eco-curating processes and what emerges. Re-working the human subject relationship to other coordinates is not a binary relation in a dualistic sense, because we have always thought relationally. Rather, re-positioning the human and human agency in digital cultural heritage is a relation of entangled and embodied connections as part of radically diverse collectives comprising new types of gatherings.

Digital cultural heritage in its humanist form is no longer solely figurations of the past that must be brought back to life; as ecological compositions they are life itself, have an ongoing life. They are world-making in a different way. The world is what Tim Morton calls the mesh,[9] a distinctive vision based on an object-orientated point of view in which things interact in complex embedded arrangements as whole objects, or what Haraway calls the compost,[10] where all things are porous bodies that become humus, each of which reflects a different orientation to the degree and intensity of worldly embeddedness. Digital cultural heritage in its ecological form is a cut into the flow of the compost of life as it connects to a wide range of things and processes. Cuts are made into the ecological composition's emergence to make sense of the world for human understanding.

The question is how will the philosophical, curatorial project and praxis of digital cultural heritage change when we move beyond subject–object relations, and a sole focus on the social and cultural conventions of language, describing, and naming, seeing heritage as bounded objects, by extending the range of coordinates that make up heritage and at the same time take the vitality of all of them seriously? Central to this is a shift in thinking from the digital object as data, as information and materiality, to a form that is multi-agential and distributed, spatially and temporally continuous and extended, and that operates in a unique rhizomic fashion involving a proliferating number of coordinates and multiple forms of rationality, all of which has far-reaching implications for digital cultural heritage practice.

The ecological composition becomes a new curatorial praxis. The reformulation of digital museology in this framing includes ecological circumstances and an expanded sense of community, curating as ecological and data production as more-than-human and other-than-human. Digital cultural heritage becomes processes that have no fixed or finite state. Compositional possibilities and alliances are extended and indeed endless and made manifest as we break the human subject–object logic. Digital cultural heritage as signs and symbols are replaced by all manner of eco-curating processes.

An ecological composition is both active and alive if it continues to be dynamic, distribute itself, self-organize, interact, copy, rescript and change itself, program other data, and gather responses within its pre-heritagization context out in the world. The thinking function that is integral to digital cultural heritage based on humanist concerns is extended to all manner of coordinates alongside heightened levels of uncertainty. Accordingly, we witness greater more-than-human user involvement inside and outside the museum.

Digital museology in its ecological form is not exclusively human but also belongs to the more-than-human and other-than-human domains of life, of elements, and of forces. Similarly, these ecological compositions unfold differently and often independently, being not necessarily subject solely to human logic but also to machine logic and elemental logic. The copy and the original's history becomes the interrelatedness of their heterogeneous coordinates, forces, and agencies – in short, of their eco-curating processes. This temporal framework, although unacknowledged as such, is a process of unfolding. It is also about what came before and what is yet to come. It no longer subscribes to a linear humanist historical trajectory. The computational dilemma of uncertainty and indeed unknowability is greatly expanded.

Curatorial interpretive and documentary work therefore becomes a matter of crafting and composing, of thinking and making ontologies. Curating the ecological composition requires new skills, thoughts, and relational capacities in practice. Curation is first a practice of identifying, acknowledging, and tracking the coordinates and agencies that make up the ecological composition. The aim here is to invoke material embeddedness and affect, to track eco-curating processes across locations and knowledge producers and their different affordances, multiplicities, temporalities, spatial relations, their cognitive, sensing, and calculative capacities, and affects activated through thingness and made manifest through their emergence.

It is not possible to map and document all the complexities of an ecological composition in its active state. When attempting to gather information through collections documentation out in the world it becomes unmanageable, unpredictable, non-linear, arbitrary, rhizomic, emergent, and processual. For example, net-based digital cultural heritage cannot be contained readily as a fixed artefact and still maintain its full integrity. Because the ecological composition is in a constant state of renewal as a series of iterative processes, documentation becomes the cut.

Cutting as documentary and interpretive procedures into the flow of the ecological composition's emergence become strategies that seek to reveal its perceptual, material, conceptual, technical aspects, often driven by curatorial intent. The cut also becomes a method that seeks to record ecological compositional processes tethered to the logic of keeping digital data active and continuing. At the same time, the cut recognizes that an ecological composition in its fixed state becomes an artefact, a representation of the complex processes that comprise it as a moment or moments in its emergence. In humanist digital cultural heritage, cutting is a process of making the artefact by which the world is made into discrete and stabilized digital objects. Objects become a form of perception in museum culture. They offer a stable view of the world, a lever through which we can know the world, and possess and contain it within a materializing heritage schema.

The digital cataloguing of historical data in the worldly archive, however, is no longer a digital memorial, no longer locked down, but again becomes emergent processes, as processes of renewal, subject to reuse, and involving the production of new creations. These curatorial interventions are directed to grasping and documenting compositions in their active, emergent states and as ongoing data streams. They are cuts in process[11] as spatial markers in the ecological composition's flow. As we shift from humanist to more-than-human ecological accounts, the ecological composition is a different type of interpretive cut into the differential, multi-scalar and multi-dimensional non-linear temporalities of its thingness. Cuts into the processes of the ecological composition itself are made up of different temporalities of deep time and geological formation, comprising the meanings and affects generated by multiple coordinates as discursive, sensing, calculative, and energetic, all uncertain, transforming, and composing.

The act of cutting is effectively achieved through the combination of more-than-human, AI, machine-curating collaborative methods and involves the cartographic mapping and tracing of the ecological composition's locations and points of contact, embodied and embedded multilayered, multi-scalar threads, and differential generative forces or power co-relations as affects as lines and meshes. Machine-curating patterns and the processing of data by similarity, by visual recognition or metadata analysis become cuts into its duration. Algorithmic tracing can be put to work to make visible, to a degree, more-than- and other-than-human cognitive processes. Cuts also represent the different angles and pathways taken through the ecological composition-in-emergence and disrupt the notion of categorical fixing and containment seen in humanist heritage. As a result, the non-standardized nature of the ecological composition defies classification in a traditional sense of fixed categories and descriptors. Ontology does not relieve us from interpretation or epistemology or the need to use language and nouns to explain things, but it can use other affective and technical, calculative, cognitive, and sensing techniques such as data visualizations as interpretive tools.

The organization of the ecological composition becomes non-categorical, chaotic and often unknowable, while making the artefact is an act of cutting as a contingent point of stabilization but is never stable in the cycles of death and renewal. The archive becomes one of duration. Duration means different things inside and outside the institutional archive, either constraining or halting duration or letting things run out in the world.

Cuts as openings onto meanings and interpretations can be a method to tell human and more-than-human stories. That is, to perceive phenomena for storytelling or to open out multiple and plural interpretations in an ecological composition's unfolding. When the cut is made differently, it can be interpreted differently. The ecological compositional cut can be used to make an artefact in the face of obsolescence, comprehend humanist temporality, try to reclaim its origin and its history. A cut can be used to invoke aura. All these cuts are momentary because digital cultural heritage always changes.

Digital cultural heritage in its ecological form can still tell human stories, but they are bound up with other coordinates that also have agency. Making statements about gender and race, as evident in Trump's tweets, most recently in his proclamations that Covid-19 is a Chinese flu, included more-than- and other-than-human alliances in their unfolding. Human stories become porous, entangled with non-human agencies many of which curate events and circumstances in their unfolding.

The ecological composition can still be considered digital cultural heritage, but of a different kind, or different ontological perspective. This is because heritage can operate as different genres, as humanist and as more-than-human, ecological forms with their own praxes and museological formations. Humanist heritage is something of value to humans and the human ego, worthy of passing on to future human generations, and operates according to distinctive modes of binary, relational forms of identification. Digital cultural heritage as ecological compositions capture their dispersed provenance, their past, present, and futuring predilections, their multiple locational politics, their multiple changing forms and combinations, their diverse and changing coordinates, ecologies, and agents of the human and non-human kind. Thingness also gestures to the way relations between the coordinates that comprise digital cultural heritage can be animated and replaced with force fields, immanence, affect, and becoming with these multiplicities of agencies, events, diverse actions, sequences, speeds, flows, and frictions. Modern history is no longer solely preserved as its bitstream. History also becomes emergent and future directed and becomes the interpretive cut or documentation cut in duration. Looking back into the past becomes an ecological composition's previous versions and cuts, as captured moments in the duration of its eco-curating processes. History is its unfolding and emergence.

Preserving an object's behaviour still inflects an obsession with obsolescence rather than renewal or the production of new compositions and reflects the desire for digital heritage to stay the same. Materializing digital cultural heritage as bits as its essence un-reveals as the ecological composition emerges, as multiple materials and materializing processes.

## From endangerment and loss to creative practice

Loss and endangerment are the founding principles on which digital cultural heritage and other types of humanist heritage rely most broadly, but the inverse is purposeful change, reuse, renewal, and new productions.

Artefactual production is indeed acts of renewal, reinterpretation, and the production of new works through software updates and system upgrades in which the original is updated and renewed and changed in an iterative process. Heritage cycles of life and death and rebirth involve multiple deaths through obsolescence and are part of the cycle of rebirth and reconstruction, reinterpretation and emulation. Emulation is presented as a process seeking to imitate the behaviour, look, and experience of the original but it is a new work. All these techniques are framed not as purposeful renewal but rather as attempts to recapture and retain the original as close as possible to its original state.

By changing, updating, and adding new tools over time, an ecological composition will become different from the original. It will no longer conform to the requirements of material, behavioural and technical authenticity. The original passes away, is superseded, and can no longer be accessible. Preserved data over time will become traces of the original. Keeping data active and emergent necessarily involves re-interpretation and re-enactment, as in the case of rogue vintage gamers. Documenting versions in GitHub is an act of renewal available for re-interpretation and as a result does not adhere solely to a saving metaphor. Viewing loss as change and renewal breaks the notion of museums and digital cultural heritage as places for archiving obsolete and inanimate things.

Digital artists often see their works as living entities that have many lives. They mutate, change, are re-scripted, re-interpreted, re-used, and re-worked. Some works are ephemeral, not meant to be kept, and instead pass away. Artists re-enact art work, re-enact past events and performances in new emulated formats while acknowledging earlier versions and incorporating these elements in new versions. This is because the idea of preserving is founded on the artist's intent first and foremost, an intent that is inherently fluid, as opposed to an intent seen in digital heritage practice to preserve the original. Change from the original in digital art preservation is still seen as a version of the original.

Curatorial principles of containment, authenticity, and history must therefore be re-worked. Wherever data is elevated as heritage and preserved as such, the idea of encapsulating the original and authentic collapses. In reality preservation acts against artefactual encapsulation because renewal, mutation and change is central to the process. Objects and bitstreams held in databases are not the original, they are mutating versions. They will always change, be renewed, and are subject to process. Digital data as heritage is to a degree removed from its pedestal. Historical data becomes something to be used and is proliferating. The whole idea of the original is under threat because of proliferating data. Each so-called original is unique in itself, but not in terms of being valuable and rare in an artefactual sense. No copy is the same as another. Provenance also loses its power especially when preservation is read differently as the production of new compositions. This idea of change and uniqueness undoes humanist heritage forms of classification, provenance, and history and its verification.

We need new thoughts, practices, procedures, notions of time and change, and must do away with our obsession with obsolescence, the original, and the authentic. Fundamentally risk and endangerment as founding principles must be replaced by change, renewal, and the production of new compositions. Working with individual instantiated objects and their specific ethnographies also highlights fractal complexity and challenges the concept of material stasis and the artefact, and instead they become living matters of interest in the broadest sense. Māori digital reals incorporate *hau*, life force, whose preservation is viewed as an act of creation, embodying living ancestors and promoting ongoing connections through the proliferation of digital *taonga*.

The development of the internet, new tools, software, hardware, machine learning, algorithms, infrastructures, and storage are all seen as elements subject to the ravages of obsolescence and are on the other hand put to work to prevent such occurrences in the context of preserving the original and maintaining the authentic. But we can view these tools and techniques differently as apparatus for renewal, for adding to existing compositions through visualization, interactivity, and automation – for example, for remixing and making new data, for tracking versions, and making duration cuts. Data in the archive can be reused for making new ecological compositions. Digital heritage enactments using historical data directed to passing on the original and at the same time keeping data active also become new compositions, in duration. Heritage then becomes anything seen as valued and worth continuing in process, in the broadest sense, rather than deleting. The production of new data overrides humanist heritage because heritage comes from the past and is something that should be brought forth to the future in its original form.

More-than-human and ecological heritage are creative acts. They are continually modified, renewed, and remixed, and self-curate through the insertion of new coordinates in their emergence, whether that be new or upgraded software, hardware, infrastructures, interfaces, new crafting practices, the addition of advanced AI automation systems and their calculations, and so forth. Data might purposely be left to pass away while its memory traces can be found in new data. Digital cultural heritage in its ecological form produces heritage, a living and earthly heritage.

In an ecological frame, web-based born-digital heritage and the archive become dynamic and open. The archive is no longer just for housing historical data and artefacts for memorialization purposes or for saving and halting decay; rather, it is put to use for updating and re-use, for the storage of new items, for enactments of historical data through reinterpretation, for remixing, emulation, and for proliferating data and data in duration. Although founded on a humanist socio-technical framework, media theorist Wolfgang Ernst's an-archive is a form of counter knowledge production in digital media art that is dynamic, algorithmically driven, unlocks the archive and develops its own momentum due to its constant updating of data and its migration onto newer formats.[12]

The world also becomes a dynamic, circulating archive enabling ecological compositions to run, to renew, to distribute, to enable their eco-curating processes to unfold, to proliferate, to use, and to create data. The intended use of ecological compositions changes from preserving the original and authentic; and once earmarked as something worth keeping active in its original form we are instead committing to its ongoing emergence, which means it will be updated, renewed and transformed. With an ecological composition in process data is added and changed all the time through its distribution, through searches, through copying, through tracing, through cutting, through interactivity, through human, algorithmic, machine calculations, through sensing, bot scripts, and human discourses. Readdressed ecological compositions are enacted or presented in different ways and often with different content. As a result, born-digital cultural heritage in its ecological form becomes something to be used, remixed, reinterpreted; it is always changing, updated and reused because it is kept ongoing and in process. Bots, algorithms, machine curating also become automated archivists. Born-digital as ecological compositions are ongoing, emergent not static, comprising traces of historical data even in their artefactual form.

There will always be new ways of versioning, making new compositions, and adding new formats. The creative and generative nature of all these practices is hidden from view due to our focus on loss and endangerment as an all-pervasive logic in heritage practice.

Digital cultural heritage, its usefulness and reuse in the future, will not be solely a legacy of preserved originals. The digital heritage legacies that will be significant for future generations are not only what we seek to make and contain as the artefactual but what is passed on as a dynamic ecological composition in duration. That is, as societal data worth continuing. All this is an invitation to redress the idea of material and stability and at the same time view digital cultural heritage as renewal and a creative practice in which new compositions are made, born out of what we currently view as multiple and never-ending cycles of death. Endangerment in relation to digital heritage is no longer solely concerned with obsolescence, loss and extinction but equally with creative practice and gestures towards difference between modern and non-representational understandings of digital cultural heritage. In a more-than-human frame, creative practice is performed by all manner of coordinates. We must shift our thinking to a practice of preservation that includes creativity as a different mode of digital heritage-making.

## Societal data worth keeping and continuing

Digital anthropology opens up a conceptual, theoretical, and fieldwork space to induct ethnographic methods into the practice of digital cultural heritage as a way of displacing the hubris of heritage value in its modern humanist form. This new disciplinary formation works to overturn universalizing concepts and can be put to work to challenge heritage and digital heritage premised on western ideas as applicable to all societies. Here I would like to acknowledge Deidre Brown and her work on the digitization of Māori *taonga*, Amiria Salmond and collaborators Wayne Ngata and Toi Hauiti in regard to Māori notions of digital life or digital reals and its purposes, and Haidy Geismar on her work at the Vanuatu Cultural Centre and database systems based on *kastom* practices, relationships, and forms of description. This work, along with others, draws our attention to Indigenous museologies and their empirical and ontological variety. Heritage is therefore part of a continuum of saving practices and processes in which digital cultural heritage in its humanist form is just one temporal, valuation, and interpretive system that works for certain types of digital data and in certain situations. Many cultural practices are not artefact-directed.

Broadly speaking, cultural practices share a common disposition towards societal data as something of significance worth keeping, worth maintaining in its aliveness. Societal data is also emblematic of a broad range of practices worth keeping and continuing. It is an important concept for various reasons. First it invokes a different set of standards and approaches to the archive, all of which are free of limited conventions. Second, it can embrace and represent many cultural values, different fractiversal concepts. Third, it can acknowledge the different agencies involved as an expression of different digital reals.

Reading societal data in its broadest sense of community and social relations brings together machine learning and organic and inanimate elements, and embraces ideas of the spiritual, the ancestral, and spectral that reside in different fractiversal configurations. Societal data worth passing on and keeping active still embodies human-ness within the broader cultural, ecological circumstances and duration of life. Most importantly, non-western digital reals see their societal data as something worth keeping active, passing on, to be renewed, transformed, transfigured, and living as an integral part of their life – as illustrated in the case of Māori *taonga* where digitizations become an ancestor. In the case of the Malagan masks, the digitizations of these were worth keeping and continuing to support cultural revitalization. Societal data broadly is a creative practice involving digital data.

People have always passed things on to the future; keeping their ancestors alive through artefacts or through digitizations is just one example. Heritage practice is and will remain a western concept, but if heritage is replaced with the more generic term societal data, this can embrace and encompass a range of meanings, attitudes, dispositions, and relations. More-than-human and humanist digital cultural heritage operates as part of a suite of practices as societal data worth continuing. Drawing on this broader definition of societal data, it opens a space to consider why data is worthy of saving, and for assessing its significance and usefulness in the context of a broader range of digital reals. This notion also embraces the likes of social bots as archivers and the logics of automated systems and their algorithmic quantifications of data processing.

## Future remittance

The past, present, and future are conventionally separate and demarcated things in humanist digital cultural heritage. Future remittance is not about passing on a singular artefact.

Saving persistent data for the future in a humanist frame is not assured. In its ecological form, pasts and emergent futures exist, but of a different kind. The past, the present, and the future refers to the convergence of events through eco-curating processes. Temporalities are unique to each coordinate, activated through their interrelatednesses that reference pasts, presents, and emerging futures at the same time. Ecological compositions as distinct from the artefact are cuts of emergent future pasts. Collecting for future generations refers to legacies based on a broader collective with whom we share a common world, not just our human relatives yet to come. Digital cultural heritage as ecological compositions are futuring through their unfolding and the eco-curating processes and affects that emerge and as actualizations of events and circumstances that are often unpredictable and unknowable. This is what future remittance becomes in an ecological frame.

## Rethinking aura

Authenticity and aura are all about modern historical thinking enabling the chronological linking of objects to the past through provenance, and through the documentation of these relationships of time. Aura becomes tethered to origin in digital heritage. This is a distinctly humanist form of identification and spatialization in which all things are identified and relationships are forged in terms of human-centred concerns and interests in their origination. The object allows us to build historicity, invoking the passage of time and then aura. Aura is tethered to the idea of modern time as a point in time and the historical specificity, presence, and the feelings incited by them.

Film historian Miriam Hansen investigates Walter Benjamin's texts to unpack what he meant by aura. She argues that Benjamin's work on aura has been read narrowly, specifically in relation to works of art, but that this was not his only interest because the development of the notion of aura also reflected his effort to reimagine experience under the conditions of technologically-mediated culture that he saw as destructive.[13] Hansen suggests that an understanding of Benjamin's aura is that it appears in all things, not just in certain kinds of things, as people imagine.[14] It is the experience of things.

In Hansen's analysis of Benjamin's aura, there is (1), aura understood as "a strange weave of space and time: the unique appearance [apparition, semblance] of a distance, however near it may be" (or, "however close the thing that calls it forth"); and (2), aura understood as a form of perception that "invests" or endows a phenomenon with the "ability to look back at us," to open its eyes or "lift its gaze. …as the distance of the gaze that awakens in the object looked at."[15]

My reading of this expanded notion of aura is that it is not an inherent property of something. It no longer exists based solely on the idea of separate states of being, the material and the virtual, nor is it entirely dependent on the accumulated history wrought by an object through visual perception. Auric processes are also not necessarily incited by human actions or necessarily human centred. Aura is a medium of perception not necessarily structured through human vision. It can be machine and algorithmic vision and aesthetics. It is an experience born out of the self-production of reality within a more-than-human framework.

Aura in a more-than-human frame as a medium of perception becomes the observed, affective, and temporal emergent characteristics of eco-curating processes. Aura can be the interpretive cut. It can be anything felt, as something that inspires an emotional connection, awe, fear, the recognition from the logic of the trace, a bond, the habitual, the familiar, a future imagining, the past projecting onto the present. It may be referred to as a spark, as an unsettling, as unease, and as anxiety.

## Notes

1 Rosi Braidotti, *Posthuman Knowledge* (Cambridge: Polity Press, 2019), 111.
2 Fiona Cameron, *Museum Practices and the Posthumanities: Curating for Earthly Habitability* (Abingdon: Routledge Environmental Humanities Series, forthcoming); Fiona Cameron, "Theorizing Digitizations in Global Computational Infrastructures," in *The International Handbook of New Digital Practices in Galleries, Libraries, Archives, Museums and Heritage Sites*, eds. Hannah Lewi, Wally Smith, Steve Cooke and Dirk vom Lehn (Abingdon: Routledge, 2019), 55–67. Fiona Cameron, "Stirring Up Trouble: Museums as Provocateurs and Change Agents in Polycentric Alliances for Climate Change Action," in *Addressing the Challenges in Communicating Climate Change Across Various Audiences*, eds. Walter Leal Filho, Bettina Lackner and Henry McGhie (New York: Springer, 2019) 647–673; Fiona Cameron, "Posthuman Museum Practices," in *Posthuman Glossary*, eds. Rosi Braidotti and Maria Hlavajova (London: Bloomsbury Academic, 2018), 349–351; Fiona Cameron, "The Liquid Museum: New Ontologies for a Climate Changed World," in *Museum Theory: An Expanded Field*, eds. Andrea Witcomb and Kylie Message (Oxford: Blackwell Publishing, 2015), 345–362; Fiona Cameron and Sarah Mengler, "Transvisuality, Geopolitics and Cultural Heritage in Global Flows: The Israeli–Palestinian Conflict and the Death of the Virtual Terrorist," in *Transvisuality: Dimensioning the Visual*, eds. Tore Kristensen, Anders Michelsen and Frauke Wiegand (Liverpool, UK: Liverpool University Press, 2015 (invited)), 59–72; Fiona Cameron, "Theorizing More-Than-Human Collectives for Climate Change Action in Museums,"

*L'Internationale Online Climate Change Special Issue* to coincide with the UNFCCC meeting in Paris, 30 November – 11 December 2015, http://www.internationaleonline.org/research/politics_of_life_and_death/48_theorising_more_than_human_collectives_for_climate_change_action_in_museums; Fiona Cameron, "From 'Dead Things' to Immutable, Combinable Mobiles: H.D. Skinner, the Otago Museum and University and the Governance of Māori Populations," *History and Anthropology* Special Issue, 25, no. 2 (March 2014): 208–226; Fiona Cameron, "We Are On Nature's Side? Experimental Work in Rewriting Narratives of Climate Change for Museum Exhibitions," in *Climate Change and Museum Futures*, eds. Fiona R. Cameron and Brett Neilson (Abingdon: Routledge Museum Research Series, 2014), 51–77; Fiona Cameron, "Ecologizing Experimentations: A Method and Manifesto for Composing a Post-humanist Museum," in *Climate Change and Museum Futures*, eds. Fiona R. Cameron and Brett Neilson (Abingdon: Routledge Museum Research Series, 2014), 16–33; Fiona Cameron, "Climate Change, Agencies and the Museum and Science Centre Sector," *Museum Management and Curatorship* 27, no. 4 (October 2012): 317–339 (Best paper award for 2012); Fiona Cameron, "Liquid Governmentalities, Liquid Museums and the Climate Crisis," in *Hot Topics, Public Culture, Museums*, eds. Fiona Cameron and Lynda Kelly (Newcastle, UK: Cambridge Scholars, 2010), 112–128; Fiona Cameron, "Object-orientated Democracies: Conceptualising Museum Collections in Networks," *Museum Management and Curatorship* 23, no. 3 (2008): 229–243.

3 Braidotti, *Posthuman Knowledge*, 14.

4 James Williams, "Process Ontology," in *Posthuman Glossary*, eds. Rosi Braidotti and Maria Hlavajova (London: Bloomsbury Academic, 2018), 372.

5 Sarah Kember and Joanna Zylinska, *Life after New Media: Mediation as a Vital Process* (Cambridge, MA: The MIT Press, 2012), 3.

6 For a discussion of Boolean distinctions and digital media see Tom Boellstorff, "For Whom the Ontology Turns: Theorizing the Digital Real," *Current Anthropology* 57, no. 4 (August 2016): 397.

7 Luciano Floridi, *The Philosophy of Information* (Oxford: Oxford University Press, 2013), 2.

8 Haidy Geismar, "Defining the Digital," *Museum Anthropology Review* 7, no. 1–2 (2013): 254; Heather Horst and Daniel Miller, *Digital Anthropology* (London: Berg Publishers, 2012); Daniel Miller and Don Slater, *The Internet: An Ethnographic Approach* (London: Bloomsbury Academic, 2000).

9 Timothy Morton, *Ecology without Nature: Rethinking Environmental Aesthetics* (Cambridge, MA: Harvard University Press, 2009).

10 Donna Haraway, *Staying with the Trouble: Making Kin in the Chthulucene* (Durham, NC: Duke University Press, 2016).

11 Cameron, "Posthuman Museum Practices."

12 Wolfgang Ernst, "Between the Archive and the Anarchival – The Anarchival Impulse," *Mnemoscape* Issue 1, https://www.mnemoscape.org/single-post/2014/09/04/Between-the-Archive-and-the-Anarchivable-by-Wolfgang-Ernst.

13 Miriam Bratu Hansen, "Benjamin's Aura," *Critical Enquiry* 34, no. 2 (Winter 2008): 338.

14 Walter Benjamin, "Protocols of Drug Experiments," in *On Hashish*, trans. Howard Eiland et al. (Cambridge, MA: Harvard University Press, 2006): 58.

15 Hansen, "Benjamin's Aura," 339.

## Bibliography

Benjamin, Walter. "Protocols of Drug Experiments." In *On Hashish*, translated by Howard Eiland et al., 17–104. Cambridge, MA: Harvard University Press, 2006.

Boellstorff, Tom. "For Whom the Ontology Turns: Theorizing the Digital Real." *Current Anthropology* 57, no. 4 (August 2016): 387–407.

Braidotti, Rosi. *Posthuman Knowledge*. Cambridge, UK: Polity Press, 2019.

Cameron, Fiona. "Climate Change, Agencies and the Museum and Science Centre Sector." *Museum Management and Curatorship* 27, no. 4 (October 2012): 317–339 (Best paper award for 2012).

Cameron, Fiona. "Ecologizing Experimentations: A Method and Manifesto for Composing a Post-humanist Museum." In *Climate Change and Museum Futures*, eds. Fiona R. Cameron and Brett Neilson, 16–33. Abingdon: Routledge Museum Research Series, 2014.

Cameron, Fiona. "From 'Dead Things' to Immutable, Combinable Mobiles: H.D. Skinner, the Otago Museum and University and the Governance of Māori Populations." *History and Anthropology* Special Issue, 25, no. 2 (March 2014): 208–226.

Cameron, Fiona. "Liquid Governmentalities, Liquid Museums and the Climate Crisis." In *Hot Topics, Public Culture, Museums*, edited by Fiona Cameron and Lynda Kelly, 112–128. Newcastle: Cambridge Scholars, 2010.

Cameron, Fiona. *Museum Practices and the Posthumanities: Curating for Earthly Habitability*. Abingdon: Routledge Environmental Humanities Series, forthcoming.

Cameron, Fiona. "Object-orientated Democracies: Conceptualising Museum Collections in Networks." *Museum Management and Curatorship* 23, no. 3 (2008): 229–243.

Cameron, Fiona. "Posthuman Museum Practices." In *Posthuman Glossary*, edited by Rosi Braidotti and Maria Hlavajova, 349–351. London: Bloomsbury Academic, 2018.

Cameron, Fiona. "Stirring Up Trouble: Museums as Provocateurs and Change Agents in Polycentric Alliances for Climate Change Action." In *Addressing the Challenges in Communicating Climate Change Across Various Audiences*, edited by Walter Leal Filho, Bettina Lackner and Henry McGhie, 647–673. New York: Springer, 2019.

Cameron, Fiona. "The Liquid Museum: New Ontologies for a Climate Changed World." In *Museum Theory: An Expanded Field*, edited by Andrea Witcomb and Kylie Message, 345–362. Oxford: Blackwell Publishing, 2015.

Cameron, Fiona. "Theorizing Digitizations in Global Computational Infrastructures." In *The International Handbook of New Digital Practices in Galleries, Libraries, Archives, Museums and Heritage Sites*, edited by Hannah Lewi, Wally Smith, Steve Cooke and Dirk vom Lehn, 55–67. Abingdon: Routledge, 2019.

Cameron, Fiona. "Theorizing More-Than-Human Collectives for Climate Change Action in Museums." *L'Internationale Online Climate Change Special Issue* to coincide with the UNFCCC meeting in Paris, 30 November – 11 December2015. http://www.internationaleonline.org/research/politics_of_life_and_death/48_theorising_more_than_human_collectives_for_climate_change_action_in_museums.

Cameron, Fiona. "We Are On Nature's Side? Experimental Work in Rewriting Narratives of Climate Change for Museum Exhibitions." In *Climate Change and Museum Futures*, edited by Fiona R. Cameron and Brett Neilson, 51–77. Abingdon: RoutledgeMuseum Research Series, 2014.

Cameron, Fiona and Sarah Mengler. "Transvisuality, Geopolitics and Cultural Heritage in Global Flows: The Israeli–Palestinian Conflict and the Death of the Virtual Terrorist." In *Transvisuality: Dimensioning the Visual*, edited by Tore Kristensen, Anders Michelsen and Frauke Wiegand, 59–72. Liverpool: Liverpool University Press, 2015 (invited).

Ernst, Wolfgang. "Between the Archive and the Anarchival – The Anarchival Impulse." *Mnemoscape* Issue 1. https://www.mnemoscape.org/single-post/2014/09/04/Between-the-Archive-and-the-Anarchivable-by-Wolfgang-Ernst.

Floridi, Luciano. *The Philosophy of Information*. Oxford: Oxford University Press, 2013.

Geismar, Haidy. "Defining the Digital." *Museum Anthropology Review* 7, no. 1–2 (2013): 254–263.

Hansen, Miriam Bratu. "Benjamin's Aura." *Critical Enquiry* 34, no. 2 (Winter 2008): 338.

Haraway, Donna. *Staying with the Trouble: Making Kin in the Chthulucene*. Durham, NC: Duke University Press, 2016.

Horst, Heather and Daniel Miller. *Digital Anthropology*. London: Berg Publishers, 2012.

Kember, Sarah and Joanna Zylinska. *Life after New Media: Mediation as a Vital Process*. Cambridge, MA: The MIT Press, 2012.

Miller, Daniel and Don Slater. *The Internet: An Ethnographic Approach*. London: Bloomsbury Academic, 2000.

Morton, Timothy. *Ecology without Nature: Rethinking Environmental Aesthetics*. Cambridge, MA: Harvard University Press, 2009.

Williams, James. "Process Ontology." In *Posthuman Glossary*, edited by Rosi Braidotti and Maria Hlavajova, 372. London: Bloomsbury Academic, 2018.

# INDEX

Page numbers in *italics* denote figures.

For Product Safety Concerns and Information please contact our EU representative GPSR@taylorandfrancis.com
Taylor & Francis Verlag GmbH, Kaufingerstraße 24, 80331 München, Germany

www.ingramcontent.com/pod-product-compliance
Ingram Content Group UK Ltd.
Pitfield, Milton Keynes, MK11 3LW, UK
UKHW020153200926
475702UK00016B/2679
* 9 7 8 0 3 6 7 6 9 0 5 8 8 *